religion

ROBERT CUMMINGS NEVILLE

religion

PHILOSOPHICAL THEOLOGY

VOLUME THREE

State University of New York Press

Published by
STATE UNIVERSITY OF NEW YORK PRESS, ALBANY

Printed in the United States of America

For information, contact
STATE UNIVERSITY OF NEW YORK PRESS, ALBANY, NY
www.sunypress.edu

Production, Laurie D. Searl
Marketing, Kate R. Seburyamo

Library of Congress Cataloging-in-Publication Data

Neville, Robert C.
Religion : philosophical theology / Robert Cummings Neville.
pages cm
Includes bibliographical references and index.
"Volume three."
ISBN 978-1-4384-5699-7 (hc : alk. paper)—978-1-4384-5700-0 (pb : alk. paper)
ISBN 978-1-4384-5701-7 (e-book)
1. Religion—Philosophy. 2. Religions. 3. Philosophical theology.
I. Title.
BL51.N443 2015
210—dc23 2014031581

10 9 8 7 6 5 4 3 2 1

for Jay Schulkin

The art on the cover of this volume, by my wife, Beth Neville, is the third and last of a suite of drawings she did for the covers of this trilogy, *Philosophical Theology*. Like the others, it is a colored-ink drawing with apparently geometrical shapes. The balanced geometry is her response to my request for "dignified" covers befitting a large, systematic, and (to many people now) untimely project. The geometrical figures are hand drawn, however, and so are inexact (though she has a good eye). This symbolizes the vulnerable tentativeness of the system expressed in these volumes. On first impression we see a series, almost a modern Stonehenge, of elongated, inward-tilting diamond shapes, suggesting the upward reaches of a cathedral, or a flight upward, as in the architecture of the United States Air Force Academy Chapel. In the history of her own work, that impression is an outworking of an earlier preoccupation with mountains, as on her cover for the SUNY Press edition of *The Cosmology of Freedom*. A second look is dominated by two horizontal bands in the lower half, the upper one narrow and the lower broad. Behind all this is a series of vertical bands signifying the infinite higher and lower pulls of the human spiritual situation. The vertical elongated diamonds of human institutions are barely rooted beneath the Earth's horizontal surface and somewhat more stable depths (like tectonic plates). They are vulnerable above. Reaching downward, they overlap and disjoin, symbolizing the tangled roots of our separate religious traditions, a major theme of the volume. But the carpentered diamond shapes are suddenly fragile, perhaps illusory, bound by the unbounded verticals and horizontals of nature. We must be prepared for the constructed edifices of religion to be temporary holding places as we realize our quotidian lives are most truly religionless religion, the volume's conclusion.

Contents

Cross References

As a systematic work, the three volumes of *Philosophical Theology* involve cross-referencing among its parts. Although each of the volumes has a primary title—*Ultimates*, *Existence*, *Religion*, the cross-references are to the volumes by number. Cross-references are in endnotes on the occasions when commentary is required; otherwise they are in the lines of the text. The general rubric for cross-referencing is this: Cross-references will always be in *italics*, and this means that they refer to volumes of *Philosophical Theology*; the first roman numeral refers to the volume. If the reference is to a chapter, the volume number will be given first, followed by a comma, then the chapter number as an arabic number, and perhaps if needed a comma followed by a section number in lower-case roman numerals. So, "Volume II, Chapter 3, Section IV" would be *II, 3, iv*. If the reference is to a part of a volume, the roman volume number is first, followed by a comma and "pt." for part and an arabic numeral for the number of the part. So, "Volume II, Part III" would be *II, pt. 3*. Often a part is referred to as a whole; but if the reference is to the "preliminary remarks" or the "summary implications," which are always keyed to parts, not chapters, then the referent to the part would be followed by a comma and "pr" and/or "si." So, "Volume III, Part IV, preliminary remarks and summary implications" would be *III, pt. 4, pr, si*. If a reference does not indicate a volume number, this means the volume referred to is the one in which the reference is made. The text spells out units of the three volumes when it discusses them directly.

Preface

Philosophical Theology consists of three volumes. *Ultimates: Philosophical Theology One* is an essay on the metaphysics of ultimacy interwoven with the development of an epistemology of symbolic engagement connecting the metaphysics to religion. *Existence: Philosophical Theology Two* is an essay in theological anthropology, interpreting the human condition with regard to ultimacy. Its principal claims are that inevitably there is something or several things ultimately wrong with the human condition in its ordinary manifestations and that religion addresses those senses of ultimate wrongness. In addition to, related to, and beyond these predicaments are ecstatic fulfillments in religion that make religion worthy, even if the predicaments cannot be remedied (and despite the downsides of many religious practices and movements). *Religion: Philosophical Theology Three* is an essay in philosophy of religion. It presents a philosophy of the nature and scope of religion. In this regard, it approaches religion in social and cultural terms. It does not primarily analyze how any one individual is religious, and in very important respects this is a serious bias and abstraction. *Philosophical Theology Two* manifests how religion is relevant to individuals in their existential predicaments and personal ecstasies. In senses discussed in *Two*, religion is an individual matter that William James and Alfred North Whitehead identify as what an individual does with solitariness. Whitehead said that if a person is never solitary, that person is never religious.[1] So, the individual's engagement of ultimate realities, as mediated by the symbolic structures that enable this engagement, is the actual locus of religion. Scientific, cultural, and other studies of religion as such do not deal with the individual and so miss the actual venue of religious engagement. Nevertheless, all individual engagements are indeed mediated by the symbolic, that is, semiotic and cultural structures, as well as by the biology involved in symbolic engagement.[2] Therefore, religion needs to be understood as well in terms of the systems within which individuals operate, thus the natural and social scientific studies of religion. The twists and turns of analysis in *Three* never lose sight of the first-order question, which is always for individuals, namely, How can I or we be religious in ways that truthfully engage what is ultimate?

All three volumes are straightforwardly theological in the sense that, for all their second-order methodological analyses and dialectical arguments, their intent is first order and practical. They (especially *Philosophical Theology One*) argue for preferred ways of thinking about ultimacy and engaging it as such. They (especially *Philosophical Theology Two*) argue for preferred ways of addressing the human predicaments that stem from, and the ecstatic fulfillments that open on to, the ultimate conditions of human life. They (especially *Philosophical Theology Three*) argue for preferred ways to be religious or live organized lives in the face of ultimacy. As the preface and introduction to *Philosophical Theology One* explain, "theology" is the intellectual work that addresses the first-order questions of religions and attempts to provide answers that might guide life in its ultimate dimensions. Although "philosophy" also in some periods and with some authors deals with such first-order questions, this is not common today. *Philosophical Theology* has its name because it is the kind of philosophy that does deal with those first-order questions. The first-order questions are mainly, although not only, important for individuals in their search for or practice of religion. *Philosophical Theology Two* focused particularly on how individuals have ultimate predicaments and ultimate ecstatic fulfillments. *Philosophical Theology Three* analyzes many of the social aspects of religion but always with reference to how individuals participate in them.

Obviously, from what is said, the trilogy is philosophy as well as theology. The introduction here says much more about the kinds of philosophy it is. A prefatory word is in order, however, about relations between philosophy and theology. The late John E. Smith was one of the most thoughtful thinkers about these relations.[3] He called himself a "Christian in philosophy" and always taught in philosophy departments, not in religious studies, and participated in philosophical professional associations rather than religious or theological ones. Although a student of Paul Tillich, he lived during the American heyday of Barthian Christian theology, during which, in many academic institutions, theology claimed to set the limits of what it could learn from philosophy, if anything. Smith resolutely resisted this, pointing out that philosophy has its own independent agenda, some items of which bear on religion and others not. Moreover, philosophy to his mind has its own modes of argument and avenues of evidence, and its own traditions of discourse. Any theology that is blind to what it might learn from these independent philosophical venues has a grievous fault: It is unnecessarily *in*vulnerable to correction. Theology, for Smith, simply should not be such a tightly revelatory-based enterprise that inhibits learning from philosophy. In particular, all revelatory sources claimed by a theology, Christian or any other, need to be interpreted, and it is the business of philosophy, Smith said, to explain and assess interpretations, providing cogent theories of what interpretation means. Most theological traditions have some philosophical apparatus already built into their interpretations. But the independent streams of philosophy involve ongoing criticisms of those philosophical elements. So, theological inquiries need to be ever vigilant for what might be learned from those ongoing philosophical developments, even when they have nothing ostensible to say about religious interpretations.

On the other hand, Smith pointed out with great force that philosophy needs to be vulnerable to learn from religion and theology as well. In his time, most forms of academic philosophy in America had turned from the large philosophical questions to small ones. Sometimes they were small in the sense of being only about higher-order issues of method, or only about logic with nothing else admitted to be clear enough for legitimacy, or only about language, taking what Smith's student, Richard Rorty, called the "linguistic turn."[4] Worst of all, in his eyes, was that most philosophy had become small in the sense of developing programs of isolated discussion stemming from certain leading figures' ideas or focused on certain popular problems. The deficit with these "program philosophies" is that they remove the consideration of their assumptions and premises from discussion and focus the philosophical venue like a working group devoted to solving a problem already set up. Good philosophy Smith knew to be "large" because it always backs up on its assumptions and brings them into criticism and reformulation, even as it proceeds to testing out solutions. This is one of the fundamental meanings of "dialectic."

What theology brings to philosophy, from which philosophy should learn according to Smith, is a concern for the first-order questions of life, most of which have to do with ultimacy and therefore religion. Those first-order issues are wild and are symbolized in all the weird sorts of ways associated with religion. Substantial knowledge of comparative religions is enough to frighten off philosophers who want to keep the philosophy professional, neat, and easy to adjudicate. But this insistence on the importance of the first-order questions is an important theological corrective to philosophy's temptation to stick to the problems that their intellectual trajectories at the moment seem suitable to solve. Theology points out that program philosophies can become a little like the drunk man who was searching for his keys under the streetlamp. Asked whether he had dropped them there, he said no, but there is where the light is. Theology calls philosophy to move out into the dark to address the really important problems.

Smith's position was to keep theology and philosophy as separate disciplines that nevertheless can learn from one another and should do so in order to keep their own integrity. While admitting his main critical points, *Philosophical Theology* does not keep philosophy and theology as separate disciplines, although many parts of philosophy have little or nothing to do with religion or theology, and vice versa. Rather, the claim is made here that theology, properly understood, needs to include within itself all the disciplines that might have something to say that would be helpful for the understanding of the first-order questions about ultimacy, the human predicaments and ecstatic fulfillments, and how to live in the light of ultimacy. This, of course, includes philosophy wherever it might be relevant. By the same token, *Philosophical Theology* holds that philosophy proper ought to include within itself both theological reflections on ultimate dimensions and also the experiences of ultimacy that are involved in religion. Philosophy is a way of engaging the world as its object, and this includes engaging ultimate realities and ultimate dimensions of human existence. In the long run, this engagement is experientially based. So, religion and its experiences, like art and its experiences, education and its experiences, and the sciences and their experiences, is a proper part of philosophy. Another way of putting this point is that philosophy should not be a "profession" in the sense that philosophers need to study only other philosophers. Philosophy needs to engage all the dimensions of human experience and the disciplines that make those dimensions sophisticated. This is parallel to theology, which is also not a profession studying only other theologians. Theology needs to engage all the disciplines that might learn something about ultimacy.[5] Rather than being a religious person such as a Christian "in philosophy," it is enough to be a philosophical theologian.

Dietrich Bonhoeffer popularized the phrase "religionless Christianity," modified in the title of Part IV as "religionless religion."[6] In his case, it was an attempt to save something of genuine religion from the failures of most of the Christian institutions in Germany to avoid complicity in the Nazi atrocities. By "religion" in the sense he wanted to dissociate from genuine Christianity, he meant the institutional forms that owed more to the culture that fell sway to the Nazi seductions than to any Christian spirit. At a deeper level, Bonhoeffer believed that mature individuals and a mature culture—humanity "come of age"—need to step beyond the authority structures of religion. Karl Barth in a similar vein and for similar reasons argued that Christianity is not a religion at all but stands in criticism of religion.[7] The nature of religious institutions relative to the authentic engagements of ultimacy that feed "authentic religious spirit" is probably more complicated than can rightly be registered in such wholesale dissociations. Of the German theologians of the Nazi era, Paul Tillich was probably closer to the mark when he argued that religion almost inevitably has a culture and is empty when it does not, but that religion always also needs a continuing critical or "Protestant" principle that holds the culture under judgment relative to renewed engagements of ultimacy. Thus, religious cultures should not be judged wholesale but part by part, a difficult matter of making assessments of complicated and ambiguous cultural elements.[8]

Nevertheless, Bonhoeffer and his colleagues gave early and influential articulation of the move to separate religion, by which they meant institutional religion, from "true religion" or the spiritual. Institutional religion has become embarrassing for many modern, late-modern, and now postmodern people. But religiosity, or spirituality, or the authoritative commands of deep faith, is held to be valid in spite of the failures of the institutions. Some Christian theologians in the generation following Bonhoeffer attempted to recognize the criticisms of institutions but to defend religious institutions in chastised modes anyway, for instance, James M. Gustafson in his *Treasure in Earthen Vessels*. Others embraced the secularization of religion, for instance, Harvey Cox in *The Secular City*.[9] This was not the abandonment of religion in favor of secularity, as Max Weber had predicted. Rather, it was the recovery of religion in forms dissociated from traditional institutions.

The movement to religionless religion in the twentieth century was by no means limited to Christianity, although the response to the Nazi corruption of Christianity was perhaps the most serious example. The Jewish side of the Holocaust led some Jewish theologians such as Richard Rubenstein to "death of God" theology. This was most directly a rejection of the idea of God as willing and able to protect his "Chosen People," but it also fed into a strong stream of secular but highly spiritual, largely nonpracticing, Jewish culture. In China the Communist revolution was harshly critical of religious institutions, suppressing them as feudal enemies of the state. Some practitioners went underground and maintained ghosts of the institutions in secret. But most interesting was the Marxist attempt to declare Confucianism to be not a religion at all but a "philosophy" and cultural resource. Even though the Communists originally were critical of Confucianism as the underpinning of the old order, they have come to recognize it as a source of Chinese identity too rich to lose. The Islamic world struggled through most of the twentieth century to balance out its institutional and spiritual forces. In several areas the primary institutions have been taken over by extremely conservative forces to the embarrassment of those bearing an interest in modernization. Or competing liberal and conservative institutions of education have coexisted uneasily. The highly spiritualized Sufi tradition has often been marginal to institutions. And the issues in Islam are complicated by the unwillingness to distinguish religious and political institutions in the ways that have become common in the West; in many Arab countries a young, educated, and otherwise secular class has arisen demanding democratic, non-sharia, governmental institutions while keeping an Islamic religious identity.[10]

Another factor in the development of religionless religion is the heritage of colonialism.[11] Western colonial powers often delegitimized the religious institutions and spiritualities of the colonized peoples. Sometimes this was by direct suppression, and other times it was by developing an educated class among the colonized people whose education was Western and who saw their own cultures through Western eyes.[12] Some reactions against colonialism were attempts to retrieve the ancient religious heritage of the colonialized people, as, for instance, in the writings of Aurobindo in the nineteenth century or S. Radhakrishnan in the twentieth. An extreme form of this is the early twenty-first-century Hindutva movement that claims that much of modern science can be found in the Vedas. Possibly a larger percentage of former colonized people, however, especially those of the educated classes, accept the Western criticisms of the ideologies and institutions of their ancient religious heritage, thus becoming "religionless" but with the will to modernize the spirit of that heritage. Thus, many people, particularly professionals, identify themselves as Hindus or Muslims, vouch for their spiritual commitments and life, but distance themselves from the institutions that are in continuity with the ancient heritages.

"Religious naturalism" is a growing movement in the West that in many respects is similar to the contemporary scientific South Asians who reject religions in most of their traditional forms but seek to revive and live in their spirit. Religious naturalism is definitely a Western religious movement, however, because of its origins in modern Western science; people from non-Western cultures, particularly religious cultures, come to religious naturalism through the adoption of Western empirical scientific commitments for their worldviews.[13] Religious naturalism is "naturalism" because it rejects all forms of supernaturalism and supranaturalism.[14] It is "religious," because religious naturalists find something sacred in nature, although the accounts of this vary widely. Some religious naturalists, such as Wesley J. Wildman, define sacred depths in terms of a metaphysical theory of ultimacy, and in this respect *Philosophical Theology* is also a religious naturalism. Many religious naturalists give a kind of phenomenological account of sacred depths without the metaphysical moment, for instance, Ursula Goodenough, Robert S. Corrington, Donald A. Crosby, and Jerome A. Stone. With respect to the sensibility toward science that functions in the worldviews of religious naturalism, a wide range of options have been chosen. Conservatively, some thinkers such as Charley D. Hardwick, Nancy Frankenberry, and William Dean hold that scientific explanation and understanding in the strict sense of the natural sciences by and large set the limits, although they also appreciate the special contributions of humanistic thinking. Others, such as Crosby, Stone, and Hogue, as well as their predecessors of a previous generation at the University of Chicago such as Bernard Meland, Bernard Loomer, and Henry Nelson Wieman, construe "science" in a broadly empirical sense, not limited to models in the natural sciences. Others, such as Wildman (and *Philosophical Theology*), develop a theory of inquiry out of the pragmatic tradition that is empirical in the sense of proposing hypotheses that are subjected to appropriate kinds of scrutiny but that treat natural scientific inquiry as but a subset of a wide range of inquiries including those usually associated with the humanities and arts.[15] The attitude of religious naturalists toward traditional religions ranges from outright rejection (usually because of a literal interpretation of supernaturalist or supranaturalist imagery) to an affirmation with a naturalistic reinterpretation of the traditional symbols. *Philosophical Theology* is a form of religious naturalism in the senses that it (1) rejects all forms of literal supernaturalism and supranaturalism, (2) gives a metaphysical interpretation of ultimacy in terms of an ontological creative act (which is not a determinate thing except in what it creates) and in terms of the conditions of determinateness within the world, (3) pursues a broad pragmatic sense of hypothetical empirical inquiry (and is rather critical of inappropriate reductionisms in the natural sciences, as discussed in Part I of this volume), and (4) holds that supernatural and supranatural *symbols* might be true and appropriate if interpreted with indexical and non-iconic reference, although whether concrete interpretive engagements are true is an empirical matter to be determined case by case.[16]

Philosophical Theology in all its volumes reflects on "religionful" and "religionless" religion from the standpoint of its analysis of sacred worldviews. When the sacred worldview orienting any individual or social religious culture becomes implausible, the result is a move toward religionlessness. When such persons or societies still are ultimately concerned and seek engagement with ultimacy, they are religious, religionlessly religious, in the sense discussed here. Part IV of this volume will discuss issues of worldview plausibility. It also makes the point that the pursuit of ultimate concern can move from participation in religious institutions as ways of ordering life toward ultimate matters to engagement of ultimacy for its own sake more directly, usually in mystical forms. In this instance, the religious institutions are not necessarily abandoned but rather made matters of merely proximate concern, not ultimate at all and thus not religious in the important sense (*III, 12*). Religious institutions can be proximate means toward ultimate ends or engagements with ultimacy, that is, genuinely religious. Or some people can pursue the ultimate religious ends without much or any employment of institutions that are socially identified as religious. This social identification of certain institutions as religious is valid only so long as some people find participation in them to be itself a matter of ultimate, not merely proximate, worth. Religionless religion thus can come from an abiding religion whose worldviews suffer plausibility problems, with resultant dissociation from religious institutions, or from religion that transcends claims for ultimacy in religious institutions, as in the case of several kinds of mystics.

The core of the Bonhoeffer call for religionless Christianity, however, was only partly the result of these two factors, implausibility in light of late modernity and a spirituality that transcends institutions. He was responding to the deep evil he saw in the Christianity of his day embodied in the Nazi movement. Religionless Christianity for him was a protest against Christianity itself. Christianity had become ambiguous in its value, appealing to a higher spiritual nature on the one hand but appalling in the ways so many Christians and their leaders pursued evil on the other. Nazism was an evil that should have been recognized as such from the very beginning. Other evils in religion have come to consciousness only slowly. For instance, the abuse and suppression of women in nearly every Axial Age religion is now recognized as an evil that prompts many people to abandon patriarchal religious cultures. The same is true of prejudice against sexual minorities. Even religious traditions in the contemporary period that recognize the "rights" of women often still have trouble recognizing the "rights" of sexual minorities, which leads many people to abandon the traditional forms of their religion in order to be faithful to the compassion in the spirit of the religion, hence, religionless religion.

Philosophical Theology Three has the task of problematizing the notions of religion that have been employed in this analysis. What are religious traditions? How can they be identified? What does participation in them mean from the standpoint of the contemporary religious person? Although some people are religionlessly religious, others are not. What are the details of this?

The organization of this volume constitutes a philosophy of religion with four main topics. How is religion to be understood in such a way that one knows with some sophistication how to be religious? How are religious traditions to be understood from the standpoint of the contemporary religious situation? What are the values involved in religion that have ultimate significance, and how are these expressed in the various ways of engaging ultimacy? How do we live with the tenuous plausibility of sacred worldviews?

I would like to thank so many people for help with this volume that the sheer number would make the thanks seem trivial. A quick look at the array of different kinds of sources in the bibliography indicates that the public to which this book relates includes a number of very different communities that usually are not in communication with each other. The first that should be mentioned is the theological community. I was raised in a Christian theological milieu, even though the theology here is much more inclusive than that. I had formal study of theology with only two persons. As an undergraduate, I studied Barth and Tillich with the late Hans Frei, a remarkably insightful and generous teacher who even then saw that I was siding with Tillich over against his beloved Barth. As a graduate student, I studied medieval theology and philosophy with George Lindbeck, who inspired me to begin a doctoral dissertation on Duns Scotus's theory of divine creation; the dissertation sprawled into a larger topic, but its published form, *God the Creator*, shows the spiritual discipline of tight argument that George taught me: Good thinking is good praying. These studies were before Hans and George became famous as the Yale School in theology, but I have been in dialogue with them and that "school" ever since. In the late 1960s I was accepted into membership of the New Haven Theological Discussion Group, which has been the nurturing home for my theological development. I owe great thanks to the members of that group, which still continues, including many from my early days, such as Louis Mink, Gene Klaaren, Steve Crites, Owen Thomas, and Gordon Kaufman, among others. Ray Hart was in that group when I joined, and he and I have been collaborators ever since, often as much in institution-building as theological conversation but always as "thinkers-of-God-together." My book *The Truth of Broken Symbols* is dedicated to him.

This book is also philosophy, grand metaphysical philosophy as well as philosophy of religion. Paul Weiss was my grand metaphysical philosophy teacher, one of the editors of the *Collected Papers of Charles Sanders Peirce* and to my mind far more original as a metaphysician than Charles Hartshorne, the other editor. When I was having trouble with some "big idea," he always pushed me to move on to an even bigger one. He taught me that "system" in philosophy means looking at a topic from as many angles as you can invent, and that system is the only hedge against parochial bias. My distinction between essential and conditional components in harmonies, and my closeness to the problem of the one and the many, comes from Paul. Robert S. Brumbaugh taught me Plato, Whitehead, and imagination. A counterweight to Weiss, he liked to say that philosophy should be concrete, but you shouldn't wait until the concrete hardens. Bigger ideas and more system can be ponderous, and so you need to come at things from *crazy* angles. He was the most imaginative interpreter of Plato I have ever found, and his book on Whitehead is entitled *The Unreality of Time*; my *Normative Cultures* is dedicated to Bob and his wife Ada, and to Paul Weiss. Richard J. Bernstein and Richard Rorty were graduate students and instructors at Yale when I was an undergraduate, and I am thankful for being in touch with them ever since. Dick Bernstein was an official teacher from whom I learned pragmatism and for whom I later was a teaching assistant. I have deviated from both of them in my development of metaphysical pragmatism but am thankful to both for their demonstration of the richness of that tradition. My deepest debt in philosophy continues to be to John E. Smith, to whom I dedicated my first book, *God the Creator*, which in fact was my dissertation that he mentored. The earlier parts of the preface indicate some of the reasons for my debt to him. He reread the pragmatic tradition through the lens of philosophy of religion, which has inspired my own interpretation. In philosophy of religion I am also deeply grateful for the collegial inspiration of Nancy Frankenberry, a dear friend who also has been my bridge to analytical philosophy of religion. J. Harley Chapman has been my friend and teacher of matters of the depths of the self, for which I am grateful. Hermann Deuser has welcomed me into the European theological community and shown me a whole new relevance of pragmatism for philosophical theology; my *Realism in Religion* is dedicated to him.

Another important dimension of this volume is history of religions and comparative theology, something that was completely lacking in my formal education. Thomas Berry taught me long ago that you cannot understand Western philosophy and religion unless you also understand the other traditions. He went on to become famous as a "geologian," a theologian of the Earth, and he is cited often in *Philosophical Theology* in that guise. But he started me in the study of Hinduism and coached me in the teaching of Sanskrit so that I stayed at least three weeks ahead of the students for the two years that I taught that subject to what he claimed must have been the largest Sanskrit class in the country (about twenty students). He also pushed me to the study of Confucianism and Daoism, arranging for me to study Chinese for a year, during which I received my Chinese name, Nan Loshan. In recent years my main teacher of Hinduism has been Francis X. Clooney, S.J., now at Harvard University, from which he is leading the burgeoning field of comparative theology and of which I am proud to be a part. Now I am learning from John J. Thatamanil, whose dissertation Frank and I directed. My first serious teacher of Buddhism was Park Sung Bae of the State University of New York at Stony Brook. Sung Bae was very patient, leading me past stereotypes of Buddhism into the nuances of its Korean and Chinese forms, mentoring our brilliant common student, Steve Odin, and introducing me to the leading figures in Buddhist studies. More recently, I have been in delightful dialogue with David Eckel, my colleague and close friend at Boston University who has been pushing me even more deeply to understand how Buddhism is so very different from what it might seem to be from the perspective of someone raised in Protestant theology. At Stony Brook I also began my serious study of Islam with William Chittick and Sachiko Murata. In more recent years I have been kindly coached in Islam by S. Nomanul Haq, whose works are cited in these volumes.

One would think that, having had a fancy education as a Christian, I would not need to learn to see it from the standpoint of history of religions. But, in point of fact, precisely because I approached Christianity through its Protestant theology, I had to learn the historical perspective. In the Comparative Religious Ideas Project, I think I learned most from the expert in Christianity, my Boston University colleague Paula Fredriksen, an orthodox Jew herself. In some kind of irony, I believe I have learned most in recent years about the actual history of Christianity from Daniel Boyarin, another Jew but one I have never met in person.

My education in Chinese religion was started by Thomas Berry and very early on nurtured in very active ways by Tu Weiming and Cheng Chungying, both of whom welcomed me into the ranks of contemporary Confucians. Extremely different in temperament and approach to Confucianism, they are both Harvard graduates and serious entrepreneurs in the advancement of Confucian philosophy and religion. I am also extremely grateful to my good friend Roger Ames, whose collaboration with another good friend, the late David Hall, has transformed Confucian studies. With our common love of pragmatism, and being non-East Asians, Roger and I are probably closer to one another than either of us is to Weiming or Chungying, despite the fact that we debate each other more in print than we do the others. In Daoist studies I am deeply grateful to Sophia Delza, my Taijiquan teacher for twelve years. I am also grateful to Livia Kohn, my brilliant colleague at Boston University who approaches Daoism not only through its medieval texts but through Taijiquan and diet! Our common student, James E. Miller, has also been extremely helpful, as evident from the citations here: How grateful teachers are for students who become their teachers! The most important debt of gratitude I have in Chinese studies is to my Boston University colleague and friend, John H. Berthrong. Our collaboration at the university over nearly twenty-five years has been Confucian in its service of ministry to the institution. But more remarkable, we have worked together to educate a generation of students in comparative studies that maintains the viability of first-order theological discourse. Bringing very different talents (John is a real scholar), he and I have enabled each other to do far more than we could have done alone. More than that, we have invented a new religion, Boston Confucianism! My *Ritual and Deference* is dedicated to him.

I would like to thank members of my doctoral seminar in Advanced Systematic Theology in the fall of 2011 for reading and commenting on an early draft of this volume; they include Sean Barley, Jonathan Heaps, Marcus McCullough, Timothy Mannes, and Lancelot Watson. A similar seminar in the fall of 2013 brought helpful comments from Lauren Hickey, Neil Hutton, Shin Myoung Kim, Samuel Needham, Stefani Ruper, Bin Song, Brian Teed, and Seth Waltemyer. Robert Corrington, Richard Peters, Christian Polke, Wesley Wildman, and Nikolas Zanetti have been in steady consultation with me during the writing of this project, and I am deeply grateful for their responses and advice.

All quotations from the Hebrew and Christian Bibles, unless otherwise noted, are from the New Revised Standard Version, copyrighted in 1989 by the Division of Christian Education of the National Council of the Churches of Christ in the United States of America. Credits for all other citations are in the bibliography.

In the early 1970s I taught at the State University of New York College at Purchase, where I had some extraordinary students, including Steve Odin and Warren Frisina, some of whose books are listed in the bibliography. I am exceedingly proud of them and treasure their friendship. Perhaps the most astonishing of all the Purchase students, however, was Jay Schulkin, whose intellectual metabolism is greater than that of anyone I have known. At Purchase he studied philosophy and became a philosopher, now with several books in the subject to his credit. But he took his doctorate in neuroanatomy and has had an extraordinary career as a scientist in both governmental and academic institutions, publishing much more than I (Roger Ames once said I published everything I thought, which is obviously false—I've published far more!). Jay masters and contributes to one field after another. But best of all, we connected with emotional intensity when he was an undergraduate and have sustained that connection in a friendship now passing forty years. He thinks of himself as a believer in "quiet religion," with Quakerish associations; he is one of the "secular, largely nonpracticing" religious Jews mentioned earlier. But in fact his spiritual life is a rampant siren, quickening (or frightening) everyone around him. His friendship is one of my greatest blessings, and I am pleased to dedicate this volume to him.

Introduction

The purpose of *Religion: Philosophical Theology Three* is to inquire into how to be seriously religious. This is a first-order question, which signals that this is a work of theology. The thesis is that to be seriously religious is to inhabit and live by a sacred worldview appropriate for orienting the particular domains of one's life, which are likely to be different from the domains of other people's lives (*II, 16*). An appropriate sacred worldview is theologically constructed, and so the work of philosophy of religion in this volume is to explore that theological construction.

I. THEOLOGY FOR WHOM?

Theology within Christianity usually has been assumed to be in and for the church community. Karl Barth began his *Church Dogmatics*: "As a theological discipline, dogmatics is the scientific test to which the Christian Church puts herself regarding the language about God which is peculiar to her. Dogmatics is a theological discipline. But theology is a function of the Church."[1] His opposite in Protestant theology, Paul Tillich, began his *Systematic Theology*: "Theology, as a function of the Christian Church, must serve the needs of the Church. A theological system is supposed to satisfy two basic needs: the statement of the truth of the Christian message and the interpretation of this truth for every new generation."[2] Karl Rahner, their Roman Catholic peer, wrote theology as *Foundations of Christian Faith: An Introduction to the Idea of Christianity*. John Zizioulis, their Orthodox peer, began his most important theology book, *Being as Communion*, with the claim that the topic of theology is really the Church:

> The Church is not simply an institution. She is a "mode of existence," *a way of being*. The mystery of the Church, even in its institutional dimension, is deeply bound to the being of man, to the being of the world

> and to the very being of God. In virtue of this bond, so characteristic of patristic thought, ecclesiology assumes a marked importance, not only for all aspects of theology, but also for the existential needs of man in every age.[3]

Theologians and religious thinkers who are Jewish and Muslim also write primarily for their own communities. To be sure, Judaism, Christianity, and Islam give very great importance to membership and to the boundaries of their communities (*III, 12*). Membership is less important and boundaries more porous in other great religious traditions, although most also have special enclaves with strict initiation procedures, for instance, into the lineages of Daoism or Buddhist monastic communities. Nevertheless, theology or religious reflection in those other traditions nearly always is oriented to those identifying with or attempting to understand those particular communities. Not all these theologians are "confessional" theologians in the sense of taking some core principles to be authoritative beyond questioning. Tillich, for instance, and Rudolf Bultmann, and other demythologizers, subject all of the basic symbols to fundamental reinterpretation. But they all write *for* their respective communities. Raimundo Panikkar is unusual in writing for at least three communities, the Christian, the Hindu, and the Buddhist.[4] His spiritual and scholarly virtuosity enables him to write for three instead of for one only, like most theologians. Yet he is writing for the faithful in each, helping them to understand their own faith as well as the faiths of the others.

Philosophical Theology is not like this. Its theology is for anyone who is interested in the first-order questions and is willing to follow all the second- and third-order inquiries pertinent to making first-order cases. People addressed in *Philosophical Theology* can belong to any religious tradition, several, none, or move about adventitiously looking for religious resources. Although *Philosophical Theology* does not take any traditional or experiential religious principles as authoritative beyond question, it does acknowledge and attempt to articulate basic revelatory claims in the major religious traditions. As the introduction to *Philosophical Theology One* argued, revelation is the condition in which something of religious value is made accessible and articulate by texts, events, and symbols through which they can be engaged and without which they cannot be engaged. The revelatory symbols "remove the veil" or make possible engagement of religious realities otherwise inaccessible.

That the revelatory symbols continue to be revelatory in this sense requires ongoing interpretation and reinterpretation, as suggested in the quotation from Tillich appearing earlier. This interpretation inevitably moves into the higher-order considerations that include philosophy, theories of religion, comparative theologies, and methodological inquiries. *Philosophical Theology* is written for people who are willing to follow the inquiries through these sophisticated dialectical turns. The arguments on all the levels of *Philosophical Theology* are accountable to the academy in all its departments that are relevant to the study and to the domains of life outside the academy—such as the arts, politics, economics, and education—that might be relevant.

The result is that *Philosophical Theology* addresses a somewhat elite audience, namely, those willing to engage the relatively sophisticated high culture of first-order religious inquiries pursued through second-, third-, and fourth-order philosophical, academic, and professional levels of expertise. It may not be for those whose religious life is lived in the thought forms of popular religion and culture or even those whose thinking has other forms of sophistication. Here is where its distinction from theology aimed at religious communities is most important. *Philosophical Theology* does not have to address or be accountable to those large numbers of people in each religious tradition who live in the forms of popular religion. It has no special responsibility to them, which is not the case for theologians who write for their whole communities. Those community-owned theologians, even the most "liberal," feel traction from the pull to support the symbols of the more popular versions of their religion that make for the formation of religious identity within the community. Even the Christian demythologizers look for interpretations of the old symbols so that those symbols can be used still by people in their community who cannot go beyond a first naiveté. *Philosophical Theology*, although aiming to be useful to religious communities and to articulate their truths so as to guide their practice, does not have any a priori loyalty to maintain symbolic or other continuity with the whole of a religious tradition or community, including both the popular and sophisticated poles of the continuum of symbols that articulate ritual and other practices (*I, 4, iii*). Rather, it aims to deal with the first-order questions where they arise and to follow the cases for and against them where they lead, regardless of transgressing community and tradition boundaries.[5]

This having been said, a serious qualification must be made. By no means should one think that only the elite can stand the truth of the sophisticated abstractions and that religious communities that include people from all classes require a different set of religious claims. Rather, there is a continuum from sophisticated to folk religion, and truth may be found anywhere along that continuum (*I, 4*), as the next section argues. Moreover, where people whose primary symbols are from folk religion make inappropriate inferences from them, *Philosophical Theology* urges that they be educated, not merely dismissed as having inadequate religion or patronized as not being able to learn better. Wesley J. Wildman believes that the metaphysical theology here is too austere for the sustenance of religious communities and that religious liberals suffer a fault of delusion in being unwilling to see that religious communities need to believe in a more supernaturalistic sacred canopy.[6] To the extent religious liberalism is true to itself, it undermines the communities that would sustain it, he argues. To the contrary, however, I argue that many people in those communities can be educated to understand themselves to be sustained by broken symbols, although whether this argument is successful is an empirical matter subject to experiment in cases where religious education is directed this way. The question is a main theme of Part IV in this volume.

Part of the novelty of *Philosophical Theology Three*'s inquiry into how to be seriously religious is its potential distance from most thinkers who assume that to be seriously religious is to actualize a thick identity within some defined religious tradition or community. Not only many theologians but also many social scientists assume this. By contrast, the argument here is that, although some tradition's name, for instance, "Buddhism," might be given to a person's sacred worldview and to a community with which that person identifies, in fact many traditions and fragments of traditions enter into that sacred worldview, not only Buddhism. At no time is a religious tradition "pure." It is already a syncretic result of previous religious resources. It takes form also as a result of secular cultural enterprises and in response to various historical, political, and imaginative literary and artistic works. Given the pluralism of the current global religious situation, each person makes up or adopts a sacred worldview tailored to that person. For many if not most people, this seems like merely adopting a familial or communal sacred worldview. But even if it seems to be this, in fact it is an idiosyncratic creation because each person's conditions and domains of life are unique and result from a heritage that is at least slightly different from that of the closest neighbor or family member. To be seriously religious thus means to have a stake in a theology that tailors a sacred worldview to one's own conditions.

Most theological thinkers and scholars of religion are likely to think of a person's religious community to be one with a named identity. Of course, many religious people do belong to religious communities in that sense, that is, they are Buddhists, Jews, or whatever. Many culturally important events such as marriage and funerals are set within communal practices shaped by a set of symbols from a traditional sacred canopy. But the reality is that for many more people, the functional set of other people with whom a person works out and practices life within a sacred worldview usually involves many individuals in many separate communities other than the person's explicitly "religious" one. Connections of education, social class, interest, spiritual longings and ways of working, playing, and achieving one's cumulative value-identity create functional religious communities that breach the boundaries of "religious" communities and establish new ones, often unnamed. This is especially true of those relatively elite people who read sophisticated theology.

Although this volume focuses a great deal on religious traditions and communities, and on problems of membership and participation, its thesis points out that there is something ineluctably individual about serious religious life. This is not new, of course, and it is not only a "Protestant" preoccupation. One way of rendering Kierkegaard's extreme claim that "truth is subjectivity" is to note that each person is obligated relative to the precise possibilities that each faces, is bound to face issues of personal wholeness for himself or herself in ways different from helping or hindering wholeness in others, has his or her own work to do with engaging others, and achieves his or her own absolute value-identity, no one else's. No other person can be grateful for existence as a substitute for each individual's gratitude. To be sure, most of these individual engagements with the ultimate conditions of existence are ritualized, expressed in common culture with others, and carried out conjointly with others. Nevertheless, each individual has the need to engage those ultimates. Here is the profound truth in Alfred North Whitehead's claim that "religion is what the individual does with his own solitariness," quoted at greater length and discussed in *Philosophical Theology Two*, introduction, Section I.[7] Whitehead is rightly criticized for downplaying the social and cultural elements of religion. But what he said about the individual in solitariness is right as far as it goes.

Philosophical Theology approaches the conception of the relation between individuals and their sociality in a way more typical of Confucians than Christians, especially "individualistic" Protestant Christians for whom a direct relation to God is more important than, and sometimes hostile to, corporate identifications. The Confucian model is that a person is made human, over and beyond biological capacities, by ritualization (*II, 13, iii*). Rituals are semiotic conventions that permeate life, from ways of standing, walking, and gesturing, to language, conscious symbols, and explicit rituals with a purpose, to the socializations that allow people to act and interpret the world meaningfully. The rituals are not externalizations of inner intentions but the already internalized semiotic processes that are vehicles for intentional action and social interaction. A person becomes humanly individualized by learning to play the rituals, which provide only vague roles that have to be interpreted in particularized ways. Confucian maturation is not only individuating a person's styles of ritual behavior but also the finding, and sometimes invention, of rituals appropriate for the context.[8] Thus, from the Confucian perspective, the true complexity of ritual social embeddedness is never to be found in membership in a community or group alone but in a vast array of interweaving ritual systems. An individual's search for a viable religious community, therefore, can never or rarely be satisfied by membership in a specific community alone. It reaches across many ritual systems and communities. To be deeply invested in a sacred worldview relevant for the domains of an individual's life should be expected to require participation in far more ritual systems than would be found expressed consistently in a given community. *Philosophical Theology* argues throughout that human beings are shaped and defined by the semiotic systems whose roles they can play, which are both social and internal to the individual. The issues for human beings seeking to be seriously religious have to do with finding appropriate semiotic systems and learning to play them in properly individuated actualizations.

II. THE QUESTION OF TRUTH IN POPULAR RELIGION

Having pointed out the elite orientation of the arguments in *Philosophical Theology*, a countervailing point needs to be made immediately. The thought forms of popular culture and religion might indeed be theologically true and thus authentic guides to religious life, despite the fact they are often unsophisticated and literally false. This can be shown through the theory of symbolic engagement of *Philosophical Theology*.

Truth, for *Philosophical Theology*, is the carryover of what is important or valuable in the object of an interpretation into the experiencing interpreter in the respects in which the signs in the interpretation stand for the object (*I, 3*; *III, 13, 14*). For reasons not to be explored here, the carryover is not necessarily of the *form* of the object into the interpreter but of the *value* or *importance* of the object.[9] The Western philosophic tradition from Plato and Aristotle onward has emphasized form, whereas the Confucian tradition has emphasized knowing as appreciation and appropriate response. *Philosophical Theology* elaborates the Confucian emphasis. A thing has value carried in its form. But the way that value is carried over and integrated into the experience of the interpreter might involve quite different forms.

In point of fact, the values of most things go through at least four families of transformation in order to enter interpretive experience. The first is that the thing is transformed into the forms of human biology. Things in nature have to be encounterable by the human body and encoded in the nervous system; people cannot hear or smell what some animals can; people extend their senses with microscopes, telescopes, and computers; forms of cognition are framed by human meat brains, not in the last instance by computers.

Second, the value-laden things engaged in interpretation are transformed into cultural forms that shape and are shaped by human interests and the particularities of place and history. All interpretations employ cultural forms, even when they involve interpreting across cultures. Cultures shape what is important to interpret and hence how the valuable in the interpreted objects is taken up and noticed.

Third, and closely related, the objects of interpretation are transformed by the semiotic systems used that provide the signs for interpretation. Without enabling signs, objects simply cannot be registered. Sometimes the signs take the form of brute resistance or destruction, secondness, as Charles Peirce would call it. Education and inquiry often are focused on attaining or inventing the signs necessary to interpret something. This is particularly true regarding religious matters where the signs that are uniquely helpful are regarded as revelatory.

Fourth, interpreted objects take on the forms of the interpreters' purposes because those purposes determine in what respects objects are interpreted. A baseline range of purposes comes from a culture's determination of what is interesting or important to interpret, and the available semiotic systems limit the signs that can be used to interpret things in those respects. But the particularities of an individual's life and affairs moment by moment give far greater determination to the purposes guiding interpretive engagement. All interpretations are in some context or other, and the context frames, and is framed by, particular purposes as well as other elements.

The distinctions among biological, cultural, semiotic, and purposive transformations of the form of objects of interpretation are crude and need to be more finely drawn. But they are clear enough here to illustrate the point that what is important or valuable to know can have one form in the object itself and a very different form in the experience of the interpreter. The point also indicates that the Western philosophical problematic of representative knowledge in which a match is required between the form in the thing and the form in mind is a misguided quest.[10] The problem for knowledge, rather, should be to determine whether the interpretive experience picks up on what is valuable, and perhaps humanly important, in the object.

With regard to religious objects, *Philosophical Theology* defines them as objects related to ultimacy, of which there are five according to the hypothesis. One, the ontological, has to do with the contingency of the world on the ontological creative act that produces the things of the world in an ontological context of mutual relevance. The other four are cosmological ultimates that are transcendental traits of anything determinate, which is what anything created must be: form, components formed, location in an existential field, and the value of having those components together with this form in this place (*I, pt. 3*).

These ultimate realities are religiously important for human beings as the boundary conditions defining human existence (*I, pt. 1*; *II, pt. 1*). The ontological ultimate is religiously significant for coming to terms with existence itself, which has many expressions in religion. The cosmological ultimate of form is religiously significant as human beings face possibilities of different value amenable to their choice and thus lie under obligation to choose well. Lying under such obligation is an ultimate condition of human existence. The cosmological ultimate of having components is religiously significant, as human beings need to comport themselves well toward the things that make up their lives when they face problems of wholeness. The value of wholeness in human life is an ultimate condition. The cosmological ultimate of having location in an existential field is religiously significant insofar as human beings need to face other people, institutions, and natural elements that are other than themselves, with their own values. How individuals engage others is an ultimate condition of human life. The cosmological ultimate of having value is religiously significant insofar as meaning is sought for the value-identity an individual actually achieves. Whether and how life is meaningful is an ultimate boundary condition for human existence. Religious objects are those things that are or can be interpreted with respect to one, several, or all of these dimensions of ultimacy, which are obviously connected with one another.

Theology is concerned with the interpretive engagements of ultimates that make up religion and religions. In matters of assessing truth in theory and practice, theology looks for the carryover of what is valuable or important in the ultimate realities in the various interpretive engagements of ultimacy. At this point, a crucial distinction needs to be recalled among three kinds of reference in interpretation, a distinction first drawn by Charles Peirce (*I, 3, ii, iii*). One kind of reference, conventional reference, is among the signs involved in a semiotic system. Any interpretation is expressed in signs that are related semiotically, and this can be called the extension of the signs. But two other kinds of reference are involved when the extensive expression of the interpretation is itself used as a complex sign to engage the real religious objects, the intension of the sign. For instance, the symbol system of sacrifice, with various semiotic expressions, is used in most religions to engage real ultimacies involved in communal life. One of those kinds of reference is iconic, whereby the object is taken to be *like* what the interpretation says it is. All iconic reference is literal in some sense, asserting that the object is what it is said to be. The other kind of reference is indexical, whereby the sign is pointed to the object so as to establish some causal connection. That causal connection, coupled with the fact that the sign is interpreted as standing for the object in some respect, is what actually engages interpretation with things.

Iconic reference can be literal, affirming a one-to-one isomorphism between the assertion and the object interpreted; mathematical science is a paradigm of this, and so is cartography—an icon is a map representing the object in a certain respect. Iconic reference can be metaphoric as well, saying that the object is metaphorically like what is said. The Twenty-Third Psalm in the Hebrew Bible says, "The Lord is my shepherd, I shall not want." This defines God as a shepherd and the speaker as a sheep. The psalmist surely did not mean this in a strictly literal sense. But the psalmist might well have meant that in certain respects, God is *like* a shepherd and the speaker is *like* a sheep, and that God takes care of the speaker as a shepherd cares for sheep. This would be a metaphoric sense of iconic reference. But, just as surely, this is false: God does not take care of us, providing us with all we need so that "goodness and mercy shall follow me all the days of my life" (v. 6): Life is filled with trouble and sorrow, the evil often flourish and the innocent suffer, a point abundantly recognized in the Hebrew Bible. So, perhaps the wise psalmist did not intend any kind of iconic reference here but rather an indexical one. Perhaps the point is that *believing* that God is like a shepherd and people like sheep, and living on this belief, establishes a causal connection with God (the ontological creative act) that gives rise to a sense of profound comfort, gratitude, and love of existence despite the violence and injustice of the created world. Iconically, the Twenty-Third Psalm is false, however literally or metaphorically interpreted. Indexically, it might be true. To determine whether it is true indexically would require determining whether its recitation does give rise to profound comfort, gratitude, and love and also whether this picks up on some true value in the gratuitous, arbitrary, undeserved, and surprising ontological creative act. A great many religious symbols, such as the psalm, are iconically false and yet might be true indexically.

The continuum from popular culture and religion to the sophistication of heavy duty philosophical theology is marked by differences in the sense in which the symbols that are iconically false but possibly indexically true are *believed*. Toward the popular culture end, the belief is, plain and simple, what Paul Ricoeur called "first naiveté." The belief is taken to be iconically true. Many religious people take their beliefs to be literally true, as in fundamentalisms. Toward the other end of the continuum the reference is known to be indexical rather than iconic, with recognition in some degree that the symbol is iconically false but believed to be indexically true. If the belief can be held to, it is a matter of "second naiveté." Many sophisticated people, however, failing to understand the truth that can be in indexical reference, give up on believing, and living on that belief, in things they come to see are iconically false. Most people engaged in organized religious practices, such as rituals and spirituality that would use psalms, abide toward the center of the continuum between popular religion and sophistication. They believe as if their beliefs were iconically true until challenged and then admit that they are not quite true and might go so far as to say they are false iconically but true in some deeper sense. The degree to which they are conscious of this determines where they lie on the continuum with respect to the symbol at hand. Few if any people who recite the Twenty-Third Psalm actually believe that God makes their lives as prosperous and safe as the psalm suggests, but they would say that it has a "deeper meaning" that still gives them comfort, gratitude, and love.

The point of this review of the theory of symbolic engagement is to show how popular religious culture might be untenable when interpreted from a sophisticated perspective as if its beliefs and practices were iconically referential. But at the same time, that culture might be true in the sense of carrying over, through indexical reference, things that are truly valuable in ultimate matters. The critique that sophisticated thinking brings to popular religion should never be only a rejection of claims that are iconically false. It should also include a careful assessment of whether living with those beliefs carries over theologically true elements through the indexical reference in the interpretive engagements.

Therefore, although the sophisticated theology of the sort in which *Philosophical Theology* engages does not define itself by an obligation to religious communities that include (probably massive) commitments to popular religion, it should by no means despise popular religion and its culture. It should rather treat popular religion as a kind of first naiveté and get on with the work of interpreting the truth or falsity of what is actually carried over in popular religious practice. This is not to suggest that popular religion is mainly true (any more than to say that all sophisticated theology is true!).

On the contrary, popular religion is often harmful and bigoted. But one of the functions of theology is to assess just where this is so and how.

The ironic countervailing point is that sophisticated thinkers are in jeopardy of cutting themselves off from true engagements of ultimate realities because their rejection of the iconic truth of certain symbols renders them emotionally and cognitively incapable of employing those symbols with indexical reference. Therefore, they cannot attain a proper second naiveté and lose the revelatory power of those symbols. The symbolic interpretations of popular religion, as well as their more sophisticated versions, are often the vehicles for grasping ecstatic fulfillments that are not so much "true" as they are perfections of the engagement of ultimates.

III. EXPLAINING RELIGION

Religion is to be understood, not explained. The chief methodological thesis of *Religion: Philosophical Theology Three* is that religion in its historical breadth and depth is to be understood in terms of engagements of ultimacy starting from the perspective of the present religious situation. Looking to the past, especially the distant past, is likely to dissolve serious questions of religion into definitional problems of what counts as religion. "Religious situation" is a somewhat technical term to be discussed at length in Chapter 3. The thesis combines two important concerns. One is to understand religion, which raises questions in methodology and definition. The other is to deal authentically with the first-order questions of religion, namely, how to be religious in these times.

Because this study is philosophical *theology*, the second concern is primary: What is a viable theology for finding serious religion today? Immediately this raises the question, What is "the religious situation today"? Because our situation today is interactive across the globe, the religious situation is global in many respects. This is obvious enough in the interaction of world religious cultures. But the situation is that finding serious religion in the global religious situation is different for different positions within that situation. For an educated middle-class American raised in a Christian culture, the situation allows borrowing from or even converting to any number of other religions, for instance, Buddhism, although always from that educated middle-class American Christian perspective, with an inevitably distinctive history of transformation. An educated middle-class Egyptian raised a Muslim might in principle have a similar set of options but would have a very different history of transformation, even if also ending up a Buddhist. A peasant in northern India is likely to have a much more limited set of options, perhaps limited to a particular heritage of rural Shaivism, as would a subsistence farmer in Chad whose worldview is filled with ancestral spirits, but both might gain access to global television news and the internet, which would make their position in the religious situation different from their grandparents'. Social class makes a huge difference to a person's position in the global religious situation, and in some positions social class is changing rapidly, such as for many in China, India, and Latin America.

Given the contemporary global religious situation, the positions within which people are located are complex, different from one another, and different in the histories of religious resources that come down to them. Chapter 3 will argue that understanding the historical religions should be guided by back-readings from various positions in the contemporary religious situation to the various intertwinings of their older roots. The ways in which different religions have encountered and learned from one another over the centuries are not given the prominence they deserve when we reduce them to labels: Christianity, Buddhism, Islam, rural Shaivism, tribal animism. Contemporary American Christianity, for instance, was much influenced in the nineteenth century by popular texts of Buddhism and Hinduism. Despite the textures of these differences, the different positions in the global religious situation can be in significant interaction. It is not at all inconceivable that the American Christian might find the Egyptian Muslim to be the most serious spiritual partner in developing a serious religious sacred worldview that has a Buddhist component. To add the Indian peasant and the Chad farmer to their spiritual circle is a bit more unlikely but not inconceivable given the increasing prevalence of internet communication. Understanding how serious religion is possible today for various positions in the religious situation is the topic of this volume, and previous volumes in *Philosophical Theology* have already provided much material.

These remarks indicate something of the complexity of understanding religion in the global religious situation, and the back-history of religions. "Understanding" means articulating the religious elements, that is, the connections with ultimacy, grasping their connections and causal relations, seeing how they relate to other things such as the political dynamics of the global situation, and so forth. The result of inquiry aimed at religious understanding is a familiarity with religion so that curiosity is stimulated and satisfied and the phenomena and their connections enjoyed. Understanding in this sense is "exhibitive" in the sense of that term used by Justus Buchler as discussed in the introduction to *Philosophical Theology One*.[11] Understanding religion means developing a "theory" within which religion is exhibited in a comprehensible way.

"Explaining" religion carries the connotation of explaining it in terms of something else. "Explanatory theory" is usually a theory about something other than religion that aims to account for why religion, a religion, or some aspect of religion, is what it is. Daniel L. Pals, in a highly influential text, *Eight Theories of Religion*, gives incisive synoptic interpretations of theoretical attempts to explain religion with some one reductive theory. He treats E. B. Tyler and J. G. Frazer's explanation of religion in terms of animism and magic, Sigmund Freud's explanation in terms of dynamic psychology,

Emile Durkheim's explanation in terms of the sacralizing of society, Karl Marx's explanation in terms of economic ideological interests, Mircea Eliade's explanation in terms of the dimension of the sacred, E. E. Evans-Prichard's explanation in terms of what Pals calls "society's construct of the heart," and Clifford Geertz's explanation in terms of cultural systems. He also treat's Max Weber's explanation of religion as a "source of social action" but notes that Weber also had a much more complex causal explanation of religion. In all of these cases, the "explanation" of religion is one particular line of inquiry, save in that of Weber, who had several. In all the cases except Eliade's that line of inquiry focuses on something other than religion as the explanation; in Eliade's case the sacred is an element within what is commonly recognized as the phenomena of religion, but it is only one element intended to orient thought about all the others.

Less focused on "classic" theories for explaining religion is Michael Stausberg's *Contemporary Theories of Religion: A Critical Companion*, which contains fifteen essays by contemporary scholars, plus an introduction and conclusion by himself, that examine important attempts in the last few years (since 1990) to explain religion more or less scientifically. The topics include E. Thomas Lawson and Robert N. McCauley's explanation of religion relative to belief in superhuman agency; Stewart E. Guthrie's explanation in terms of animism and anthropomorphism; Walter Burkert's explanation in terms of the need for violence; Roy Rappaport's explanation in terms of ritual; Rodney Stark and Roger Finke's explanation in terms of rational choice and religious economies; Niklas Luhmann's explanation in terms of communication; Andrew Newberg, Eugene D'Aquili, and Vince Rause's explanation in terms of exotic experience and its neurological bases; Pascal Boyer and Ilkka Pyysiainen's explanation of religion as an unintended by-product of the evolution of brain functions according to a dominant model in cognitive science; Scott Atran's evolutionary explanation; David Sloan Wilson's explanation of religion as a function of group evolution; David Lewis-Williams and David Pearce's explanation in terms of paleoanthropology; Thomas Tweed's explanation in terms of boundary maintenance; Loyal Rue's explanation in terms of the evolution of myth; Daniel Dennett and Richard Dawkins's explanation of religion as a great and wicked mistake as understood from the standpoint of their versions of cognitive science; and Martin Riesebrodt's explanation in terms of religion's interventions in life. Some of these theories are discussed directly in Chapter 1 of this volume. Here it is to be noted that all of them have interesting promise to explain something about religion. Much is to be learned from following them out.

But each is partial in its explanation, and most are partial in many senses. Most, for instance, try to explain why religion arises or has evolved without much explanation of what religion has turned out to be. Most but not all assume that religion has to do with belief in and comportment toward supernatural beings, despite the fact that Buddhism, the Advaita Vedantic forms of Hinduism, Confucianism, and philosophical Daoism do not ascribe religious significance to supernatural beings, even when their cultures acknowledge them. All forms of Hinduism believe that personal gods are subject to the law of Karma and hence are not as ultimate as something else. Christian theologians such as Paul Tillich, Wesley J. Wildman, and this author deny the religious significance of putative supernatural agents. A longstanding tradition of religious naturalism exists that is not associated with historical religions, as described by Jerome A. Stone in *Religious Naturalism Today: The Rebirth of a Forgotten Alternative* and exemplified in detail by Donald A. Crosby in *A Religion of Nature* and *Living with Ambiguity: Religious Naturalism and the Menace of Evil*. So, most of these "theoretical explanations" of religion deal only with a few aspects of religion and do not deal with certain religions at all.

Therefore, these theoretical explanations of religion have limited value unless integrated within a larger "understanding" of religion that shows how their various reductionisms work. By themselves, even when they do explain something important in religion, they can cause religion to be seriously misunderstood because of what they leave out or because of what they suggest religion is in some essential or definitional way (for instance, belief in supernatural beings). Without being integrated into a larger understanding of religion, these approaches through theoretical explanation can give rise to the "drunk man and the streetlight" phenomenon.[12] Like the drunk looking for his keys where the light is rather than where the keys were dropped, the reductive explanatory accounts can deal only with those aspects of religion enlightened by the explanatory models at hand. Ann Taves's *Religious Experience Reconsidered* is a thoughtful approach to what she calls a "building-block" approach to the study of religion that attempts to assemble studies of what various people think is "special" in religion, especially as related to religious experience. How the blocks fit together is not likely to be a matter of mere assemblage (not that she suggests that it is) but requires understanding on its own.

IV. UNDERSTANDING RELIGION

To review and to preview the task of *understanding* religion, *Philosophical Theology* delimits the understanding of religion with an heuristic hypothesis of definition. Religion has been defined throughout *Philosophical Theology* as *human engagement of ultimacy expressed in cognitive articulations, existential responses to ultimacy that give ultimate definition to the individual and community, and patterns of life and ritual in the face of ultimacy (I, introduction, ii)*. This hypothesis about how to define religion was put forward in *Philosophical Theology One*, the volume devoted principally to analyzing ultimacy itself and carried forward in *Two*, which elaborates some of the existential responses to ultimacy. It guides the philosophy of religion in *Three.* With this much of the *Philosophical Theology* in hand, it is appropriate to reexamine the strategy of defining religion philosophically in order to understand it.

Much philosophy of religion has been anticipated in *Philosophical Theology One* and *Two.* In *One* a complex first-order metaphysical hypothesis about ultimate reality was defended in detail. That volume also introduced a philosophical theory of symbolic engagement that exhibits how the interpretive elements of engagement might be true or false about first-order issues of ultimacy. It articulated a program for philosophical theology that centers on being able to address those first-order issues with the aid of all the other considerations that might enter into it, including the study of religion and the development of a philosophy. And it introduced some analytical terms for understanding religion in its cognitive articulations as sacred canopies functioning within sacred worldviews.

Philosophical Theology Two focused on the first-order claims that are to be made about the human predicament, or predicaments, and how religions articulate and offer remedies. It also articulated how religion organizes the human experiences of ecstatic fulfillment relative to the ultimate conditions of human life. *Two* employed the metaphysics of ultimacy from *Philosophical Theology One* to define four cosmological ultimate predicaments for human life and one ontological ultimate predicament. Insofar as the "personal and communal existential responses to ultimacy that give ultimate definition to the individual and community" deal with ultimate human predicaments, that volume fleshed out this part of the definition of religion. *Philosophical Theology Two* said much about how religions are shaped by the realities of human predicaments and how those predicaments open into positive experiences and expressions of ecstatic fulfillment. But it said little and presupposed much about the internal structures of religion or religions, which is the main topic of *Three.*

What is the significance of defining religion philosophically as the engagement of ultimate reality or realities? The idea itself is not new, having been developed in profound ways by Paul Tillich.[13] Whether religion is best defined in relation to ultimacy is a question that will be answered in the long run by seeing how fruitful this strategy is compared with other ways of defining it, say, in reference to the sacred or holy, or to supernatural beings, or to special kinds of experience. The answer to this question is given through the whole of the argument of *Philosophical Theology*, although it is summarized in various places. Whether the strategy of defining religion through a philosophical conception is helpful is the more immediate question to be asked here.

The philosophy of religion in *Philosophical Theology* is conspicuously different from most contemporary forms of philosophy of religion by virtue of its use of philosophy (*I, preface; I, 1, iii, iv*). Analytic philosophy of religion tends to use philosophy as a kind of methodological tool with which to analyze religious topics, often but not always for apologetic purposes. Continental philosophy of religion focuses on a kind of philosophical analysis of religion as a phenomenon or set of phenomena, with philosophy functioning in a phenomenological manner. For some, philosophy of religion is the extension of the philosophical tradition of German idealism with a heavy dose of explication of mysticism. In *Philosophical Theology*, by contrast, philosophy is a kind of systematic, dialectically unfolding, multilayered, complex hypothesis addressing a broad range of philosophical topics, "a philosophy" in other words that turns to address religion. In particular, this philosophy is used to define or circumscribe religion so as to set the context within which phenomenological, historical, and conceptually analytical inquiries can be conducted.

To understand religion through "a philosophy" of this systematic, dialectically unfolding, multilayered, complex hypothetical sort is not only different from other common philosophical approaches: It is positively objectionable to certain kinds of postmodern thinking. The postmodern worry is that large-scale philosophical concepts are logocentric, that is, that they force reality to conform to a conceptual theory. Or to put the complaint in reverse fashion, whatever in reality does not register within the logical concepts at hand is marginalized or forced out of view. Behind much postmodern thinking is an ethical impulse to bring to light and defend those experiential perspectives that are marginalized or obscured by any large-scale theory. This objection is not a general objection to metaphysics, which is supposed to have been delegitimized by Kant: Simply to say that metaphysics is hypothetical rather than apodictic, and to show how this is so, for instance, by the example of Whitehead's metaphysics, is sufficient to answer Kant. Rather, the postmodern objection is a defense of the marginalized and otherwise obscured or delegitimized *(I, 2, iv)*.

The answer to this postmodern objection is to come down to cases: Point out some experiential perspective, say, that of women, or the poor, or the colonized, and then the hypothetical philosophy should be amended to lift them up and give them a proper place. The postmodern rebuttal of this answer is that access to those experiential perspectives is to be gained only by entering into the languages and thought worlds of those perspectives themselves, which in practice means micro-studies. To ask how those experiential perspectives relate, through marginalization or negation, to some larger philosophical theoretical structure is already to distort them. The micro-studies unfold the experiential perspectives from within and in literal and in-principle senses are incomparable to one another or to a theoretical structure.

The answer to this postmodern rebuttal is that those micro-studies are legitimate and can stand on their own. The attempt also to relate them within a larger philosophy of religion does not delegitimize them. But there is nothing wrong with also attempting to think them in comparative categories, working them into the larger philosophy of religion. And, in fact, this is what happens anyway. If the micro-studies of experiential perspectives were really to be isolated and limited to their internal languages and thought forms, then there could be no postmodern theory, no theory of the evils of logocentrism and the effects of marginalization. The theory of postmodernism itself is an example of a very large logocentric philosophy, arising from Marxism and concerned about economic power and control of the intellectual agenda, as in the work of Terry Eagleton, Michel Foucault, and Edward Said, to take some classic examples. Much of the evidence for validity of the postmodern theory comes from the accumulation of microstudies of various experiential perspectives that show that they indeed have been marginalized or obscured by the dominant philosophical theories. So, the question is whether the large-scale theories in postmodernism are better than the larger and more complex philosophies that might also define the tasks for understanding religion. *Philosophical Theology* as a whole constitutes a cumulative argument for the superiority of the philosophy elaborated here.

At this point it is possible to draw a sharper focus on the character of the project of philosophical theology as intended here. On the one hand, philosophical theology needs to be vulnerable to learning from all the reductive sciences and other disciplines that approach religion with special methodologies and theoretical tools. Not to be so vulnerable, indeed not to seek out actively what reductive approaches can reveal, is to tempt philosophical theology to fall back into a philosophical defense of some prior religious commitment. Nevertheless, philosophical theology needs to be alert to what is left out in each of the reductive approaches, and for this reason it always needs a working definition of religion of the sort that has been developed here. On the other hand, philosophical theology needs to be open to all the sources of religion, including the vitality of scriptures, revelations, and traditions. It especially needs to be open to the search for ecstatic experience that provides the spirit and power of religious life. Karen Armstrong writes,

> An increasing number of people find traditional religious doctrines and practices irrelevant and incredible, and turn to art, music, literature, dance, sport, or drugs to give them the transcendent experience that humans seem to require. We all look for moments of ecstasy and rapture, when we inhabit our humanity more fully than usual and feel deeply touched with and lifted momentarily beyond ourselves. We are meaning-seeking creatures and, unlike other animals, fall very easily into despair if we cannot find significance and value in our lives.[14]

Openness to these first-order issues of religious life is extremely uncomfortable for most of the reductive approaches to religion. To be sure, philosophical theology needs to be in a position to not only criticize the innocence of some first-order claims and experiences but also to recover it. A large part of the contextualizing of these first-order claims and experiences is comparative theology in which different religious situations and tradition are brought into comparative contact. Francis X. Clooney, S.J., one of the most accomplished comparativists, clearly is open to the authenticity and inspirational base of religious life.[15] Yet his work is rooted in his own religious tradition, and his questions ask what can be learned about other religions from that basis, including what the study of other religions teaches about his own. In practice, perhaps that is about as "catholic" as a philosophical theologian can be. Yet in theory the investigator might encounter a religious source or experience that uproots the beginnings. Of course, mature, sophisticated thinkers are not likely simply to dismiss their roots and adopt a whole new system or path. Far more likely, they will return to reconfigure their own roots, introducing newly learned elements. Nevertheless, it is always possible, especially in this time when the old forms are so impotent or even offensive for so many people, that openness to first-order sources of religious inspiration, in teachings, practices, and experiences, will lead to taking on what is essentially a new religion, or a new version of deeper religious life that displaces the old. To be open fully to first-order sources of religion one needs a posture of inquiry and experiment that is willing to move away from antecedent commitments. This point is especially important in light of the problems discussed in the final two chapters of *Philosophical Theology Three*, concerning living on the cusp between an inhabited sacred worldview and the lack of such a worldview.

Philosophical Theology Three focuses on religion itself as a locus of first-order theological topics. Those topics all involve symbolic engagement of ultimacy by means of cognitive, social, and existential expressions. The pursuit of this agenda requires the development of rudiments of a theory of religion. It needs also to recalibrate the references to religion that are made in *Philosophical Theology One* and *Two*. In those two volumes, the discussion is controlled by philosophical argument with the development of categories for articulating ultimacy, predicament and fulfillment. Accordingly, religious concepts, practices, experiences, and phenomena are cited there to illustrate the philosophical points. These citations are often cross-cultural and comparative, and examples are snipped out of concrete religious traditions in such fashion that they become abstract illustrations of philosophically expressed matters. Actual religion is much more complicated than this, and the eliciting of illustrative snippets distorts even the snippets.

The direct study of religion in this volume needs to recalibrate the approach to actual religion and religions. The first step toward doing this is to examine basic issues in understanding religion, the topic of Part I. The second step is to examine some actual religious traditions, problematic as the notion of religious tradition will have been made in the prior discussion. The focus is on the different unifying themes in various traditions that are operative when the integrity of the tradition is at stake. A claim throughout *Philosophical Theology* is that religion is the symbolic engagement of ultimate realities that are rather much the same for all people, and that religions are different symbolic systems for doing this. The differences among religions in embodying symbolic engagements are what need to be brought into focus. This will be the topic of Part II.

Part III will take up the topic of how religion and religions engage the ultimate in normative issues, particularly ethics, spirituality, and religious belonging. A philosophical theory of possibilities, values, obligations, self-integration toward wholeness, the engagement of others through causal influences, and the achievement of personal and communal value-identity is developed in *Philosophical Theology One* and *Two*. But this theory is not brought to address the great normative issues characteristic of religious life until *Three*.

Part IV will note that the interpretations of the predicaments, remedies, and ecstatic fulfillments discussed in *Two* come from religious worldviews. Religious worldviews are also the key interpretive notion for the social dimensions of religion and its engagement, according to *Philosophical Theology*. But what happens when the religious worldviews become implausible, many aspects of which are addressed in *Three*? Implausibility produces an ontological crisis on top of all the cosmological predicaments. Moreover, the relativity of all worldviews, their inadequacy in times of certain crises, and the need to live between worldviews pushes religion into the class of proximate concerns and refocuses ultimate concern of the mystical sort on living on the boundary. Part IV will analyze explicitly what makes worldviews plausible, what makes them implausible, the special ontological crisis this occasions, and the religious virtuosity of living on the cusp of having and not having a plausible sacred worldview.

Part I

Understanding Religion

Part I

Preliminary Remarks

Religion is to be understood as the symbolic engagement of ultimacy by means of signs expressed cognitively, existentially, and socially. Such is the hypothesis elaborated throughout *Philosophical Theology* and defended in detail in *Philosophical Theology Three*. The engagements are real activities and what is engaged is real. Perhaps what is engaged is not well interpreted by the symbols in the engagement; this might be because it is misidentified in the reference, because it is interpreted in respects other than the ones the engagement intends, because it is interpreted in unimportant respects, or because the interpretation is muddied, too ambiguous, or just plain wrong. Nevertheless, what is putatively engaged, the ultimates, are real; otherwise they could not be badly interpreted or be interpreted mistakenly.

That religion is the symbolic engagement of ultimate reality (or ultimate realities, or ultimate dimensions of mundane domains of experience, or any of the other cognates we have discussed) is justification for beginning the study of religion with what science can tell about how human beings engage the ultimate boundaries of their natural and cultural environment. Evolutionary biology and cognitive science, including neuroscience, have made interesting proposals about how to understand the origins of religion in the evolution of human biological and social structures. Religion always is *symbolic* engagement, however, which means that it is guided by symbols or signs that take their meaning within cultural semiotic systems. Therefore, a crucial task is to understand the evolution of semiotic systems capable of engaging ultimate matters. In certain respects, this too is a scientific question about a phenomenon more or less universal to all human beings. In other respects, however, it is a question calling for study of the actual semiotic systems that provide symbols of ultimacy. These are the symbolic systems studied by the social sciences involved with religion, including history of religions; they also are studied by the interpretive disciplines of the humanities and arts. The rudiments of religion might be understood in evolutionary terms, such that what "explains" is the adaptive advantage for carrying on genes for those rudiments. Yet, to the degree that religion has evolved with symbolic engagement, that which "explains" is how human beings learn from their symbolic engagements so as to symbolize better. Symbolic culture evolves, too, not just by forces of adaptive advantage but through the correction of symbolic interpretations in engagements. These are the topics of Chapter 1.

How do the scientific approaches identify religion in the first place, however? The Pleistocene rudiments of religion—ritual behaviors, beliefs in supernatural agents, and so forth—are also the rudiments of science, government, art and literature, and most other dimensions of civilized experience, just as much as they are rudiments of what we now understand as religion. How do we track the development of those rudiments into religion as opposed to their developments into those other dimensions? The argument in *Philosophical Theology* is that religion is the engagement of ultimacy. Therefore, those rudiments are religious insofar as they can be tracked to the symbolic engagement of ultimacy. This is to say, we read back from a current understanding of religion, defined as engaging ultimacy, to see the history of religion as it developed in some distinction from those other dimensions. The most important historical nexus in that development was the Axial Age, in which, for the first time, large-scale cultural conceptions of ultimate conditions were formulated in what became the dominant religious traditions of East, South, and West Asia. Pre–Axial Age religions had symbols that functioned as symbols of ultimacy, demarking and describing boundary conditions for worldviews. But Axial Age religions formulated conceptions of the world as such, the nature of human obligation, of human wholeness, of relations of people to other people, of ultimate personal identity relative to the principles of the cosmos, and of the contingency of all this. These considerations shape the agenda of Chapter 2.

The great religious traditions of the Axial Age have different symbolic systems from one another for engaging ultimate matters. It would seem, then, that each tradition would have theologians who explicate these symbolic systems, interpret them for various circumstances, and, in particular, develop interpretive tapestries that connect the popular symbols that have such intimate forms that they can orient life in proximate detail with the transcendent symbols that more directly engage the ultimate conditions of life. Following the current language in Christian theology, these can be called "confessional" theologians because they start with ("confess") the symbolic system of their tradition and elaborate this for the circumstances of life and history, including the history of their community defined by their symbolic system. Accordingly, there are Buddhist, Confucian, Christian, Daoist, Hindu, Jewish, and Muslim theologies, each with sub-branches. Also there are theologies of Axial Age religions such as Jainism, Paganism, and Zoroastrianism that have shrunk in importance compared to the others. The organizing principle of this particular way of thinking about tradition-defined theologies is that each flows from some defining source—person, text, event, and so forth—and ramifies in various directions that can be described in a chronological narrative. Because of the source, the religions can be defined by their names.

This organizing principle is misleading, however. At any given historical situation for a religious group, the causal, especially symbolic, antecedents are not just those identified with the semiotic symbolic system that might name the group but come from a wide variety of other sources. Buddhism's roots are in Brahmanical religions, and renouncer traditions, and in Dravidian resistance to Aryan religions, and in social conditions to which Jainism also responded at about the same time as early Buddhism with somewhat different symbolic resolutions. To study traditions organized around their name, or uniquely identifying founding symbols, is like doing a genealogy by studying a man's male *descendants* for many generations, all bearing his name (in a patrilineal culture). Much can be learned from that. The study, however, is not likely to be very alert to what is brought into the succeeding generations by the women who come from other lineages. Perhaps more to the point would be to do a genealogy by studying a person through the branching of *ancestors* through many generations. That is, the study of religious traditions should begin with their concrete characters now and look to the interweaving of factors that have led to them. In this way, far more of the interactions and multiple locations of religious practices, beliefs, and motifs of spiritual and social life will become apparent. The current symbolic systems of religious practitioners are not exclusively those of the founding systems, even when they include interpretation of early or original texts. The current systems reflect the influences of many interpretive strands coming from "other" traditions. To be sure, strong movements to purify religious practice in terms of a quasi-immediate relation to a founding text or person occur, as in the seventeenth-century Christian Puritans or the twentieth-century Muslim fundamentalists. But even these have internalized reactions to the intervening developments. To read religious traditions starting from some "beginning" and tracking them to the present is to run great risks of missing the actual mixtures of religious life and thought. Far better it is to read the present religious situation and to back-read into the interactions of its sources. This task itself points up the necessity, often obscured in historical research, of taking responsibility for assessing what is important and true for understanding the present symbolic systems available for engaging ultimacy. Perhaps the most profound lesson of postmodern critical studies, particularly the liberationist approaches of feminism, queer theory, and postcolonial studies, is that our contemporary assumptions about both religion and methodology require reflective analysis and critique. Our views of the past and of the current lay of the land with respect to religion and religions depend on the ever-fallible but ideally thorough vulnerability to critique and amendment. These considerations are the topic of Chapter 3.

If reality does have ultimate conditions, if these can be known at least in part through the metaphysics of ultimacy developed in the other volumes of *Philosophical Theology*, and if there is an historical evolution of different symbolic systems for engaging those ultimate conditions, then a central philosophical theological task is the development of sacred worldviews that are adequate for our time. Because of the importance of intimate symbols of ultimacy that are connected with the diverse symbolic systems and cannot be reduced to one another, such sacred worldviews will legitimate several different embodiments in traditional practices. What will be common to all will be the transcendent symbols of ultimacy, phrased in terms of some common metaphysics of ultimacy. Where the different embodiments diverge will be in their intimate symbols and the hermeneutic procedures for relating the intimate to the transcendent. The viable sacred worldviews thus build in explicit tolerance for different embodiments. Many viable worldviews can exist with Buddhist, Christian, Confucian, Daoist, Hindu, Jewish, and Muslim embodiments. Or, since those names are likely to be misleading, there might be many more embodiments reflecting diverse versions and new combinations, plus adaptations of pre–Axial Age religions, such as shamanisms of various sorts. Of course, not everything that has been associated with these "named" traditions and their subgroups can become embodiments within viable sacred worldviews. In fact, everything that resists interpretation in consistency with the transcendent metaphysical symbols of ultimacy is likely to be rejected from a viable sacred worldview. Still an extraordinary diversity exists in the ways to be religious within the viable sacred worldviews, and recognition of that diversity is part of the worldviews. These are the topics of Chapter 4. The chapters of this part present the rudiments of a theory of religion as well as sacred worldviews for how to be religious as best we can now.

Chapter One

Science and Culture

What does "understanding religion" mean? This has to be an underlying question from the beginning, as the introduction of this volume pointed out and it remains a contested issue throughout the inquiry. If the inquiry can be said properly to end, the question can be rephrased to ask what the understanding of religion has turned out to be. The discussion here will be to start with the proposal popular among evolutionary biologists and cognitive scientists interested in religion that understanding religion means to "explain" it in terms of some more primitive concepts from which it is derived.

I. COGNITIVE SCIENCE WITH EVOLUTIONARY BIOLOGY

Biological evolution concerns the ways in which traits carried in human DNA that favor the reproductive capacity of those who carry them get passed on with greater prevalence than traits with less favorable reproductive capacities. Part of the complexity in this idea has to do with the different senses in which individuals and populations carry the adaptive traits. A population might carry a suite of traits that does not favor the reproduction of all individuals but that, when mixed with other suites of traits in the population, gives adaptive advantage to the reproductive capacities of the entire population.[1] The suites of traits, for instance, that typically are expressed in homosexual impulses and behavior, and those expressed in sterile intersex anatomy, do not favor the reproductive capacity of those who bear them but must have some adaptive advantage for the population. Otherwise, they would not have been passed down so universally in so many animal groups, including humans. Apparently, situations exist with some steadiness in which the genetic palette of the population has greater adaptive force for reproduction if not all individuals in the group are breeders.

Some controversy exists over whether religion, or its early elements, is adaptive in the sense of biological evolution, or whether it is a side effect of something else—for instance, the development of language—that is adaptive for other reasons.[2] Such side effects are called exaptations or spandrels.[3] The likelihood is very high, however, that the early roots of religion are indeed adaptive in the biological evolutionary sense. Consider two examples.

Anthropologists argue that ritual behavior is essential for the biological evolution of the human (*II, 13, i*).[4] Ritual, of course, is present in a number of "higher" animals and in all cases serves the purposes of group solidarity either well or ill. Group solidarity is adaptive in the ancestral environment in which the disposition of human genes was worked out. Now, to be sure, ritual is not only religion: In the ancestral environment it was the government, the artistic output, and economic structure too. Confucians have known that learned ritual behavior reaches down into patterns of posture and meaningful eye contact up into language and imperial court rituals to celebrate the seasons.[5] But the genetically adaptive disposition to ritual behavior continues in religion to the present day and has become distinct from many dimensions of government, the arts, economics, and other elements of social life. The specific cognitive elements in religious ritual today might make little adaptive difference to contemporary group solidarity compared with the simple cohesiveness of the war band and child-rearing cadre.

Patrick McNamara, a neuroscientist, argues that religious experience is biologically adaptive to human evolution in the following sense.[6] By religious experiences he means psychological states that "decenter" the self; these include states produced by exercise and posture, by prayer and meditation, by drugs, music, and other mind-blowing activities. His hypothesis is that the self is ordinarily a dicey achievement of partial integrations of many cognitive, emotive, and physical factors, and that under ordinary circumstances the self is stuck with that achievement. Religious experiences decenter that stuck self and allow for a better integration that is more ideally rational, integrated, and capable of self-control. This characteristic of religious experiences contributed over time, he argues, to the evolution of higher executive control functions that are mediated mainly in the right prefrontal cortex and right anterior temporal lobe, precisely the neural organs mediating much of the kind of religious experience at stake. Although the evidence is sometimes indirect and speculative, McNamara not only shows that the evolution of executive control functions is aided by religious experiences but also describes some of the underlying neural mediation of that. Here is an instance of a universal religious practice—decentering religious experience—that is adaptive to the evolution of more rational, integrated people who therefore have an evolutionary advantage.

Some people who worry about religion as genetically evolutionary identify religion not with ritual or cultivated religious experience but with beliefs, particularly beliefs in the supernatural, which they immediately classify as false beliefs and therefore lacking in direct adaptive value. Most cultures, at least in their early forms, do include beliefs in supernatural agents, particularly agents who "know what you are thinking." But these beliefs are likely not to be adaptive for their intellectual religious content as much as for their advantage in imputing agency to external things in the face of uncertainty: Wildman's example is the sound in the bush that might be a tiger or the wind; people genetically disposed to impute agency (It's a Tiger!) will run away to pass on their genes another day.[7] Children of wholly secular parents who have been taught nothing about religion still develop beliefs in supernatural omniscient agents until they are taught otherwise.

Cognitive science with evolutionary biology is a relative newcomer to the disciplined study of religion. Insightful attempts to understand religion in terms of its evolution in human nature and society are not new, however, notable milestones being Lucretius's *De rerum natura*, David Hume's *The Natural History of Religion*, and Friedrich Nietzsche's *On the Genealogy of Morals*. What is new in recent decades is the attempt to study religion within the clearly reductive tools of evolutionary biology; the psychology in cognitive science is closely connected with biology. Biology includes neuroscience, both as it understands neural-mental human functions and as it understands the genetic evolution of these neural structures and functions. Evolution is understood in Darwinian and Neo-Darwinian senses having to do with the passing on of genes. This is to say, what is taken to "explain" religion, strictly speaking, is some human function that evolved as part of human nature because it was adaptive in the Paleolithic environment for the passing on of genes.[8]

The significance of this sense of understanding by reductive explanation needs to be noted *(I, 2, ii)*. First, hardly any scientifically educated person for the last century or so has doubted that the cognitive and emotional aspects of religion are made possible by the evolution of the human brain that can perform them. The great promise of contemporary cognitive science, especially its neuroscientific strains, is that it is developing exact theories of what these religious brain functions are and how they evolved. Some of these new explanatory concepts will be discussed shortly. Understanding how these mental/brain functions evolved and work helps to explain how religion is possible, insofar as religion employs them. Perhaps it even understands why religion is prompted by the development of these functions, why it is natural, although that is controversial.

But in no way does this particular kind of reductive explanation explain everything that is interesting to understand about religion. Pascal Boyer, one of the leaders in this field, takes pains to reject other senses of explaining or understanding religion because they do not appeal to evolved mental/brain modules; for instance, he rejects the understanding of religion as itself a mode of understanding or explaining things (he cites puzzling natural phenomena, puzzling experiences such as dreams, the origin of things, and why there is evil and suffering).[9] But this is bizarre! Of course, religion has attempted to understand things like these, and it would be remiss not to study how this has been and is so now. He rejects the explanation of religion as providing comfort, "making mortality less unbearable" and alleviating anxiety; but, of course, religion has done this, and it is important to understand this aspect of religion. He discards the explanation of religion as providing social order, an approach dear to sociologists of religion, accounting for religion's contribution to holding society together, "perpetuating a particular social order," and supporting morality. But, of course, religion has done this, and it is bizarre not to appreciate this line of interpretation. He rejects the skeptical approach that explains religion as a cognitive illusion based on superstition, the employment of irrefutable beliefs, and the greater ease of believing than refuting beliefs. But, of course, religions have superstitions of many kinds and often have attempted to make their beliefs invulnerable to refutation. This, too, is important to understand about religion. He does not even consider the interpretation of religion in terms of its meanings, the meanings of its symbols in culture and the arts, its presence in music, the bearing of religion on other aspects of life, and other lines of interpretation practiced in the humanistic disciplines. Why is it even intelligent for him to disregard these various ways of understanding aspects of religion that have been practiced by accomplished scholars for ages?

His motive is that these approaches other than his own "all fail to tell us why we have religion and why it is the way it is." This, too, is bizarre, since in various senses we have religion because it explains some things, provides comfort, provides social order, and in some respects is the result of certain cognitive illusions. These approaches do answer certain important questions about why we have religion and why it is the way it is. But they do not answer the question in the only sense in which Boyer and many of his colleagues understand explanation, namely, that given the evolved mental/neural structures, religion necessarily follows. The model of explanation in his kind of scientific reductionism is the "forward causation" approach: If *a*, then *b*. If the right mental/neural modules evolve, religion is the necessary result. To be sure, this is an important sense of explanation if, in fact, it can be developed plausibly in detail. If we are to understand religion, we need to know what mental/neural capacities are required for it and how they evolved. But would it be a vast mistake to take interest also in other approaches to explanation that reveal other important aspects of religion?

A second significant point about the cognitive science approach to understanding religion is that it scrupulously avoids any responsible consideration of the reality of putative religious objects. Its account of evolution treats the natural environment as that which puts pressure on the adaptiveness of various mental/neural modules. This is consistent with a physicalist or materialist inventory of what is real. But it assumes without appropriate argument that religious objects (which are usually characterized by cognitive scientists interested in religion as supernatural agents) are not real, calling them "counterfactuals." What if part of the way religions come to be and are the way they are is that they have learned something about what is real? That surely is how most reflective religions understand themselves. Often this learning takes the form of rejecting false gods, inappropriate objects of devotion, and the like. As soon as human beings evolve semiotic systems complicated enough to think in terms of boundary conditions, they have symbolic tools for engaging those boundary conditions and they can learn something about which tools are inappropriate. This supposes that religions evolve for cultural reasons as well as for those of evolutionary biology, which they do, as any historian would say. But this point is difficult to register within the cognitive science approach when it is devoted to its own exclusive sense of explanation of religion.

A third significant point about that sense of explanation has to do with its definition or delineation of religion as the phenomenon to be explained. Boyer and Scott Atran, another leader in cognitive science, are anthropologists who are vastly learned in cross-cultural religious phenomena, as is Justin Barrett, a psychologist. But, strangely, they define religion as belief in supernatural agents, noting the cultural ubiquity of those beliefs. Why define religion as belief in supernatural agents, or rather, as they really do, define belief in supernatural agents as religion?[10] Belief in supernatural agents is a belief about what the universe contains, along with strategies, where appropriate, for relating to those alleged supernatural agents. As such, that belief is science, albeit folk science. Why associate it with religion? Western monotheisms, the home cultures for most of the cognitive scientists, do indeed symbolize the principal religious object, the ultimate, in personalistic metaphors ascribing supernatural agency in some sense or at least in certain parts of their symbolic systems.[11] On the other hand, the Western monotheisms also have conceptions of God as far transcendent of anything that might be called a supernatural agent, for instance, the Neo-Platonic One, the Thomistic Act of To Be, the Kabbalistic Ein Sof, and the Tillichian Ground of Being. At the very best, the identification of religion with belief in supernatural agents can apply only to symbols toward the folk religion end of the folk religion–sophistication continuum of worldview symbols (*I, 4*). Outside of the Western monotheisms plus some forms of Hinduism, most forms of Buddhism, Hinduism, Confucianism, and Daoism explicitly reject any ultimate status for supernatural agents of any sort. The metaphoric systems of consciousness and spontaneous emergence for ultimacy give little if any religious play to supernaturalism. Emptiness, Brahman, Heaven and Earth, the Dao, and their variants are not supernatural agents. In fact, in many of the cultures in which these religions are embedded, agents of any sort, supernatural or natural, are subject to the round of reincarnation and the law of Karma. These East and South Asian religious cultures have had robust beliefs in supernatural agents of many sorts, good and bad, and in the transformation of living people through death into honorific ancestor status. But these supernatural beings were not conceived to be ultimate: Rather they were conceived as also subject to the boundary conditions of ultimacy defined in non-agential ways.[12] Again, belief in supernatural agents might well be a universal cross-cultural phenomenon, but that in itself is a scientific (perhaps folk-scientific) factor, not necessarily related to religion. It is related to religion only if ultimacy is ascribed to supernatural agents, that is, if they are taken to be boundary conditions.

This illustrates the point made in the introduction to this volume and in *Philosophical Theology One*, introduction, that a defensible definition of religion is needed to orient and legitimate reductionist studies of religion. The cognitive scientists and evolutionary biologists interested in explaining religion really are aiming to explain its origin. But they do not have good control over what it is whose origins they attempt to explain. Their ideas of religion come from their own commonsense understanding of religion in their own culture, not from a disciplined analysis of the round of their religious situation.

Another way of putting this point is that the discussion of the origins and nature of religion within evolutionary biology and cognitive science has not internalized the lessons of Michel Foucault and the postmodern, poststructural, postcolonial, feminist, and queer theories that have been inspired by Foucault's understanding of the social construction of categories. One does not have to agree with those postmodernists who say that every category is a social construction and that there are no natural kinds in order to accept the lesson that one should look for the historical embeddedness of categories in both science and religion that gives rise to bias and distortion. The critical discussions of the category of "religion" as such make it irresponsible to assume any commonsense notion of religion with naiveté, as so often happens in the scientific discussions. Therefore, the failure to understand in a subtle way what religion is when explaining its origins is a serious matter.

The seriousness has to do with a misunderstanding of legitimate reductionism in science. Scientific reductionism is legitimate when it is clear that it is talking only about those elements in the subject matter that are amenable to analysis in the terms of its theories, instruments, and traditions of inquiry, and that it is not talking about the subject matter in any sense that is not so amenable. Moreover, scientific reductionism is legitimate only when it is clear that even those aspects of the subject matter that are amenable to its particular inquiry might be distorted when abstracted from the rest. Clarity about this second point requires the scientific inquiry to have a subtle grasp of the whole of the subject matter in order to understand the force of the abstractions in its inquiry. For this subtle grasp, the science needs to collaborate with the humanistic disciplines whose very heart is the protection of the whole of the subject matter from abstractive distortion. The correct force of the postmodern critique of science as well as older forms of humanistic study is the protection of the marginalized and obscured elements. Postmodernism is so extreme in its attempt to delegitimize any abstractions that it undermines its own work in the eyes of many scientists. Nevertheless, it is a fault of the sciences of religion not to look to the humanistic discussions of the contours of religion, the difficulties of defining it, the history of the categories of analysis, and all the other arrows in the postmodern quiver, to gain a sense of the limits of their own reductionisms. The cultural dissociation of the sciences and humanities is definitely not a good thing for the sciences of religion.

By defining religion in terms of the symbolic engagement of ultimacy, we can gain traction on understanding religion as a contemporary phenomenon. Sophisticated Hindus, Buddhists, Daoists, and Confucians, as well as sophisticated Jews, Christians, and Muslims, can reject much if not all of the supernatural imagery associated with past cultural contexts for their traditions while still affirming those traditions. The traditions need to be interpreted so as to contain plausible transcendent symbols of ultimacy and plausible intimate symbols as well, and the latter might not include supernatural agents to whom existence is ascribed. Rather, "belief" in supernatural agents might well be an interpretive symbolic engagement whose reference is indexical, not iconic.

A fourth significant point about the paradigm of explanation in cognitive science of religion is that the distinction between the natural and supernatural is extremely problematic. For many if not most scientists in the field, the natural means what is material and can be measured by the tools and theories of biology and psychology. Barbara Herrnstein Smith has shown how confusing and question begging this is.[13] Any conception of nature is relative to the science of its day. A first-century scientist in the Mediterranean countries would have believed that nature includes the stack of heavens above the earth and the hells beneath, each with its own proper physical properties, including angels and devils of various ranks; none of the angels or devils would be considered supernatural. For certain cognitive scientists to define religion in terms of belief in supernatural agents and to say that these are false beliefs, and then to explain religion as an interestingly false set of beliefs arising from evolved cognitive capacities, is entirely question begging. The reason usually given for the definition and for the claim that those beliefs are false is the citation of the authority of the presuppositions of cognitive science, not an appropriate study of what is going on with alleged supernatural agents.

Given these critical observations about the significance of the particular reductive sense of explanation in these cognitive scientists of religion, it is important to return to their positive contribution, namely, the research program to determine how the mental/neural system evolved that makes religion possible. They should not be looked to for helpful definitions of religion.[14] Nevertheless, their studies might well open up new aspects of religion not noticed otherwise.

The most important new aspect, new at least in the contemporary situation, is that to the extent that cognitive science of religion can explain how mental/neural structures evolve that make religion possible and play roles in religious life, it locates religion as a more or less universal phenomenon. Religion in its mental/neural substrates underlies religions that employ them in their diversely symbolized cultural ways.

The current status of the research program of those cognitive scientists of religion whom Barbara Herrnstein Smith calls the "New Naturalists" is at a highly speculative stage. She points out that they model mental/neural activity on the analogy of computer functions and postulate "modules" of behavior that evolve for specific functions in the evolutionary environment. These modules, say for recognizing agents, connect with others that bring a train of inferences about agents, which connect with others that make agents fearsome or welcome in the environment. The modular approach to modeling mental/neural activities has limited usefulness. What is needed is a model that can describe semiotic activity, which is interpretive of things in terms of purposes and intentions. The computer model is "forward causation" exclusively, whereas semiotic causation is a much more complicated, teleologically involved, causal process, which Dewey called a "reflex arc." There is good hope that cognitive neuroscience can move from the reductionism of computer modeling of modules to the more expansive reductionism of semiotic modeling of interpretive symbolic engagements. Nathaniel Barrett, for instance, proposes an "interactive model" that rejects the computer analogy in favor of a strategy of embodied cognition.[15]

Not all cognitive scientists are preoccupied with explaining religion as belief in supernatural beings with computer models of mental/neural modules. Neuroscientists such as Patrick McNamara, for instance, study certain kinds of religious experience, the cultivation of ecstatic or transcendent states, to see how they contribute to the evolution of the modern brain. His research suggests that at least this kind of religious practice contributed to the evolution of higher executive control functions in the prefrontal cortex.[16] In this sense, religion is not "explained" by evolution but helps to explain human mental/neural evolution itself. His finding is an extremely interesting thing to know about this kind of religious experience, even if it does not "explain" the experience.

Related to the cognitive science and evolutionary approach is a neuroscientific concern with religious experience. It does not attempt to explain religion but rather the neural basis of certain kinds of religious experience. Its most important spokesman now is Andrew B. Newberg with his *Principles of Neurotheology*. The "principles" that he lays out, unfortunately, illustrate the failure of the discussions of which he is a part to internalize with much precision the historicist lessons that are so important to humanistic ways of thinking. Wesley J. Wildman examines religious experience in a much broader sense, relating the neurological to other scientific approaches in his *Religious and Spiritual Experiences*.

Extraordinarily delicate questions arise about the differences between biological evolution understood scrupulously in terms of fitness for passing on genes and the evolution of human nature and religion that comes from learning. These questions will be raised in various sections to follow in this chapter and the next.

II. SOCIAL SCIENCE AND PHENOMENOLOGICAL UNDERSTANDINGS OF RELIGION

The study of religion in American universities has come to be dominated by the social sciences, perhaps mainly because they can claim that their scientific objectivity fits a university setting better than theological approaches that include discussions of first-order religious issues. *Philosophical Theology* argues that theological discussions of first-order religious issues are entirely appropriate for the academic study of religion if they make themselves vulnerable to correction. In fact those discussions are necessary if proper academic attention is to be paid to religiously important first-order issues. To leave out the theological discussions is to leave out very basic elements of the topic of religion. Nevertheless, not all approaches to the study of religion need to be theological, and the social sciences have contributed enormously in their own ways. This section comments on what can be learned from them, although it is by no means a comprehensive commentary.

The social sciences studying religion can be named, in an old-fashioned way, by their departments: anthropology, sociology, psychology, and in rare cases political science and economics.[17] In the study of religion, philology in the sense of the editing, contextualization, and interpretation of texts is developed as a social science as much as it is as a literary study. This way of naming is old-fashioned because so much real research and teaching are carried out across disciplinary lines.[18] Important things are to be learned, however, from the developments of these disciplines and their interactions.

The nineteenth- and early twentieth-century origins of the social sciences were much influenced by the interests of the positive sciences in objectivity. As such, they were reductive in form, as discussed in the previous section in connection with cognitive science. When clear about their reductionism, they were careful to say that what they were explaining is religion, or some religious phenomenon, only insofar as it registers in their theories and methodologies. Much was learned about religion as part of culture and as contributing to social stability, or instability (e.g., Durkheim). Similarly, the various approaches to psychology (e.g., James, Freud, Jung) differed radically among themselves and lifted up important aspects of religion that were explained according to the disciplines involved. Some psychological approaches treat religion as a coping mechanism, in which capacity it might or might not be delusional. Others focus on religious experience, which also might or might not be regarded as delusional.[19] All the limits to reductionism discussed in Section I apply to the reductive social sciences, raising questions about what is left out in the reduction and how the results of the sciences need to be amended when what is left out is brought back in. In particular, all the social sciences left out disciplined consideration of the first-order theological questions, often with the presumption deriving from their theories and methods, even more from their own scientific cultures, that the first-order questions have no real reference (*I, 2*). Sometimes they had strong views about some of the first-order questions but did not subject them to disciplined analysis.

The various forces feeding into the development of postmodernism, however, had their critical influences on those disciplines as they developed. In particular was a critique of "essentialism," to use the pejorative term. For instance, can anthropologists impose a uniform notion of culture on all the societies they study? Or should the nature of culture be an empirical question? Perhaps culture means different things in different cultures. More particularly, is the anthropological goal of describing "the culture" of a given society, as in a thick description, a proper one? Or does it distort by highlighting common elements in a society while obscuring divergences and margins? Does it distort the actual situation by suggesting that individuals are more defined by a dominant culture than they really are, given the many ways people relate to cultures?[20]

Questions such as these have been pressed with particular force by the liberationist intellectual movements, especially ethnic and minority studies, feminism, queer theory regarding gender identities, and postcolonial studies. By paying attention to those who are marginalized in a society, and by calling attention to the plays of power within those societies that cause the marginalization, these liberationist movements have called into question the steadiness of the theoretical and methodological tools of the classic social sciences. Just as queer theorists queer (to use the verb form) the distinctions between genders and gender roles, so many of the liberation movements queer the theoretical categories as well as the methodological practices for gathering evidence, assessing it, and employing it to explain the religious phenomena.[21]

Although postmodernism has not entirely carried the field in challenging essentialism, to the extent it has, it has turned the whole goal of obtaining objectivity into an undesirable orientation. The very grounds for claiming scientific objectivity in the first place is that the social science disciplines have clear ("essential") theoretical categories and methods of analysis. The "object" they study is a methodological construct of the phenomenon reduced to what can be formulated in the disciplines' theoretical terms and is accessible through its methods of empirical analysis. The defense against vicious reductionism is always to say that the disciplines do not study the phenomenon in itself and do not say anything about it; they study only the phenomenon as reduced to their disciplinary structure.[22] Of course, this has not been how the social sciences have been viewed by outsiders, who see them as studying real religious cultures, social influences, psychological effects and manifestations, and so forth. Sometimes philosophers try to say what is left out in the reduction and what the consequences are of integrating the social scientific results with what had been left out. By and large, however, the social sciences have been viewed by their insiders as well as by outsiders as studying their subject matters without much reduction. Just that far, then, they cannot lay claim to objectivity. The result of the postmodern critiques of essentialism is decisive on this score: If the categories and methods of the social sciences, and their own cultures of scholarship and argument-making, are problematic, then the phenomena cannot be reduced to them. The subject matter cannot be turned into an "object" about which the sciences can have objectivity. Postmodernists view the modernist social sciences as distortions that implicitly carry over the power structures of their intellectual social and political arrangements.

The postmodern critique of the social sciences, like its critique of the natural sciences, often carries an animus that goes beyond the intellectual critique of obscured reductionism. Many postmodern thinkers speak for people who have been brutalized by the sciences in the nineteenth and twentieth centuries. Distinguished scientists such as Harvard's Louis Agassiz in the nineteenth century, for instance, certified the "racial inferiority" of non-white peoples.[23] Science in the age of European colonialism objectified the colonialized cultures as inferior and the peoples as in need of Europeanizing. Medical science thought it was making a humanitarian scientific advance by proving that homosexuals are diseased rather than morally "disordered" (the latter remains the position today of the Roman Catholic Church).[24] Medical "treatments" of homosexuality as a disease included electroshock and other brutal forms of aversion therapy as well as psychosurgery.[25] The empirical studies that made the disease model of homosexuality implausible were done in 1956, and yet the American Psychological Association did not declassify homosexuality as a disease until the early 1970s; even then the declassification debate was regarded by both sides as more political than "scientific."[26] From the perspectives of these different groups who have been "objectified" by the sciences, all of the claims for objectivity are tarnished by political values and interests that are hurtful to them but hidden behind the ideology of objectivity. So, these groups and their postmodern spokespersons view the sciences with a strong dose of suspicion and skepticism, even when they acknowledge that in certain instances the sciences are self-correcting. Identifying with those who are scientifically "objectified," the hostility, or at least allergy, of many postmodernists to the sciences is understandable and legitimate to a certain extent.

In the name of the marginalized and objectified, postmodernists launch a countermovement to change the power structures, giving up claims to objectivity in favor of staying closer to the truth. The postmodern emphasis on studying very local communities and discourses through learning to read their narratives is an attempt to stay closer to the truth by letting the analytical categories emerge from interactions between the scientist and the subjects. The cultures, social structures (especially power structures), and the psychological and historical characteristics of the local subjects—often those marginalized by the "essentialist" categories that reflect and reinforce the larger social power structures—are clarified and brought to voice in the close interaction. The results of these micro-studies in principle are difficult to generalize beyond the local populations studied (although generalizations are often made!). But such postmodern studies are attempts to achieve a greater realism by sweeping the artificially imposed essentialist categories out of the way. Much of postmodernism is a self-conscious philosophical nominalism, arguing that no overarching universal categories can be legitimate. But it need not be nominalistic. It needs only to say that the essential categories and methods should not be used to reduce phenomena to the questions and terms imposed by the scientists. Perhaps in empirical fact there are some universal categories.

Postmodern approaches, however, agree with the reductive social sciences in bracketing out first-order questions of theological interest. If a social group experiences the world as filled with spirits and supernatural agents, that experience should be understood on its own terms without asking what would be represented as an outsider's question, namely, whether there are any such things. Whereas cognitive scientists such as Boyer, Dennett, and Dawkins (to the extent he belongs to the group) would hold beliefs in spirits and supernatural beings in mild to harsh derision, because they conflict with the more objectively sound scientific culture, most postmodern anthropologists, sociologists, and students of psychology would say that it is fine to hold those beliefs if that is your richly textured experience.

Another approach to the study of religion is that of phenomenology, and it has done far more than the social sciences to provide a common fund of understanding about religion in the Western world. Associated most prominently with Mircea Eliade, but with massive earlier contributions from Edward Burnett Tylor, James George Frazer, Rudolf Otto, and Gerardus van der Leeuw, phenomenology had its roots in the Cartesian philosophy of consciousness, German idealism (Kant, but most especially Fichte), and the great philosophical phenomenologist, Edmund Husserl.[27] Although the methodological definitions of phenomenology of religion are extremely complicated, it rejects the reductionist claims of other social sciences that involve the reconstruction of the phenomena into the disciplines' categories. Instead, phenomenology of religion claims a kind of objectivity that comes from examining the phenomena on their own terms and laying that out descriptively. As Husserl insisted that philosophical phenomenology "bracket" out all judgments of whether the phenomenon had existence beyond its appearance in experience, or whether the terms have reference to experientially transcending realities as would be supposed by the "naturalist" posture, so phenomenology of religion brackets out first-order theological truth questions.[28] Its great advantage is that phenomenology of religion provides descriptions of enormous amounts of data, describing many, many religious practices and beliefs, in many contexts, and attempting to develop comparative categories inductively.

Of course, the standard criticism of phenomenology of religion is that, despite its inductive intent, it describes with biased categories. The great summary characterizations of religion and religions provided by Eliade have been appreciated as wonderful organizing principles for the masses of data he and others bring forward. But still they reflect his own theoretical interests. Indeed, Eliade is accused of being too theological![29] Gavin Flood states the situation this way:

> The most important paradigm in the academic study of religion has been phenomenology. Through the adoption of its method religious studies hoped to reach an objective, unbiased, empathetic understanding of religions that moved away from the traditional Christian attitude to other religions either as wrong, or as pale reflections of its truth. In this sense the phenomenology of religion offered a welcome antidote to theological dogmatism and opened the way for the West to encounter other horizons of possibility. But the objectivism of the phenomenological research program can be brought into question from the perspective of postmodern indeterminism, and an argument presented that the understanding and/or explanation of religion is always historically contingent; knowledge is always produced from a social base, though this base is rendered invisible by objectivist science.[30]

What Flood calls "objectivism" is phenomenology's attempt to let the phenomena appear as objects on their own terms. He rightly says, however, that even phenomenological description is biased by its social base, is historically contingent in its terms and methods, and is fallible ("postmodern indeterminism" is his phrase).

Flood's own proposal is that religious studies embrace its historical contextuality and practice in what he calls (following Bakhtin and others) a dialogical research program. By "dialogical" he means an explicit interaction between the historically located self of the researcher and the subject matter, such that the outcome of the research is as much about the researcher as about the subject matter, at least with regard to the hermeneutical presuppositions. Thus, he aligns himself with the hermeneutical tradition of Gadamer and Ricoeur (especially the latter).

One very important point about the program of dialogical hermeneutics is the emphasis on language, texts, and practice as performance of narratives. Flood writes:

> The critique of phenomenology means the recognition of the interactive nature of research, which firstly entails the recognition of the centrality of narrative in any research programme, and secondly that all research programmes are dialogical, constructed in interaction between self and the 'data' or subjects of research. The dialogical nature of research places

> language, and particularly utterance, at the center of inquiry and provides the tools for the analysis of religious utterance. The dialogical nature of research entails that it is impossible to get behind language and its reference systems. The dialogical nature of research entails an ethic of practice which reflexively recognizes the contextual nature of research and its implicit values and is sensitive to the power relationship in any epistemology.[31]

Much in Flood's hermeneutical approach is consonant with the pragmatic theory developed in *Philosophical Theology*. Pragmatism is historicist in the sense of noting that all interpretations are contextual, with signs that are contextualized in the semiotic systems at hand. All knowledge is in the logical form of hypotheses that are fallible, or "indeterminate." Inquiry has as its moral ideal the making of itself vulnerable to correction, which includes the back-and-forth correction of the method and categories of analysis by the subject matter and the articulation of the subject matter by means of the questions of inquiry.

Nevertheless, hermeneutics for Flood and the traditional stream with which he identifies is caught by its model of interpretation. "The dialogical nature of research entails that it is impossible to get behind language and its reference systems." Interpretation is the interpretation of texts by other interpretations. By "reference systems" he does not mean the realities engaged interpretively but the texts—the language, utterances, practices—by which the realities are engaged. He does not mean that the texts refer to the things they seem to refer to, but that texts refer to other texts that give them meaning. So, his hermeneutics, like reductive science and phenomenology, cannot deal with first-order theological issues. It limits itself to the extensional meanings of interpretation and does not recognize the intentional meanings. Real engagement involves intentional meanings (*I, 3, ii*).

Jason Blum, although not citing Flood in his recent article, "Retrieving Phenomenology of Religion as a Method for Religious Studies," agrees with him about the importance of dialogue with neighboring disciplines in the social (and perhaps cognitive) sciences.[32] But he takes the greatest challenge to phenomenology to be the claim made by many phenomenologists, for instance, Eliade, that there is an "essence" to religion, for instance, the sacred. The postulation of such essences is arbitrary, and non-empirical, according to phenomenology's critics, and Blum accepts the criticism. Of course, essences are out of fashion these days precisely because of their perceived arbitrariness. But what is it that makes religion irreducible to its social aspects, for instance, or its psychological, cultural, evolutionary, and other aspects? Even if these disciplines were complementary and, together with other reductive explanatory theories, exhaust the most salient traits of religion, what unites them so that they are all about the same thing? To justify the study of religion and seek out these multiple explanatory models requires some integrating components that exhibit how the various theoretical analyses fit together. These, of course, are "essential components" in the technical terms of *Philosophical Theology*. No essence of religion exists, of course, because the varying conditional components of religion—for instance, the social, psychological, cultural, and evolutionary ones—have important components outside religion, and those are just as necessary to religion as its essential components.

But the essential components, according to the hypothesis in *Philosophical Theology* (*I, introduction, ii*), are those that relate engagements of various things to ultimate realities, either in direct engagement or through the religious dimensions of various domains of life. The argument in *Philosophical Theology* is not that the essential components are phenomenologically given or perceived, but that engagement of ultimacy is the best heuristic hypothesis for defining religion because, among other things, it indicates just what is religious in social, psychological, cultural, and evolutionary approaches to understanding what has been called religion. Engaging ultimacy is a "natural kind," because there are ultimate realities and ultimate dimensions of experience to be engaged, and a sophisticated culture in the long run can no more escape engaging ultimates than it can escape engaging the weather. The long-range empirical question is whether studying engagement of the ultimate with all its social, psychological, and other components is a useful way of getting at more or less unified human cognitive, existential, and practical activities people have come to call religion. *Philosophical Theology* bets it does.

Instead of needing an "essence," Blum argues the phenomenology of religion both unifies itself and is able to relate in fruitful ways to other approaches to religion by focusing on the meanings of things in religious experience and consciousness. He agrees with the phenomenological tradition that the discipline should "bracket or enact an 'epoche'" on the question of whether what is experienced in the way of religious objects is really real and concentrate instead on what those things mean in the experience of religious believers. This point hides a crucial ambiguity we have noted before. Does "experience" mean engaging the real objects, however those objects are interpreted or misinterpreted? Or does it mean merely the content of consciousness, so that the interpretation of "meaning" means interpreting only what is internal to consciousness? If the latter, then it makes sense to bracket out the real objects to which experiential signs refer. But if it means the former, then the attempt to bracket out the question of the religious objects is sophisticated obfuscation and distorts the intentionality of the experience itself. Of course, even interpreting the meaning of symbols within the experiential symbol system is needful and helpful, regardless of the fact that it is a truncated sense of experience.

The hypothesis elaborated throughout *Philosophical Theology* is that religion is the symbolic engagement of ultimacy as expressed in cognitive, social, and existential ways. Of course, there are no noninterpretive ways to get at ultimacy. But there are many ways of triangulating in on what given religious interpretations are getting at. In particular, the metaphysical arguments defining ultimate reality provide a way for discerning how symbolic engagements interpret them in certain respects, with certain forms of reference, and with various elements of truth. Truth, as argued here, is the carryover of what is important in the subject matter into the interpreter in the respects defined by the symbolic engagement (*I, 2, 3*).

III. EVOLUTION AND SEMIOTICS

Reference has been made several times to the transition within human evolution to semiotic behavior, a point that needs to be explored in greater detail. If religion is symbolic engagement of ultimacy, nothing in human life is religious unless it is interpretive or meaningful. But this is not true only of religion. Thinking of any sort is interpretive. Attempts to explain religion, or to explain anything at all, are interpretive. Models of mind based on analogies with computers, with strictly "forward causation," might have some utility in explaining some things. But they cannot explain the kind of thinking that goes into explanation, understanding, inquiry, and other forms of truth seeking. A judgment that is believed only as the end product of a mechanical set of calculations, and is explained by that mechanical set by analogy with a computer, cannot be believed to be true or false because it is not believed to be about anything. It has no intentionality. It is only the last thing a person is caused to say in a causal process of mental operations, a burp with syntax (for those with the intentionality to interpret syntax).[33]

So, a crucial question for the study of the evolution of mental/neural structures is when and how the various sensory impingements on and within the human body are causally responded to with semiotic structures of causation as well as neurological ones. No one doubts that all mental responses have a neurological undercarriage. But the mental responses, insofar as they are intentional, are organized by causal connections of a semiotic sort. The semiotic causal connections are not possible without a sufficiently complex set of neural connections. They add a layer, or a great many layers, of causal connections on top of the neural ones, by means of organizing the neural connections, so that responses to the various sensory impingements are intentional.

Intentionality itself is by no means limited to human beings. A frog sits on a lily pad at the edge of a pond. An insect comes within its field of vision. The frog shoots out its sticky tongue, catches the insect, and dines. A mechanical description can be given of this incident, like the jerk of a patient's leg when the doctor strikes the person's knee with a rubber hammer. But a far more natural description is with a primitive form of intentionality: The frog is moved by the purpose of assuaging hunger to take up an habitual hunting position; the insect comes into view and is taken as a sign by means of an interpretation that consists of shooting out the tongue, catching, and eating. The mode of reference of the sign is mainly indexical, prompting an interpretation that establishes a complex causal relation between the frog and the insect. Probably there is little iconic reference: The frog probably does not think, "I see something that looks like dinner—let me taste to make sure." But consider a fox, similarly hungry and in a hunting mode, who sees a rabbit by the pond downwind; the fox thinks, "That looks like a good dinner, but the rabbit will bolt before I get close enough, unless I can get downwind of the rabbit." So the fox sneaks around to approach from the other direction, catches the rabbit, and dines. The fox takes the complicated sensory field as a sign that refers iconically to the position of the rabbit relative to the wind, rotates the sensory image of the rabbit so as to imagine sneaking up behind, and does so. This interpretive engagement has much iconic reference. Whereas amphibians such as frogs probably cannot rotate iconic images in their imagination, advanced mammals such as foxes can. The fox engages the rabbit with a complex icon involving an image of the rabbit, wind direction, and habits of successful hunting from a downwind direction and interprets that icon with a successful hunting-and-eating ploy.

A camouflaged naturalist with binoculars crouches quietly, watching all this a few yards away, chuckling while trying to imagine the frog sneaking around behind the insect, hop, hop, hop. She thinks about all the layers of natural evolution at the pond, from the slime mold at the edge to herself in the blind, and wonders whether Thoreau could have thought of that biological complexity while meditating on Walden Pond. Prompted by musement about the stretch of a world picture from cosmic gasses to this pond's nexus of biological ecosystems, by the literature on meditation she's read, and by this moment in her watchful, reflective life, "What hath God wrought?" she asks. Her symbolic engagement of the pond at this moment, probably taking less than a minute, involves many indexical and iconic references but is most important for the ways the conventional symbols in her highly evolved semiotic system, with its particularly rich knowledge of nature, literature, and signs for reflecting on Big Theological Issues, allow her to engage the pond with highly civilized breadth, discernment of differences, and intensity. What distinguishes her as human from the fox and frog, among many other things, is that her intentionality employs a vastly superior semiotic system of conventionally interdefined meanings. Her semiotic system with all its meanings from different spheres of life can be articulated in a large, complex sign whose parts refer to one another in many kinds of extensional reference. And that single complex sign embracing indexical perceptions, iconic understandings, evolutionary and ecosystemic theory, literature, theology, and her own particular habits of meditation instanced on this one day at this paradigmatic moment, is the sign by which she intentionally engages the situation at the pond. Of course, many different interpretive judgments are going on at once, watching, hearing, and smelling many things while struggling to keep still, balanced in a crouch, and the engagement takes time moving not quite seamlessly from thought to thought; but all these are integrated into a single experience by many qualities of continuity and integration that are also parts of her semiotic resources.[34]

Human experience is intentional, with indexical, iconic, and symbolic or conventional references. To engage something symbolically is to employ a complex sign, set within a semiotic system (in fact, probably within several systems only loosely coordinated) to interpret the thing engaged. The engagement is guided by situational, cultural, and personal purposes as enabled and limited by the resources of the semiotic systems, the sensory apparatus for observation and action, and the continuities of the interpreter's self through the interpretive time. The engagement is an interaction between the interpreter and the thing interpreted, mediated by the signs. It is intentional in the sense that the interpreter takes the thing to be as the signs say when interpreted in this context for this purpose as relevant to this interpreter. The great promise of neuroscience and cognitive science is that it might someday soon show how the causal models for understanding the nervous system and body can evolve to the complexity that the relevant causal models are those of the intentionality of semiotically charged interpretive engagement.

One of the functions of philosophy is to render a characterization of human intentional experience such that the reductive accounts of mental/neural models can be understood in terms of what they leave out. Then it is up to the neuroscientists and others to develop explanations of mental/neural functioning that do not leave out anything.[35]

With regard to religion, our scientific understanding of its origins and development needs to articulate the transition from those elements of religion that are most usefully explained by evolutionary biology to those that are to be understood in terms of the intentionality of symbolic engagement. Suppose it is true that among the important components of religion is the development of mental/neural modules for attributing agency to things based on certain cues, and then to have ready-made templates for what agents are likely to do. Even if agency is not necessarily attributed to ultimate realities in religion, it surely is attributed to other people, and the engagement of other people is an ultimate condition of being in an existential field with them. That these modules and templates evolved in human beings is explained, perhaps, by the fact that they have greater adaptive value than their previous alternatives in the matter of passing on genes to the next generation. Suppose this is a correct theory for explaining certain experiential properties. Nevertheless, this theory does not understand them, for understanding them would have to include showing how intentionality is involved in taking something to be an agent, how that act of "taking" is a complex sign in a larger symbolic engagement with the thing so construed, related to contexts, purposes, and the like. For the elements of religion to be understood in terms of their roles in religion, most of them must be construed intentionally. The basic form of this is to understand religion as doing and believing what it does because of what people have learned about their environment in the relevant matters.

IV. THE CULTURAL EVOLUTION OF RELIGION

Given the definition of religion as symbolic engagement of ultimacy, the cultural evolution of religion takes its first significant step in the development of symbols for ultimacy. The question is how ultimacy in the sense of boundary conditions can be conceived or symbolized. The reflections here are highly speculative but lay out the logic of the problem.

Semiotic systems complicated enough for ordinary everyday communal life involve causal chains, sometimes very long ones. The conception of something happening because something else happened, which happened because something else happened, exhibits a rough rule of conditions with prior conditions. The same thing can be said for conceptions of a chain of consequences. A similar rule of conditions is exhibited in nests of contexts—meals take place in the home that is in the village that is in the territory. These seemingly linear sorts of conditions in real experience are mixed without confusion. Seeing affairs as a set of causes from the past, with potential consequences in the future, as nested in various sets of overlapping contrasts, is not rocket science. This kind of thinking does not have to involve reference to items not found in isolated village life and culture.

But it does involve thinking of things in ordered series of conditions and invites the thought of the outermost or last condition. Kant was perhaps overly rationalistic in his claim that reason itself cannot think of a series of conditions without thinking of the total series, or the series as totalized. He thought this was an intrinsic but dangerous element of thinking because we should never think we know anything in a series beyond that for which we have empirical evidence. But he did say that we cannot help but think of the series as a totality, with an ultimate (for him unknowable) boundary condition.[36] Somewhere in the evolution of human thinking processes it became possible and common to think about boundary conditions. The candidates for those boundary conditions might seem extremely primitive. The boundary conditions for the cause of illness might be witches, or imbalances of humors, or yin/yang elements, or germs that attack like an invading army, or a natural consequence of an intensely deep layering of nature underlying human life. The boundary condition for the past causes that determine present life might be the natural round of seasons, or a visit by the ancestors, or a creation as understood in a myth involving productive gods, or a Big Bang physical theory, or an ontological act of creation. Candidates for chains of contexts might be a mythic geography, as in the upside-down tree of Norse mythology, or an image of the plain of Earth with many levels of heavens above and hells beneath, or an island in an infinite sea, or a globe resting on an elephant, on another elephant, such that it's elephants all the way down, or a conception of existential media constituted by the things that are in it to the entire extent of any determinate relations. Perhaps the most significant chain of conditions is that which constitutes human life and whose boundary condition is death: Death is the condition beyond which more food, better medicine, or more intense prayers for more life do not help.

Religions codify various symbols of ultimate boundary conditions in their sacred canopies, connecting them in ways that make sense of the interactions of the different lines of conditioning. Or rather, the sacred canopies often do not make sense of the integration of the various fields of conditions for which they symbolize ultimate boundaries but exhibit resonances and dissonances among the various symbol systems of ultimacy involved. Sometimes the sacred canopies become so inconsistent as to be implausible (*III, pt. 4*).

A crucial element for understanding religion thus is to understand how religion or religions learn from their experience and modify their sacred canopies appropriately. According to some cognitive scientists discussed in the first section, religion is formed in its earliest components by factors best understood in terms of biological evolution. But as soon as religion takes an intentional stance, interpreting affairs in terms of symbols of ultimacy, the structures of religion and its significant changes need to be understood in terms of what people learn about ultimate realities and ultimate dimensions of mundane domains of life.

The history of religions is filled with accounts of how changing situations cause people to change their religious practices and conceptions. Subtle histories of religion show how changing situations ramify throughout a given people's cognitive, social, and existentially embodied semiotic systems. A standard story form is that one religious culture learns from another. Another story form is that a "people" is moved from one territory to another, perhaps to a very different kind of territory. Or the conditions of nature change. In these and many other situations, changes prompt new learnings, new interpretations, new practices, and new religious forms generally. Of course, cultures cannot change completely without total disorientation; religious cultures are the embodiments of sacred worldviews, and these change. Anthropologists of a previous generation were impressed with the synchronic organization and diachronic stability of groups of people living in isolation from one another, as in New Guinea and Australia before the coming of Europeans. Nevertheless, those centuries-old, mainly stable religious cultures are to be understood in part by what the people learned as they arrived in the South Pacific from East Africa, having crossed Asia from Africa.

A more generalized statement of the point is that understanding religion means understanding how it symbolically engages ultimate reality in cognitive, social, and existential semiotic ways. To understand this in any particular case requires understanding how the people corrected their previous ways of symbolic engagement so as to arrive at their present one. Included in this is the need to understand the diffusion of cultures. This, too, is understood as learning from interpretive experience.

The history of the learning adventures of religious people(s) is not enough to understand their religions, however. One of the things most important to understand about them is how they, with their semiotic systems and sacred canopies, engage what is really ultimate, what they discover to change their engagements about that, and how to get on the inside of their concern for proper, truthful, authentic engagement of ultimacy. To do this it is necessary to see their engagements in the intentional stance, related not just to their conceptions of ultimacy (which would be only extensional reference) but to what is really ultimate as symbolized by them. Therefore we need metaphysical means of gaining access to a position in which we can see the practice of religion as an interaction between religious people and ultimate reality. The great literate traditions had metaphysical ways of addressing this problem. Insofar as these metaphysical ideas became parts of their sacred canopies, they were unable to stand outside and query the truthfulness or validity of their engagements. But standing outside is not the issue. The issue is conceiving of the religious activity in which we human beings are religiously defined from the "natural standpoint," as Husserl derisively called it. Religion is not about interpreting its religious ideas. It is about interpreting ultimacy by means of its religious ideas, even when it identifies ultimacy only with its ideas. This is the intentional stance regarding ultimacy. The understanding of religion needs to acknowledge this intentional stance.

Chapter Two

Axial Age Religion

Whereas the first chapter introduced considerations about the approaches for understanding religion, the purpose of this chapter is to frame the development of religion historically. As we look back on that history from the present standpoint, a decisive turning point was the revolution that took place across the entire Eurasian continent that Karl Jaspers labeled the Axial Age, to which reference has been made throughout *Philosophical Theology*.[1] This chapter provides a reading of the history of religion from the perspective of the distinction between Axial Age and pre–Axial Age religions. It is, of course, a reconstruction of the history on philosophical grounds stemming from Jaspers's distinction, not a chronological or even "history of religions" history.

I. THE AXIAL AGE REVOLUTION

Pre–Axial Age religions were (and are where they continue to exist) primarily tribal.[2] For various reasons, some of which are discussed in the previous chapter, pre–Axial Age religions are not to be distinguished clearly from pre–Axial Age cultures, religion not being clearly distinguished from culture in a larger sense. Inferring from many sources, particularly from what anthropologists find in studying tribal religions, certain characteristics mark the pre–Axial Age situation.[3]

Tribal religions are closely tied to place, to a traditional home territory, or to being driven from such a place, or, as in the case of ancient Israel, on the quest for a home place. Burial grounds are extremely important because individuals are defined much in terms of their roles within family systems, perhaps extended clan systems. Sacred places for rituals are also important. Markers of place are common symbols of ultimacy in pre–Axial Age sacred canopies. So are constructions of kinship with ultimately important definitions of kinship relations, eligibility for marriage within or without one's kinship group, and identification in terms of ancestors. Often the belief in supernatural beings is augmented by the interest people have in staying in contact with, or buying off, their ancestors and living so as to prepare the way for themselves becoming "ancestors" in the future with needs from future generations. Hence, great importance is placed on tribal in-group definition and clear, easily recognizable distinctions between in-group and out-group. These distinctions are made through grooming, clothing, perhaps tattoos, special prescriptions for body hair, as well as through specialized cuisines that treat certain foods (those of the neighbors) as unclean. The distinctions also are made through definitions of gender roles and sexual customs, as well as specialized rituals that mark the stages of life.

Social psychologist Jonathan Haidt proposes that very early in the evolution of human society were the development of five "moral projects."[4] His point is to understand why our moral judgments tend to be so immediate and operative prior to deliberation, although they might be affected after the initial judgmental impulse by subsequent reflection.

The first of the moral projects is to develop care and compassion for people in one's in-group. This includes cultivating feelings of hurt and shock when others are hurt, long-term devotion to people who are needy, not just children—although that is a significant group—but also those who have been injured or disabled. Fellow feeling and love, over and above sexual love, are part of this project. "Love" is a good summary word from Axial Age religions for this moral project, although love is complex and takes many forms. In pre–Axial Age cultures, love is more or less restricted to the members of the in-group. Such in-group solidarity has obvious advantages for inclusive evolutionary fitness in early human history. Loving friends and hating enemies is a maxim of pre–Axial Age religious cultures that Plato analyzed in critical detail in book 1 of the Republic.

The second moral project is to develop a sense of fairness and reciprocity for those in one's in-group. Keeping bargains and contracts, giving others their due, and demanding of others their due contributions to the whole, are given great weight. By contrast, people in one's in-group who do not pull their own weight or who cheat others are despised. "Justice" is a good Axial Age word for this moral project, although in the evolutionary conditions of pre–Axial Age religious cultures it is limited to sensibilities directed toward members of one's in-group. Cheating people from the out-groups is more or less acceptable and, in fact, a mark of virtue and accomplishment.

The third moral project is to develop a strong sense of in-group loyalty and the ability to discern quickly in-group/out-group distinctions. Some common markers for this were mentioned earlier. As a moral project, however, the point is to develop a sensibility of identifying with one's group as opposed to the others. In many tribal contexts, competition with other groups for scarce resources is heightened into ritualized, fairly continuous intertribal warfare. In many instances the boundaries of the in-group are defined by hostility toward the out-groups. The sensibility of liking those who are like oneself and hating those who are different is well-grounded. Objectifying out-group people with bigotry was, and still is, common. Bigotry is dislike of others based on a group characteristic that in itself is no ground for dislike other than the fact that it indicates that group's status as outside the in-group; the reason for the dislike is that the others belong to some out-group, which makes their race, dress, cuisine, or sexual habits seem bad. In pre–Axial Age religious cultures, being a member of an out-group was reason enough to be thought bad.

The fourth moral project Haidt outlines is the cultivation of respect for the in-group in terms of its structures of authority. Tribal organizations have complex hierarchies of authority to which allegiance is owed by those lower down and responsibilities for protection and support are held by those higher up. Many different kinds of hierarchical structures have existed, but the moral project is the cultivation of patriotism for one's own tribe's authoritative cultural identity. This patriotic loyalty is particularly important when it has to do with military and defense matters, in which warriors are expected to put their lives at risk for the good of the whole under the orders of the leaders.[5]

The fifth moral project is the development of deep visceral responses concerning purity, mainly feelings of disgust at what one's tribe construes to be impure. The capacity for disgust reactions developed early in mammalian evolution as a way of staying away from toxic food, and disgust reactions still center about food. But also they have come to be directed at the things identified with out-groups by means of which the in-group distinguishes itself from them. Sexual practices, modes of dress and comportment, and customs associated differentially with out-groups come to be objects of disgust. Save for matters of genuinely toxic food and hurtful customs, most matters distinguishing cultural groups are conventional, such as cuisine. Most readers of this book would be disgusted by a diet of bugs and worms, despite the fact that this was the principal diet of our ancestors who were evolving these moral projects; the disgust is real, although bugs and worms can be a healthy diet. Parallel to visceral disgust at things deemed to be impure are things deemed to be pure to which one is viscerally devoted. In all this, what is deemed to be impure or pure is *felt* to be that before it is *reasoned* to be that, and Haidt is concerned to account for the evolution of these feelings with his moral theory. That these traits would be adaptive in strengthening in-group solidarity, and hence greater facility for survival in a competitive situation, seems to be common sense.

Pre–Axial Age symbols of ultimacy mark the boundaries of the cultural world. Symbols having to do with the ultimacy of place have been mentioned. Symbols having to do with the tribe's real or mythic history also can have ultimacy, as in ancient Israel's experience of itself as a Chosen People. Ultimacy also is given to the five moral projects as defining the human.

The moral project of compassion and love is akin to the ultimate condition of having to relate to others in an existential field, albeit limited to others within one's in-group (*II, 3*). The moral project of justice is akin to the ultimate condition of obligation stemming from value-laden possibilities, albeit limited to one's in-group (*II, 1*). The moral project of distinguishing one's group from others is akin to the ultimate condition of groundedness in components, stemming from the fact that people need to integrate themselves into whole identities (*II, 2*). The moral project of loyalty to one's group's authority structure and integral culture is akin to finding absolute value-identity in identifying with that group (*II, 4*). And the moral project of internalizing the pure-versus-impure distinctions is akin to the ultimate condition of relating to existence as such: Is one worthy to be a creature? This depends on staying pure (*II, pt. 1, pr, si*).

The Axial Age, which Jaspers put between 800 and 200 BCE, marked a rather different social circumstance from the earlier situation of competing tribes in local geographic spheres. It was a time of consolidation of tribes into kingdoms and kingdoms into empires. By the end of that period, most parts of China, India, and the Eastern Mediterranean had been brought into large empires. Alexander the Great's empire was in transition to the even larger Roman Empire. The areas on the Arabian Peninsula that were not brought into empires at the end of this time were united under Mohammed in the seventh century CE. In an imperial situation, intertribal warfare is no longer adaptive. In fact, it is counterproductive and likely to be violently suppressed by the imperial forces. In-group/out-group distinctions, while necessary in some obvious senses, only cause trouble when associated with ultimacy. In all three imperial areas, a common language of empire was laid down on top of the countless tribal languages and dialects, so that people in Jesus's circle, for instance, spoke "tribal" Aramaic and also "imperial" Koine Greek, Paul and the other New Testament writers being literate in the latter. The Chinese emperors standardized the characters for writing and imposed the ancestor of Mandarin over varieties of dialects. The Indian empires adopted Sanskrit as the court language in which most philosophy and theology, as well as governmental business, was written.

During this period, Jaspers pointed out, philosophy developed in East Asia, South Asia, and West Asia. Confucius, Laozi, Zhuangzi, Mencius, Mozi, Xunzi, and others wrote in China, giving rise to, or at least giving the intellectual substance to, what later became Confucianism and Daoism. In South Asia, Buddhism and Jainism arose in contest with Brahmanical religion, which revived itself as the religio-philosophical path of the Upanishads and the development of the orthodox and heterodox Hindu schools. In West Asia, the Jewish prophets—Elijah, Isaiah, Deutero-Isaiah, Ezekiel, and Jeremiah—the Iranian reforms of Zoroastrianism and later Manichaeism, and Greek philosophy in Sophism, Socrates, Plato and Aristotle, converged to produce the Axial Age religions of diasporic Judaism, Christianity, and a bit later Islam. Jaspers pointed out that most of the great teachers traveled widely for their time, spreading their teachings. Probably there was much more communication between those cultures than Jaspers knew about or was willing to acknowledge.[6]

Among the ideas that occurred to these philosophers and became embedded in the religions they formed were the following. First, the world was conceived as a universe, not a local territory with vague surroundings. In East Asia this was expressed as "all under heaven," as the five cardinal directions "north, east, south, west, and here," and with conceptions of time that pulsed with recurrences to ancient predecessors back and back.[7] In South Asia, the Upanishads had several conceptions of the creation of the universe, including the gods, along with the conception of the expansion of the universe from the "golden egg," through its flourishing, then a collapse back into the golden egg to begin the cycle again. In West Asia were the Semitic creation conceptions as in the Enuma Elish, Genesis 1, and the Platonic and Aristotelian conceptions of the cosmos.

Second, and correlated with the first, was the development of conceptions of first principles or causes underlying the whole cosmos. In East Asia these included the conception of the Dao that cannot be named and Heaven and Earth as the principles of order and motion. In South Asia was the conviction expressed throughout the Upanishads and elsewhere that any plurality testifies to a deeper unity beneath, as consciousness underlies the objects of consciousness, such as Brahman, or cosmic mind, or the Emptiness in diversity and apparent change. And in the West were ideas of monotheism and the creative transcendence of the Form of the Good in Plato and the conception of God as Thought Thinking Itself in Aristotle. What was historically significant for the Axial Age in all of these was that philosophy in these cultures developed ways of thinking through the problematic of ultimacy. Whereas all cultures with sacred canopies have symbols for what they take to be the boundary conditions of their world, the Axial Age religious philosophies thematized this as a problem. In ancient Israel the development of monotheism was a move away from the older polytheistic demand for loyalty to the Israelites' God rather than to the other gods, to the Axial Age critique of competitive conceptions of God as being too small, too idolatrous. The search for grounding first principles was part of the problem of the one and the many that arose across the Axial Age cultures (*I, 9*).

Third, along with the conception of a whole cosmos, however imagined, and a unifying principle or set of principles, went a new conception of the individual. Whereas the pre–Axial Age religions identified people mainly with kinship relations and locales relative to that, the Axial Age religions said that individuals are most importantly defined by their relations to the first principles, to the Dao, to Heaven, to Brahman, to Emptiness however construed, to the Good, to God. Of course, there were also local points of identification, and the Axial Age religious cultures differed in how to construe this. Belonging to "the people of Israel" was different in texture from the Chinese belonging first to family, then to local community, then to king and empire. But the rise of individualism, as characterizes the Axial Age, comes through the identification of individuals with the ultimate, not only the proximate, a distinction difficult to make in the localness of pre–Axial Age religions. For the latter, even the ultimate boundary conditions are rather proximate, not as high as heaven nor as indeterminate as Nirguna Brahman.

Fourth, because of the primacy of the relation of individuals to the ultimate principle, and because all individuals are so primarily identified, the relation of individuals to one another is mediated by the universal relation with ultimacy. In-group/out-group distinctions are still real but not as important as the relations of people to one another through their common identification with the ultimate principle or set of principles. In East Asian Axial Age thinking, to be humane is to be humane to all people, although some distinctions in kinds of relation are appropriate. In South Asian thinking, compassion should be directed to all sentient beings in the karmic cycle of life, death, and rebirth. In West Asian thought, all human beings are to be regarded as children of God or beings with intrinsic dignity.

Fifth, because of the previous point, all beings should be subject to compassion and love, not just those within one's in-group. The moral project of compassion, love, and fellow feeling was universalized. Humaneness in Confucian thought meant, among other things, sincere love. Although the conception of the self that might engage in love is a matter of much debate in South Asian Axial Age thought, a persistent theme is love of every living being but without attachments that would bend love toward possessiveness. In the West, Jesus advocated loving even your enemies.

Sixth, also following from the fourth point, all the Axial Age religions advocated universal justice. The idea of being fair with one's in-group but ready to cheat the others was rejected in all those cultures. Justice is not compatible with special pleading.

Seventh, the three moral projects other than love and justice were relativized. To be sure, local communities and families remained with special responsibilities. But the distinction between them and the "others" in out-groups was denied ultimacy. Recognizing cultural differences, including the specifics of one's own culture, the religions also advocated tolerance of cultural diversity. Of course, this did not mean that all cultures were accepted equally; issues of justice would prevent that. But the in-group/out-group distinction was less important by far than the universality of humaneness and justice. Similarly, all groups need a social structure with some kind of authority. But no authority structure should be given ultimacy and in all the Axial Age cultures the philosophers provided tools for subversive criticism of the existing structures. And with regard to visceral feelings of disgust at impurity, recognition grew that cultures simply are different and that what disgusts some cultures delights others. For instance, homosexual acts are disgusting to some people but the very point of sexuality for homosexuals.

One of the most poignant illustrations of the Axial Age recognition of the relativity of disgust reactions regarding impurity was the story of Peter's dream in Acts 10 in the Christian New Testament. A non-kosher Roman centurion, Cornelius, was prompted by a divine dream to invite Peter to dinner. Peter, a kosher-observant Jew, would never have accepted the invitation. But he, too, had a divine dream of a bedsheet lowered from heaven containing all sorts of foods, especially non-kosher ones. He learned from the dream that all foods are clean and that the kosher prohibitions are not of ultimate significance. So, he accepted the invitation, a significant move for transforming Christianity from a form of Second Temple Judaism to a religion for the gentiles too. (But he still probably did not each much shrimp.)

Although the Axial Age religions that had developed by 200 BCE and their quick sequelae, such as Christianity and then Islam, had many differences among them, in both practice and philosophical conceptions, they were in vague but extraordinarily important agreement on these things: The world is one; it has some ultimate conditions; people are defined primarily in terms of relating to those ultimate conditions; one's relation to other people as standing under the ultimate conditions is more important than in-group/out-group relations; love should be universal; justice should be universal; in-group/out-group distinctions can have only proximate importance, in their distinctions, in their demands on loyalty, and in their visceral feelings of disgust. Extraordinary differences existed among the religions as to how they expressed and embodied these points. But even more extraordinary was their agreement upon them, and in their rejection of the pre–Axial Age alternatives.

The historical changes that allowed for the Axial Age religious ideals are important to stress. Considering our ancestors when they were small bands competing with one another and other animals for flourishing subsistence in a dangerous land, the pre–Axial Age religious sensibilities, so focused on in-group solidarity with concomitant hostility toward out-groups, were evolutionarily advantageous. Human beings to some extent are hardwired for in-group protectiveness and for violence to maintain the boundaries. Only when a great many problems of human security, cooperation across cultural differences, and massive social stability (despite wars between organized armies) were resolved with the beginnings of civilization were the Axial Age conceptions and religious ideals possible. In pre–Axial Age conditions, Axial Age religions seem vacuous and unrealistic about the problems immediately at hand.

II. THE TRIBAL UNDERGROUND OF AXIAL AGE RELIGION

The rise of the ideas and ideals of Axial Age religions, as Jaspers stressed, was a function of their philosophies, or at least of the interaction of new ideas in imperial conditions with a new professional class of philosophical thinkers. The actual transformation of pre-Axial Age religions into Axial Age ones was far more complicated. The Axial Age ideals were laid down on top of the existing tribal religions. The new ideals modified the tribal religions, changed names, and to some degree changed their course. Moreover the sense of identification with religious membership grew from tribal religions to more inclusive membership. But the tribal religions were not overturned quickly and still have not been to this day.

China through most of the Axial period was in a state of turmoil with the central authority broken and tribal or clan loyalties reasserting themselves. Religious practices were varied, but during the early Han dynasty there was a kind of showdown at the imperial court. The ruthless fifteen year Qin dynasty brought unity to the empire, and the Han consolidated this over the next four centuries. The culture of shamanism and magicians characteristic of the pre–Axial Age religions vied with the new Axial culture of Confucianism.[8] The latter was literate and anti-supernatural. The Confucian political side won, though never eliminating their opponents. In the evolution of Chinese religion, Daoism drew heavily on the tribal shamanistic side, with an uncertain connection with the highly literate philosophies associated with Laozi and Zhuangzi. Buddhism also entered into the Chinese scene by the first century of the Common Era as a kind of folk religion mixed in with popular Daoism. Confucianism, and also Buddhism when it reached ascendancy in the Tong dynasty, attempted to impose the universalistic elements of their philosophical ideas with only moderate success. Chinese religions now go by the universalistic names but are local and idiosyncratic in their actual practice. In China the distinction between the literate class, both Confucian and Buddhist, and the nonliterate classes may well have been more important for actual religious practice than the distinctions between those two Axial Age religions.

In India the situation was much the same. The society during the Axial Age was very much organized along tribal lines, and the establishment of the Mauryan Empire in the fourth century BCE, though unifying political control, did not much affect the vast diversity of languages and local cultures. Gautama Buddha, at least by legend, had led a religious revolution against what he regarded as the corrupted Brahmanical religion that was based on the Vedas and that enshrined caste differences. In response to Buddhism and Jainism, the very many parts of the Vedic traditions reorganized themselves into the schools of Hinduism, all with many local variations and still laid down on top of indigenous or older religious cultures.

West Asia saw a series of empires: Babylonian, Assyrian, Neo-Babylonian, Persian, Greek (Alexander's), Parthian, and Roman. Though they each tried to establish more or less a common political and linguistic culture, including their versions of Axial Age religions, many strong tribal elements remained. The life of the Christian St. Paul is instructive. He was a devout Jew—and considered himself to be all his life—with a pharisaical education of which he was proud that probably had many Hellenistic elements because he was something of a Stoic in his philosophy. He was the first great spokesman for the religious reforms of a rural Galilean, Jesus from Nazareth, but he spoke to urban centers around the Mediterranean. He was a full Roman citizen and so traveled with state protection. When he was attacked toward the end of his life for impiety against the Roman gods by a Jewish puppet king who was allowed to rule his state with Jewish customs under Roman law, Paul appealed to the imperial court in Rome and was allowed to take his case there. Paul argued that gentile Christians did not have to become Jews in the ritual sense (circumcision for men, kosher food rules, etc.), but he also dealt with a great variety of different Christian cultures in Palestine, Syria, Asia Minor, Greece, and Rome. A somewhat fractious personality, Paul criticized other forms of Christianity than his own, principally the school later associated with the Gospel of Matthew. The diversity in Christianity based on differences in local, if not tribal, cultures was extraordinary in the early period, a point sometimes obscured by the relative unity of the New Testament (notwithstanding Paul's rejection of the Matthean point of view or the significantly different perspective of the Gospel and letters of John). But the New Testament is a fourth-century anthology of first- (and perhaps early second-) century texts. It reflected Constantine's interest in imposing unity on a deeply divided empire, which he prosecuted also by initiating a series of councils to decide orthodox doctrine.[9]

Religions have continued to develop to the present time by diversifying for contextual reasons while at the same time being more or less committed to philosophical or theological principles that would unite contexts. Scholars such as Samuel Huntington can speak of the great religions as civilizations and articulate world conflicts in terms of their clashes.[10] But, in actual practice, the religion in a local context is likely to be an amalgam of many different religions' traditions, not through strict and authorized lines of inheritance (as, for instance, Christianity arose out of Judaism and Hellenism) but through the accidents of religious elements that find themselves useful in the context.

The situation today is that people tend to think of themselves as belonging to one of the Axial Age religions, but the version they have is very much located in their community, which might have a tribal culture. In many parts of the world, tribal cultures in the literal sense are still prevalent, as in the Islamic lands from the Straits of Gibraltar to the Straits of Malacca, and in nearly every part of Africa and many parts of South, Southeast, and East Asia as well as the indigenous areas of South America. American religion in the later years of the twentieth century went through "culture wars" that replicated competing tribal identities in some ways.[11] The forces defending the tribal ways tend to be conservative, whereas those defending the more universalistic ideals of the Axial Age religions tend to be liberal.

At least this is the conclusion the social psychologist Jonathan Haidt draws from his empirical research in the United States, Latin America, and Europe. Asking people to code themselves as more or less liberal or conservative, he surveys attitudes about controversial topics in which the five moral projects he defines are weighed against each other in importance. The more conservative people label themselves, the more they tend to put just about equal weight on the projects of love, justice, in-group/out-group distinction, patriotic loyalty to in-group culture and authority structures, and visceral reactions about purity and impurity construed as direct moral intuitions. The more liberal people label themselves, the more weight they put on the first two, love and justice, and the less they put on the last three, tending to undermine the importance of in-group definition, loyalty, and instincts. These tests allow Haidt to determine in interesting ways just how conservative and liberal a given population is, and on what issues.[12]

Roughly, then, and noting that many qualifications need to be made, contemporary religions are a mixture of Axial Age ideals laid down on top of tribal in-group/out-group religious cultures. The Axial Age ideals of universal love and justice are severely compromised by the power of in-group/out-group thinking. In nearly every one of the major world religions now a deep tension exists between conservatives who want to defend a specific religious culture over against competition, often demonizing the competition, and liberals who insist on tolerance of other religions, precisely because they are the ultimate identifying markers of other people who should be respected on their own terms. The official ideologies call for universal love and justice, but the pressure is to limit love and justice to those close to one's in-group. Consider the unfortunate countries whose English names begin with "I," all beset in our time by internal religious wars among neighbors: Ireland, Israel, Iraq, Iran, India, Indonesia. Perhaps there is an ancient name beginning with "I" for Sri Lanka, where the Hindus, whose slogan is "Shanti, Shanti, Shanti" ("Peace, Peace, Peace"), have recently battled the Buddhists, who believe that all attachments to self-identity and self-possession should give way to compassion for the liberation of all sentient beings. In these and very many other instances, the universalizing themes of the Axial Age religions with regard to compassion and justice are compromised by "tribal" cultures that want to limit them to the in-group.

III. RELIGIOUS MEMBERSHIP AND PRACTICE

This then raises the question of religious identity. Actually, two kinds of questions of religious identity arise. To which Axial Age religion, if any, does one belong? In one's specific context, does one have a more conservative, that is, tribal, or more liberal, that is, universalistic, version?

As to the first, top-down religious identities are complex to understand. In nineteenth-century America, for instance, nearly everyone considered themselves to be members of the Christian community, with a few distinctly standing out for Judaism, a few more for Native American religions, and a very small smattering of others, including dissenters. African Americans to some degree held on to African traditions, including Islam and tribal religions. But Christianity itself had absorbed enormously influential ideas from Hinduism and Buddhism as they were understood by the English-speaking world in those days. The ideologies of secular self-help movements, as well as communes and experimental educational ventures, entered into the cultural practice of Christianity. In actual practice, Christianity was a shifting amalgam of a great many religious "identifying" motifs that would not have been associated with Christianity two centuries earlier.

This was nothing new. Nearly every religion, at every stage, has been an amalgam of different influences. The amalgam of the philosophical principles of an Axial Age religion with the tribal religious cultures within which it is influential has already been mentioned: Christians celebrate "Easter" as the center of their liturgical calendar, named after a Norse goddess. Often the Axial Age religions have influenced one another and adopted, with adaptations, many ideas and practices from one another. Early Christianity in the Roman Empire interacted with Roman paganism and continued to do so for centuries after it became the official religion of the Empire. Each of the Axial Age religions, as it spread across diverse cultures already influenced by other Axial Age religions, became diversified in its own constitution by those different interactions. Christianity defined itself in its first millennium not only by its European interactions. In India it interacted with Hinduism, particularly the Shaivism of the southern part of the continent where Christianity flourished until suppressed by the Portuguese in the fourteenth century.[13] In Iran, Christianity interacted with the Zoroastrian tradition, giving rise, among other things, to the syncretic religion of Manichaeism. Along the Silk Road and into China, Nestorian Christianity developed in relation to Daoism and Chinese Buddhism. Similar stories could be told of the other great Axial Age religions. Buddhism developed new forms in Tibet, China, Korea, and Japan. Hinduism developed through Southeast Asia into Indonesia. Confucianism expanded into Korea and Japan and followed Chinese migrations into Southeast Asia, Indonesia, and as far east eventually as Boston. Islam worked its way from the Arab cultures to the Western edge of North Africa, west and south into Egypt, the Sudan, and Sub-Saharan Africa, east through Iraq and Iran into India, the tribal peoples of southern Siberia, and from India south and east to Indonesia. Although Islam insisted on the central importance of one language, Arabic, which the other Axial Age religions did not, it nevertheless adopted different cultural forms in each of the major areas in which it became invested. Then all of these religions have come to the Americas in the last two centuries, mixing as they never did on Eurasian soil.

What does it mean to be a Muslim, Buddhist, Christian, or Confucian today? This depends entirely on which branch of the Axial Age religion is at stake, in what cultures, learning from what other religions. An American Muslim physician perhaps has much more in common regarding ultimate matters with American Jewish and Christian physicians than with Muslim peasants in the Philippines or Indonesia. Christians and Jews together in New

York City might have more in common with each other than they do with Christians and Jews together in Indonesia.

Furthermore, membership in a religion might not be exclusive. It is commonly said that most Chinese are Buddhists for some things, Daoists for others, Confucians for yet others, and all the while shamanistic underneath.[14] It is possible to be some kinds of Christians and some kinds of Confucians at once. John Berthrong has examined the phenomenon of multiple religious identity in some detail.[15] So, what does it mean to belong to a religion, especially an Axial Age religion laid down on top of some but not all the tribal religions in which that religion is invested?

Yet one more complexity should be added to this question. The very meaning of membership differs among the Axial Age religions. Most forms of Judaism, Christianity, and Islam, plus the caste-ordered versions of Hinduism, treat membership as very important: You either are a Muslim, confessing the same, or you are not. Belonging to each of these religions, for many of their traditions, means explicitly not being something else. This is not true for all forms of these religions, of course. Liberal Jews often practice yoga, liberal Christians embrace multiple religious identities, and liberal Muslims are sampling these kinds of extension. Of those who are strongly exclusivist, the motive is not always to say that "salvation" lies only with membership in one particular religious confession. Judaism has long said that its practice and membership are for Jews only and that Gentiles have their own means of salvation; yet there have been traditions of Jewish thinking that have thought all Gentiles to be idolaters. Christianity has long understood Jews to be under the same dispensation as Christians without having to give up Jewish ways, although a strong anti-Semitic tradition within Christianity has claimed that the Jewish religion has been superseded by Christianity and is no longer valid. Muslims have often and officially given special protection to Jews and Christians as "People of the Book" and have not thought they are denied salvation because they are not Muslims, although there have been many instances also of intolerance.[16] Nevertheless, Judaism, Christianity, and Islam tie religious identity very closely to explicit membership, indeed, confessing membership.

By contrast, Confucians, Buddhists, Daoists, and many kinds of Hindus treat membership as less important than depth and virtuosity of practice. For them, it is less important what official religion one belongs to than it is whether one's practice is deep enough to bring freedom, release, harmony, and spiritual achievement. Each, of course, has its own sacred texts and symbolic systems, as well as distinct spiritual practices, and each defines the spiritual goals in its own terms. Yet each can conceive of "members" of the other religions achieving virtuosity according to its own ideals. In fact, for each of those four Axial Age religions, it is safe to say that important intellectual and spiritual traditions would claim that the reason it is best to practice the religion is because it better fosters spiritual practices than the others, agreeing to a surprising degree about what the spiritual practices should be. These generalizations should not be pressed too far, because each has many counterexamples. But they do reflect an important distinction: For some, religious membership in a confessing sense is very important, whereas for others the confessing membership is not as important as how adept one is at religious practice within whatever tradition one is in. So, again, what does it mean to belong to a religion?

To answer this question it is important first of all to recall the discussion of sacred worldviews in *Philosophical Theology One*, Chapter 4, and elsewhere. Three important variables are discussed there regarding the participation of individuals in sacred worldviews, and each variable allows of degrees and thus could be described as a continuum. The variables were sharing, comprehensiveness, and intensity.

Part of the answer to the question of what it means to belong to a religion has to do with the degree to which one's sacred worldview is shared with others, and with what part of it is shared. Is it just part of one's worldview that is shared with others who also belong to that religion, such as the Five Pillars of Islam (but not necessarily whether one insists on sharia), or belief in the authority of the Vedas (but not at all on the meaning of the Vedas), or confessing Jesus Christ as Lord (but interpreted in very contradictory ways). Or does membership require sharing one's worldview across many domains, such that those who do not share in this are not part of the religion of which one is a member, even though they might practice the Five Pillars, accept the Vedas, or take Jesus to be their Lord? Around the world at the present time, many very conservative Christians and very liberal Christians believe they do not belong to the same religion.

Comprehensiveness refers to the extent to which one's sacred worldview orients multiple domains of life. This is particularly important with regard to whether the worldview relates its sacred canopy to much in life or to only a little. Part of the meaning of belonging to a religion has to do with how much of one's life is affected by it. A "Sunday Christian" is a Christian in a different sense from a person whose whole life is permeated with significance from some Christian sacred canopy. *Philosophical Theology Two* argued that every domain of life that might be oriented by a worldview is set within the ultimate conditions of possibility, integration, engagement, and value-identity, as well as radical contingency, and therefore *should* be touched by ultimacy as articulated by the sacred canopy the worldview *should* have if it is to realistically engage ultimate reality.

The third existential continuum regarding sacred worldviews is the intensity with which they are held. For some people the orientation toward ultimate dimensions of life within their worldview is of minor significance, whereas for others it is of greater significance. The meaning of membership in a religion depends in part on how intense one's religious commitment is as registered in its sacred worldview, noting also the variables of sharing and comprehensiveness.

The argument of *Philosophical Theology Two*, Part IV, especially Chapter 14, is that to engage the remedies religion offers to various dimensions of the human predicament, deep participation in religion is required. A preliminary answer to the question of what it means to belong to a religion can now be offered. Nominal membership is always possible. That would be a minimal sharing of ultimate matters in the worldview defined by the religious name (Buddhist, Christian, Hindu, and so on), a minimal range of comprehensiveness of that named worldview over one's life domains, and a low-intensity commitment to the named worldview in its ultimate dimensions. These nominal senses of membership are sufficient to allow one to identify as being a Buddhist, Christian, Hindu, and so on, or even as belonging to such a tradition as a member. But nominal membership is not effective membership.

Effective membership in a religion requires participating with the shared breadth so as to have a reinforcing community, with the comprehensiveness that covers all the domains of life in which ultimate human predicaments might appear and with the intensity to carry through with the remedies. Any ineffective membership is not particularly significant religiously. It might be significant demographically, so that one "counts" as a Buddhist, Christian, Shaivite, or secular humanist. It might be significant in terms of family solidarity or in the dissolution of a family or community religious tradition. But that by itself is not significant religiously as a function of engaging ultimate reality in cognitive, social, and existential ways.

Is there not more to the integrity of a religious tradition to which one might belong than whether it can be engaged effectively? Chapter 3 will explore the theological meaning of a religious worldview to which one might belong. Part II as a whole explores ways of characterizing the integrities of Axial Age world religions, noting their unities and internal diversities, as well as crossovers. The present chapter has already noted that one's worldview lies somewhere in the complex ways in which the theological identities of the Axial Age religions overlay local tribal religions. But does not religious membership mean that one needs to commit to some one religion or sacred worldview defining a religious life? This is the question for the final section here.

IV. SACRED WORLDVIEWS OF AXIAL AGE RELIGIONS

In order to participate in religion effectively, so as to address the many dimensions of the human predicament and find venues for ecstatic fulfillment, it is necessary to participate in some particular religious life, relevant to those dimensions. To do this, it is necessary to have a sacred worldview in which one can participate effectively, as defined in the previous section and *Philosophical Theology Two, Part IV*. How can one have such a worldview?

The most obvious answer to this question is to belong to one of the great Axial Age religions or to as many as one can manage with some consistency. These religions each provide a varied set of well-developed sacred worldviews that can be adapted to the particular circumstances of one's community and personal life. To say the traditional sacred worldviews are well developed is to note four things.

First and perhaps most important, the traditional worldviews have evolved the basic symbols of ultimate reality that allow us to engage ultimacy at all. Without them, and the dialectic among those symbols and among the traditional religions themselves, we would be at a loss for symbolizing ultimacy. This *Philosophical Theology* is a strain of religious thinking that arose, as Jaspers said, in the Axial Age as part of the great revolution. This strain has now evolved to having a comparative base among many of the world's religions.[17] Its articulation of ultimacy in philosophic terms is commended here as something that should be part of the sacred canopies of all religions, particularly in the ways in which it dialectically connects the various traditional symbols of ultimacy. Even if an individual does not commit to membership with attendant effective practice in a traditional religion, that individual's capacity to symbolize ultimate reality is a legacy of those traditions. The prudent question is whether one can inherit that legacy regarding the historical dialectic creating symbols of ultimacy without taking much of the rest of the religion too.

The second well-developed element in the traditional religious worldviews is that they have developed symbols of ultimacy that are also intimate enough to relate effectively to the important domains of life. The religions differ radically in those intimate symbols. Devotion to the Buddha, to Christ, or to Krishna means very different things, and the intimacies are in the differences. The Torah, the Vedas, and the Confucian and Daoist scriptures might well be getting at similar dimensions of ultimacy (obligatory possibilities, integration of the self, engagement of others, achievement of value-identity), but they do so in very different ways. Unless the ultimate can be engaged through some particular intimate symbols of ultimacy, it cannot be engaged with intimacy and therefore not with effectiveness. So, the traditional religions offer particular paths defined by intimate symbols of transcendence. To be sure, these intimate symbols need to be tailored to one's circumstances, but they are deep, rich, and malleable in their possible deployments.

Third, the great traditional religions offer a host of different kinds of communities within which one can live out an effective religious life; communities necessary for the effective practice of ritual; communities ready to receive, structure, and reinforce commitment; communities that recognize and give public place to the life of faith; and communities within which one can come to understand and work through the achievement of absolute value-identity (*II, pt. 4*). As *Two*, introduction, discusses, Whitehead had a point, in *Religion in the Making*, about religion having to do with facing ultimate reality in solitude (*II, introduction*). Nevertheless, the larger point to note is that even religious solitude needs some community in which to be contextualized.

The great religious traditions offer many versions of their own communities.

Fourth, the plain fact is that a given religious culture is what a person is born into and acculturated to as part of the person's identity. Despite all the circumstances noted in which any given individual needs to modify an inherited religious culture in order to have any functional religion, a person's first religious identity is as a member of a religious community with identifying markers. This is so overwhelmingly important that anthropologists, historians, and sociologists are able to study "religion" as a function of group culture, disregarding the tiny deviations of the individuals within it. Most people, most of the time, think of "religion" in terms of a cultural identity. Yet, any cultural identity needs to involve an engagement with ultimacy to be religious, and many cultural identities allow individuals to play the cultural roles without any such significant engagement with ultimacy.

On four counts, therefore, a traditional sacred worldview offers astonishing resources for an individual's effective participation: a long tradition of careful imaginative thought about symbols of ultimacy that articulate their proper transcendence; long-developed varieties of paths of practice and reflection defined by intimate symbols of transcendence; communities within which to learn, practice, and receive correction in symbolically engaging ultimate realities; and just being born into a social group with a religious culture. Great wisdom therefore lies in embracing one (or more) of the great rich sacred worldviews and adapting it to one's circumstances.

Not only does great wisdom lie here but so does cultural inertia. Social scientists sometimes say that the most important factor in determining a person's religion is the religion of the parents. Part of decent parenting is passing on a religious culture so that adolescent commitments of existential self-identification have some prudent shape. Parents with no religious culture to pass on leave their children without anchor or orientation to ultimate matters when adolescence brings them to the point of having to define themselves ultimately (*II, 14*). Although no one exactly repeats a parental religion, to reject it requires extra effort. Most people accept the parental religion with the intent to modify it for their own circumstances, including their own community, which might be quite different and far from that of their parents.

Nevertheless! Chapters 13 and 14 will review some of the conditions of plausibility in sacred worldviews that are difficult to fulfill in the contemporary situation. Most of the traditional religious sacred worldviews, those that developed during the Axial Age, are difficult to make consistent with the science of our age. Often their focus is on being relevant to conditions that no longer obtain, and they do not provide guidance for many conditions that do obtain. Perhaps most intractable is the problem of finding ways to interpret back and forth between the transcendent symbols of ultimacy and the particular intimate ones that are unique to each religion. Without the transcendent symbols that are able to indicate what is truly ultimate, and not some proximate condition, a sacred worldview will turn out to be false. Its "gods" will be too small, its saviors subject to the law of Karma and rebirth themselves. On the other hand, without the intimate symbols of transcendence, the sacred worldview will find it difficult to make ultimacy relevant to life, effective in remedying the human predicament or giving expression to ecstatic fulfillments. The problem is that the intimate symbols usually are false when referred literally. How can they be interpreted so that they are true indexically, and how can this be known (*I, 3, iii*)? When any of these plausibility conditions is failed, the very authority of a sacred worldview is undermined.

Sometimes people find that their inherited Axial Age religious traditions simply do not provide a sacred worldview that they can embrace so as to deal effectively with the ultimate predicaments of life. The transcendent symbols are not transcendent enough; the intimate symbols are too particular, no longer address the important issues of life, and cannot be connected with the transcendent symbols so as to have their own indexical truth. Local religious communities are not attuned to these difficulties, it often seems, and also are too often corrupt. All this gives an unhappy consciousness about membership in one or several of the great world religions.

Therefore, seriously concerned religious people attempt to patch in elements of other world religions, of secular culture, of poetry and the imaginative arts to work out an effective sacred worldview. Often this takes them back to identification with a traditional religion as a member, bringing in the corrections and supplements. Sometimes this ultimate quest for a religion to which to be committed lasts a lifetime. And at any given point "membership" in a religion has ambiguous identifications with actual communities of members. For the vast majority of people in any land, such a religious quest in the context of ambiguity cannot be pursued with much theological sophistication. A religious community requires the theological work of specialists thinking on behalf of the rest. It is to that theological task that the argument now turns.

Chapter Three

Theology and the Religious Situation

What is the role of theology in understanding religion? This is a late-modern question. The more traditional question would be: What is the role of theology in understanding ultimacy? "Ultimacy" in this question would explicitly mean both ultimate realities, the finite/infinite contrasts constituting the boundary conditions, and the bearing of ultimate realities on other, mundane, dimensions of life, making them ultimate dimensions in some sense or other. As argued throughout *Philosophical Theology*, however, the traditional question about ultimacy cannot be addressed without an understanding also of religion.[1] Religion, and the religions, constitutes the context within which ultimacy can be engaged. Theology is directly about the engagements, only indirectly about the doctrines that might express some of those engagements. So, the study of religion is part of theology even when theology focuses on the first-order questions of ultimacy.

I. CONFESSIONAL THEOLOGIES

An original function of theology has been to bring the suppositions and thinking of the practices of religions to some kind of intellectual discipline. Theology in this mode is usually within and for the sake of a community or tradition. Of course, many different senses of community exist for which a theologian might speak. Christians—Orthodox, Roman Catholic, and Protestant—tend to have strong senses of authority defining theological communities resting in councils, assemblies, and other centralized forms of leadership. Muslims do not have centralized forums of theological authority, and the very strong sense of Muslim community is tied more to political leadership than to theological authority.[2] South Asian religions have schools or traditions of interpretation that develop and speak for practitioners who identify with those schools. Confucians also have schools of interpretation but rarely limit themselves to addressing only those within their schools. Monastic Daoism, like monastic Buddhism, tends to organize traditional schools around key texts.[3] In all these cases, however, an important mode of theology is and usually has been the interpretation of the religious practice and its sources for the contemporary situation of its time.

From the beginning of the Axial Age, the roots of theology lay in the interpretation of ritual. The Vedas are organized in four parts: the Samhita, mainly hymns sung in rituals; the Brahmana, mainly ritual instructions; the Aranyaka, mainly elementary interpretations; and the Upanishads, mainly discursive and sometimes highly theoretical interpretations. The actual literatures have many exceptions to this neat, but traditional, classification. In China, the Book of Rites and much of the other classical books upon which later Confucianism drew are concerned with rituals and their meanings. The Torah of ancient Israel was concerned in considerable measure with the establishment of cultic ritual, one aim of which was to distinguish Israel from neighboring peoples.

An important twist on the role of theology to interpret rituals within communities practicing them was a theological objection to certain of the conditions for traditional rituals, especially exclusivist conditions. In Hinduism these are known as the "renouncer traditions," meaning Buddhism and Jainism most conspicuously but also strands within the authority of the Vedas, in which the external sacrifices have been internalized so that most do not have to be performed anymore.[4] About the time in Israel when Ezra and Nehemiah were compiling the Torah and carrying out their purifying exclusivist reforms, anti-exclusivist books were written and incorporated into the biblical canon that relativized or ignored the ritual: Ruth, which showed David's grandmother was a Moabite; Jonah, which was about a divine mission to Nineveh, Israel's most vicious enemy; Job, which was about a non-Jew; and Esther, which does not mention God. In China the early Confucian and Daoist texts, while emphasizing ritual in the former case (later "medieval" Daoism also emphasized cult ritual), focused on the roles of ritual in life rather than on ritual as the bearer or revealer of transcendent ultimacy.

All these variants on ways in which theology functioned in and for religious communities have in common the task of giving verbal and usually intellectual expression to the religious practices and their suppositions of people, most often but not always in community. They articulate the relevant sacred canopies and how these sacred canopies bear upon the religious dimensions of various mundane domains of life. For the purpose of *Philosophical Theology* this mode of theology can be called "confessional." The term comes from Protestant Christian theology and refers in a narrow sense to the early Protestant confessions that distinguished Protestantism from Roman Catholicism and one sect of Protestants from others. In the twentieth century, however, the term was generalized to mean theology that begins with a commitment to a particular tradition or religious community and interprets what that commitment might mean in contemporary circumstances. The model behind this approach was Anselm's "faith seeking understanding," which meant a commitment to the identity of the particular community that might not be fully understood and needs theology to flesh out that understanding.[5] The identity of the community and of its members does not mean only theological identity; indeed, there can be serious theological disagreements within the community so that the theology does not serve well to define identity. Identity rather means the community of practice, often ritual practice, and a sense of belonging to a religious way of life. However the identity of a community and of its members might be stretched by confessional theology, the theology would never allow a supposition that the identity is plainly mistaken. Confessional theology assumes, "confesses," the core identity. When theologians in the confessional mode engage in interfaith dialogue, as has been popular for the last century (since the 1910 Edinburgh World Missionary conference), it is as "representatives" of their traditional identity.[6] The general characteristics of Protestant confessional theology hold for similar theological functions in all literate religions.

Rowan Williams distinguishes three styles of what is called here "confessional theology": celebratory, communicative, and critical.[7] "Theology begins as a *celebratory* phenomenon, an attempt to draw out and display connections of thought and image so as to exhibit the fullest possible range of significance in the language used."[8] He goes on to say,

> [T]here is an *appropriate* rigour to this enterprise that will be familiar to anyone who knows anything about the composition of poetry or the attempt to find a proper aesthetic congruence in creative work.[9]
>
> The problem comes when that congruence becomes so densely worked that the language is in danger of being sealed in on itself. The cross-referencing of images and patterns, in more and more intricate ways, the displaying of an ever-more complex texture to the language of belief, will risk 'freezing' the reflective process and denying it the possibility of actively illuminating and modifying the concrete historical discourses of its environment, and of being renewed and extended by them.[10]

Thus, Williams sees the limitations of celebratory theology leading to "communicative" theology: "a theology experimenting with the rhetoric of its uncommitted environment." He writes:

> Theology seeks also to persuade or commend, to witness to the gospel's[11] capacity for being at home in more than one cultural environment, and to display enough confidence to believe that this gospel can be rediscovered at the end of a long and exotic detour through strange idioms and structures of thought. . . . The assumption is that this or that intellectual idiom not only offers a way into fruitful conversation with the current

> environment but also that the unfamiliar idiom may uncover aspects of the deposit of belief hitherto unexamined.[12]

He illustrates communicative theology with the use of Greek philosophy by the early Christian apologists and the use of Marxist categories by many twentieth-century Christians.

Critical theology, for Williams, is what arises when serious questions are raised about whether the traditional categories can be carried forward even when reinterpreted. He illustrates this with the negative or apophatic theology of Pseudo-Dionysius, Hegel's dissolution and reformation of categories, John Hick's relativizing of categories in the pluralistic context, the Yale School movement, the "atheous" theologies of Don Cupitt and Mark C. Taylor, and the revisionary theologies of Maurice Wiles and Gordon Kaufman.

Williams draws upon David Tracy's emphasis on theological publics to clarify these styles of theology.[13] Williams notes that the main public for celebratory theology is the believing community, which the theology helps to inhabit its heritage more richly. The public for communicative theology includes those whose main thinking is in idioms other than that of the believing community and therefore cannot be addressed with the rich symbolic vocabulary of that community. The public for critical theology is that for which the critical theologian "should not be deflected by considerations of conventional piety from challenging and testing the language of celebration, or even the language of communication when this latter takes for granted a stable and unproblematic native tongue, never unsettled by the enterprise of translation."[14] All three styles, for Williams, are undertaken by theologians who themselves inhabit a theological identity, even those whose critical work puts that theological identity at risk. All three can be called confessional.

The importance of confessional theology, in all its modes, is that it presents and makes a preliminary case for those founding persons, events, and scriptures that reveal elements of ultimacy. The practices of religions attempt to repeat the inspirational and revelatory beginnings, and, although the "bureaucratization of charisma," as Weber called it, sometimes makes this difficult, the vitality of the religious community exists in part because confessional theology and the practices following from it rereveals the ultimate sources.

Having said this, the limit of confessional theology even in the critical mode is the bias it brings for one theological tradition or another. What about the others? Do they challenge one's own? Whether they do is an empirical question of comparative theology. At the very least, the rhetoric of the alternatives is different from and often exclusive of one's own. When there is conflict, how does one go about assessing that conflict and determining where the truth lies, if anywhere?

But before moving to the question of the limits of confessional theology, it is important to stress that no theology gets off the ground without some confessional theology in this sense, some theology that articulates primary symbolic engagements of ultimacy. Some theologians nowadays are allergic to confessional traditions and rely instead on direct religious experience. However, few if any religious experiences are untutored by confessional traditions concerned about the identity of being faithful to the founding revelatory elements.[15] Philosophical theology cannot get far without incorporating confessional theologies within it, the more the richer.

II. INTERPRETING BETWEEN TRANSCENDENCE AND INTIMACY

With what might appear to be the possible exception of Confucianism, the center of gravity of the theologies of the religious traditions lies in the clusters of symbols that engage ultimate realities with intimacy. No symbolic engagements of ultimacy would have taken hold in religious life in any tradition if it did not have the capacity to give meaning to people's lives and make the ultimate relevant to the mundane. So, although prophetic Judaism of the Axial Age recognizes Yahweh as the one creator of the entire cosmos and the God of all peoples, it is the story of Israel in this regard that counts and Judaism does not expect that story to have much intimate significance for other peoples distant from that story. Jews define their ultimate reality intimately through the story of Yahweh's relation to Israel. Similarly, with Christianity: The high God, invisible, of whom Jesus Christ is the image and firstborn of all creation (Colossians 1:15), is met intimately in Jesus Christ; Christian life is all about how to relate to God in Jesus, and Jesus has been symbolized to reach throughout a very wide range of ultimate conditions.[16] So, with Islam: The absolutely high creator of everything is to be met through the mediations of Mohammed and the Qur'an. In crucial ways, the intimate symbols of Judaism, Christianity, and Islam contradict or marginalize each other, while the transcendent symbols are explicitly in accord.[17] In South Asia, the ritual and meditative practices, which are the intimate symbols of ultimacy, are front and center; the more transcendent metaphysical symbols of ultimacy are limited to the intellectual elites; nearly all the traditions practice yoga.[18] In East Asian Daoism, the intimate symbols are cultivated feelings of non-action in various contexts, which is how most people relate to the Dao that cannot be named. In Confucianism, despite the transcendent symbols of ultimate Heaven and Earth, the intimate symbols for the cultivation of sagehood are what define the main rhetoric.[19]

The result of this is that the intimate symbols of the religious traditions are those that bespeak their separate and particularistic revelatory origins and their particular developments. These are most likely to be different across traditions, perhaps even incommensurate with one another, and sometimes even contradictory. Therefore, in order to ask the question of whether the different religious traditions are addressing the questions of truth in the same or different ways, we need to investigate the connection in each tradition between the intimate and transcendent symbols of ultimacy.

As Chapters 13 and 14 will elaborate, theology makes the connection between intimate and transcendent symbols of ultimacy through interpretation. The intimate symbols, as mentioned, are those that have inspirational and revelatory power. Many pressures exist to symbolize the ultimate in intimate ways, and the intimate symbols are the ones by which a given religious tradition or community is most usually identified (*I, 7*). They are the symbols central to celebratory theology and are found in the rituals and in the folk-culture expressions of the religion. Contravening pressures exist to develop transcendent symbols of ultimacy (*I, 6*). These pressures may not register in confessional theology except in its critical mode, and then in nearly every tradition these pressures have given rise to symbols of ultimacy that place it beyond determinateness in something like the metaphysics of the ontological act of creation and the ontological context of mutual relevance. How, within a given tradition, can theology interpret between the idiosyncratic intimate symbols and the more metaphysically neutral transcendent ones?

The answer offered by the theology of symbolic engagement is given through its theory of reference (*I, 3*). The intimate symbols of ultimacy might very well be false when referred iconically. This is to say, they are not literally true. Yet they might be true indexically in the sense that living with them carries over what is important and valuable in the ultimate objects engaged into the interpreters. Symbolic engagements of the ultimate usually are not discrete events, although they are always concrete and contextualized and shaped to the readiness of the engaging person. They are intentional engagements that use vast extensional interpretations within semiotic systems as the operative symbols for the engagements. Thus, whole clusters and networks of symbols are involved in concrete engagements, mixed and resonating with one another, perhaps as thoroughly interpreted by celebratory and communicative styles of theology. The interpretation of their truth, however, is tied to showing how they relate to engagements with the transcendent symbols.

Although different traditions have different sets of transcendent symbols, *Philosophical Theology* argues that the ultimate conditions to be symbolized are the five finite/infinite contrasts of form, components, existential location, absolute value-identity, and radical contingency/ontological creation. Thus, for instance, a Christian puts on a vast intimate symbology about Jesus (there are many symbologies of Jesus) that includes reference to the atonement, to the Cosmic Christ, to the Second Person of the Trinity, to the historical Jesus as known one way or another, to the piety of imaginatively knowing Jesus as friend, and to the life-directing symbols of Jesus as the Way, the Truth, and the Life. The person might or might not believe that these symbols refer in a literal, iconic, way. But the person's life engagements with ultimacy as shaped by these symbols can be true if the following conditions hold. First, the symbols as they bear upon the person's possibilities and issues of choice are true if they carry over the sense of lying under obligation; they also carry a dimension of truth if they emphasize the Axial Age values of the moral, social, personal, and natural aspects of obligation. Second, the symbols of Jesus are true if they carry over the ultimate importance of being grounded in one's components of life and integrating them with integrity: Can the symbols of Jesus heal the important forms of disintegration and bring wholeness? Third, the symbols of Jesus are true if they carry over the ultimate importance of engagement with all the awareness, appreciation, courage, and love that are involved, central elements of the teachings of Jesus. Fourth, the symbols of Jesus are true if they engage the importance of absolute value-identity and the redemption (to use the Christian term) or ultimate happiness this involves and carry over the resources for achieving that. Fifth, the symbols of Jesus are true if they facilitate engaging the world's and one's own radical contingency upon the ontological creative act and provide the medium for apprehending the gratuitous, arbitrary, undeserved, and surprising character of that.

Hardly anyone would be able to shape a life around the abstract metaphysical symbols of form, components, existential location, value-identity, and radical contingency on an ontological act of creation. But people can shape their lives richly in the engagement of those metaphysical things through the symbols of Jesus. When that happens, those intimate symbols are good interpretations of the transcendent ones and truthful engagements of those five aspects of ultimate reality. The symbolic engagements are not simply believing in the symbols of Jesus (or in the metaphysics for that matter). They are rather the living of life in the face of ultimacy, articulating that ultimacy through the symbols of Jesus. To determine whether the ultimacy in form (possibility, obligation), components (grounded wholeness), existential location (engagement), value-identity (achievement of happiness), and radical contingency on the ontological creative act (awe and bliss) are carried over in fact requires particular determination in each case. A vital religious community is where this complex of carryovers takes place generally and for the most part. What is said about the possible truth of the intimate symbols of Jesus in Christianity holds true for the possible truth in the intimate symbols of Israel's special place in Judaism, the special mandates of the Qur'an, and the intimate symbols idiosyncratic to all the other traditions. If they are not used to refer literally, they do not contradict one another. Their real meaning is in what they carry across about the five ultimate conditions. Their possible truth lies in whether they carry across what is important in those ultimate conditions, in what respects, and with what implications.

The theological function of interpretation relative to the tension between the particular intimate symbols and the transcendent ones is not so much a tidying up of connections within a religious semiotic system as it is providing criticism in particular cases of whether the indexical reference carries across what is important. Nevertheless, much of theological interpretation is concerned with preventing the wrong implications from being drawn from the symbols, particularly the intimate symbols. Anthropomorphic conceptions of the ontological act of creation can carry across powerful elements of the gratuitous, arbitrary, undeserved, and surprising qualities of that act. But if it is inferred from those symbols that God has intentions and that these intentions include individuals suffering from disease or natural disasters, then those symbols are in that respect false. They are false because their interpretation supposes for a moment a literal iconic reference rather than a nonliteral indexical one. For many people, to employ the symbols at all is to employ them iconically, which makes many of those symbols false. Not all intimate symbols of ultimacy are literally false, of course, but many are. The interpretive function of theology is to see to it that the intimate symbols are not interpreted in such a way that implies literal falsehood.

One of the functions of confessional theology is to employ this kind of interpretation in religious communities, especially in preaching, which is common to many though not all traditions. But it should be possible to do this nonconfessionally with respect to the employment of the intimate symbologies in many traditions, not just one's own. This is the ground of the possibility of philosophical theology operating out of a comparative base.

The theological identity of a religious person or community is not defined only by the prominent intimate symbols that conspicuously shape the particular religious life. It is also defined by how those intimate symbols are interpreted relative to the transcendent ones. Both together are needed for critical symbolic engagement of ultimacy.

III. BACK-READING HISTORY

Now the question of religious identity can be reformulated. How can religions be identified from the standpoint of the present? How can personal religious identity be formed in the present by appropriating a religious heritage? Although obviously different, these two questions are closely related.

The preliminary remarks to this part distinguished two metaphors for understanding the evolving identity of religion and religions. One is to do a genealogy of descendants, starting with some founding event, person, or text, such as the Vedas, which developed branches in many directions. This is the way the history of religions is usually studied and presented. Often the religions are "named" after some founder or founding text. Two major problems lie in the approach defined by the metaphor of genealogical descendants. One is that the account loses track of descendants who lose the name and sense of commitment to the founding source. The other is that no religious culture or person within the history is defined only by the inheritance from the named source. The real identity is an amalgam from many different sources.

The other metaphor is to do a genealogy of ancestors, starting with some present religious reality, a back-reading. Each of the ancestors can be understood through a back-reading of its ancestors, and so on back. This allows for maximum empirical study of the ancestral influences. It also requires the interpretation of the tangled roots of each "tradition" in others. Moreover, it provides the means for a theology of religions to take responsibility for its critical assessment of first-order religious claims. How a theology defines the identity of a contemporary religious reality such as a community or movement includes defining who its ancestors are. Who the ancestors are depends in part on what ancestors contributed to the health or woe of the contemporary reality with regard to its capacity to embody symbolic engagement of ultimacy. This point shall be explored in several stages.

The definition of religion that has governed *Philosophical Theology* in all the volumes is: human engagement of ultimacy expressed in cognitive articulations, existential responses to ultimacy that give ultimate definition to the individual and community, and patterns of life and ritual in the fact of ultimacy. This definition of religion arises from contemporary reflections on religious issues and phenomena: It is not a description of anything to be found as a separate and bounded reality in prehistoric times, say, or savage societies studied by anthropologists. Consider the highly ritualized life of an isolated tribe in New Guinea whose rituals include much traffic with supernatural beings. Those rituals might be identified with religion, as is common in anthropology. But, as Chapter 1 in this volume pointed out, those rituals considered inclusively were also the educational system, the government, the economic system, and the expression of the tribe's science or understanding of nature. Only from the standpoint of a contemporary definition of religion such as that given earlier can we say without reductionism what aspects of that tribe's ritual life are religious. The answer that follows from the definition is that those aspects are religious that have to do with ultimacy, where ultimacy is defined in terms of the boundary conditions as perceived by the tribe. Anthropologists might identify the religious rituals with those that involve stepping across a liminal boundary into sacred space or time. These rituals might in fact have to do with ultimacy, but they might also have to do with proximate, non-ultimate, albeit spooky, elements of life. By the same token, ritualistic changes in agriculture that follow the changing of the seasons might involve no liminal crossover into sacred space-time but still be ways by which people relate to the ultimate boundary condition of the existential field. With regard to the supernatural beings, some of them might be associated with ultimate boundary conditions, but others might not be. In the former case, an overlap exists between the scientific belief in supernatural beings and the religious evaluation of them as ultimate. In the latter case the belief in supernatural beings is interesting from the standpoint of the origin of science but not from the standpoint of the development of religion. These points can be made because of a back-reading of the savage society from the standpoint of a contemporary definition of religion. No way exists by which one could give a thick description of the tribal life and then say which parts were its religion, which its science, or government, or educational system, without back-reading from contemporary definitions of those dimensions of life.

Serious problems arise when an inquiry is not self-conscious about the contemporary definition by means of which it reads back. For instance, the cognitive scientists who define religion as belief in supernatural agents are usually not properly responsible for that identification. It usually comes from their own personal beliefs that religion is about supernaturalism and that supernaturalism is false, and then they identify any supernatural belief as religious, and religion as bad science, or a belief system refuted by science. Then they cannot recognize as religious those religions that reject supernaturalism nor those that accept the existence of all sorts of supernatural beings but consider them simply items in the universe, possibly problematic, but not as important as much deeper realities. Since the scientific revolution and its spread across the world, important strains have arisen in nearly all the religious traditions that reject supernaturalism in the name of naturalistic science but redefine their religious objects in ways that are not supernaturalistic. Supernaturalism is a shortsighted contemporary definition of religion, even though it can be found in savage societies. Reference to ultimacy is a far better hypothesis for how religion should be defined in terms of present considerations. The fact that ultimacy in rituals perhaps cannot be distinguished in savage societies from education, government, and economics in those same rituals is not a fault of the definition of religion as engaging ultimacy. It is only to point out that in those contexts the boundary conditions were not much separated off from those other domains of life. The moral is that inquiry needs to take responsibility for its definitions in contemporary terms so as to back-read the phenomena of its interest.

The study of particular religious traditions, by the same argument, needs to take responsibility for its identification of present religious realities with which to start. The temptation is to begin with specific religious communities and analyze the congeries of ancestral influences that have given rise to them. Postmodern studies of religion, anxious to avoid reading in large theoretical categories that bias and marginalize people and practices, often focus on local communities. The theoretical basis for this, carried to something of an extreme, is the Yale School's belief that religious communities are identified by their deep structure or grammar, each being unique to its own deep structure that has evolved from various sources. But this paints an unrealistic picture of religious communities as having sharp boundaries when in fact they do not.

So the study of a particular religious community needs to identify the community in part in terms of its interactions with other religious communities and with secular cultures. Moreover, the religious character of the community is formed in part by the ways it takes in and draws implications from science and from the community's interactions in world politics, and economics, and a host of other factors. Many complications exist regarding what contributes to the sense of ultimacy in a sacred worldview (*I, 4–8; II, 13–16*).

Perhaps a better starting point than a religious community for the study of the twisted roots of ancestral religious realities is an analysis of the "religious situation." Analysis of the religious situation was the mode of inquiry by which Paul Tillich began his theology.[20] His own analysis was biased by his existentialist philosophy at the time (early in his career), but it was helpful for locating what the concrete reality of religion is: not a community but a situation within which communities exist, more or less, and to which individuals belong, more or less, and in which symbolic engagements of ultimacy are not to be limited to those defined by communities with explicit traditions. The next section here analyzes the concept of the religious situation.

What is said about identifying religion and religions as objects of study through a back-reading from an analysis of the contemporary situation applies with even greater intensity in the case of individuals taking on a religious identity. The responsibility for the identity lies with the individual, not with authoritative antecedents. If one becomes a Buddhist, or Christian, or Kashmir Shaivite, the rich texture of historical tradition in each case will have enormous effects on one's engagements with ultimacy, for better and worse. Each of the ancestral elements in each of those traditions will be important. But the responsibility for putting oneself into the influence pattern of these traditions belongs to the individual. This is so even when one just finds oneself in a tradition because of one's family or society. Moreover, one becomes a Buddhist, say, in a certain situation where Buddhism is of a particular sort, where it relates in particular ways to other traditions, and to science, politics, and so forth.

The act of giving oneself a religious identity then is an extremely complicated way of defining oneself in a religious situation. One's subsequent (or continuing) engagements of ultimacy in all its dimensions are functions of how one constructs identity in that situation. That construction is primarily a function of groundedness with respect to the components of that situation. The existential choice of a religious identity is part of the predicament of wholeness. But it also has obligatory dimensions, since that identity will largely affect how one behaves. And it also has dimensions relating to how the world and other people are engaged. And, of course, it affects, but is not the whole of, one's absolute value-identity. Some religious traditions, for instance, many evangelical Christian ones, believe that one's choice of religious identity—say, accepting Jesus Christ as one's Lord and Savior—determines the whole of one's absolute value-identity. That is a difficult case to make, however, given the complexity of the value and disvalue one achieves through life. Nevertheless, the choice of religious identity defined in one's religious situation does have bearing on all the points of ultimate reality

IV. THE RELIGIOUS SITUATION

The question for theology in religion, then, is how to sort out the understanding of the religious situation relative to religions and religion and what this means for individuals and their own religious identity. How should we understand the concept of the religious situation, with an eye to ordering theology to its study?

A good place to begin is with Paul Tillich's understanding. True to the nature of the concept of the religious situation, Tillich's own situation should be noted first.[21] He published *The Religious Situation* in German (*Die Religiose Lage Der Gegenwart*) in 1926 at the height of the Weimar Republic when he was forty years old. The son of a Lutheran minister, he had received a PhD in philosophy from Breslau in 1910 and a licentiate in theology from Halle in 1912, writing on Schelling for both dissertations. He served as an army chaplain in the First World War, resulting in a nervous breakdown. In 1924, when he would have been planning *The Religious Situation*, he moved from Berlin, where he had been a *Privatdozent* for five years, to take up a professorship in systematic theology at Marburg. There he befriended Rudolf Otto, who had published his *The Idea of the Holy* in 1917; he also met Rudolf Bultmann and Martin Heidegger. In Berlin he had been very much part of the intellectual, artistic, political, and scientific scene. In the summer of 1925 he moved to the Dresden University of Technology as professor of religious studies. A major theme of *The Religious Situation* was an attack on what he called "the spirit of capitalism," which he regarded as a (bad) religious movement because of its claims to ultimacy and its capacity to inspire ultimate commitments.

In this context he analyzed the religious situation of the Weimar Republic and Europe more generally, with vague reference to global issues. He took the religious situation to be comprised of many components beside religious traditions. Listing only the general titles of his chapters, these included science, metaphysics, art, politics, ethics, mysticism outside the churches, eschatological movements, and the religious situations in the churches.[22] Tillich regarded the churches to have failed, especially in their responses to the war. So they were not, for him, the primary loci of the symbolic engagements of ultimate reality. Rather, he analyzed the ultimate dimensions he found in the other cultural domains as well as in the churches; sometimes he called this mode of analysis "theology of culture."[23] In fact, he regarded religion as only one domain of human spiritual reality: The first chapter of his *Theology of Culture* is entitled "Religion as a Dimension in Man's Spiritual Life."

The situation at the beginning of the twenty-first century is very different from that at the beginning of the twentieth. For one thing, the causal interactions of those domains Tillich discussed are now global, and his concentration on European culture seems strikingly parochial. For another, whereas Tillich was influenced by Max Weber's secularization thesis according to which organized religion would diminish, the second half of the twentieth century saw a great resurgence in organized religion, especially in Africa and Asia. Christianity, Tillich's concern, had enormous growth (though not in Europe). Conservative forms of Islam and Hinduism have been burgeoning. The removal of Marxist strictures against religion in China has led to a resurgence of Daoism and Confucianism; it is estimated that there are 130 million Christians in China, making it one of the largest Christian nations in the world. Therefore, the religious situation of our time is dominated by the revival of traditional or organized religion, even as the sciences and arts that are sometimes hostile to organized religion go on apace.

For the purposes of *Philosophical Theology*, the religious situation is to be defined as the various interrelated contexts within which there are symbolic engagements of the ultimate expressed in cognitive, social, and existential ways, wherein people define their ultimate identities. These contexts include practicing traditional religious life, and the syncretistic fashioning of new forms of explicitly religious practice, but also all those dimensions of the sciences, philosophy, arts, politics, ethics, mysticism outside organized religion, and apocalyptic movements, as Tillich said. These contexts interact, as detailed in many ways in *Philosophical Theology*. All of the symbolic engagements of ultimacy, in any context, involve something of a sacred worldview that contains a sacred canopy, which directly symbolizes ultimacy and which connects that sacred canopy to at least some of the other, more mundane, domains of life. The sacred worldviews might lean heavily on sacred canopies deriving from traditional religions, but they might also have sacred canopies that expressly reject such traditional views, as Tillich found in the "depths" of some antireligious secular cultural enterprises.

The toolkit of theology, then, needs to include the intellectual resources for understanding all those domains and contexts in which ultimacy might be found, including being on the inside of the sciences, philosophy, the arts, and all the rest. This is a far cry from theology as the study of theologians. Theology also needs to be able to understand the concrete contexts of the current situation, global in scope. Then it might be able to see just what is going on with respect to symbolic engagements of ultimacy, those that are strong and good and those that are weak or demonic (Tillich's great fear, having lived through Nazi spirituality).

But theology will not be able to understand what it sees of the contemporary situation without grasping its historical depths. In this regard, theology needs to do a back-reading from the manifestations of religion in the contemporary scene to their ancestors. Thus, it needs to grasp the history of science, philosophy, the arts, and so forth, as well as the historical developments of the traditional religions. These historical developments are best understood through the study of ancestors and historical conditions of the distant past, not through leaping back to some prior age and tracing descendants down to the present religious situation. Any given past "ancestor" can be understood in terms of its own religious situation, with multiple factors, mixing in their own ancestors.

Theology as well cannot understand what it sees in its religious situation without understanding something of its future, how it can develop, how it probably will develop, and how in various senses it should develop. Of course, predicting the future can be a silly game and is almost impossible, as the "exact science" of economics has taught us. But part of understanding a present reality, the religious situation, is to understand where it is tending.

With disciplined resources for analyzing the present religious situation, understanding its historical depths and its future tendencies, it is possible for theology to address the first-order questions of religion for the present religious situation. Because the present situation is always contextual, as it has to be for actual symbolic engagements of ultimacy to take place, general judgments about first-order issues are difficult to make. In the case of particular individuals, perhaps only a spiritual advisor can bring discipline to assessing the meaning and validity of those persons' symbolic engagements of ultimacy.

This chapter has argued that theology's role in the understanding of religion and religions is to provide a reading of the present religious situation and then to provide a back-reading that shows how this has developed. The implications of this approach for understanding the history of religions, including beginning with a contemporary definition of religion and reading back to find its roots in the ancient past and in the development of religious cultures, set it at odds with approaches for understanding religion that want to begin at the beginning. There is no beginning of religion, only things in the past that give rise to the present religious situation or that would have given rise to a different religious situation if things had been different. Because the present situation contains religions in traditional forms as well as religious dimensions in many different cultural spheres, there exists a history of religion and religions ready for investigation. Theological inquiry is always hypothetical, however, and is best when vulnerable to correction. The ways we might best understand religion in its historical depths today might seem amusingly, or tragically, limited from the standpoint of theology in religious situations centuries hence.

The discussion here has progressed to the point where many of the complicated issues theology needs to address in articulating the possibilities for religious identity have been explicated, those possibilities that shape the existential decisions about wholeness, obligation, engagement, value-identity, and one's contingency. Among other things, the discussion has shown how the existential choices constituting religious identity involve taking on elements of the past as authoritative, a matter of one's own (and one's culture's) responsibility. Thus, the quest for theological truth trumps, and is the authorizing source for, the quest for religious identity.

The next question is whether theology can articulate a sacred worldview appropriate for the present religious situation.

Chapter Four

A Viable Sacred Canopy

I. THE PROBLEM OF TRANSCENDENT AND INTIMATE SYMBOLS

A sacred canopy needs both transcendent and intimate symbols of ultimacy. It needs the former in order to be true to the nature of ultimacy, the boundary conditions beyond which are no others. It needs the latter in order to be relevant to the ordering of life in its many domains. Other conditions of plausibility remain, as do obstacles of implausibility; these will be discussed in Chapters 13 and 14.

To order life, a sacred canopy needs to be embedded within a worldview, making it a sacred worldview. The worldview provides orientation for most or all of the events, things, and affairs of a person's life. But people across the world live such diverse lives that no one worldview could orient them. This is not to say that there are no questions of truth regarding worldviews: there are. It is only to say that a worldview appropriate for the affairs of one person's life is likely not to be appropriate for all the affairs of another's. So, the religious situation requires a great number of sacred worldviews. These sacred worldviews can be overlapping in many respects, especially those common within a given culture. Moreover, the worldviews of most people have to include interacting with people with other worldviews, and so there is orientation from one worldview to another. Yet, because of the differences in the intimacies of life, there need to be many different sacred worldviews.

Can there be one sacred canopy common to all the worldviews relevant for the religious situation, allowing for diverse rhetorical modes of expression? If the sacred canopy contained only the most transcendent symbols of ultimacy, the answer might be yes. An argument will be made in the next section to the effect that the transcendent symbols should express the metaphysical theory of the ontological act of creation; otherwise they are false or not transcendent enough. But the sacred canopy also needs the intimate symbols of ultimacy.

Philosophical Theology One, Chapter 7, outlined four generic pressures in real life that push toward intimacy in symbols of ultimacy. One, called "nature's depths," is that in our personal biological, cultural, and environmental reality lies the ultimacy of being created.[1] The ultimate therefore is within us and needs to be interpreted in the terms with which we interpret our own bodies, cultures, and natural environment. Creation is not only of the cosmos in its general sweep but also in the bones and fluids of who we are individually and what we do. A second pressure for intimacy comes from the fact that many aspects of life, in their particulars, have an uncanny side, an intimate intimation of transcendence. The language for this often comes from anthropology, which talks about the uncanny aspects of the world of primitive peoples. Even postmodern sophisticates, however, know about sacred places, uncanny pivotal times, strange encounters. A third pressure comes from the need for human meaning relative to ultimate matters. Any worldview sets affairs within some scope of meaning. But at least some people wonder whether their lives have any meaning in ultimate senses. They might have, or seek, highly transcendent senses of ultimacy, but these need to be tied to the details of their own lives. So, ultimacy needs to be conceived in ways that relate to those intimate details. A fourth pressure comes from the need to correct or reorient individual and communal lives. Sometimes the ultimate meanings of the details of life signify that people ought to change, or to be grateful in specific ways, or to increase their ultimate concern, reordering priorities. So, some symbols of ultimacy need to be intimate in ways that give direction. These are all generic pressures toward intimacy in symbols of ultimacy, exerting themselves in the situation of any sacred canopy in just about any human personal or social condition.

Within those generic pressures are particular pressures that are specific to the contemporary religious situation at the beginning of the twenty-first century. This is not the place to attempt to describe the current religious situation, only to mention some of its factors, each of which is particular. A particular state of affairs obtains with respect to the development of capitalist economies around the globe after a century of competition between capitalism and communism, with different situations in various parts of the world, including the rise of China and India as capitalist economies, the continued underdevelopment of African countries and some other countries, and the roles of the oil-producing nations in the strategic competition among countries and blocks of countries. Associated but not identical with the economic aspect of the religious situation is the military-political dimension, again with different configurations and shifting historical allegiances and conflicts. The two wars being fought at the beginning of the twenty-first century by Americans and their allies in Iraq and Afghanistan on one level reflect the Western, particularly American, fear of terrorism by Islamic militants. A century hence, those two wars mostly likely will be seen as chapters in the story of Western colonialism and the revolutionary push-back from the humiliated Muslim colonies, of which terrorism is a part. Or they will be seen as annoying Western interruptions of the much larger and more basic struggle within the Islamic world over the political and theological disposition of Islam's many parts. On another level these wars are matters of economic dominance, with the other countries trying to control the oil found in Iraq and other Middle Eastern countries and also trying to control the export of opium from Afghanistan; powerful economic forces determine much of the motive and power for military action, particularly in the former situation. These conditions obviously have great significance for the religious situation.

Related to the economic and military-political conditions, and partly a function of them, is the education/information situation. In rapidly changing ways, due to the development of the internet, cheap computers, smart phones, social media, and the like, some large numbers of people are sophisticated in Western ways of understanding the overall situation, with access to scientific data and to institutions of higher education. Other people in large numbers are sophisticated in various religious traditions whose views of the world are somewhat orthogonal to the dominant Western views. Yet other great numbers of people exist in countries with educated elites of one type or another and yet who themselves, for economic and political reasons, do not have access to sophisticated education and who therefore live in the symbolic world of folk cultures with blinkers shutting out the electronic world. Many other people live in countries where hardly anyone has elite education of any sort, where "elite" means nurtured through media that are more universal than what is conveyed in folk cultures.

Within these economic, military/political, and educational/informational conditions, the situation of the world religions is extremely particular and not to be understood well by tracing the history of those religions as such, whatever that might mean to scholars. In the first place, wherever modern, late-modern, or postmodern economic and political cultures have been influential, strong forces are present that tend to undermine traditional religions in their authority, relevance, and consistency. In the second place, all of the major religions, for a century or more, have been going through the struggles to address the issues of modernity. Many of China's intellectuals in the twentieth century tended to believe their traditional religious cultures were decadent and enfeebled, and for them the Western philosophy and (anti)religious culture of Marxist communism was a heady dose of modernism. Now it seems that the religious cultures more indigenous to China are in resurgence: Confucianism and Daoism, and even Buddhism, which, though foreign, was dominant in China for nearly a millennium. Moreover, Christianity is growing in China. British colonization of India gave rise in the nineteenth century to movements to recover (if not invent) precolonial Hinduism, movements led by Western-educated people. The Gandhian revolution against British rule was fueled by a universalist Hindu religious movement that led easily to the establishment of a secular state. Since then, however, centuries-old tensions between Hindus and

Muslims have led both Hinduism and Islam to become much more defined by competing nationalist interests than by their universalist strains that were extremely powerful before independence. Islamic developments in the Middle East in the nineteenth and early twentieth centuries had important modernizing movements embracing central aspects of Western education, including both science and the understanding of religion. With the establishment of the State of Israel, however, which was taken to be a Western colonialist affront to Islam, the nationalizing pressures on Islam overwhelmed the modernizing movements. Tensions between Islam and Christianity continue to play out in Africa, although the dominant religions there are local and tribal, even when fitted into and modified by Muslim or Christian categories. The religious situation in Latin America a century and a half ago was dominated by Roman Catholicism but in a social construct that put great distance between the economic and ruling elite (including those ruling in the churches) on the one hand and the peasants on the other, whose Catholicism was a dense mixture of missionary Christianity and pre-Christian religions. The development of an economic middle class during the last century has tended to fill the distance between the peasants and the elite, although the middle class has associated itself rather often with the elite. The explosion of Protestant evangelicalism in Latin American during the last half century or more, especially among peasants and lower-middle-class people, has altered the dominance of Roman Catholicism. North American religion has been dominantly Christian but has also found explicitly welcoming places for Judaism, Buddhism, Confucianism, Daoism, and most recently Islam. North American Christianity over the last century and a half, however, has fractured into liberal and conservative wings, and this in nearly every denomination, including Roman Catholicism. The liberals have tended to emphasize tolerance of other religions, and of nonreligious secularism, and to foster change of social structures to bring about greater economic justice. The conservatives have tended to emphasize the salvific truth of their version of Christianity over that of the others, taking the others to be candidates for conversion, and to desire the preservation of social structures that bear their sense of cultural identity over against others.

This very general sketch of the global religious situation is surely wrong in many details, would require a thousand qualifications before being asserted as a good hypothesis about the religious situation, and will doubtless be outdated very soon because the situation constantly lurches through changes. The purpose of the sketch here is to illustrate the following point. Any individual in the world has a particular place in this situation, in a particular country, with a particular social class, particular religious heritages, and with particular problems of finding religious identity. No one simply inherits a religion. Even when one chooses the religion of one's parents, that choice is the partial construction of a sacred worldview from the particular perspective one has within the global religious situation. One's sacred worldview needs to be shaped so as to orient the affairs of one's life within the particularities of one's situation. A sacred worldview that addresses the intimacies of a middle-class office worker in Belgium whose family has not practiced any religion for several generations, but whose family was originally Jewish, would not address the intimate details of life of an unemployed Kurdish Muslim in Iraq, nor that of a Confucian scholar returning to a university position in Beijing after a long career teaching philosophy in the United States. Each needs a sacred worldview with intimate symbols of ultimacy that address their positions in the religious situation that embraces them all. The perspective of each on that situation might be almost incommunicable to the others.

The result of this is that religious pluralism is an indelible part of the global religious situation. Religious pluralism does not mean only "membership" in some named religious tradition, as the issue of pluralism is so often framed. It means that being religious requires a sacred worldview whose intimate symbols of ultimacy are relevant to one's own situation and that therefore one's authentic religious practice needs to be different from the authentic religious practices of others. Many kinds of Buddhism are needed, as are many kinds of each of the other traditions, and combinations of traditions, and economic, political, and educational social locations of the mixtures of traditions.

Recognizing the need for idiosyncratic intimate symbols of ultimacy, which make one's sacred worldview idiosyncratic, entails at least two things. First, one's own sacred worldview should be regarded as a project for personal development relative to one's own situation within the larger religious situation. Second, everyone else has the same religious need.

Therefore, a viable sacred canopy today needs to recognize this pluralism. Internal to one's sacred canopy should be both recognition of the irrelevance of one's own sacred canopy for people in other traditions and recognition of their need to have a sacred canopy with symbols of ultimacy intimate to the details of their lives. On a crude level, this means recognizing that people with different religious heritages, for instance, Buddhism, Confucianism, or Christianity, need to have sacred canopies that cope with one another's heritages, which are different from their need to cope with their own religious heritages. Insofar as a viable sacred canopy becomes sophisticated, this means developing serious understanding of those other religions as they are exemplified in their various social locations. Academic and denominational conversations among religious traditions have been developing categories by which each might be understood in terms of one another, although this process still is in its infancy.

The intimate symbols of ultimacy, which would express different religious heritages and social locations for their embodiment, need to be related to the ultimate symbols of ultimacy, the topic of the next section.

II. TRANSCENDENT CONCEPTS OF ULTIMACY

As argued throughout *Philosophical Theology*, the transcendent symbols of ultimacy are under pressure to engage the ultimate boundary conditions in as literal a way as possible. *Philosophical Theology One*, Chapter 6, argued that the great religions had strains that attempt to do this and that can be given contemporary interpretation in terms of the theory of the ontological act of creation. The argument of this section is that a viable sacred canopy, regardless of the diversity of its intimate symbols of ultimacy, should have symbols that reflect the metaphysics of ultimacy.

Philosophical Theology One, Part III, elaborated a metaphysical theory of ultimate reality in detail. The main points of that argument will be summarized here as a statement, in metaphysical form, of the most transcendent symbols of a viable sacred canopy. Ultimate reality, or the ultimate conditions of reality, is to be understood in both ontological and cosmological senses.

The ontological sense of ultimate reality has to do with the question of why there is anything at all rather than nothing, or with the nature of being-itself.[2] The first question to ask about being is about what it is to be a thing, a determinate being. The nature of determinateness is the most abstract topic that is intelligible. It is more abstract than any philosophical theory about what kinds of determinate things there are. It is more abstract than mathematics and logic, which suppose that *a* is not non-*a*, a statement expressing sheer determinacy. Whatever is concluded about determinateness must be true of whatever might legitimately be said about anything else.

The theory of determinateness proposed here is the following: Something determinate is this rather than that. To be this rather than that is to be a harmony of two kinds of components, conditional and essential. The conditional components are those by which the determinate harmony is related to other things with respect to which it is determinate. The essential components are those by virtue of which the determinate harmony is itself as the harmony of the conditional components. Without conditional components, a determinate thing could not be determinate with respect to anything. Without essential components, a determinate thing would not be itself so as to be able to be determinate with respect to anything. For any thing to be determinate, there must be a plurality of determinate things that are determinate, at least in part, in respect of each other.

How is the plurality of determinate things together? This is the problem of the one and the many. A cosmological answer to this question is that the plurality of determinate things is together by virtue of their conditional components with which they mutually condition each other so as to be determinate in respect to each other. The conditional components constitute the causal and interdefinitional structures of the cosmos, whatever those might be. But the cosmological answer cannot be sufficient. Each determinate thing is a harmony of essential and conditional components. Whereas the cosmological connections account for the togetherness of their conditional components, they do not account for the deeper togetherness the determinate things must have in order for their essential components to be together. Their essential components are explicitly not together in their mutual conditional components. This is how the determinate things can be other than one another. If the essential components of one were contained in the other through conditional components, they would be only one thing, with parts. So, there must be some ontological context of mutual relevance within which separate, mutually conditioning, harmonies can be together with their essential components but with their essential components separate. The determinate things could not be at all without each being a harmony of its essential with conditional components. Therefore, for there to be anything determinate there must be a plurality of determinate things existing as related to but other than one another in an ontological context in which they can be mutually relevant. That ontological context of mutual relevance is the "being-itself" by virtue of which there can be determinate beings. It is the most ultimate reality that makes possible determinate realities.

But what can be the ontological context of mutual relevance? If it is determinate itself, then it is a harmony that presupposes existence in a yet more basic ontological context of mutual relevance by virtue of which it is together with the original plurality of determinate things. And if that further ontological context of mutual relevance is determinate, there must be a yet further context, and so on; the plurality of determinate things would be impossible. Put in more prosaic terms, if the "ultimate reality" that grounds the possibility of determinate reality is determinate, then it presupposes a more ultimate reality. No God, Heaven, Dao, or Brahman that is determinate can be truly ultimate.

What could be an indeterminate ontological context of mutual relevance? The only candidate would seem to be a creative act that creates the determinate plurality simply as together. Each of the determinate things is an end product of the ontological creative act, mutually conditioned by and conditioning other determinate things but existing with its own essential components along with each other determinate thing with its essential components within the ontological creative act. The ontological creative act itself is nothing apart from creating; if it were apart, it would be absolutely indeterminate, not even an "it." Its determinate nature comes about in the act of creating itself, whereby it makes itself creator of the things it creates. What is interesting about the act itself is not its nature but its making. The act of making something new is a kind of primitive perception. *Philosophical Theology One*, Chapters 13 and 14, analyzed what can be known about the ontological act; Chapters 15 and 16 explored the mystical senses involved in engaging the ontological act itself.

Because determinate things exist, there is an ontological context of mutual relevance, which is an ontological act that creates the determinate things together. The ontological creation is not in time or space but creates them. Because there is no nature motivating or constraining the ontological act, and no context motivating or constraining it, the ontological act is gratuitous, arbitrary, undeserved, and surprising. The ontological act creating all determinate things is the most ultimate reality. This is the ontological sense of ultimate reality.

Given the existence of determinate things, however, the very conditions of determinateness provide cosmological ultimates. To be determinate is to be a harmony, and there are four transcendental traits of harmony: form, components formed, existential location, and value-identity. For the ontological creative act to create anything at all, it must create determinate things, and therefore the four transcendental traits of harmony are ultimate conditions for the creation of anything.

Any harmony must have a form or pattern by virtue of which its components are together. A form integrates the components with the traits of complexity and simplicity. Complexity refers to the differences among the components and simplicity to the ways they are combined to create new components over and above the given ones. Complexity without simplicity is sheer conjunction; simplicity without complexity is sheer homogeneity. A harmony has a kind and degree of elegance by virtue of how it maximizes complexity and simplicity together, and that elegance is value. Every form bears value in the ways by which it arranges components. Forms as future possibilities are possibilities for instantiating value. Forms as being actualized actualize certain values and exclude other values in the alternative forms rejected. Forms as actualized are the values of actual achievement, of the past as bearing on the present and future. So, form is an ultimate condition for there being any determinate thing at all, and with form comes value: To have a form is to have a value.

Because human beings are harmonies with some freedom to determine what they do and the effects they have, they face the ultimate reality of form as possibilities for choice. Because choices sometimes are between possibilities with different values, human beings give themselves a value character by the choices they make, and this is the ultimate ground of obligation. An ultimate condition of human life is to live under obligation because of how human freedom relates to value-laden form (*II, 1, 5*). This is an ultimate issue in all religions.

Similarly, to be determinate is to have an internal plurality of components, among them conditional and essential components. In respect of being components, however, the distinction between conditional and essential components is not particularly important. What is important in this respect is how the harmony as a whole comports itself toward its components. What does being harmonized within the harmony do to the nature and value of the components? The harmony's form integrating the components might embody the nature and value of the components either well or to their detriment. To the extent the harmony embodies the components well, it is well grounded in them; to the extent it does not, the harmony fails in groundedness. The integration of the harmony is a function of the overall harmony comporting itself to the nature and value of its components so as to be well grounded in them.

In respect of human beings, this is the ultimate condition that poses the problems of integration and wholeness, an issue of wide proportion in all religions. The issues of obligation in the actualization of diverse possibilities also show up as problems for human wholeness as being integrated and well grounded in the components of life (*II, 2, 6*).

By virtue of being determinate with respect to other determinate things, each harmony is located in an existential field constituted by their mutual relations among conditional components. At this point, the distinction between essential and conditional components becomes particularly relevant, because a harmony's engagement of other harmonies involves not being able to include the others' essential components without making them mere components of itself.

For human beings, location in an existential field with others constitutes an ultimate problem of engagement, namely, how to engage things so as to respect them as others with their own essential components. Religions have thematized many issues under the headings of relating to other people, to social institutions, and to the larger natural environment (*II, 3, 7*).

A final cosmological ultimate reality is that every harmony achieves the value of getting its components together with its form in its existential location. Some aspects of this value are within the harmony's own nature, and others are the effects it has on the values of other things that are genuinely other because of their essential components. For human beings, this constitutes their value-identity in ultimate perspective, which is usually what is meant by talking about the meaning of life or salvation (*II, 4, 8*).

Thus, the four transcendental traits of determinateness as such—form, components, existential location, and value-identity—constitute ultimate conditions for the human world. The human world is, of course, part of the larger natural world. As argued throughout *Philosophical Theology Two*, sacred canopies need symbols that relate these conditions to human life, and they are, generically stated, symbols for obligation, integration, engagement, and the achievement of absolute value-identity.

In addition to these four ultimates, the ontological ultimate reality is the ontological act of creation that is encountered by human beings in the radical contingency of the world. Not only are the particulars of this world contingent, the radical contingency is that there could be nothing determinate at all unless it were plural and created by an ontological creative act.

A viable sacred canopy, therefore, needs symbols for the one ontological ultimate reality and the four cosmological ones. For people of a philosophical bent, the terms of this metaphysical argument constitute such a set of symbols. But the metaphysical dialectic here is a reaction to real conditions and all of the literate religious and philosophical traditions have had to engage these conditions with some kind of symbolic vocabulary (*III, pt. 2*). The underlying dialectic, which this section has attempted to summarize, is the attempt to be true to the ultimate conditions as best as possible. The ultimate ontological condition has been expressed metaphorically through the symbol systems of personhood, consciousness, and spontaneous emergence pressed to extraordinarily transcendent interpretations. *Philosophical Theology One* and *Two* have presented the arguments for why the worldview described in this section is plausible.

III. THE CRITICAL INTERPRETATION OF INTIMATE SYMBOLS OF ULTIMACY

Nevertheless, a sacred canopy cannot live exclusively on these highly transcendent and metaphysically abstract symbols of ultimacy. It needs intimate symbols in order for the ultimate realities, ontological and cosmological, to be engaged. The intimate symbols are conceptual but not only conceptual. They are also embodied in feelings and activities. Symbols for engaging the ontological creative act, for instance, include building up the experiential facilities of meditation and contemplation (*I, 16*). Complex symbols are required for addressing obligation as an ultimate dimension of life, and the same is true for addressing wholeness, engagement, and the achievement of absolute value-identity.

The religious situation is filled with candidates for the intimate symbols that can function in a viable sacred canopy. There are, of course, the symbols that have developed through the great religious traditions. They have the density and polyvalence to relate to all the ultimate realities. As we saw earlier, any form of Christianity that is involved with the symbols of Jesus in the New Testament and in the various separate traditions has ways of expressing Jesus's relation to obligation, wholeness, other people, and one's standing in ultimate perspective, as well as to the gratuity, arbitrariness, undeservedness, and surprise of existence. This is true for the central figures and texts in all those traditions. From the standpoint of the present religious situation, those figures and texts are appropriated in ways reflective of the history of the needs of different religious situations, down to the present day.

In addition to the great religious traditions, the events of our time provide intimate symbols for the transcendent. Perhaps most striking is the symbol of martyrdom in Wahhabi Islam that has come to mean defending the faith through the bombing of noncombatants, in the attempt to destabilize governments and ethnic groups thought to be anti-Muslim or contrary to one's own sect of Islam. In many parts of Africa and Latin America, religious symbols are evolving, often from earlier traditional symbols, that give great heart and encouragement in the face of brutalizing poverty. As Tillich noted, the arts have provided many new symbols for religious engagement, although he would likely not have appreciated the way Hip Hop has given voice to deeply marginalized and antisocial people.

Consider, for instance, these poems by the explicitly Christian poet, the Jesuit Gerard Manley Hopkins.[3] The first is an evocation of God the Father, in Christian terms, or the utterly gratuitous, arbitrary, undeserved, and surprising ontological act of creation:

Pied Beauty

Glory be to God for dappled things—
    For skies of couple-colour as a brinded cow;
        For rose-moles all in stipple upon trout that swim;
Fresh-firecoal chestnut-falls; finches' wings;
    Landscape plotted and pieced—fold, fallow, and plough;
        And all trades their gear and tackle and trim.

All things counter, original, spare, strange;
    Whatever is fickle, freckled (who knows how?)
        With swift, slow; sweet, sour; adazzle, dim;
He fathers-forth whose beauty is past change:
                Praise him.
For poetic representation of Christ,

The Windhover

To Christ our Lord

I caught this morning morning's minion, kingdom of daylight's dauphin, dapple-down-
                drawn Falcon, in his riding
    Of the rolling level underneath him steady air, and striding
High there, how he rung upon the rein of a wimpling wing
In his ecstasy! Then off, off forth on a swing
    As a skate's heel sweeps smooth on a bow-bend: the hurl and gliding
    Rebuffed the big wind. My heart in hiding
Stirred for a bird,—the achieve of, the mastery of the thing!

Brute beauty and valour and act, oh, air, pride, plume, here
    Buckle! And the fire that breaks from thee then, a billion
Times told lovelier, more dangerous, O my chevalier!

No wonder of it: sheer plod makes plough down sillion
Shine, and blue-bleak embers, ah my dear,
    Fall, gall themselves, and gash gold-vermilion.

Then there is Hopkins's poem to the Holy Spirit:

God's Grandeur

The world is charged with the grandeur of God.
    It will flame out, like shining from shook foil;
    It gathers to a greatness, like the ooze of oil
Crushed. Why do men then now not reck his rod?
Generations have trod, have trod, have trod;
    And all is seared with trade; bleared, smeared with toil
    And wears man's smudge and shares man's smell: the soil
Is bare now, nor can foot feel, being shod.

And, for all this, nature is never spent;
    There lives the dearest freshness deep down things;
And though the last lights off the black West went
    Oh, morning, at the brown brink eastward, springs—
Because the Holy Ghost over the bent
    World broods with warm breast and with ah! bright wings.

These three poems articulate not only the three basic symbols of ultimate reality in Christianity but also, in their poetic consonance, a sense of the Christian Trinity. They enfold brute senses of human predicament in ecstatic aesthetic senses of fulfillment. Yet they do not require any doctrinal belief. Their power does not depend on anyone's prior commitment to Christianity. Someone with no prior history with Christianity, or only a hostile one, might read these poems and say, "Ah, so this is what Christianity is about!" So also with the great literature inspired by other religious traditions that does not itself employ what might have become jaded and dogmatic, noncommunicative representations of the intimacy of the ultimate.

A viable sacred canopy thus has, on the one hand, the transcendent symbols attesting to the engagement of the ontological and cosmological ultimates that were sketched in the previous section. On the other hand, it has as well some one or several sets of intimate symbols that can shape concrete life like the symbols of Jesus, the poems of Hopkins, the dharma of the Buddha, or the Confucian way of the sage, with all of these reinterpreted for much more specific locations within the contemporary religious situation. One has to be very good at the English language, for instance, to hear the song in Hopkins's poems, to grasp the way his poetic distortions of words and grammar create a new symbolic reality. So it is also with living into the depths of the specific symbol systems of any religious heritage. Because the worldviews of people need to differ so greatly, their sacred canopies need also to differ and to register the legitimate differences of others.

But how can the legitimacy of the intimate symbols be assessed, since often they are not very literal representations of the ultimate conditions? Hopkins's poems summon an intimate grasp of ultimacy with only the most indirect allusions to the customary Christian transcendent symbols. Often the images from folk religion are far too literal to be meaningful on their surface. How can we know that they are not demonic?

The first response in answer to this question is to recall that what is at stake is the truth about ultimacy that comes (or does not come) through engagement with the intimate symbols. The truth is very likely not to be conveyed through iconic reference but rather through indexical reference. That is, one has to see whether engagement with the intimate symbols transforms the person so as to enable whatever is pertinent in the ultimate to be carried over into the person. Thus, in "Pied Beauty" the power of the poem is in bringing to attention the stunning absolute particularity of what is fathered forth by the creator, the creator whose act is eternal and "past change." "The Windhover" represents Christ as the spectacular beauty that rides the world like a falcon on the wind and in so doing transforms the world's "blue-bleak embers" into "gold-vermilion." The poem depersonalizes Jesus Christ into something along the lines of the tradition of the Cosmic Christ but makes cosmic beauty intimately compelling and ultimately important. "God's Grandeur" charges the world "like shining from shook foil"; for all the human hiding of this grandeur in shod feet that no longer feel the ground, from the black night (West) springs the eastward morning with the grandeur anew, an evocation of the renewing power of the Holy Spirit in Christian symbology. Lovers of poetry, who know how to read, feel these things, which are also expressed metaphysically in the transcendent symbols reviewed in the previous section. The point about truth is to identify what readers of the poems actually pick up in the poems about ultimacy and to ask, in other language, whether what they pick up is right. The standard readings of these Hopkins poems are in accord with the Scotistic metaphysics of the ontological act of creation.[4]

The second response to the question of how to assess the legitimacy of the intimate symbols is to engage in the elaborate act of interpretation that makes sure that nothing in those symbols' reference be allowed to lead to inferences that contradict the more nearly literal, if too abstract, truth of the transcendent symbols of ultimacy. For this, a theory of interpretation is needed, for instance, something like Thomas Aquinas's theory of analogy. In this *Philosophical Theology*, the theory of symbolic engagement functions as the theory of interpretation. In practice, this involves a twofold move. First is some kind of demythologization of the intimate symbols so that the wrong inferences from their iconic references are short-circuited. Second is a remythologization of the symbols so that they have indexical reference, as in Hopkins's poems.

At this point a crucial objection needs to be considered. The problem with most religious language in our present religious situation is that much of it is dead to many people, and the folk-religious symbols, or folk interpretations of traditional religious symbols, which are alive for so many are embarrassments for the elites who ask how they might be true. Tillich was worried that secular people find no intimate life engaging the ultimate in traditional Christian symbols.[5] With the resurgence of various religions, the vitality found in certain symbols seems very often to lead to the denial of vitality for others in other religions' symbols. And yet, as Tillich pointed out for his religious situation, many things indeed point to the ultimate in ways that produce ecstatic, life-transforming responses. How then does it help to break the first naiveté of vital and engaging intimate symbols—the soaring beauty of Jesus or the promise of heaven for militant martyrs—to ask whether they are true to the ultimate as defined abstractly? Does not analysis destroy the very power of intimate symbols to engage with intimate consequences?

It must be admitted that this is a great possibility and that it is destructive to religious life that cannot attain a second naiveté. On the other hand, religions' intimate symbols have led all too often to vicious, human disasters. As we shall see in the next section, this often has to do with them being employed in a pre–Axial Age religious context. Nevertheless, theological criticism needs to be woven into the multifarious engagements of ultimacy with clusters of intimate symbols, not applied afterward, or only to elite classes.

The third response to the question of how to assess the intimate symbols of ultimacy that come from traditions, experience, poetry, music, and the arts, or wherever, is to use the theory of ontological creation as the control. The vast extensiveness and intensiveness of the creation require that transcendent symbols of ultimate reality not be too small to indicate that the ultimate reality of the ontological creative act creates them. But the intimate symbols are likely to be of much-reduced dimensions, symbolizing the ultimate with personal terms, or natural movement of the Dao scaled to human affairs, or the practices of yoga that lead to the cessation of the movements of thought. The use of the intimate symbols thus needs to be set in the context where the larger extension and intension of creation are also in mind. The gripping story of Jesus Christ, for instance, presented as a lure to bring one's disordered life to wholeness, need make no mention of saviors on other planets. However, when the question about saviors on other planets arises, the context of one's intimate personal history needs to be connected with at least imaginings of what might be salvific elsewhere. The "elsewhere" for Christians might be Jewish or Buddhist communities.

The legitimacy of intimate symbols of ultimacy within a sacred canopy can only be determined when that canopy is understood to be part of a larger worldview. Sacred worldviews need to be plural in this religious situation. Sacred canopies as well need to be plural, with perhaps common transcendent symbols but diverse and possibly exclusive intimate ones.

IV. THE RELIGIOUS SITUATION AND THE AXIAL AGE

Yet another factor needs to be laced into the complex theory of a viable sacred worldview. Chapter 2 of this volume discussed the distinction between pre–Axial Age and Axial Age religions. One characteristic of the latter is that they arise with and are filled with philosophy. This *Philosophical Theology* is thoroughly philosophical and has used the metaphysical theory developed in the first volume to articulate ultimate reality, a theory that has been the basis of the study of religion in the second and third volumes. Thus, the conceptions of the singular ultimate reality of the ontological act of creation and of the four cosmological ultimacies of determinateness per se reflect this universality at the heart of Axial Age religions.

A viable sacred worldview thus needs to give expression to these universal elements. Part III will elaborate some of these in detail, but the principle for them can be expressed here as a requirement of a viable sacred worldview for our religious situation. Because lying under obligation is a universal condition for human life, all people need to be represented in a viable sacred worldview as obliged agents, with the responsibilities and dignities this involves. Because every person faces the need to be grounded in the components of life, becoming whole with them, all people need to be represented as in need of and deserving of wholeness. Because every person is in an existential field with other persons, social institutions, and larger reaches of nature, human engagements with others should recognize the otherness, constituted by the essential components, of those other things. Because every person is working out an absolute value-identity, each is to be conceived most importantly as a creature in the cosmos created within the ontological creative act. From this it follows that justice, care for wholeness, love, and respect should be accorded universally.

The rub for this, of course, is that social life is organized by necessity into smaller units, a point Confucians understand perhaps better than those of other traditions. Therefore, viable sacred worldviews need to incorporate articulations of those smaller units and how people are treated differently within them, all acknowledging at basic practical levels the universality of justice, care for wholeness, love, and respect.

Finally, to repeat a point we have met again and again, every viable sacred worldview should acknowledge that there can be no single sacred worldview for everyone. Because of the diversity of intimate ultimate realities in the complex religious situation, there need to be many different sacred worldviews if they are to involve ultimate intimacy. Because of the need for universal justice, care for wholeness, loving engagement, and respect for others in ultimate perspective, each viable sacred worldview needs to be able to represent within itself enough of those other sacred worldviews to allow for the informed engagement with others. Therefore, not only need there be an external plurality of sacred worldviews, the plurality of sacred worldviews needs to find expression in each sacred worldview, to the extent that they might interact. This calls for a vast expansion of cultural knowledge and theological interpretation, only barely begun with the dawning of the Axial Age three millennia ago.

One characteristic of the global religious situation of the early twenty-first century is the interconnectedness of different locations within it. As we've seen, this requires the diverse sacred worldviews of those different locations to include reflection on each other in at least the respects in which they might interact. This point needs no emphasis for the elite educated people who might be readers of *Philosophical Theology*. The projects of "theologies of world religions" have gone on for decades in the form of interfaith dialogues and academic discussions.

The need for sacred worldviews to reflect on one another is not limited to elites, however. Given the actual interactions of nonelites taking place within the global economy, the military situation, and other factors discussed earlier in this chapter, the sacred worldviews rich with the symbols toward the folk religion end of the continuum need also to reflect one another. However, often the sacred worldviews rich in the symbols of folk religion are tied to the mores of pre–Axial Age tribal religions that emphasize in-group/out-group distinctions. So, for instance, such sacred worldviews are sometimes exclusivist, denying much legitimacy to alternatives. Sometimes they are chauvinistic, taking themselves to be radically superior to others without taking into account that their own sacred worldviews would not be relevant to order the domains of other kinds of lives. Sometimes they are even defensive, taking themselves to be under attack by people and cultures representing alternative sacred worldviews, as is characteristic of many fundamentalists in Christianity, Islam, and other religions.[6] Because of these and related factors, the development of helpful reflections of other sacred worldviews within nonelite sacred worldviews is difficult, often filled with obstacles. Three points need to be made about possible responses to this kind of difficulty.

First, what might be called the "Methodist response" because of the emphasis on education in the Methodist Christian tradition, is to push against the legitimacy of the distinction between sophisticated elite religion and folk religion by actively trying to bring everyone into the elite sphere.[7] Such educational movement is gradual and takes different forms in different circumstances. It amounts to actual transformations of social class structures. Perhaps something like this is inevitable because of the astonishingly quick and thorough elaboration of electronic media of communication and learning. The first naiveté of many folk religions is hard to maintain online. There are drawbacks to this strategy, however. Because of the destructive effects of education on the first naiveté intensity of folk religious forms, for many people the folk religious engagements of ultimate reality will be rendered impossible when they in fact function truly, through indexical means, as well as when they function falsely. Although this is a generalization needing many qualifications, the vitality of folk religious expressions likely involves a much denser engagement of ultimacy in the five orientations discussed here than the more sophisticated expressions with their limping second naiveté. In many cases, education makes it more difficult, not less, to be religious through engaging ultimate realities. Another drawback to the education strategy is that not everyone will be brought along, and the distance between the elites and unreconstructed nonelites can widen.

The second response to the difficulty of engaging other sacred worldviews helpfully within sacred worldviews rich in folk symbolism is to emphasize the embracing quality of religious communities that operate along the vast stretch of the sophistication–folk religion continuum between the extreme poles. Most religious communities include people who are extremely sophisticated and those who are less sophisticated, perhaps even blinkered with first naiveté. The Sunday morning ritual analyzed in *Philosophical Theology Two*, Chapter 9, exhibits elements from a wide swath on that continuum, shared by all. Although the ritual is experienced differently by different people in a given congregation, it provides them with a common experience. The swath on the continuum is large enough that individuals can move from one position to another in terms of their own sophistication without losing contact with one another. And if the preaching is authentic and intelligent within the liturgy, the various parts of the service are interpreted to one another on all levels. The downside of this response, however, is that not all religious people function within communities that have a broad range within the folk religion–sophistication continuum. Many people do not organize their religious lives in terms of congregational ritual. This is as true for religions other than Christianity as it is for Christians.

The third response to the difficulty of relating sacred worldviews to one another in the face of in-group/out-group distinctions is the work of theological interpretation itself. The work of theology is not only within the genre of philosophical theology but often undertakes the social and cultural criticism necessary for assessing the truth value of particular engagements of the world with concrete elements of sacred worldviews. This hermeneutical work is epitomized in preaching but requires the full panoply of disciplines necessary for assessing religious engagements. The social location of hermeneutical theologians requires that they float with sensitivity and tolerance among the sacred canopies that require definition in one another's terms. Such theologians of course can practice one or several religions defined by sacred canopies. Yet they also need interpretive openness to those they cannot or will not practice.

This chapter has addressed the question of what might be a viable sacred worldview today, both true and effective in orienting life. The answer has been complicated. On the one hand, a viable sacred worldview needs to have symbols addressing the ultimates such that the dialectic of their close interpretation is able to yield engagement with the five ultimates discerned throughout *Philosophical Theology*. On the other hand, sacred worldviews need to be intimate to the domains that require orientation, and these are different for different social locations across the globe, different historical heritages, and different accidents of local needs and personal purposes. No general specification of this side of sacred worldviews is possible, except to note that in our pluralistic situation, each sacred worldview needs to understand enough of the other relevant sacred worldviews so as to be able to engage those who hold them with respect and compassion. Another point general to any viable sacred worldview in the contemporary global situation is that each needs access to hermeneutical practices that allow for the mutual interpretation of the local intimate circumstances and the transcendent symbols relative to which truth might be measured with some universality.

Part I

Summary Implications

The chapters of this part address in an unfolding order several questions concerning how to understand religion. The first considers the contributions of cognitive science, broadly construed, and the social sciences (Sections I and II). Both kinds of approach are important for understanding religion, and yet both are reductive. So, in various ways, philosophy is needed to indicate in what the reductions consist and to reconstruct religion in light of what has been left out. The main lesson from these considerations is that, however religion developed in its early evolution, the result from early on was that it involves intentional engagement with whatever it symbolizes as ultimate. Chapter 1, Section III, fleshed out the theory of symbolic engagement developed in *Philosophical Theology* (*I, 3*). Section IV discussed how religion is to be understood as itself having an intentional stance. Many other things are to be understood about religion, but its intentional engagement with reality is what allows it to learn and to develop through learning, not only through contributing to the successful transmissions of genes of religious people.

Chapter 2 considered the understanding of religion in an historical mode, discussing at length the distinction between pre–Axial Age and Axial Age religions. It developed that distinction beyond Karl Jaspers's use into the terms of *Philosophical Theology*. The Axial Age religions saw the rise of philosophy with its universalistic understanding of the world, its basic principles, human individuality, and imperatives for universal justice and compassion. Fundamentally, the Axial Age religions began the undermining of the sharp distinction between in-group and out-group in pre–Axial Age religions. Nevertheless, the Axial Age religions were laid down on top of the tribal religions and continue to this day to be in tension with them. This raises the question of what it means to belong to a religion. Is it to belong to an in-group as opposed to the out-groups of other religions? For many people, this is what it means. But for the principles behind the Axial Age religions, the universality of human nature, the universal relation of each individual to the ultimate conditions of the universe, the universality of the imperatives for justice and love, all militate against that. Many distinctions were drawn in Chapter 2 concerning the nature of belonging to a religion, which in turn help to define what a religion is such that one can belong to it. One conclusion is that belonging to a religion involves choices that define the individual, even when the religion chosen is inherited from culture (*II, pt. 4*).

Because of the role of choice in religious life, the role of theology as guiding choice is important for religion. Using Rowan Williams's distinction between celebratory, communicative, and critical theology, Chapter 3 gave an interpretation of "confessional" theology. Confessional theology is done by thinkers within a religious tradition for the sake of expressing, communicating, and criticizing that tradition's theology. The symbols of ultimacy at the heart of confessional theology, especially the celebratory genre, are usually the very intimate ones. The intimate symbols are those that can directly relate to people's lives. Still, the point of the symbols is to engage ultimate reality in its various dimensions, and this transcendent sense of ultimacy also needs to be expressed. The great religious traditions all have highly transcendent, metaphysical symbols for most dimensions of ultimacy, even when they stay in the background of their popular sacred canopies. A crucial theological problem for the guidance of religion, or of any religions, is to weave a set of interpretive connections between the intimate and the transcendent symbols. The problematic character of this task is that the circumstances within which a sacred canopy needs to function continue to change; the ways of balancing intimate and transcendent symbols in the past often no longer work later because the worldview within which the sacred canopy exists changes. At this point theology needs to analyze the religious situation to discover what the conditions are for the legitimate weaving of the transcendent and intimate symbols. The suggestion made in the preliminary remarks to this part, that religion is to be understood through a back-reading from a given point to the influences from various sources, is spelled out as an heuristic device for understanding the resources for the present religious situation.

Chapter 4 analyzed something of the contemporary religious situation as the problematic context in which a viable sacred worldview might be developed. It restated the metaphysical theory of ultimate reality that has been developed throughout *Philosophical Theology* (*I, pt. 3*). Any viable contemporary sacred worldview would have to have transcendent symbols for those dimensions of ultimacy, the chapter argued. But what about the great diversity among the conditions of people within the overall religious situation? No one worldview is adequate to be intimate to all the conditions of human life. Therefore, every viable sacred worldview needs its own symbols of ultimacy, often coming from the inherited religions, contemporary events, and the arts. Theology thus needs to be able to interpret legitimate connections between the transcendent symbols, more or less universal among viable religious worldviews, and the different sets of intimate symbols relating to different human conditions.

To deepen the discussion, the next topic is a study of the rhetorical symbols of some of the most important world religions of the Axial Age.

Part II

Historical Religions

Part II

Preliminary Remarks

The conclusion of the previous part was that viable sacred worldviews might agree on the most literal, transcendent symbols of ultimate reality, however rhetorically expressed. But they could not agree on the diverse intimate symbols of ultimate reality because the intimacies of the lives of people are so radically different, context by context. The religious situation is such that people need to engage ultimacy from different contexts, which means different sacred worldviews, which in turn means different sacred canopies, especially with regard to the intimate symbols of ultimacy.

The purpose of this part of *Philosophical Theology Three* is to indicate in general and schematic ways some of the theological resources that certain Axial Age religions bring to the religious situation, especially in respect of the interplay of transcendent and intimate symbols. "Theological resources" means primarily the concepts and symbols that might be employed in a viable sacred canopy and beyond that in a viable sacred worldview. A great many qualifications need to be expressed at the outset about the purpose of this part.

First, the *concern* for multiple worldviews probably has very little traction for most people, say, for five billion of the over seven billion people on Earth at this time (2014). Most people in South and East Asia, and Africa, and many if not most people in Europe and the Americas, live in rural and small-town settings in which the religious situation is densely layered but fairly homogeneous. They most likely live within the sacred worldview of their parents and local community with little known alternatives. Such a sacred worldview itself is the result of millennia of overlayering of cultural shifts, including new religious ingredients, and can be understood by the kind of back-reading discussed in Chapter 3. But electricity is coming even to the most remote rural areas of India, China, and Africa, and with electricity comes the internet that brings the alternatives to the local worldview. More important, with electricity and its technological and economic accompaniments come serious challenges to the local worldview. Jared Diamond built his remarkable biocultural study, *Guns, Germs, and Steel: The Fates of Human Societies*, in answer to the question of a tribal New Guinea politician, Yali: "Why is it that you white people developed so much cargo and brought it to New Guinea, but we black people had little cargo of our own?"[1] That question is being asked all over the globe by people encountering modernity for the first time. In whatever different ways that question is answered, alternatives are posed to local worldviews, and the concerns for a viable sacred worldview will arise in the religious situation as a consequence.

Second, theological resources are but a small part of the array of resources that traditional religions as well as various forms of secular society, for instance, secular humanism, Marxism, and secular Zionism, bring to different positions within the religious situation. Traditional religious resources include pre–Axial Age religions as well as the Axial Age traditions discussed in this part. Most important are the forms of community and dense culture that are resources for living religiously. For the most part, however, this study prescinds from these to focus on the theological or intellectual resources. Although the theological resources in sacred canopies and more broadly in sacred worldviews are extremely important for guiding communal life, especially in times of crisis, they are not the communal life itself. A broader study than *Philosophical Theology* is needed to cull the resources for the religious situation beyond theology.

Third, the selection of traditions to study here is narrow, although surely it is broader than makes for a neat discussion. In the present religious situation, many powerful and obvious theological resources are left unnoticed in the discussion. Moreover, starting from the present religious situation with its very many different locations, the resources even of those traditions that are discussed are far richer than can be treated here. Specialists in those traditions need to take a charitable view toward the simplifications the discussion requires, which leave out whole lines of religious and theological life. Many people identifying with the traditions discussed will not recognize themselves in the representation here and perhaps will take offense. The discussions to come are also selective in the sense that they employ categories from the philosophy in *Philosophical Theology* to sort the resources. In no way are the chapters of this part to be construed as histories of the theologies of the traditions discussed or thorough, balanced representations of them in the present religious situation.

Rather, the purpose is to examine selected cases of theological symbolism that through some extended historical development have dealt with the tensions between transcendent and intimate symbolism. Fundamental rhetorical tropes have shaped theological thinking differently. The analyses of Axial Age religions in this part usually will treat their symbols more as motifs than as theologically sharpened concepts. Given the present religious situation, how are these useful for different positions in the matter of building sacred canopies that are as true as possible to the realities of ultimacy and at the same time include symbols that can be made intimate to human life and shape the religious dimensions of the various domains within a sacred worldview?

The tactical clue to the organization of the discussions in this part is the metaphysics of ultimacy developed in *Philosophical Theology One*, Part III, and summarized in *Philosophical Theology Three*, Chapter 4, Section II. The ontological ultimate is the radical contingency of everything determinate on an ontological creative act, and this is discussed in a prologue to each chapter. The cosmological ultimates are the transcendental traits of determinateness as they bear on human life: form/value/possibilities/obligation, components/groundedness/wholeness, existential location/engagement/love, and absolute value-identity. Each of the chapters has four sections, dealing with how the religions under consideration have symbolized the cosmological ultimates in various ways, including the integrations of transcendent and intimate symbols. The ontological ultimate appears in various guises as the background for the cosmological ultimates.

The religious traditions selected for discussion are Axial Age religions. The so-called Abrahamic religions—Judaism, Christianity, and Islam—are treated together for several reasons. They are historically connected and claim to be worshipping the same God as ultimate reality. The rhetorical center for symbolizing God is personification, although all three have ways of speaking of God as beyond personal characteristics. Yet they are very different in the ways they deploy many of the same symbols of ultimacy, especially the intimate ones, and these differences are instructive for the religious situation.

Buddhism is treated as a kind of polar opposite to the Abrahamic religions because of its hostility, in varying degrees, to the religious importance of ontological ultimates at all. Rather, it focuses on the ultimacy of the quest to overcome suffering, although in different ways within its own branching traditions. Theravada traditions offer a focus on psychological achievements over suffering, whereas Yogacara and Madhyamaka traditions stress the ontological emptiness of consciousness and all dharmas, respectively.

With respect to Hinduism, the traditions that have grown up as Shaivism and Vaishnavism are studied, with an emphasis on the former, constituting a kind of combination of theistic themes, often personalistic, and transcendent themes that stress the indeterminate and move over into the metaphors of consciousness. Both traditions embrace contradictory tendencies, and both provide dense intimate symbols for religious life. Illustrations from several of the orthodox Hindu schools—including Vedanta, Mimamsa, Yoga, and Samkhya—have been discussed elsewhere in *Philosophical Theology.*

Chinese religions are studied as integrated more or less in Chinese cultural and philosophic life, as well as in religious organizations such as temples. Confucianism and Daoism are laid on top of primal shamanistic cultures and are mixed with the influence of Chinese Buddhism, particularly of the Yogacara sort.

In all these discussions, the rhetorical tensions between the transcendent and intimate symbols are noted, with the explicit purpose of determining viable intimate forms for the contemporary situation. Perhaps even more important is the exploration of the implications of central core texts and motifs in each tradition for engagements with each of the ultimates. This is to say, within most traditions, the central notions are used for the interpretation not only of one of the ultimates but also the others, in different contexts. Whereas the multiplicity of ultimates, cosmological and ontological, make the religious traditions internally diverse, requiring different interpretations of the same core symbols, the unity of the texts and stories brings many forms of coherence to the traditions, even if not consistency of symbolic meaning.

A word should be said about the neglect of African religion in this study, which is surely a fault and weakens the claim of *Philosophical Theology* to be interpretive of religion and religions. In the nineteenth century, European and American scholars regarded Africa as home to tribal religions, plus the extensions of Islam and Christianity in certain territories. Thus, it could be dismissed as what later would be called pre–Axial Age religion. A consensus now is emerging, however, especially among African scholars, that there is more of a universal African religion or spirituality with tribal and other variants than a loosely connected set of different tribal religions. Moreover, African religion does have a strong belief in a single supreme deity above other deities and spirits. It has a more or less common strong sense of spirituality associated with life force and a powerful ethics of community responsibility. These and other considerations led Laurenti Magesa to declare that African religion is a world religion.[2] The other considerations include the fact that Judaism, Christianity, and Islam took their own rise on the margins of African religion and owe some of their elements to that. African religion was included as the topic of the third volume of Ewert Cousins's magnificent series, *World Spirituality: An Encyclopedic History of the Religious Quest*.[3]

Moreover, students of Christian missions in Africa are now recognizing that the mission field was not chaotic, empty, or degenerate until the missionaries arrived but rather a rich religious culture of its own. Christianity in modern times must change itself as much when it goes into sub-Saharan Africa as it did when it went from the Mediterranean to northern Europe.[4] Kwame Bediako goes so far as to say that modern Christianity in Africa, by virtue of its interaction with African religion, is itself "the renewal of a Non-Western religion."[5]

All of these considerations signal the importance of African religion in the contemporary global religious situation. The practical reason for its neglect here has two levels. First, there is no tradition of a literature of African religion, no scriptures, no commentaries, no literate history of debates about various interpretations of the basic symbols of ultimacy. Therefore, this author is at a serious disadvantage in coming to terms with African religion in a philosophical theology. Second, the lack of a literary tradition also has meant that philosophy failed to develop in African religion, even though some of the great philosophers of Judaism, Islam, and Christianity worked on its margins. Therefore, intellectual reflection within African religion has not developed its symbols of transcendent and intimate ultimacy against the background of a self-conscious dialectic. Although African religion offers many illustrations of the tensions between transcendence and intimacy in its symbols, it does not present much by way of a philosophy about these tensions. Why African religion did not develop a philosophical literary heritage, when it was surrounded by and interacted with religious cultures that did, is something of a puzzle. Contemporary African scholars are working hard to fill in that lacuna. Surely, future developments in philosophical theology such as in this project will have to take it into account.

Chapter Five

Abrahamic Religions

PROLOGUE

The Abrahamic religions—Judaism, Christianity, and Islam—have in common fundamental identifying references to Abraham and Abraham's God in the book of Genesis. Jews trace the history of Israel from the descendants of Abraham's son Isaac, and Muslims trace their heritage from Abraham's son Ishmael. Christianity followed the Jewish line, accepting the whole of the Hebrew Bible (to which Islam also accredited revealed authority, though not so important by any means as the revealed authority of the Qur'an). Beginning as a form of Second Temple Judaism, Christianity was very early Hellenized and addressed its main concern to Gentiles, asking them to accept the story of Israel (in the Septuagint) leading up to Jesus Christ as their story in place of their own Pagan narratives. In the Christian retelling of the story of Israel, Abraham was the model of faith in God's promises, which were extended then to Gentiles in Jesus Christ.

The Hebrew Bible exhibits the struggle within the history of Israel occasioned by the dawning of the Axial Age. In opposition to Axial Age ideas, pre–Axial Age ideas such as the polytheism assumed in the imperative to hold first to Yahweh rather than to other gods and an emphasis on the exclusive uniqueness of the people of Israel as an in-group distinguished from Gentiles dominate some parts of the Hebrew Bible.[1] The Axial Age prophets claimed that there is only one God who created the whole of the world and that justice is due to everyone; as we saw earlier, texts such as Job, Ruth, and Jonah are orthogonal to the interests in in-group exclusivity. By the first century, both Judaism and nascent Christianity assumed that there is only one God, known through the history of Israel, who created the entire cosmos. In the seventh century, Islam arose in explicit agreement with this in a context of competitive polytheism on the Arabian Peninsula, emphasizing the oneness of God, recognizing Jews and Christians as "People of the Book," and beginning a long theological tradition of articulating the comprehensiveness of divine creation, providence, order, and control, all in relation to a strong doctrine of human freedom and responsibility.[2]

Thus, the Abrahamic religions from the Axial Age onward gave expression to conceptions of the totality of the world as created by a single ontological creator. The conception of creation, of course, is relative to the conception of the world as created. In the first century, due in part to the influence of Greek and Persian philosophies, the High God was conceived to be very high indeed, beyond imagining in fact. The Christian letter to the Colossians says (1:15) that Jesus Christ is the "first image" of that High God. With the development of Neo-Platonism in the next two centuries, a clear criterion emerged regarding creation: If something is determinately what it is, the "dyad" that distinguishes one thing from another, it is created or derivative from that which is beyond determinateness. Neo-Platonism was important if not dominant within Christian theology through the medieval period and was formative for Islamic philosophy from its first century.[3] The subsequent influence of Aristotle in Christianity, Judaism, and Islam did nothing to change the general view that the Creator is simple, that is, not determinately complex, and that everything with any determinate complexity is created.

The history of theology in these traditions is much more complicated than indicated here, of course, with competing conceptions of the cosmos created and often conceptions of intervening or mediating creators, albeit derivative or created creators. Christianity was particularly interesting in this regard because of its interest in identifying both Jesus Christ and the Holy Spirit with God, although not as the creator in exactly the same sense.

Complicated, confused, and often contradictory as they were, the transcendent philosophical conceptions of God as creator of the entire cosmos did not provide the rhetorical center of gravity for the Abrahamic religions. All three set that center of gravity on stories in which God acted in history to reveal the divine character and provide standards for the identification of individuals and communities as normatively related to God. God as an actor in history was personified as an agent with intentions, although many passages in all three sets of scriptures represent God as transcending personhood in many if not all respects. The personifications drew upon much older pre–Axial Age symbols of gods as mighty but finite forces; Yahweh was originally symbolized as a storm god, like Shangdi in China. A complicated historical dialectic is needed to account for how forces of nature can be personified, and how images of the gods as super-humans can be integrated with these naturalistic personifications.

The great attraction of the personification symbols is their intimacy to human life. If God acts and calls upon people to react in some way, that makes ultimate reality intimate to the prioritizing of human life. It also helps to understand one's situation, especially one's history, as having ultimate dimensions. Moreover, it gives ultimate shape to the human desire to have one's situation changed by God, perhaps motivated by prayer. From ancient times to the present religious situation, the conception of the creator as an actor within history and potentially within one's own life, an actor with respect to whom one's own identity can be defined for better or worse, has served as a powerful family of intimate symbols of ultimacy. The center of gravity of the personifying language of ultimate reality as a divine actor within history dominates the Jewish, Christian, and Islamic scriptures, although they give expression to the much more transcendent symbols also.

Jewish, Christian, and Muslim theologians, therefore, have had to cope with the fact that the scriptural language within which their people lived is highly personifying at the same time that the God who is supposed to be personified is beyond the mutuality with others presumed in personal reality. Many coping mechanisms have been employed. One, perhaps the most common, is to assume that the creator of all determinate things is to be modeled on a creator of finite things, an agent, but somehow transcending the limits of agency. In this context, theologians such as Jonathan Edwards can talk about the "end" for which God creates the world, as if God created out of divine intentions. This, of course, is not a metaphysical possibility: If God has intentions, God has potentials that are not fulfilled, and there is nothing that can possibly fulfill them if God does not have them fulfilled in the first place. But the analogy of God the creator with an intentional, personified being has been a steady, if metaphysically unsupportable, theological strategy. Another strategy, developed at length by Thomas Aquinas, is that the analogy works the other way: God is the completely fulfilled Act of To Be, and creatures are analogues of pure act by virtue of having finite limitations of act. Creatures can be understood as participating in infinite divinity in finite forms, and God can be understood as the positive virtues of finite creation expanded to infinite fullness. Thus, there are "two truths" for the Thomistic tradition. With respect to the ultimate reality of God apart from the world, the metaphysics of simplicity and infinity holds; with respect to the reality of God as related through analogy to the world, the biblical language of God acting (but in a hidden infinite way) holds. Whether this solution to the tension between intimate and transcendent symbols of the ontological act of creation holds for the present religious situation is a matter we will discuss further on.

I. FORM/VALUE/POSSIBILITIES/OBLIGATION

The primary motif of ontological creation in Genesis 1:1, common to Jews, Christians, and Muslims, is that God creates by giving form to an aboriginal chaos: God created in the beginning by making formal distinctions, beginning with that between light and darkness. Some but not all important theological traditions in all three religions amended this motif to say that God creates everything in the world, including primal chaos, in order to emphasize various conceptions of God as the absolute source. *Philosophical Theology* agrees with this amendment in its claim that everything in determinateness is created, not only the form but the components, existential location and achieved value-identity. Nevertheless, in the rhetorical development of the Abrahamic traditions, a certain priority or special importance of form is to be noted. Perhaps the popularity of Neo-Platonism, according to which the first move of creation (or emanation) is the making of distinctions (or the Dyad), is related to this special importance of form. Theological traditions also exist that maintain that creation involves the imposition of form on aboriginal stuff.[4]

In the first Genesis account of creation, God creates the ordered world and sees that it is good. The most obvious reading of this is that goodness arises with the order or form created, which accords with the claim in *Philosophical Theology* that value is a function of form (*II, 1; III, 9*). Many of the Abrahamic theological traditions, however, have attempted to say that value is primordial in the divine nature prior to and apart from creation and that the goodness in creation derives from the goodness in God. Some of these proposals say that God is required by the divine nature to create a good world, others that God has some freedom in the matter. All these traditions imputing value to God prior to the creation of things with form, however, are seriously questioned by the arguments in *Philosophical Theology* to the effect that apart from creation the ontological act cannot be determinate.

That God creates a world where form itself carries value and constitutes possibilities that human beings face means that how human beings respond to alternative possibilities with different values is extraordinarily important for the fundamental relation of human beings to God. The second creation story in Genesis is about, among other things, how Adam and Eve were placed in a situation of choice and chose wrongly. Judaism, Christianity, and Islam give very different interpretations of the "fall," but for all three with their subtraditions the definitive relation of human beings to God their creator is to be under obligation with regard to things about which they have choice.[5] The root of human dignity in the Abrahamic religions is that all beings who are under obligation regarding choice have the dignity of being persons in some honorific sense.

The question for the contemporary religious situation is how Judaism, Christianity, and Islam provide intimate symbols for existing under obligation as an ultimate constituent of human existence. Little question remains as to whether all three provide transcendent symbols for living under obligation. What about the intimate symbols?

In several (somewhat mutually contradictory) senses, the story of Adam and Eve is paradigmatic and can be adopted as one's own story. This provides an intimate sense of identity as living under obligation. What are these senses? As part of the Hebrew Bible appropriated by Jews (rather than Christians or Muslims), the story of Adam and Eve is part of the first section of the book of Genesis (Chapters 1–11) that apply to all humankind. With Chapter 12 and continuing throughout the rest of the Torah and the books of history, the discussion turns to Abraham and his descendant who become the Jews, with little attention to the rest of humankind, who are viewed simply as non-Jews (or non-Israelites), the Gentiles (except when they border Israel in problematic ways). So, the sense of lying under obligation is taken by Jews as applying to all human beings, not just to themselves as, say, the Mosaic covenant applies only to them. For people self-identified as Jews, however, being a Jew has a special bearing on this universal sense of living under obligation. The special bearing has a wide range of interpretations. For contemporary secular Jews and many liberal, for instance, Reconstructionist or Reformed, Jews, the articulation of being under obligation and the very rich sense of justice that is developed in the Hebrew Bible are Jewish contributions to a wider culture. For Jews who identify themselves with more or less detailed forms of Jewish observance, moreover, the Jewish people, however defined in terms of observance, play the additional special role of being the central symbol of obligation and justice, perhaps even the agent of teaching justice to the other "nations." Jews toward the more orthodox end of their spectrum can couple the ontological condition of living under obligation with symbols of divine commandment that establishes the obligation and its contents. *Philosophical Theology* has argued that God as the ontological act of creation cannot have intentions as might be implied in a literal interpretation of divine commandments. But divine commandment symbols might be metaphors for the gratuitous, arbitrary, undeserved, and surprising aspects of the ontological act. The divine commandment symbols, in turn, are connected with the symbols of a special covenant relation between God and the Jewish people that give perhaps even greater intimacy to the expressions of lying under obligation in the Hebrew Bible.[6]

A tension arises here, however, (that takes equally problematic if somewhat different forms in Christianity and Islam as well) namely, between the universality of obligation and justice on the one hand, and identification with a religious in-group as the intimate identity of one's obligation on the other. Not only is every human being (assuming normal mental capacities, maturity, and so forth) under obligation to choose well, but every person affected by one's choices has a right to have their own values and interests respected. This right is merely an expression of the fact that one's choices should be for the better rather than the worse, noting the complications and ambiguities in this. The better and worse include the values and disvalues implicated in all those who are affected by one's actions. Therefore, justice should be dealt to all people, not only those who belong in one's in-group. Justice at this point does not mean only, or even, equality of principles of reciprocity but rather calculating the good of all involved who are affected by one's possible actions. Of course, this calculation is complicated by many factors, including specific duties to certain individuals such as those belonging to one's in-group just by virtue of that membership; Confucianism is particularly adept at parsing these complications. The general point, however, is that justice is not to be limited to or heightened for those in one's in-group. This is a point reflected in all the Axial Age religions.

The tension is posed by the intimacy of the symbols of obligation and justice in this sense. That intimacy comes from the particular symbols related to one's in-group, for instance, Jewish identity, or membership in the Christian church, or belonging to those who submit as Muslims to Allah. To the extent that the in-group is symbolized as, in part, the group whose role is to foster universal obligation and justice, that tension is a healthy one, connecting both the intimate symbols, say of the story of Adam and Eve interpreted as Jews, or Christians, or Muslims variously do, with the transcendent symbols of creation, form, possibilities, and value. But to the extent that the intimate symbols detract from the universality of obligation and justice by suggesting the greater importance of the in-group, to that extent the intimate symbols become treacherous. They do not automatically become wrong just because, when interpreted literally, they suggest the slighting of recognition of people in out-groups as obligated and deserving of justice because they are marginalized and objectified as "Gentiles." After all, these symbols might be used indexically to foster universal obligation and justice even when iconically they suggest limited obligation and justice. But the iconic pull makes such symbols treacherous.

In practical terms, each of the Abrahamic religions (as well as several of the other Axial Age religions) has legitimate concerns about its own community. As noted, in Judaism, that "community" stretches broadly from people who are observant in Orthodox ways, and take part in specific communal rituals with fairly literal belief in the symbols and stories of the tradition, to those whose observances are light, or who are explicitly secular Jews rejecting all observances but clinging to a biocultural identity as Jews.[7] Similarly, within Christianity exists a lumpy continuum from those who are deeply involved in Christian church life to those who do not attend church or believe traditional Christian doctrines or symbols in any literal way but identify with and draw their worldview from Christian cultural elements.[8] At the present time (2014), it would have seemed until recently that within Islam no sizable group of people exists who consider themselves Muslims but who have a light-handed, mainly cultural connection to Islam. The sudden arising of the Arab Spring, however, has revealed many people who do fit this description, those who are culturally Muslim but anxious to participate in a larger secular world. Partly this perception is due to the fact that Enlightenment liberalism has been slow to develop within the Islamic world. But largely it is because the meaning of being a Muslim for so many has been to be part of the political movement of Islam, relative to its political leadership. The Arab Spring demonstrates a loosening of the connection between Islam and specifically Islamic government, although the reaction against the Arab Spring has attempted to reinforce that connection. Given this spectrum of meanings of community identification with an in-group in each of the Abrahamic religions, it still is true that in appropriately various ways there are temptations to place the good of the community above recognizing the dignity of obligation and the universality of justice for everyone. To the extent people succumb to those temptations, their symbols of intimacy regarding obligation and justice are questionable, if not just wrong.

The ideals defining the Axial Age religions, including their names, have been laid down on top of tribal religions that emphasize the in-group/out-group distinction (*III, 2, ii*). In some instances, the Axial Age religions have been adopted as newly named tribal religions, often with considerable compromise of the Axial Age ideals. Tribal conflict in Africa to this day in some cases is clothed in terms of conflicts between Christians and Muslims, as in the Sudan. Tribal warfare is surely outlawed by the Christian ideal of loving enemies, and the Muslim ideal allows for war only in the case of self-defense and spreading the faith, not the continuation of tribal conflicts over power.

The distinction to draw is between issues of obligation and justice, on the one hand, and issues of comportment toward the components of one's religious life, on the other. Concerning the former, everyone with choices is under obligation and is to be respected as a person for that. Moreover, everyone is to be treated justly insofar as they are affected by one's actions, regardless of whether they belong to one's in-group. Concerns for one's in-group legitimately have to do with comportment.

But an even more intimate set of symbols regarding the unconditioned character of facing possibilities has been developed in the Abrahamic religions. Each defines what is, in its context, a new possibility for being human. Compared with all the other peoples of the world, who have vastly different cultures, histories, interests, places, and powers, the people of Israel have the possibility of a special relation to God that the Gentiles lack, according to Jewish belief. Of course, a range of Jewish interpretations of this special relation exists, from the view that the Jews are the only people who can enter into the divine presence to the view that God relates to different peoples in different ways and that the Jewish relation through the Sinai covenant is the way God relates to the people of Israel. Thus, membership in the Jewish community, by birth or, in rare instances, conversion, is a particular possibility for an intimate relation with God different in notable respects from the intimate (or not so intimate) relations other people have. Being Jewish is a special possibility.

In the case of Christian belief, membership in the community is secondary to the fact that Jesus Christ offers a new possibility for being human, which Paul called a "new being." As in Judaism, Christianity offers many interpretations of this new being, and individual Christians identify with Jesus differently. But for all, the new possibility has to do with commitment to justice even when Christians remain (redeemed) sinners and with finding the person of Jesus to be a model for and symbolic partner in achieving wholeness and integration. The new possibility also has to do with the elaborate "new commandment," according to the Farewell Discourses in the Gospel of John, to love one another "as I have loved you," including loving enemies, and with accepting the rightness of one's absolute value-identity even when it turns out to be crucifixion. Christianity in its many guises is a family of cults of personal relation to Jesus Christ as a new possibility for personal and communal identity.

The case of Islam is closer to that of Judaism than to the Christian fascination with the person of Jesus in that it offers a new possibility for being part of Allah's work. The Muslim community has the task of bringing the entire world to acknowledge and submit to Allah. Even if this means only living in one's context according to the patterns of Muslim life, it is still a special purpose. Islam offers the new possibility of a very great definiteness in how one should live in relation to Allah, spelled out in the Qur'an and codified in sharia.

II. COMPONENTS/GROUNDEDNESS/WHOLENESS

Issues of groundedness are as complex as the kinds of components that make up a person's life. In the case of the Abrahamic religions, the distinction between components of a group and those of individuals is important.

Considering the components of communities of Jews, Christians, and Muslims, three kinds are especially important and have been from the beginning: membership issues, traditional authority and definitions, and territory.

Concern for identifying who is a member of the group is higher for the Abrahamic religions than it is for most other religions, although there are exceptions; the distinction between church and sect applies beyond the Christian case. For Jews, the distinction between Jews and Gentiles is fundamental because the covenant—and issues concerning adherence, disobedience, and neglect—does not apply to Gentiles. For Christians, Christian identity has to do principally with the voluntary establishment and institutional development of relations with Jesus Christ and his traditions. For Muslims, Muslim identity has to do not only with accepting Allah as the one and only God but also accepting Mohammed as the capstone and complete revelatory prophet who began the lineage of leadership defining the Muslim communities to the present day.

As noted previously, these distinctions are not as obvious as they might seem. There are many degrees and kinds of Jewish observance, especially of those things such as kosher diet that are supposed to distinguish Jews and Gentiles. Christians have many different meanings of adherence to Jesus Christ, who in turn is interpreted in many different ways with different senses of obligation. Muslims have complicated ways of distinguishing between non-Muslims and Muslims of the wrong sort, for instance Sunnis versus Shi'ites.

The very difficulties of operationalizing the in-group/out-group religious distinctions are major concerns for the Abrahamic religions, whereas they are not often so important for the differences among Hindu religions or among the Chinese religions. For all three Abrahamic religions, being a member of the community is a particularly powerful form of intimacy in relation to the ultimate.

In part the importance of the intimacy of membership is due to the fact that, in these religions, many of the traditions concerning their pasts have revelatory force. Although many Jewish ways of relating to the history of Israel have been pursued through the centuries, they all have to do with how Jews today are related to the God who identified Israel as a special people in the Mosaic covenant and how that history worked out through time. Similarly, many Christian ways exist of relating to Christian history, especially to the person and work of Jesus Christ; but whatever the way, it is the most important connection of Christians today with God the Father, the creator of the universe. The historicity of Allah's revelation to Mohammed, while controversial both in its content and in the sense of historicity involved, is still crucial for identifying the authority of the Qur'an, the sayings attributed to Mohammed, and Muslim law, acceptance of which in some sense or other defines membership in the Muslim community. Furthermore, membership in the Muslim community is deeply tied to the acceptance of the authority of the leadership of that community, which has been controversial since the first generation after Mohammed.

Because of the focus on membership in the religious community, which is defined by giving some considerable authority to its history, however interpreted, the territory on which that history took place has special importance for the Abrahamic religions. Tragically, that importance has been compounded by fights over much of the same territory. All religions have their sacred sites and monuments, but the Abrahamic religions share the core history of the search for the Promised Land and the subsequent events each religion associates with that land. The medieval Christian crusades against the Muslims in Palestine, including the establishment of the Christian Kingdom of Jerusalem, are to be seen in geopolitical terms as a push-back against earlier Muslim expansion into Spain and through much of the Byzantine Empire. Nevertheless, the rationale given on the Christian side, perhaps sincerely believed by the majority, was to reconquer the Holy Land, which was identified as the homeland of Jesus and much of the rest of Christian history and therefore "belonged" to Christians. Most Christians today, except on the extreme evangelical Protestant right, do not make that claim about the Holy Land.[9] Nevertheless, all Christians to some degree or another adopt the history of Israel as in the Old and New Testaments as their history with its important places.

In the contemporary religious situation, membership in a disciplined, tight-knit, culturally specific group is especially attractive to people whose social and political lives are chaotic or under threat by modernization. Both

Christianity and Islam are growing in such areas in Africa and Asia; China is witnessing a great growth in Christianity after the Communist decimation of traditional Chinese religions, which are also experiencing revival and growth. The stability of a well-organized in-group is extremely attractive for containing an otherwise chaotic situation and can be an important component of the religious organization of a community. Moreover, the specifics of the in-group provide intimate symbols that are tied to the transcendent symbols in both religions. The problems to be settled case-by-case, however, are similar to those raised regarding the predicaments of obligation: Does the adoption of a tight in-group community require the negation of those in the out-group so that justice toward the latter is impossible?

The components of individual lives in the Abrahamic traditions depend on their social and historical circumstances. They also include how the individuals relate to the components of their communities. Yet the components that deserve special mention here are interestingly different among the three religions. What is the chief motif for the problems of wholeness? For Judaism, the problem is a tension between peaceful, just, impulses and aggressive impulses that often lead to violence. This is a tension, not a contradiction, and God is believed to have created people to be both just and aggressive. The apparent dangerousness of aggression is offset by the belief that without aggression, sexual reproduction would languish. God is thus imagined, in parallel with this, to insist on justice on the one hand and yet to be merciful on the other.[10] For Christianity the root problem for wholeness is not a tension but a contradiction. As Paul said in his letter to the Romans, "I do not understand my own actions. For I do not do what I want, but I do the very thing I hate."[11] The nature of good and evil is very complicated and in respect of components it has much to do with issues of faithfulness, loyalty, respect, and honor. But the main problem for achieving wholeness is overcoming that contradiction in the soul regarding will and knowledge of the good. For Islam, the motif central to attaining wholeness is obedience or submission to God. The theme of obedience is also important in Judaism and Islam but not in such a central, powerful way.

A negative comparative point is worth noting here. Several of the Axial Age religions give great importance to the integration of bodily and mental components of the individual. The Abrahamic traditions generally do not give great importance to this, even when they hold to dualistic conceptions of human beings as they sometimes have. Christianity in particular has had traditions that denigrate the body, and sometimes these have resulted in strange conceptions of sexuality. Of course, there are martial themes in the Abrahamic traditions, as in all traditions, and the martial themes involve disciplining the body. All the traditions also have ascetic components, which often require "conquering" bodily desires. But, generally speaking, the integration of the physical and mental or spiritual is not as important in the Abrahamic traditions as it is in some of the others.

Extremely complicated are the various ways in which the Abrahamic religions comport themselves, and teach their members to comport themselves, toward the important components of the nature of membership, the authority of historical traditions, and territorial identifications. For people in the present religious situation, they differ according to various social locations. Yet, the issues of being grounded in these and other important components of the religions are the source of some of the intimate symbols of ultimate reality. These intimate symbols, in a viable sacred worldview, are necessary in order to allow the ultimate realities to be relevant to the important mundane domains of life.

III. EXISTENTIAL LOCATION/ENGAGEMENT/LOVE

The peculiar themes of engagement in the Abrahamic religions need to be understood against the background of their more general agreement with the Axial Age religions about universal justice, universal respect for all people, and the need of all people to find wholeness. Furthermore, the Abrahamic religions in their mature Axial Age forms are explicit in their recognition that the whole of reality is God's creation and therefore to be treated with the respect due to that creation. They agree that nature, institutions, and individuals are worthy of being engaged with care and respect. In this, they affirm the ultimacy of the existential field and of the human orientation to it as respectful of the whole of creation.

The intimate ways by which they shape engagement differ from some other religions and in part among themselves. Judaism, Christianity, and Islam have primary and pervasive metaphors that stress the importance of humanity within creation, sometimes as the apex or central purpose of creation. Both creation stories in Genesis 1–3 represent human beings as the completion of creation, and God passes on to them the divine work in caring for it as stewards; at least the stories can be and very often have been read this way. Furthermore, the Abrahamic religions agree, as we noted earlier, in giving their respective defining histories primary revelatory roles in the formation of their communities and senses of personal identity.

The result of both of these points is that affairs on the human scale are given much more importance than engagements with nature. Some advocates of ecological and environmental consciousness have been sharply critical of the Abrahamic religions in this regard.[12] This is not to say, of course, that the Abrahamic religions neglect environmental nature completely. All three traditions have given rise to strains of nature mysticism that are alive today. The theology of Thomas Berry has been cited in *Philosophical Theology* as a reformulation of the ways Christians, indeed all human beings, ought to relate to nature, respecting it on its own terms and taking seriously in a new way the role of stewardship toward nature's own flourishing.[13] Nevertheless, the center of gravity of Jewish, Christian, and Islamic rhetoric has been on the importance of the human story with the affairs of larger nature treated as more of a background, or even as the mere enabling conditions, for the human. This is particularly true of the apocalyptic elements of these traditions.

All the Axial Age religions give great importance to the human in relation to nature, but in different ways. The Daoist and Confucian traditions stress the embeddedness of human interests and social affairs within a larger nature that is a function of the interactions of Heaven and Earth in the Dao.[14] Most forms of South Asian religions suppose a background concern for all sentient beings, among which human beings are located as a grade or as a form through which sentient beings pass on their way to release or nirvana.[15] The Abrahamic religions, by contrast, symbolize human beings primarily not as nestled in nature or as involved in a multi-species migration of souls but as having a history and present story. Of course, all peoples have histories and present stories, but these are not always taken to be what is most salient about human life as they are in the central rhetoric of Judaism, Christianity, and Islam.

The intimate symbols for engagement of other things in the existential field thus reflect the ways by which the Abrahamic religions interpret their stories. For Jews, the distinction between Jews and Gentiles, particularly the preservation of Jewish identity in the face of living conditions radically different from the rabbinic interpretations of the Torah, and often in the face of hostility from surrounding Gentile groups, is very important for defining the issues of engagement of other people. Even secular Jews who are barely if at all observant of the covenant mandates identify themselves as Jews because of their history. Thus, fellow Jews sometimes are engaged differently from the ways Gentiles are engaged, at least at some level. This is particularly true of observant Jews, some of whose observances, such as kosher laws, are designed to inhibit contact with Gentiles.

Christians do not necessarily have a close identification with the history of Israel as depicted in the Hebrew Bible, regarded by many of them as the "Old" Testament. Because the great majority of early Christians were Gentiles, even in the first generation (as addressed by Paul), their adoption of the history of Israel as their history, rather than their assorted native Pagan histories, was secondhand. Nevertheless, for many Christians from Paul to Karl Barth, the frame of the existential field is a history of creation and redemption; this is true today for many Christians across the spectrum from conservative to liberal. The centrality of Jesus Christ makes a human being the prime mediator between God the creator as ultimate reality and the human condition, which for many is a history of having lapsed into sin. What is important about Jesus Christ is the difference he makes to the story. This is not the same as the Hindu appreciation of Krishna in the Bhagavad Gita, who was a human being, an avatar of the High God Vishnu who could have given his advice to Arjuna at any time, so to speak. Although the Mahabharata was an epic drama that instantiated many different Indian conceptions of the world, it did not represent world history as turning on the speech and activities of Krishna talking to Arjuna.

To be sure, for Christians Jesus is not to be understood exclusively in terms of his role in the drama of creation and redemption, particularly in its apocalyptic versions. In particular, Jesus's advocacy of a way of love, including love of enemies, puts the primary emphasis on nonhistorical conditions in matters of engaging others in the existential field. In fact, when historical conditions would suggest that one should engage Gentiles with neglect or hostility, for instance, Jesus stressed that the context in which love is an option is more important than the context in which those historical roles might be played out. Jesus's story of the Good Samaritan was one in which a Jew with historically hostile relations with Gentile Samaritans was helped by a Samaritan after Jewish leaders had neglected to help, even despite their Jewish in-group obligations.[16] As argued earlier, an important strain in contemporary Christianity is to subordinate the grand creation-redemption narrative to a less historical but metaphysical relation of human beings in context to God and to one another as creatures deserving of respect and care.

Islam, as already noted, construes world history to be wholly under the control of Allah and to be a continuous, ordered story.[17] The role of Islam within that story is to bring all people to recognition of Allah's sovereignty and to recognize this in explicit submission to Allah. The Qur'an and the teachings of Mohammed detail how this submission is to be lived out. But the process of converting the world is a story, and the people of Islam are identified by their "journeying" under the proper leadership in succession to Mohammed.[18] This last reason is why the internal disputes within Islam over the authority of the leadership, as between the Sunnis and Shi'ites, are so very important. The intimate symbols of engaging others thus have to do, in considerable part, with how Muslims relate to the various traditions of authoritative succession.

At the present time, of course, the history of Islam's part within Allah's world history is unsettling. That Allah controls and wills everything that happens is a comforting intimate symbol of ultimacy when Islam is in the ascendance. But when it is in decline, particularly when subject to colonialism by an historical enemy, the Christian West, those symbols of ultimacy become problematic.

Participation in stories provides powerful intimate symbols for engaging other people and groups, and their social institutions, for people who think of historical interactions and their narrative forms as primal symbols of ultimacy. For cultures that do not think of human history as having this ultimate importance, the historical details of life are not likely to provide such powerful symbols of ultimacy. The Abrahamic religions, in their different ways and at least in some of their more important traditions, do give history a kind of ultimate seriousness. Therefore, for many people in these religions, their own stories, placed within a larger history, provide important symbols of ultimacy.

Limitations exist to the viability of symbols of ultimacy arising from the places of people in an allegedly ultimate history (*I, 7, 8*). The extent of the cosmos is so vast that human history is a miniscule part of cosmic history. Human beings are involved in historical roles, necessarily, and yet the intension of nature in their biological, chemical, and physical conditions is so much greater than the possible outcomes of any story except some kind of mass annihilation that human history is rather trivial in the overall human constitution. God as the ontological creative act of the entire cosmos needs to be symbolized in ways that grasp the extensiveness and intensiveness of nature, with the attendant humbling of the human place within creation. Such a God cannot literally be a player within the cosmos in any history. Therefore, the symbols of ultimacy need to reflect the scope of creation.

This is not to say that the intimate symbols coming from the human social and historical order cannot viably engage people with the ultimate conditions of engagement in the existential field. They can be effective indices of ultimacy even though they cannot be icons. But judgments have to be made in each context of engagement whether this indexical carryover is effective and some implicit iconic reference is not used to distort valid metaphorical reach.

A qualification of this point needs to be registered. Engagement with others in the existential field is normatively shaped in part by considerations of justice, under the ultimate conditions of obligation. The considerations of justice necessarily are functions of social and historical conditions. The social and historical conditions might not themselves have anything ultimate about them except through their background traits of determinateness. Nevertheless, the social and historical conditions are primary considerations for determining how to give people the justice due them, as well as for determining how to relate to institutions and sometimes to nature beyond the human sphere.

IV. ABSOLUTE VALUE-IDENTITY

The discussion of the importance the Abrahamic religions give to human history carries over into the topic of intimate symbols of absolute value-identity. Absolute value-identity is the combination of value achieved in oneself and the value that one causes in things and people other than oneself, the subjective and objective modes, respectively. This combined value-identity exists only in the ontological context of mutual relevance where the separate though mutually conditioning things that bear one's value are together (*II, 4*). Whereas it might be tempting to think of one's value-identity as being lodged exclusively in one's own identity, in fact one's value-identity is the value in oneself and also that for which one is responsible in other things. Value-identity is a descriptive, not normative, term. One person's value might be very high relative to what might be expected, whereas another person's value might be very low relative to expectations. Value is not a quantitative measure but a quality, and hence it has an identity. Who a person "ultimately" is, is the value the person achieves both subjectively and objectively.

Although, because of the externality of the objective and subjective components of value-identity to one another, there is no finite standpoint that contains a person's whole value-identity, the whole indeed can be symbolized in many ways and regularly is in the Axial Age religions. What is one's identity in ultimate perspective (the metaphysical meaning of "ultimate perspective" here means the ontological context of mutual relevance or the ontological creative act)? A wide variety of answers has been given to this question, including the denial, as in most forms of Buddhism, that there is any substantial value-identity, or the denial, in nondualistic forms of Hinduism, that it is finite and different from Brahman. But for the Abrahamic traditions, a first line of answers has been that one's absolute value-identity has to do with one's role in the social and historical orders that define the community of which one is a member. Thus, the question of absolute value-identity is to be answered by citing how one has or has not been a faithful Jew, Christian, or Muslim, under the many meanings of faithful membership involved. The answer consists in elaborating the roles one has played in the history and social context.

Although this is a first line of answers, it is not a very deep one. The deep answers have to do with the intimacies of life within which the ambiguities of identity and achievement are registered. Consider the following senses of ambiguity that come from the philosophy in *Philosophical Theology*.

First, one's absolute value-identity includes the character one acquires through all the choices one makes in contexts of obligations. As distinguished here, these include moral obligations, social obligations, obligations to oneself, and obligations to nature. In all these contexts, one's objective value-identity consists in the effects of the choices on the objects of choice as well as the effect of the choices on the character of the chooser. Ideally, one would always make the optimum choice in each context. But even if that were so, every choice that actualizes one possibility excludes its alternatives. The alternatives, having the nature of also being forms of harmony, have their own values, and these are excluded. The value-identity of the actualizing situation is a composition of the value-identity actualized as well as the loss of the value-identity excluded. Given the frailties of human reasoning about the different value-identities of alternative possibilities, plus the wild accidents of history, what seems the optimum choice for a while might turn out to be a significant disaster down the line. The value-identity of actualized decisions in the past is always changing as subsequent events alter their significance. Therefore, the character of one's achievement regarding obligations is ambiguous throughout life with gains and losses in nearly every important decision. This point is particularly important for the Abrahamic traditions that emphasize historical action and achievement so much.

Second, one's comportment toward the components of life, needing to respect them, is also ambiguous. Consider the component of membership, so important for the Abrahamic traditions. Although no individual is responsible for what everyone else in one's religious community does, virtually every religious community has ambiguous value, recognizing as members people who betray the ideals, or misunderstand them, or are insincere, or ineffective. Membership in a group commits one to the overall value of the group. Jewish, Christian, and Muslim histories are filled with spiritual and moral disasters, not least of which is a tendency to bigotry toward those not in the in-group that has often led to violence. In all three religions are many robust traditions of self-criticism and "prophecy." But membership is always tainted, even when one's own efforts are above reproach.

Consider also the ambiguities of engaging others. Efforts to respect others through being aware of them might still be clouded by ignorance or bad ideas. Appreciation might be mixed with selfish distortion. The courage to carry through with engagements might be compromised with disabling fear. Love in intentions might result in hateful consequences, all mixed with good and bad. What should we think of St. Francis, who, during the devastating plague, crowded his congregants into the church to pray, thereby enabling the plague-bearing fleas to circulate through the whole crowd?

And then with regard to the achievement of absolute value-identity itself, the Abrahamic religions all provide many sacred worldviews that members might inhabit so as to achieve saving value. The opportunity deeply to inhabit a rich sacred worldview is what religions have to offer as means to achieving optimum value-identity. And yet is it not more human to recognize that even the sacred worldviews are constructions with less than ultimate authority? Being human in the depths is being able to live on the cusp of a worldview taken for granted and a recognition that it is arbitrary and possibly mistaken. The heroes of faith in the Abrahamic religions all wrestled with the meaning and validity of faith itself, which is to say, among other things, the meaning and validity of membership in the community and its story.

So, the truly deep intimate symbols for the ultimate condition of value-identity wrap themselves around these senses of ambiguity. What they point to is the inscrutable mystery of an individual's absolute value-identity. On the one hand, the mystery is that there is no finite position that registers both the objective and subjective components of value-identity. On the other hand, the mystery is that, even if there were, the ambiguities of value would render any expression of that value-identity impossible to parse.

The Abrahamic religions have a strategic response to this that comes from the anthropomorphic conceptions of God at the center of gravity of their rhetorics. God is the judge who registers each person's absolute value-identity and "renders judgment." Moreover, such judgment belongs only to God, not to any individual, not even to the individual thinking about himself or herself. Although each individual should be as discerning as possible in all the contexts affecting value-identity, the judgment of its sum is not appropriate for human beings.

Now Judaism, Christianity, and Islam have a wide range of interpretations of the consequences of divine judgment. They all have traditions depicting an afterlife result of divine judgment. Jewish images of heaven tend to the metaphors of a courtroom, Christian images to banqueting, Muslim images to the enjoyment of gardens. Similarly, there are diverse images of hell, and the religious cultures have exercised extraordinary imagination in depicting what "everlasting punishment" might be. Dante's *Inferno* is a masterpiece of art. The religions also have traditions that take the afterlife destiny of individuals to be metaphorical for nontemporal relations with God or Allah, either coming into the divine presence or being thrown into the outer darkness. The distinction between sophisticated and folk culture symbols is important for sorting these images, and their meanings are much dependent on different contexts of social location. The very great importance of the symbols of divine judgment is that they indicate the absolute, that is, the ultimate, significance of value-identity.

Philosophical Theology has argued that the anthropomorphic symbols of God as the ontological act of creation can at most be metaphors and not be literally true. God cannot have intentions apart from the world and cannot sum up a person's record and pass judgment in any literal sense. Taking those symbols literally often has resulted in the opposite of what they truly mean, namely, the ultimate importance of one's value-identity, and fostered a kind of plea-bargaining. Nothing in a person's absolute value-identity requires that it be literally judged by some divine intentional agent. It simply is what it is, ambiguities and all. What it is, is registered necessarily in the realities of the individual and the effects in other things. One is what one is, taking into account the issues of achieving what one is.

What is the religious significance of this? In the long run, for the Abrahamic religions, the religious significance of one's absolute value-identity is the acceptance of it as part of creation. Without denying personal responsibility for its achievement (although all three traditions have great debates about free will and providence at precisely this point), one is enjoined simply to accept oneself as a creature of God, ambiguities, failures, and guilt included. Sometimes the traditions say that there is some inscrutable purpose behind God's creation of people with dubious value-identities. The inscrutability, however, renders the appeal to purpose helpless to explain much beyond the need for the sheer acceptance of creation, oneself included. No appeal to divine purpose is needed to justify acceptance, which is identical with being created with others in the ontological context of mutual relevance.

Now it would seem as if this point about mystery and acceptance has moved from the question of intimate symbols of the ultimacy of value-identity to very transcendent ones. In rhetoric, this is so. Nevertheless, the intimate symbols are those ways by which individuals come to identify themselves as who they are, mysterious, ambiguous, and not identifiable plainly from any finite perspective. For each individual, these intimate symbols are particular and perhaps unique. Each person needs to work them out in the contexts of their own lives. The Abrahamic religions offer many candidates ways of identifying oneself, both as a participant in a larger story and as having the idiosyncrasies of a very personal and perhaps private life. But they also, all three, invite individuals to image their own story.

Chapter Six

Buddhism

PROLOGUE

In contrast to the Abrahamic religions, Buddhism places little focus on the discovery of ultimate realities to which individuals or communities should submit or conform. To be sure, Buddhism has very rich metaphysical traditions developed in close conversation with both Hindus and Jains in India and Chinese traditions in China. Also significant contact was made with Greek philosophy in the states in the Indus valley and north established by Alexander the Great, exemplified in "The Questions of King Milinda" (King Menander).[1] In certain respects, the diversity of contexts and conversation partners for Buddhist metaphysics has made it extraordinarily cosmopolitan in its philosophy. And yet, the metaphysical analysis of ultimate reality has not been the primary focus of Buddhism.

The primary focus rather has been on the soteriological problem of overcoming suffering. Suffering is the most prominent part of the human condition, according to Buddhist thought, and the Buddhist analysis of suffering is complicated. Malcolm David Eckel points out that the ancient Abhidharma analysis of suffering distinguishes three kinds. The first is the suffering of hurt or pain, mental or physical. The second is the suffering of loss of something pleasurable because of change. The third, and most complicated, is the suffering that consists in the impermanence of things because they are wholly conditioned. In a variety of senses, all three kinds of suffering arise from "beginningless ignorance." The first two, of course, have many different kinds of instances but are generally comprehensible. The third takes a bit of explanation and has received many interpretations. Before entering into that explanation, it is worth noting Eckel's placement of the problem of suffering:

> The notion of beginningless ignorance has led the Buddhist tradition to avoid unnecessary speculation about the origin of things and focus instead on how to make them better. There is a well-known story in the Pali Canon about a disciple named Malunkyaputta who approached the Buddha and asked him ten questions: Is the universe eternal? Is the universe not eternal? Is the soul different from the body? Does the Buddha exist after death? Does the Buddha not exist after death? Does he both exist and not exist after death? Does he neither exist nor not exist after death? Rather than answer the questions directly, the Buddha responded with a story. Suppose someone is shot with a poisoned arrow and brought to a physician. Would he say: "I will not let this arrow be pulled out until you tell me the caste of the person who shot me, how tall he was, the color of his complexion, what kind of bow he used to shoot it, what kind of bowstring it had, what the arrow was made of," and so forth. If he insisted on getting answers to all these questions, he would die before the questions could be answered. The same is true of Malunkyaputta's questions about such things as the finitude of the universe. They are not helpful for the task at hand, which is to pull out the arrow of suffering by applying the insights of the Four Noble Truths and the Noble Eightfold Path.[2]

Keeping in mind the primacy of healing people from the wounds of suffering, Buddhism does have metaphysical motifs by which, in various competing ways, it understands the nature of suffering.

Perhaps the best way to orient the Buddhist metaphysical motifs is to place them in contrast with certain fundamental motifs from the Upanishadic traditions. In particular, a common motif in Upanishadic thought is that whenever a plurality is noted, including a plurality of changes in time, this testifies to an underlying reality that is one and that does not change. Thus, for instance, whereas many things pass through consciousness, consciousness itself is a background substratum; or, whereas there are many things dealt with in the world, there is a background unified and unchanging reality that holds these together, for example, Brahman; or, whereas there are many selves, the substrate reality is Brahman, atman (self) is Brahman. The motif, of a plurality of components presupposing a substratum that holds the components, is not limited to Indian thought. Aristotle's theory of substance is a version, for instance, that says matter underlies changes in form; perhaps Aristotle's view itself was influential in the development of Indian thought, since he traveled to India with Alexander. (Perhaps King Milinda, or Menander, was an Aristotelian. Or perhaps the influence went the other way: Aristotle might have picked up the substratum theme for his theory of substance from the Indians. Plato does not appeal to that motif of thinking about the one and many.)

The Buddhists of most schools generally reject the changing-form/unchanging-substrate model completely. Buddhism, of course, is as internally diverse as the Abrahamic religions or the collection of traditions called "Hindu." These schools argued vigorously with one another in different contexts and historical periods.[3] Yet sometimes certain principles or doctrines are vaguely true of all or most schools, even when they interpret them in mutually opposing ways. For the Buddhist analysis, things simply are components (dharmas) that come together because of antecedent causes, abide briefly in harmony, and then change and disappear, to be replaced by other components that come together. This process of causation is *pratitya-samutpada*, "conditioned" or "dependent co-origination," and is often expressed in terms of denials of any self or own-being behind the forms that momentarily come together. Nagarjuna, the great original thinker of the Madhyamaka Mahayana School, is the best-known exponent of *pratitya-samutpada*.[4] A substratum self would explain nothing for these Buddhists. The only explanation of the phenomena of experience is the tracing back of the causal lines upon which they depend. Of course, this motif about the nature of phenomena and their causal explanations has had many interpretations in Buddhist schools that have developed over the last two and a half millennia, some of which have survived and others gone the way of impermanent dharmas. One of the most important problems that have led to multiple traditions of interpretation is how the mind can have enough continuity to note the arising and ceasing of the phenomena, a crucial question when it comes to meditation.

For most Buddhist traditions, the "beginningless ignorance" that is both the origin and reinforced consequence of suffering is mistaken belief in some substratum behind the phenomena, some self or own-being.[5] Pain is suffering when it is mistakenly believed to be the property of an enduring suffering self. Loss is suffering when it is mistakenly believed that there would be some permanence in what is prized. The very reality of encountered things is suffering when it is mistakenly believed that there is something other than the contingent, conditioned array of things that arise, have momentary existence, change, and cease, one after another. To be attached to "something more" in the phenomena causes a kind of suffering of false existence.

Escape from suffering involves a release from attachments to the substratum quality erroneously believed to be in things. This release is a kind of knowledge or enlightenment but is not a merely cognitive adoption of a non-substratum metaphysics. Rather, it is the acquisition of the means actually to see and experience the world as *pratitya-samutpada*, always in change with no own-being. Malcolm David Eckel has analyzed in detail the conception of the Buddhist journey as coming to see, in the work of the outstanding sixth-century Buddhist philosopher Bhaviveka, who left a record of his debates with other schools of philosophy, Buddhist and Hindu. Eckel comments on Bhaviveka's work:

> One final way in which Bhaviveka can serve as a catalyst for useful reflection outside the narrow confines of the Indian tradition has to do

> with the connection between metaphor and thought. Bhaviveka's arguments are situated in a much larger picture of the world. He thought of a philosophical argument not just as an "idea," a "position," a "proposition," or any of the other conventional terms that can be used to name the currency of intellectual disputes. He pictured it as a trajectory of thought or an "approach" that led eventually to a distinctive "vision" of reality. The metaphor of vision (of following a path in order to see) generates many of the important components of Bhaviveka's thought. How do philosophers typically go wrong? They wander off the path by falling into "extremes," or they are deluded into seeing things that are not there.[6]

This position on philosophical argument is accepted and reinforced by the understanding of the religious meaning of philosophical work in the symbolic engagement theory of *Philosophical Theology (I, 3)*. The various more popularly recognized Buddhist practices of meditation, disciplined ways of perhaps monastic life, and cognitive turns, as in koan meditation, are also means intended to acquire this way of envisioning or experiencing the world. Given the great diversity of interpretations of this motif of causation and reality, the approaches to Buddhist practice are varied.

One way of interpreting *pratitya-samutpada* is with the theory of harmonies in an existential field that has been developed throughout *Philosophical Theology (I, 10)*. The components of a harmony do not have a substratum but just fit together. The components are the outcomes of streams of causation from the past. They have a form together for as long as they last. In present experience, they are experienced as coming together and then being past. Some extreme forms of Buddhism emphasize the deconstruction of the harmony into its components. For instance, in the early Buddhist dialogue with King Milinda mentioned earlier, the Buddhist monk Nagasena answers the king's question about the meaning of the no-self doctrine by asking about the king's chariot.[7] Is the chariot the wheels, floor, and other components or something over and above that? Assuming that the parts are the real things, the king answers that the "chariot" is a conventional name for the parts together, and that it is not real in the way the parts are. Similarly, "Nagasena" is a conventional name for the parts of the monk. Some lines of Buddhist thought have supposed that the really real is the components of the components down to the smallest experiential fragment, and for some of these lines of Buddhism, even the reality of the smallest parts disappears. Other lines of thought have emphasized that the conventional truth that grasps the whole chariot, or person, or harmony is just as real and true as the "higher truth" that disaggregates harmonies. The force of the Buddhist polemics about this topic is its continued opposition to the substratum theory. Because the philosophical cosmology in *Philosophical Theology* is not preoccupied with rejecting substratum theory, it does not give priority in reality to the components, the form, the existential location, or the achieved value-identity of the harmony, however large or small scale it might be.

Through all the divergent schools of Buddhism is another common motif, which is that, however the reality and unreality of phenomena or selves are interpreted, liberating experience is the ability to grasp the world "such as it is." "Suchness" is the character of ultimate reality as accurately apprehended. Suchness is empty of any kind of own-being beyond the phenomena that have come together in their various dependent co-originations. Of the many interpretations of this, perhaps the most thorough and cumulatively influential is that of Nagarjuna.[8] Many different Buddhist cosmologies illustrate the general basic point.

Bearing in mind the relative unimportance of the metaphysical issues, the essential components in the theory of harmony developed in *Philosophical Theology* correspond roughly to the dynamics of arising and ceasing of formed conditioned pluralities. Generally, however, Buddhism has not been exercised to understand how really different things can be experienced together as mutually conditioning but separate. Rather, for most analyses what arises and ceases is the complex field of consciousness. Therefore, there has not been much Buddhist concern for the possibility of really distinct things being sufficiently together that an ontological context of mutual relevance would be required as an assumption. The question of the one and the many that motivated the argument in *Philosophical Theology One*, Part III, is quickly interpreted by Buddhists to be an attempt to find a substratum. But a substratum would have to be determinate to do the work of unifying across plurality and change. The ontological act of creation is not a substratum in any sense but rather the creative cause of the existence of the mutually conditioning empty dharmas. This would be an interesting ontological interpretation of the Buddhist philosophy, if the Buddhists were interested in that sort of thing. But they are interested rather in the practice of attaining the capacity to achieve an enlightened and therefore liberated mode of personal life.

I. FORM/VALUE/POSSIBILITIES/OBLIGATION

Like all the Axial Age religions, Buddhism holds to a universal ethic of justice for all and respect for all who are under obligation. The background cosmology presupposed in Buddhism, at least in its ancient versions, is the karmic theory of the transmigration of souls. This means that all sentient beings, in whatever state—human, subhuman, or superhuman—are under obligation, and the quality of their succession of lives depends on the choices they make. Similarly, the justice due to human beings according to most of the Axial Age religions is also due to sentient beings in other states, according to Buddhism, although, of course, taking into account differences in the meaning of justice: Justice is defined vaguely as optimizing the value of the possible effects of one's actions on other sentient beings.

Perhaps the most striking aspect of the Buddhist traditions' engagements with the ultimate condition of form and possibility, however, is its promise of the special possibility of radical change. Whereas Christianity, for instance, promises the possibility of becoming a New Being in Jesus Christ, which is a way of living ordinary life with full acceptance of its created status, Buddhism in some of its forms promises a path for getting out of ordinary life altogether. Whereas Christianity promises a way of intensifying the dynamic extension and intension of life, Buddhism promises a way of being released from that dynamism while still situated and engaged.

These contrasts are complicated and problematic. The transmigration of souls theory that Buddhism shares with most forms of Hinduism seems to suppose that there are continuous souls with own-being that go from one life to another. Buddhism, and most nondual forms of Hinduism, reject the metaphysics of the finite continuity of soul stuff. But that situation of transmigration shapes the rhetorical context for the Buddhist (and nondual Hindu) projects of release or liberation from life's changes. Some forms of Buddhism, such as Pure Land, symbolize nirvana as the release of the soul from the process of more rebirths according to karmic law and the soul's immediate transportation to the Pure Land of the Buddha; in the Pure Land, there is no more rebirth, only everlasting bliss. This is similar to conceptions of heaven in some other Axial Age religions and involves obviously intimate symbols of the ultimacy of change from the round of karmic life. Other forms of Buddhism take different routes, most of them attaining intimate symbols through the actual practices of meditation. Meditation is physical as well as mental and involves specific steps that are felt intimately. The various stages of meditative progress tracked in different forms of Buddhism are extremely intimate to human experience.[9] Whatever their order and nature, they constitute concrete changes in human reality relative to the unmediated, aboriginally ignorant states.[10]

Nevertheless, in the classic statement of the Middle Way in Gautama Buddha's first sermon, the practice of meditation comes late in the list of the "moral" conditions that Buddhists are supposed to master in the Eightfold Noble Path that leads to the cessation of suffering: "right views, right intentions, right speech, right action, right livelihood, right effort, right mindfulness, right concentration."[11] Only the last three have much to do with meditation in its customary forms. The possibilities for the transformation of the self so as to escape the wheel of rebirth require beginning with learning how to live right within that cycle of temporal life.

The great missionary power of Buddhism is the possibility it offers for radical personal change. This is so especially in the contemporary religious situation where many people in diverse social contexts feel their lives to be disintegrated. Buddhism does not have much appeal to people in non-Buddhist cultures whose social situation is chaotic and whose lives are filled with violence and crippling poverty; evangelical Christianity seems more attractive in those chaotic situations because of its strong emphasis on building tight, ritually organized communities. But for people whose primary troubles are personal and somewhat internal—though no sharp line can be drawn between the internal and external—Buddhism offers the possibility of radical change.

Moreover, precisely because the methods of change involve intimate practices of the reorganization of life and then of meditation, often with group support, Buddhism in its many forms has little difficulty cultivating intimate symbols of the ultimate conditions of how to be just, to integrate oneself, to relate to others with compassion, and to be real in value-identity according to some Buddhist interpretation of what that might be. With some important exceptions in Mahayana, Buddhism has not spent much energy on developing sophisticated transcendent symbols of ultimacy. But then, the transcendent symbols are not so important in Buddhism: What is important is pulling out the poisoned arrow by means of the practices that constitute the intimate symbols.

II. COMPONENTS/GROUNDEDNESS/WHOLENESS

The rhetorical center of Buddhism's most ancient and still-dominant symbols is the transformation of the self so as to surmount suffering. To be sure, Buddhism has many important strains that address issues of justice and decision-making regarding possibilities. A preeminent theme is compassion for others. Buddhism addresses issues of absolute value-identity. But most of all, Buddhist symbols focus on the ultimate condition of proper wholeness of self.

The centrality of the philosophical cosmology of *pratitya-samutpada* calls attention first and foremost to the components of life. All the things that make up life are conditioned phenomena, each with its many histories of conditions. To be grounded in these components, for many Buddhist schools, is to accept them for what they are, let them be, and let them go, without attachment to them. No special harmony of the self, such as a metaphysically unified consciousness, should be posited that comports itself to the components except for the facility of allowing the components to be, enjoying or suffering them for what they are. The self in metaphysical truth has no own-being over against the components, and only the ignorant projection of an overarching ego would lead one to think otherwise. Wholeness of life is the enlightened acceptance of the components as they arise and the release of them as they cease.

The components are, of course, real: One has one's particular body with its strengths and ills, one's family, social situation, economic conditions, and all the rest. The images of Buddha common in the West often depict him in meditation, as if meditation neglects the body. He often looks soft and fat from too much sitting. But John Powers points out that the assumption of development through countless lifetimes means that the Buddha's body improves along with his spiritual powers. He is born to royalty for the life of his enlightenment and is "a bull of a man," exhibiting all the characteristics of hypermasculinity prized at the times of the characterizations of him.[12] Buddhism is also the source of important martial disciplines for improving the body. These physical as well as mental components of human beings are such as they are and need to be engaged as such. But the way an enlightened Buddhist should comport toward them in the ultimate sense defining the self is to accept them as they arise and as they cease. This posits no substratum self beyond the acceptance of the dependent co-origination of the components of one's life.

Buddhist schools variously interpret how this integration is to be conceived and attained. They all would caution against taking "integration," the term developed in *Philosophical Theology*, to suppose a substratum unitary self, such as a transcendental unity of apperception or a primal personhood. Rather integration is an harmonic patterning of the disparate components of the self and is itself a dependent co-origination. Consider as an example the approach of a particularly powerful contemporary school, deriving from the Korean "Son" Buddhism (Chinese, "Chan," Japanese, "Zen") as interpreted by the Korean-American Buddhist monk and professor of religious studies Park Sung Bae. Zen was one of the first forms of Buddhism to become popular in the United States. It is a form of Yogacara Buddhism and is coupled with the Chinese Hua-yen Buddhism for deep philosophical analysis, as in the work of Fa-tsang (643–712) commenting on the *Hua-yen ching*, or *Flower Adornment Scripture*. Also important in Park's analysis is the *Ta-ch'eng ch'i-hsin lun*, which he translates as the *Treatise on Awakening Mahayana Faith*, especially as this is interpreted by the Korean Buddhist Wonhyo (617–686). Although Yogacara is a major tradition of Mahayana Buddhism alongside the Madhyamaka, Park holds his interpretation to be general enough to apply across the whole Mahayana movement.

Given the miserable life of suffering, just how can one achieve the transformation to enlightenment? Park answers, through faith. As he points out, "it is well known that Buddhism is a religion of meditation and of enlightenment; yet few are aware that it is also a religion of faith."[13] Most Westerners think of faith as "faith in" something, such as faith in God. Pure Land Buddhism can also be construed as "faith in" the Buddha of the Western Land, although it need not be interpreted that way. Faith in the dominant Buddhist conception, according to Park, does not take an object. Rather, it is based on the classical Chinese conceptual construction *ti-yong*, or "essence and function," as it is usually translated.[14] Faith in this sense is the *function* of the inner *essence* or Buddha-mind. Faith is the name of the way the Buddha-mind functions in the world.

Buddhist faith, in general, is the commitment to the practice that leads to enlightenment and transformation, "abiding firmly with resolute conviction in a state of clearness, tranquility, and freedom."[15] Yet there are two senses of this founding faith: doctrinal faith and patriarchal faith. The former is faith that the person can become Buddha (enlightened), and the latter is faith that one already is Buddha. Doctrinal faith is expressed in the rhetoric of transformation. Patriarchal faith is expressed in the rhetoric of arousing faith in the first place. Doctrinal faith requires confidence in the cause and effect processes of practice toward enlightenment. Patriarchal faith

> only stresses that there be faith that everyone is originally Buddha; that all people intrinsically possess the perfect Buddha nature; and that the marvelous essence of *nirvana* is perfectly complete in everyone. Hence, there is no need to search anywhere else, because since the beginning, those have been complete in oneself.[16]

Doctrinal faith requires a passionate attachment to the future as determined by practice. Yet that attachment is itself counterproductive. To be attached to the attainment of enlightenment is one of the worst possible attachments, one that will give one constant grief. Far better, Park argues, to conceive of the Buddhist path as that of awakening patriarchal faith that one already is Buddha, that is, enlightened and free, but without realizing it. Patriarchal faith itself is already one's nature and one only need be awakened to it. Patriarchal faith in this peculiar sense is the state of being enlightened, of experiencing the world with Buddha-mind, seeing it such as it is, *pratitya-samutpada*.

The process of awakening patriarchal faith is what Buddhist meditative practice is all about. The Hua-yen scripture suggests that there are fifty-two stages toward the awakening of such faith. But the Zen tradition has also always believed in sudden enlightenment, as sometimes happens in koan meditation. Park interprets patriarchal faith to be identical with practice in a certain sense, namely, that to the extent one is committed in practice, to that extent patriarchal faith is aroused and one's consciousness is the function of the Buddha-mind. To that same extent, one is enlightened. Complete enlightenment would consist in having no mental functions that are not the functions of the Buddha-mind that accepts things as they are, in their suchness, and without attachments. Practice in meditation simply for its own sake, without attachment to using it to attain enlightenment, is the Buddha-mind functioning.

Yet obviously there exists the purposeful process of meditation in Buddhism. Buddhist sermons incite people to practice, and teachers teach people how to do it. If no one suggested that meditative practice might relieve the misery of ordinary life, no one would do it. Park appeals to the Buddhist doctrine of two truths at this point. The ordinary, practical, truth is that one has to work at enlightenment through perhaps many stages of practice. The higher truth is that what is happening in this work is that the enlightenment that is always already present, the ability to experience things as nothing more than empty arisings and ceasings of dharmas, needs to be awakened.[17] But, in point of fact, ordinary consciousness must be changed radically for the Buddha-mind to function in consciousness. Even if nirvana already lies within, it is not accessible to consciousness unless consciousness is changed in what Park calls a "revolution of the basis."[18]

This change in consciousness is a function of practice; that is, practice is the "essence" whose "function" is a changed consciousness. Although one begins practice as a novice, only with the improvement of practice (in fifty-two steps!?) does the essential practice function with enlightened consciousness.

The philosophy of consciousness and its objects is extremely complicated in Buddhism, and different schools take widely divergent tracks even when dealing with the same basic motifs. An analysis of Buddha-mind deals with highly transcendent symbols of ultimate reality. And yet the Buddhist connection between those transcendent symbols, however interpreted in Yogacara or Madhyamaka, and the intimate symbols involved in the details of practice is extremely close. Whereas the Abrahamic religions have much distance and tension between the intimate symbols of their special characters and stories and the transcendent symbols of a viable metaphysics of ultimacy, Buddhism has powerful intimate symbols that in no way contradict the viable symbols of ultimacy. What is Buddha-mind but harmony grasping its conditions with perfect pitch for what they are? What are the essential components of harmony except whatever is involved in allowing those conditional components to arise and cease within the harmony as they do, however that is interpreted by various Buddhist schools? What is the experiential engagement of things such as they are but the expression of the ontological context of mutual relevance in which different things can be together registering one another in their interactions?

To be sure, most forms of Buddhism have not pursued the ontology of ultimacy much beyond the conditions for consciousness. There have been serious disputes about how much reality dharmas have over and above their being perceived in consciousness. The debate as to how much continuity consciousness can have so as to notice arising and ceasing of dharmas without becoming a substratum for their appearance is an element that distinguishes the Yogacara and Madhyamaka traditions. Buddhist philosophy has generally addressed the problem of the one and the many in terms of consciousness, not in terms of a realistic view of different things. So, Buddhist notions of certain aspects of ultimate reality are underdeveloped, precisely because to develop them would be distractions from the task of removing the poisoned arrow.

As far as the ultimate project of attaining enlightenment, realizing nirvana, or obtaining liberation from the cycle of samsara goes, the Buddhist practices of meditation based on a disciplined moral life provide powerful and intimate symbols for the ultimate concerns for wholeness or an integrated life. The very intimacy of the practices of meditation, and the relative unimportance of the transcendent metaphysics behind the practices, make Buddhism attractive to people who hold to different transcendent symbols of ultimacy. A common kind of syncretism, especially in late-modern "developed" cultures, is the practice of parts of Judaism, Christianity, Islam (with reservations), and Confucianism along with the meditative practices of Buddhism. One of the geniuses of Buddhism is that this is perfectly satisfactory: If the meditative practice gives rise to the revolution in the base that allows consciousness to see things such as they are, the other symbolic trappings of historical Buddhism are not needed.

III. EXISTENTIAL LOCATION/ENGAGEMENT/LOVE

Nevertheless, the pursuit of one's own relief from suffering through a proper integration of the components of life in an enlightened consciousness by itself does not address all of ultimate reality. Another ultimate human condition is the engagement of others. This is affected deeply by the integration or wholeness of the self, or lack of it. But engagement of others is not to be reduced to how one behaves as a whole person: The *other* things are involved.

Buddhism addresses engagement through its motif of compassion. Compassion is not merely the unattached acceptance of dharmas as they arise, linger, and cease. It is a genuine engagement of other things for their own sake. As the central virtue or character ideal of Mahayana Buddhism, compassion is supposed to be directed to all sentient beings. Whether or not contemporary Buddhists accept a literal version of the reincarnation theory of lives moving through many sentient species, that motif forms the background of contemporary Buddhist symbolic rhetoric. At the level of basic motif, compassion is a commitment to other sentient beings to aid them on the way to their own enlightenment and liberation from the round of samsara. Compassion means both empathizing with the suffering of others and helping them to achieve their own liberation.

In Mahayana Buddhism a principal character role is that of a bodhisattva. A bodhisattva is a sentient being who has vowed not to take his or her own release from samsara into nirvana until all other sentient beings have been so released. The process of a bodhisattva's life extends perhaps through many lifetimes. Important Buddhists texts (the Jataka tales) describe the previous lives of Gautama Buddha before he was born into the one during which he was enlightened and from which he entered into nirvana. The details of the image of the bodhisattva have been very important for Buddhist art, even if they do not bear literal scrutiny; if every bodhisattva is waiting for the liberation of all the others, none could go first and no one would become Buddha. The overall effect of the bodhisattva ideal, however, is to emphasize the point that the purpose of Buddhist practice is not only to develop an integrated self that experiences life as the Buddha-mind but to live a life of compassion that actually helps others escape the miseries of suffering.

Compassion involves feeling compassionate toward others. Much Buddhist meditation, especially coming from the Madhyamaka School, is aimed at developing feelings of compassion. In part, this is because compassion, caring for others, appears as something of an opposite to attachment. The meditative practice of being able to experience others without attachment but with compassion for their own welfare is part of the cultivation of enlightened wholeness.

But compassion is not only feeling. It is behavior toward others that is aimed to make a positive difference for them. For the most part, Buddhists have not paid much attention to compassion toward the nonsentient environment, although they have understood the liberating effects of beauty in nature and cultivated gardens.[19] They have paid somewhat more attention to affecting institutions that in turn affect individuals; during the Tong dynasty in China, they were a dominant force in the imperial government. For the most part, Buddhist compassion has been directed toward individuals.

In our time, one of the most powerful expressions of Buddhist compassion was manifested among the American gay community at the time of the AIDS crisis at its worst in the 1980s and '90s. Because of the stigma against homosexuality, particularly male homosexuality, many gay men had been disowned by their own families, often because of the religious culture of those families. The intense religiosity of evangelical Christianity and some Roman Catholicism at the time was often coupled with bigotry against gay people. When the AIDS crisis struck, many of its victims were rejected by their families and many of those families interpreted the affliction as divine punishment for what they saw as a sinful lifestyle. Yet the victims themselves had been cultured to be explicitly religious, and so the rejection by their familial religious cultures was all the more devastating. In this context, many gay people in America drew together to create new communities of compassion for one another and a significant number of these people were drawn to Buddhism. Buddhist compassion thus became a prominent American religious way of helping people die and grieve.[20]

No formula exists for how to love with compassion in Buddhism, or in any of the other Axial Age religions, all of which emphasize the importance of love for engaging other people. The needs of love are always particular to individuals and contexts, such as the special needs occasioned by the AIDS crisis. Compassion requires effort, however, and does not come easy (*II, 3, 7*). It requires, first, that one's own attitudes are free of hate and self-interest. It requires also cultivated awareness of others, overcoming the ways in which people objectify one another so as not to have to be aware of others as human beings. It requires learning how to appreciate others, to see their values clearly and dispassionately, to understand the lives and circumstances of the others so as to grasp what is good and bad in their lives. It requires also the courage to stay with all this when there are so many reasons to be in denial about the demands that loving others places upon one's life. No wonder the Buddhist mythology says that it takes very many lifetimes to learn how to be compassionate toward all sentient beings!

Buddhism is particularly attractive in our time for focusing on the practical steps required to practice compassion, not just to cultivate the feeling of compassion but to act on it concretely. This Buddhist emphasis on getting the job done helps trivialize the larger narratives that people use to relate themselves to others, often to distance themselves from others, to treat others merely according to the roles in some story. These are all excuses for not having to do the work of being particularly compassionate, and Buddhism undercuts them. The limitation of Buddhism in our time with regard to compassion is its hesitance about compassion toward nonsentient things. Because compassion ultimately, for most forms of Buddhism, means helping people achieve their own enlightenment, the nonsentient natural environment has no issues for compassion to address. The current scientific and philosophical movements that see sentient being arising within a nonsentient environment are forcing reflective Buddhists to rethink the meaning of sentience.

A crucial connection exists between the integrating experience of enlightenment and the capacity for compassion. As argued in the previous section, enlightenment for most Buddhist schools involves coming to see things such as they are, without the distortions that come from egoistic attachments. Appreciation of things such as they are is also a crucial ingredient in compassionate engagement, both in being aware of others in their details and understanding their values appreciatively. Therefore, a cultivated experience of the suchness of nature, often expressed in aesthetic media, is the foundation for compassionate engagement of others that goes beyond sentient beings.

IV. ABSOLUTE VALUE-IDENTITY

Buddhism is as various in its approaches to one's absolute value-identity as Christianity and Hinduism. Its many schools approach the issue differently. And the popular practice of Buddhism runs from very sophisticated anti-supernatural versions to popular devotions to Guanyin or to Amida Buddha of the Pure Land. In the latter, the absolute value-identity to be sought is something like heavenly presence before God popularly imagined in Judaism, Christianity, and Islam, as well as in some popular forms of Hinduism. The image of absolute value-identity is to be brought to the Buddha of the Pure Land with one's own identity accepted with perfect compassion. On the other hand, most forms of Buddhism, particularly the Mahayana, hold to the metaphysical view that there is no underlying self that might travel to the Pure Land. Nirvana is the extinguishing of the self that moves through samsara from moment to moment. Nothing exists of one's life, really, except that it is such as it is.

The root meaning of value-identity in most schools of Buddhism is the realization that one's life is simply what it is, moment by moment. It consists of the values and disvalues experienced and of the effects of one's actions on others. Their true value-identity includes contributions from all those who have affected them, in one way or another of understanding the causal doctrine of *pratitya-samutpada*. The transcendent philosophical question of value-identity is how to conceive its wholeness in light of the fact that subjective value-identity is encompassed within the harmony of a person's life, whereas the person's objective value-identity is within the harmonies of other things and is ordered by the essential components of those other things. A person's value-identity is more than the person's harmony and exists only in the ontological context of mutual relevance in which things external to one another but mutually conditioning can be together. Buddhists have a number of symbols for this ontological context, none of which is quite an ontological creative act as described in the metaphysical dialectic of *Philosophical Theology*. Among these symbols is emptiness as nothingness in which things can simply be together.[21] Also there is the symbol of the Buddha-mind, or the omnipresence of dharma in all finite consciousnesses. One of the most influential expressions of this is in the baroque imagery of the *Lotus Sutra*. In chapter after chapter, the Buddha addresses or immediately communicates with an incomprehensively large number of consciousnesses: In Chapter 15, tens of millions of billions of bodhisattvas alone are called into conscious communication by the Buddha.[22] In the introductory chapter of the *Lotus Sutra*, the Buddha was staying at Rajagriha on Holy Eagle Peak with twelve thousand monks; six thousand nuns; eighty thousand bodhisattvas; Indra, king of the gods, with twenty thousand of his followers; Brahman, king of heaven with fifty-two thousand assorted children of heaven; eight dragon kings; four chimera kings; four centaur kings; four griffin kings (each king with several hundred thousand followers); plus many others.

> From the tuft of white hair between his eyebrows, one of his characteristic components, the Buddha emitted a beam of light, illuminating eighteen thousand worlds in the east, so that there was nowhere that it does not reach, down to the lowest purgatory and up to Akanishtha, the highest heaven.
>
> In those worlds, all the living beings in the six states could be seen. Likewise the Buddhas existing at present in those lands could be seen, and the sutra teachings those Buddhas were preaching could be heard. Monks and nuns, laymen and laywomen, who had attained the Way through practice, could also be seen. Further, one could see bodhisattvas, the great ones, walking the bodhisattva way due to various causes and conditions, with various degrees of faith and understanding, and in various forms. Likewise Buddhas who had entered complete nirvana could be seen. And one could see there stupas made of the seven precious materials, stupas that had been built to hold the remains of these Buddhas after they had entered complete nirvana.[23]

The light from the Buddha's white hairs opens up an instant complete comprehension of the entire world, conceived to be vastly larger than even modern physical science suggests, to the great mass of sentient beings of human, subhuman, and superhuman sorts in the Buddha's courtyard. Although the personal and cosmic circumstances of the revealed beings are mentioned, what they have in common is their possession of the Buddha's teaching of enlightenment, possessed aurally as well as conceptually and through relics. Again and again, throughout the *Lotus Sutra*, the Buddha is surrounded by worlds within worlds of sentient beings to which he communicates enlightenment. In many instances each of those sentient beings has identity through eons upon eons of multiple lifetimes. The struggles of each sentient being provide intimate connections with ordinary Buddhists' lives. But the symbol of the incredibly numerous arrays of such beings with whom the Buddha is in an enlightening relation breaks the symbolism of personal striving, doctrinal faith, as Park would put it. One's absolute value-identity is to be in an enlightened relationship with all other sentient beings, *being in nirvana together.*

The fantastic imagery of the *Lotus Sutra* is not easily taken to be literally true in the contemporary world. But it can be taken to be symbolically true, literarily true, and indexically effective by those for whom the Buddhist scriptures and teachings constitute the important real world.

The themes of transcendence and immanence discussed concerning the Buddhist traditions are only a few among the many that provide resources of contemporary positions in the religious situation.

Chapter Seven

Hinduism

PROLOGUE

With only a little irony, Hinduism can be said to be a bit like the Buddhist idea of the self, a construction placed on a vast and confusing multiplicity but itself without an essence. Although many things are Hindu, Hinduism is no one thing. This, of course, can be said of all the other Axial Age religions, which are far more diverse internally and interconnected than might be thought when indicated by their names (*III, 3*). But this diversity is even greater in what passes for Hinduism than in the other religions. Consider the following dualities.

First, "Hinduism" is a theoretical construction developed in the late eighteenth and nineteenth centuries as part of a reaction against foreign colonialism.[1] The immediate colonial opposition was Britain, its intellectual "orientalism," and more broadly Western Christianity. Behind that was the millennium of occupation, sometimes in a colonial mode, by Muslim forces. Hinduism reflects a nationalist move to bring unity to an "indigenous" Indian religion. "Nationalism" has meant, on the one hand, a kind of exclusive nationalism to be distinguished from other cultures in opposition to them, as in the Arya Samaj of Dayananda Sarasvati and its later offshoots. On the other hand, Hinduism is known more in the West as a universalizing spiritual contribution of India, as in the Brahmo Samaj of Ram Mohan Roy and its sequelae, including Ramakrishna and Vivekananda. The universalizing Hinduism was more popular in the West but has returned to India as an important religious entity for middle-class Indians.[2] Contrasted with the modern invention of Hinduism are all the religious movements in India with often separate but sometimes intertwining careers that have been claimed for Hinduism.

Second is the contrast between the Aryan and Dravidian traditions, the former associated with migrations of ethnic Aryan peoples into India from the northwest, speaking a proto-Sanskrit language and with a Brahmanical social order expressed in the Vedas as revealed texts, the latter with the previous peoples who held out longer in the south of India and whose dominant religious language turned out to be Tamil.

Third is the evolution of Indian religions into two main movements, Vaishnavism, based on the "worship" of Vishnu, and Shaivism, based on the "worship" of Shiva. These movements continue to organize Hindu thought and practice today, though qualified in the middle class by universalizing senses of Hinduism. The conceptions of Vishnu and Shiva evolved from both Vedic and Dravidian sources, and the worship of each of them often involves recognition of the other and their "relatives." Yet many contexts involving competing lineages mark them as different religions.

Fourth is a contrast between an emphasis on different lineages, especially as marked out by lineages of gurus and their communities, and ancient texts that are common property of nearly all forms of Hinduism such as the epics, the Ramayana and the Mahabharata, including especially the Bhagavad Gita. The Vedas were anciently reinterpreted in various forms of Dravidian religion, and Tamil-based worship practices were accepted in communities that also identified primarily with the Vedic traditions.

Fifth is a contrast between the householder religion associated with Brahminism and the renouncer traditions, including Buddhism and Jainism, but also elements clearly identified within Hinduism.[3] The householder religion gives great emphasis to duty or dharma, with a rich set of traditions of duties to family, society, and to the gods through sacrifice. The more ascetic renouncer traditions in various ways reject the social components of dharma and some of the obligations of sacrifice. This distinction is ancient.

Sixth is a contrast between the householder and ascetic renouncer religious movements together on the one hand and the bhakti movements of religious devotion and passion. Perhaps there is something to the customary claim that the former originally were the province of the Aryan cultures and the latter of the Dravidian. But both sides are now present in a great many Hindu religious forms.

Seventh is a contrast between highly sophisticated Hindu philosophy and theology, on the one hand, and the wild folk practices of devotion to local deities, on the other. Sometimes the local deities are associated with "high gods" such as Shiva, Krishna, or Vishnu. But in many of those instances the association is somewhat strained and much more local gods are involved.

Eighth is a contrast between metaphysical monism and metaphysical dualism. This takes many forms and appears in various schools of thought. Most schools of Hindu thought believe that there is an underlying unity beneath the diversity of the world. The monists or nondualists say that this underlying unity is the only real reality, accounting for diversity as a function of some kind of ignorance. The dualists acknowledge the unity but say that diverse individual things are also real in some way or other and that liberation or *moksha* from the grind of time does not mean losing one's individuality.

Ninth is a contrast between positions that say that the absolute (Brahman) is beyond determination altogether and those that give Brahman or the high god some determinate theistic character. This contrast is related to different forms of spiritual practice or piety.

Tenth, identifiable continuities of philosophical or theological positions weave back and forth among different religious communities. For instance, the Vedanta tradition's most prominent thinker, Shankara, was associated with Shaivism, whereas other Vedanta thinkers such as Ramanuja and Madhva were associated with Vaishnavism. Yoga is a philosophical and spiritual school of its own, but it is present in many other forms of Hinduism as well as Buddhism and Jainism.[4]

Dualistic contrasts such as these serve to indicate some of the great variety in Hinduism, or its roots, and thus to prevent easy generalizations. But they are also false in that the interactions between the sides have produced many variations and that often there are not two things in opposition but rather a multiplicity only vaguely to be compared as different. To get beyond introductory observations such as these, a somewhat deeper immersion in the particulars of communities, practices, and texts is in order.

As an example, consider briefly the nondual Kashmir Shaivism of the late tenth-century philosopher and aesthetician Abhinavagupta. Shaivism itself, the worship of Shiva, is generally thought to be a post-Vedic movement, although Shiva is associated with Rudra, a Vedic deity. A form of Kashmir Shaivism directly descended from Abhinavagupta has a following in the United States today. For Abhinavagupta, Shiva is a male personification of ultimate reality that is wholly indeterminate, unmanifested, consciousness.[5] Shiva is inseparable from Shakti, however, the female personification of the power of manifestation. Just as, for the metaphysics of *Philosophical Theology*, the ontological creative act is indeterminate apart from creation, so Shiva is indeterminate apart from Shakti. And just as, for the metaphysics of *Philosophical Theology*, the ontological creative act is always determinate as that which gives rise to, or "manifests," the determinate world, so Shiva is also always Shakti manifesting the world. The general characteristic of things in the world is that each is a *kula*, which Muller-Ortega translates as "group."[6] Individual persons are such groups, as are families, social institutions, and human-environmental relationships. The point is that to be a thing, manifested from Shiva/Shakti, is to be a plurality with internal differentiation and yet a unity that hangs together. Without claiming too much for a parallel of conceptualization, this notion of "group" is very close to the notion of "harmony" developed in *Philosophical Theology*.

Abhinavagupta articulates the power of consciousness to "manifest" the "groups" of the world with a notion of "vibration" (*spanda*, in Sanskrit). Vibration is a little like the Chinese motif of yang and yin in which the determinateness of "groups" is a function of patterns of assertion and retreat. But it also has the connotation of vibrating into manifest existence and then back into indeterminate Shiva so that there is always a connection between the ultimate indeterminate reality and the proximate determinate realities of groups. Vibration is an exercise of power/Shakti, of which there are three fundamental kinds: willing or desiring, knowing, and acting.[7] Each of these is a power of consciousness, which is not conceived at all in the dualist fashion of Samkhya for which consciousness is pure passivity. Rather, the repose of consciousness is just a beginning of a vibratory, free, cognitive act that also includes the full manifestation of determinate realities. Paul Eduardo Muller-Ortega writes:

> The level of cosmic manifestation is very important here. In terms of the non-dual Kashmir Shaiva scheme of the female potencies or powers of Siva, each of the three *sakti-s* is respectively associated with a corner (*kona*) of the inverted triangle [of the heart]: the *iccha-sakti*, the willing or desiring of Siva; the *jnana-sakti*, the cognitive function of Siva; and the *kriya-sakti*, the active-creative function of Siva. This triad of powers is the triple function of the Heart of Siva, by means of which Siva is free to create, enjoy, and destroy the myriad universes that appear in the great ocean of consciousness. This triple function reduplicates on the level of ordinary life as our finite capacities for willing, knowing and acting.[8]

One of Abhinavagupta's fundamental metaphors for "vibration" is sexual emission, *visarga*. As an esoteric tantric tradition, his form of Kashmir Shaivism does involve ritualized sexual union. But that is by no means the only meaning of "emissional power." The union of the male and female, the lingam in the yoni, means both the ejaculatory power of creation and the receptive and returning power of repose. In this way, and with many other conceptual and metaphorical approaches, Abhinavagupta attempts to employ the metaphor of active consciousness—outward-moving and also self-reflexive—to articulate what *Philosophical Theology* articulates in its metaphysical way as the ontological act of creation, nothing in itself without its production but not reducible to the manifest things apart from their source (*I, 12*).

This brief presentation of the ontology of Abhinavagupta's nondual Kashmir Shaivism has prescinded from many elements that are intrinsic to it but would require much greater elaboration than can be attempted here. For instance, central to his exposition is an elaborate scheme of Sanskrit phonemes, both spoken and orthographic, that correspond to elements in the theory. The analogies drawn here between his theory and that of *Philosophical Theology* obscure the very many differences in intellectual context between his and that developed here. The differences between Abhinavagupta and other Hindu schools are also remarkable. For instance, the insistence on the monistic character of Shiva as active consciousness distinguishes him from the dualistic philosophy of Samkhya and many other schools. It also distinguishes him from Shankara and other nondualistic schools for whom ultimate reality is fundamentally nonactive. Abhinavagupta raises the question, "How can the

Ultimate, which is devoid of temporal succession and is only consciousness, grant the *kaulika* [groups] perfection, linked to temporal succession, by the mere knowing of which, one would obtain the nature of the Goddess?"[9] That question would not make sense to Shankara, for whom the multiplicity is an illusion of superimposition and not a reality to be perfected.

For the further purposes of *Philosophical Theology*'s inquiry into the role of Hinduism in the present religious situation, the guide to understanding the potential roles of various forms of Hinduism shall be the philosophical conceptions based on the analysis of determinateness, lifting up the theological significance of form, components, existential location, value-identity, and radical contingency. Furthermore, the operative question is how various forms of Hinduism might offer connections between intimate and transcendent symbols of ultimacy in each conception.

I. FORM/VALUE/POSSIBILITIES/OBLIGATION

The form of life, insofar as that is expressed as possibilities for action, is fundamentally that of duty or dharma. On the notion of "dharma," Gavin Flood writes:

> The term '*dharma*' is untranslatable in that it has no direct semantic equivalents in any western languages which convey the resonance of association expressed by the term. It has been variously translated as 'duty,' 'religion,' 'justice,' 'law,' 'ethics,' 'religious merit,' 'principle' and 'right.' More particularly *dharma* is the performance of vedic ritual by the Brahmans. It is 'the ritualistic order of Vedic sacrifice,' which refers especially to the performance of the 'solemn' rites (*shrauta*) enjoined on all Brahmans, to the domestic rituals (*grhya*), and to obligations appropriate to one's family and social group. *Dharma* is an all-encompassing ideology which embraces both ritual and moral behavior, whose neglect would have bad social and personal consequences.[10]

In all of these variants of meaning, the importance of dharma is that human beings lie under obligation. Although the renouncer traditions might claim to escape certain aspects of dharma, this claim defines them as seeking to get out from under the obligation that otherwise would define them.

Without for a moment suggesting that much uniformity exists among various parts of Hinduism as to what particular patterns of life dharma enjoins, especially ritual and domestic life, the tighter the prescriptions, the more intimately powerful and helpful they are. This is so in several senses. First, dharma provides important guidance for the living of the moral life, helping with decision-making. No set of moral rules can be complete or can work without interpretation. Nevertheless, detailed moral codes as characterize many segments of Hinduism are both intimate and helpful.[11] Second, the ideology of life as governed by dharma is psychologically and spiritually containing. In perilous conditions of nature, society, and personal life, dense containing worldviews are very helpful. Third, because dharma is public, even if different codes apply to men and women and to different castes, it provides a tool for understanding and relating to the actions and beliefs of others, helping to harmonize society. Although dharma is extremely prominent in many forms of Hinduism, it has analogues in many other religions with highly scripted codes for living.

Dharma, of course, is taken to define ultimacy in important respects. Its derivation is ascribed to the Vedas, among other sources. For the classical orthodox Hindu school, the Vedas are divinely authoritative. Moreover, insofar as some of the root metaphors of dharma come from the obligations and rules for sacrifice, it plays a role in the maintenance and even existence of the gods that depend on sacrifice. Not all Hindus devoted to dharma today might hold to notions of Vedic authority or to the classical interpretation of sacrifice. Nevertheless, the more generalized point stands, namely, that with respect to what is to be done, most or all aspects of life are under obligation.

The specific patterns of dharma for a person give intimacy to what it means to be defined ultimately as being under obligation. The sacrality of being under obligation points toward the transcendence of being under obligation over and above any specific obligations, although there is no obligation without specifics. The theological question concerning dharma today is whether it can be justified as transcendently ultimate.

The philosophical argument in *Philosophical Theology* is that possibilities with alternatives for choice are value laden and that, therefore, any choice among them actualizes some values and excludes some others (*II, 1; III, 9*). Obligation derives from the fact that it is better to choose the better, however that is constituted, and that one's moral worth relative to that choice depends on the values chosen in comparison with those excluded. Choosing gives the chooser the motive of choosing the value chosen; if the choice is free, the chooser might have chosen to adopt the motive of choosing an alternative. Lying under obligation depends on there being a value-difference between options chosen.

In the case of prescribed dharma, perhaps there is a question of acting according to one pattern of duties (or ways of conducting the sacrifice) rather than another. Conflicts among the duties of dharma abound in the various Hindu movements fixed on dharma as they do in any religious system of rules. But the deeper question is whether there is a value-difference between acting on the basis of dharma and doing something else contrary to dharma, such as abandoning one's family or failing to perform the sacrifice. If a renunciant, for instance, makes a case that it would be better for him or her to abandon family than to fulfill domestic dharma, this would align the focus of obligation to the choice between following dharma and doing something else that would reject dharma. In such an instance, with which the Hindu traditions that include renouncer movements are replete, obligation does not lie with dharma per se but with the value of dharma, which must be more important than the alternatives that might justify a renouncer choice. Thus, it would seem that dharma alone is not sufficiently ultimate to frame the human condition of lying under obligation.

In point of fact, arguments are made for the value of dharma itself, providing containment within a wild cosmos and perhaps even supporting the gods. Perhaps these arguments might always be successful, such that renouncing dharma is always a mistake, occasion by occasion. But this does not allow dharma itself to be a sufficiently transcendent symbol of the ultimacy of obligation because the case needs to be made for it each time.

The general point is that adequately transcendent symbols of ultimacy in reference to form and possibilities need to be sensitive to the locus of value, namely, in the alternative possibilities facing choice rather than antecedently given rules for choosing. Translating this to symbols of dharma or moral (and cultural) rules more generally is a step away from the adequately transcendent. So is the translation of ultimacy regarding possibilities to the various kinds of virtue ethics exhibited in religions, including forms of Hinduism. And the same is true of symbols of general policy. The advantage of these translations is that they provide more intimate symbols of duty that can be learned and applied with some generality; the disadvantage is that any might lead to the distortion of the real choice points between competing options. These issues will be revisited in Chapter 10 in this volume.

II. COMPONENTS/GROUNDEDNESS/WHOLENESS

Of equal importance to dharma in the multiple roots and branches of Hinduism is the concern for the career of the soul. Like Buddhism, the Hindu forms of South Asian religion suppose as the background for framing the human predicament the metaphors and intellectual tropes of the reincarnation of the soul in many lifetimes and life forms. Modern Western-educated Hindus might well have given up explicit belief in reincarnation, but the symbols of reincarnation are deep seated in the ways people think about themselves and their life, just the way personifying symbols of divinity provide rhetorical background framing for Jews, Christians, and Muslims who might have explicitly adopted a highly transcendent, nonpersonal conception of God or rejected belief in God completely.

So, the first problem within the Hindu matrix for thinking of how to relate the self to the components of life is relating the self to its many lives and life forms. In the early development of South Indian religious culture, the chief form of this relation came to be articulated in the doctrine of karma. The Mahabharata, for instance, has some expressions of reincarnation that are connected with karma and others that are not. Although complexly developed in many ways, not all consistent with one another, karma is the determination of the form of life, its nature, and situation, by the moral quality of previous lives. "Moral quality" is not always a precisely defined trait and is as large in scope as dharma.

Karma has many dimensions, four of which are important to notice here. The first is that it serves to give meaning to the diversity of situations, particularly the inequalities, among sentient beings. The ambient reality of inequalities is particularly reinforced in the suppositions of caste systems that derive from the influence of Brahmanical Aryan culture on the various strains of Hinduism. The caste into which one is born is determined by the karmic legacy of past lives. Even if the caste system is explicitly rejected, inequalities of birth are obvious. Some religious responses to the fact of inequality construe it to be just an expression of the arbitrariness of the world, a tough absurdity. Karmic religion, by contrast, gives inequality a meaning based on moral deserts.

A second point to notice about karma is that the continuity through all life forms of sentient beings itself creates a moral community that extends beyond the human. Although this means many things in different contexts, and is perhaps expressed more strongly in forms of Buddhism and Jainism than in many forms of what we identify as Hinduism, the karmic moral community includes all living sentient beings, requiring appropriate forms of respect and deference to souls in life forms radically different from the human. Given the metaphoric base of the caste system, human beings are separated into different classes that have rules for separating them one from another, with proscriptions of cross-caste touch, talk, marriage, business, and many other things. Within this caste-oriented metaphoric base, the differences between the species of sentient beings do not have such a radical cut-off between the human and other species as would be expected within the West Asian and East Asian Axial Age religions that do indeed consider the human to be a status radically distinct from the rest of sentient nature. In the contemporary religious situation, with increasing sensibilities about the embeddedness of human life within a larger nature and concerns for moral relations with nonhuman nature, this dimension of karma offers an intriguing possibility for conceptions of the self and its moral community as components of the self. The underlying continuity of reincarnation of continuously identified selves might be hard to make persuasive to people from cultures without the background of reincarnation, however. Perhaps biological continuity would be enough.

A third dimension of karma is that it intensifies the issues of relating to one's past as components of one's life. Nearly all religions have symbols for articulating an individual's past and that of his or her groups and perhaps their environments. Coming to terms with these things are important elements of the groundedness component of the human predicament. Often, comporting oneself toward one's past has a contemporary moral side to it, determining how one fixes one's own moral character, as in making amends for past misdeeds or affirming or rejecting the history of one's group. The karmic connection, however, intensifies this by its conviction that one's past lives have determined one's situation in this life by their moral (in the very broad sense) qualities. If one's situation is very bad, the karmic conviction requires taking responsibility for making it this way in previous lives. One also can take credit for one's previous lives if the situation is very good. This is an intensification of the moral community with oneself as well as with others.

A fourth dimension of karma is that it intensifies one's moral responsibility for the future. Most forms of karma are not strict determinisms: Although one's situation in this life is determined by the influence of past lives on one's soul, there is some freedom in this life to affect future lives for better or worse. In fact, moral responsibility, which is at the heart of the karma doctrine, requires that one be somewhat free in how to act in this life. In addition to the consequences of one's action that determine one's moral status regarding the values affected by choice, one's choices affect the quality of one's own future lives. This can mean many things, not all consistent with one another; but it still is an important consideration that distinguishes the rhetorical and symbolic base of karmic religion from the range of moral factors open to those religious systems without the karmic connection.

What is the goal of life's integration of components within the sensibilities of karma? Different strains of Hinduism frame the issue in different ways. For some, the point is to attain an improved life next time, with less suffering than in this life. Others take a longer view and aim at a superhuman life cycle as a divine being. Yet others look for the attainment of a life within which one can be released from the whole cycle of karmic reincarnation. For this last approach, *moksha* is the attainment of a kind of integration that does not require the components that force change and rebirth. The conception of the self involved in this will be discussed at greater length in conjunction with value-identity.

The religious variants on karmic reincarnation symbols usually have a rather tight interpretive integration between the transcendent and intimate symbols. On the one hand, the symbols that define the soul as having morally freighted continuity through a vast number of lifetimes are highly transcendent with respect to the nature of the soul and the abstract array of issues of integrating its components. On the other hand, one's life is always particular, and its very particularities are the intimate symbols of its ultimate nature and karmic tasks. Everything one does, having moral or dharmic significance, is ultimately important regarding how one grounds oneself in the components of life.

One problematic question for the contemporary religious situation in regard to the Hindu dimensions of karma is whether a robust conviction of continuity from life to life can be maintained as we learn more about how personhood, personality, and consciousness are embedded in biological processes. Although those processes give rise to elements of self that are not to be understood in reductive ways, can those elements of self survive total replacement of their biological enabling?

A second problematic question for the contemporary religious situation is whether the obvious differences in life's situations can be attributed plausibly to each person's own past responsibility. Can it be made persuasive that the millions of Jews, Gypsies, homosexuals, and Christians who were killed in the Nazi Holocaust in fact deserved to die because of their own past actions? Can people believe that those born to riches, power, loving families, and intelligence deserve that, whereas those less fortunate do not, because of their past-life achievements? The moral effect of the karmic sensibility is that there is no innocence. These questions are rhetorical, of course, because millions of people for millennia have in fact given a moral explanation based on karma for inequalities. Can this remain persuasive in the contemporary religious situation?

III. EXISTENTIAL LOCATION/ENGAGEMENT/LOVE

Like the other Axial Age religions, the traditions and communities of Indian religions that have come together as Hinduism advocate the engagement of others in the existential field with respect. As already discussed, the respect that other religions extend to human beings, most forms of Hinduism (and Buddhism) extend to the whole range of sentient beings. That respect, involved as it is with the moral community of karma, is not extended in the same way to the nonsentient parts of nature, although there are other ways of engaging nonsentient nature that will be mentioned shortly.[12]

As also discussed, for many strains of Hinduism the engagement of sentient beings as others is very much mediated by the social structures of the caste system and other ritualized relations with animals. All human relations, of course, are shaped by the institutions of society that give meaning to human interactions. Indeed, the very possibility of civilized human interactions depends on the evolution of social structures that enable family and community life, a point to be developed at greater length in the discussion of Confucianism in Chapter 8. Not just the caste system but the whole social/ritual array of dharma determines the channels by which the dharma-oriented strains of Hinduism engage others, including the gods. Insofar as the gods are sentient beings, themselves subject to reincarnation and karma, they are not ultimate and are to be engaged among the other things in the world's complicated existential field.

The intensity of modes of engagement varies widely among traditions and strains of Hinduism, ranging from passionate devotion to ascetic withdrawal. Traditions of passionate devotion, bhakti, have been associated historically with the ancient Dravidian or Agamic roots of Hinduism, although the strains of bhakti can be found in a great many Hindu movements now. Bhakti practices of worship and devotion involve cultivating intense passions of love, expressions of devotion in song and poetry, often with erotic metaphors as in devotion to Krishna, the flute-playing, seductive cowherd. Sometimes bhakti devotion is intensified in special ceremonies. For some people, the whole of life is organized around ceremonies for the cultivation of ecstatic emotional transport in love.

Most objects of bhakti engagement are divinities. Many forms of Hinduism make easy identification of divinities with their representations in temples, however, and so bhakti can be fixed on the statue, or lingam, or sacred grove, as itself divine. Moreover, perhaps because of the symbolic background of the moral community of karma, passionate, ecstatic devotion can be directed to an ordinary person, or to a guru, as in the guise of a divinity. Any sentient being, in principle, can be the object of devotion for the sake of the divinity their life might sometime embody.

The Bhagavad Gita is a text common to nearly all subsequent traditions within Hinduism, even though it has been interpreted in wildly contradictory ways. In the symbolic structure of the Gita, Krishna appears as a man who serves the warrior Arjuna as his charioteer. When the latter has an emotional breakdown at the prospect of going into battle against his friends and relatives, Krishna counsels him, slowly revealing himself to be a god, in fact the embodiment of Vishnu: At one point. Krishna transfigures himself as Vishnu, the transcendent creator who is in all things but also above them. Although complicated, the Gita discusses and recommends three paths or "yogas" of salvation: through action, through knowledge, and through devotion. Krishna says:

> Those who fixing their minds on Me worship Me, ever harmonized and possessed of supreme faith—them do I consider most perfect in *yoga*. But those who worship the Imperishable, the Undefinable, the Unmanifested, the Omnipresent, the Unthinkable, the Unchanging and the Immobile, the Constant, by restraining all the senses, being even-minded in all conditions, rejoicing in the welfare of all creatures—they come to Me indeed [just like the others]. The difficulty of those whose thoughts are set on the Unmanifested is greater, for the goal of the Unmanifested is hard to reach by the embodied beings. But those who, laying all their actions on Me, intent on Me, worship, meditating on Me, with unswerving devotion, these whose thoughts are set on Me, I straightway deliver from the ocean of death-bound existence, O Partha (Arjuna).[13]

This is to say, devotion to the figure of Krishna is better and easier for the "embodied" than devotion to the transcendent of which Krishna is the avatar. Nevertheless, Krishna as the avatar pervades all things, and so worship of him in a personal way is the worship of the entire creation:

> Of creations I am the beginning, the end and also the middle, O Arjuna; of the sciences (I am) the science of the self; of those who debate I am

> the dialectic. Of letters I am (the letter) A and of compounds (I am) the dual; I also am the imperishable time and I the creator whose face is turned on all sides. I am death, the all-devouring and (am) the origin of things that are yet to be; and of feminine beings, (I am) fame, prosperity, speech, memory, intelligence, firmness and patience.[14]

With this symbolic background, it is possible to see how bhakti devotion to the person of Krishna (and similarly to Shiva, who is also symbolized as creator of all) is a powerful way of engaging all the things in the world as other. All things embody the God and are to be engaged as means of devotion to the God.

Here is Krishna's description of the ideal devotee:

> He who has no ill will to any being, who is friendly and compassionate, free from egoism and self-sense, even-minded in pain and pleasure, and patient, the *Yogi* who is ever content, self-controlled, unshakable in determination, with mind and understanding given up to Me—he, My devotee, is dear to Me. He who from the world does not shrink and who does not shrink from the world and who is free from joy and anger, fear and agitation—he too is dear to Me. He who has no expectation, is pure, skillful in action, unconcerned, and untroubled, who has given up all initiative in action—he, My devotee, is dear to Me. He who neither rejoices nor hates, neither grieves nor desires, and who has renounced good and evil—he who is thus devoted is dear to Me. He who [behaves] alike to foe and friend, also to good and evil repute, and who is alike in cold and heat, pleasure and pain and who is free from attachment, He who holds equal blame and praise, who is silent [restrained in speech], content with anything that comes, who has no fixed abode and is firm in mind—that man who is devoted is dear to Me. But those who with faith, holding Me as their supreme aim, follow this immortal wisdom—those devotees are exceedingly dear to Me.[15]

Devotion in personal faith is the best kind, according to Krishna at that point in the Bhagavad Gita.

In contrast with this complex sense of engagement, at the opposite extreme, are the renouncer strains in Hindu practice, the ascetics who seek to disengage as much as possible from human and natural interactions, perhaps even from most ritual duties. Asceticism does not only mean disengagement—the Bhagavad Gita's yogas of action and knowledge require extraordinary ascetic discipline. Nevertheless, the serious renunciants who leave home and most dharma for the sake of realization of some sense of self-integration stand at the opposite pole from the existential engagement enjoined by the Gita, based on its metaphysics of creation. The practices and beliefs of contemporary forms of Hinduism occupy many positions on the continuum from ascetic disengagement to the virtuoso yogic realizations advocated in the Bhagavad Gita. Consideration of issues of absolute value-identity helps sort the reasons for this continuum.

IV. ABSOLUTE VALUE-IDENTITY

What is a person's ultimate value-identity? This is to ask, what is the self, not only as an achieved integration of components but as ultimately real? Hinduism offers many answers to this question, not only the well-known answer that the self is consciousness, which is atman, which in turn is identical with Brahman, the ultimate reality. The first historical point to make is that the early, pre-Upanishadic Vedic literature was much more interested in ritual than in the nature of the self. The Vedic Upanishads, probably written between 700 and 300 BCE, can be divided into the earlier and later ones, with the careers of Buddha and Mahavira (founder of Jainism) in the sixth century BCE marking the division.[16] The importance of this distinction is that, roughly speaking, for the early Upanishads the problem for the self was how to achieve immortality (which itself had several sorts), whereas for the later ones the self was conceived as caught in the wheel of samsara, reincarnated from life to life, and the problem was *moksha* or release from immortality. The previous discussion of reincarnation supposes the worldviews of the later Upanishads, although symbols of reincarnation were reinforced from many directions.

For purposes of the present discussion, the following general point can be made. In highly diverse ways, most strains of Hinduism that have come down to the present define the ultimate identity of the self in relation to a deeper ontological reality. That deeper ontological reality has been symbolized on a wide spectrum of objects, from local temple statues with whom one might be joined in devotion, to transcendent images of Vishnu or Shiva beyond determination, to Brahman without qualities. Many more or less determinate theistic conceptions of God or gods as ultimate reality lie in between. One's absolute value-identity consists primarily in how one relates to such an underlying ultimate reality.

Roughly speaking, there are two forms of this relation, dualism and nondualism. In the dualistic conceptions (and symbolic networks), the individual maintains something of his or her own identity in the relation to the more ultimate reality. This might be by coming into the presence of the God with an individual consciousness. Or, in the ingenious theology of Ramanuja, usually characterized as a "qualified nondualist," the individual is part of the body of God, individuated as such a part but integrated with the others as individual dance steps are integrated with one another in being the movements of the dancer.[17] For the dualistic positions, release from the wheel of samsara means an exiting from life and change while still maintaining an individual consciousness whose object is the ultimate reality.

The nondualist traditions, associated most strongly with Shankara, say that the true reality of the self is not different from Brahman without qualities. With some symbol system or other the nondualists say that *moksha* is the obliteration of any individuating elements, such as perspectival consciousness, and some sense of dissolving into the ultimate. The more strictly philosophical nondualisms have to argue that no real independence of unchanging Brahman is possible and that the appearance of separation, including the appearance of change and the life-death-life cycle of samsara, is somehow an illusion. How then is this illusion accounted for? It must be a very powerful illusion in order to power the entire project of obtaining release from samsara. Furthermore, the practicalities of daily life require treating reality as if it were complex and changing. Shankara's solution explains in complicated ways how the play of items changing within consciousness is superimposed on reality as its object. One of the important points of debate within Shankara's Advaita Vedanta is whether *moksha*, the realization that superimposition causes the illusion of dualism and change, is possible within this life, or whether one must die (and thus cease to need to deal with changing things) in order for it to be possible.[18]

For the question of individual value-identity, what is remarkable in the nondualist position, and even to a larger extent in the dualist, is that the relation to Brahman is so vastly more important than the particularities of achieved identity that those particularities drop out as important at all for absolute value-identity. Indeed, for most forms of nondualism, the particularities of identity are unreal, illusory.

The symbolic matrix that lies behind this ease of rejecting the particularities of achieved identity is that of consciousness. An ancient and very powerful motif of Indian thought, present in Buddhism as well as the many forms of Hinduism, is that the self is primarily consciousness. The contents of consciousness are particular but consciousness itself is not. Removing the particularities of consciousness, the consciousness that is I is also the consciousness that is you. Moreover, the underlying ultimate reality is what gives rise to consciousness and has the form of pure consciousness. This analysis of consciousness as pure and non-intentional is problematic to most Western understandings because of their usual commitment to the dynamics of intentionality. The Advaita Vedanta conception of consciousness involves no dynamism; the movement of consciousness is interpreted entirely in terms of the arising and ceasing of contents of consciousness. Pure consciousness is the model for ultimate reality in these strains of Hindu thought. Even where the individuality of conscious perspectives is maintained, the particular contents of consciousness are rendered inoperative except, in some instances, where they become transformed into a kind of bliss at having nothing as their object except Brahman. The absolute value-identity of the particular self is to disappear.

The nondual philosophy of Abhinavagupta's Kashmir Shaivism pushes consciousness in another direction, however, as indicated in the prologue to this chapter. For Abhinavagupta, the finite consciousness is capable of coming to see itself as a part of, indeed identical with, the creative willing, knowing, and acting vibratory powers of Shiva/Shakti, suspended between pure indeterminacy, symbolized as conscious (rather, *un*conscious) complete repose and engagement with the groups of things constituting the manifest order. Through various esoteric practices, including meditation, mantras, and rituals involving sexual union, individuals can be awakened to their true reality as Siva. Or, the awakening is to the fact that Shiva/Shakti is the true and only reality. Thus, as argued in *Philosophical Theology One*, Chapter 15, and *Philosophical Theology Two*, Chapter 11, a person can become a self-interpreting material sign of the ontological creative act, in Abhinavagupta's view. A person's absolute value-identity can come to be appreciated as the value-identity of Shiva/Shakti. That appreciation is bliss. Or, the reality of Shiva/Shakti is bliss. Or, "actualizing" the true Shiva/Shakti consciousness is bliss.

Surely, it would be a mistake to make summary judgments about the intimacy and transcendence of Hindu symbols of absolute value-identity. Like all the Axial Age religions, Hinduism has many symbols to articulate the achievements for better or worse of an individual with regard to particular obligations, with regard to integration and wholeness, and with regard to dealing with other people and things. For many people, the operative conception of their value-identity is simply to get a better life next time. But for those people influenced by the Advaita Vedanta tradition, perhaps through Sri Aurobindo or through the Ramakrishna movement, the question of absolute value-identity is peculiarly unimportant. What one has achieved by way of ultimate identity is trivial, and perhaps a distraction, in comparison with entering into a unifying relation to ultimate reality, merging with it, or disappearing. The deep experiential elements in the transformation of consciousness involved in properly relating to ultimate reality makes the many different kinds of efforts at establishing that relationship intimate. And yet the transcendence of ultimate reality conceived in these ways goes beyond the particularities that make individual identity important, for the Advaita Vedanta position. For Abhinavagupta's Kashmir Shaivism, the particularities of individual identity merge with the indeterminate repose of Shiva in the dynamic vibratory reality of the powers of Shakti.

This chapter has focused on the diversity of resources within Hinduism considered generally, resources that are often in conflict with one another. Yet they are manifestly addressed both to the engagement of transcendence and to the needs of intimacy.

Chapter Eight

Chinese Religion

PROLOGUE

The Chinese religio-philosophical traditions are as internally multifarious as any other Axial Age religion or religion family.[1] Building on pre–Axial Age shamanic bases, what we now know as Confucianism and Daoism, along with many other schools such as Moism, Legalism, and institutional devotion to yin/yang thought, arose during the Axial Age. After a period of considerable contestation, sophisticated anti-supernaturalistic Confucianism emerged as the dominant spiritual power of the court during the early Han dynasty. Buddhism from India began to be influential in the first centuries of the Common Era, developing Sinicized forms and achieving important recognition at the court during the Tong dynasty. Daoism, too, in its medieval institutionalized form, achieved recognition at court during the Tong. At the same time, Christianity flourished, particularly in the Western regions along the Silk Road, and it has been said that during the Tong dynasty there were more Christians (of the Nestorian branch) in China than people in all of Europe.[2] Islam came to China, too, along the Silk Road during the Tong.

The situation was, of course, was much more complex than this because of all the local religions, some of which have continued down to this day, sometimes taking on the official language and some of the practices of the larger Axial Age groups. But it was not until the late Tong dynasty, in the decades surrounding the year 800, that the Confucian revival led by Han Yu and Li Ao began to sort the activity into the schools we know today, distinguishing earlier Confucians from Daoists and both schools from Buddhism and the other "foreign" religions. Buddhism and Christianity suffered official suppression during the late Tong, and Nestorian Christianity almost completely died out; Roman Catholicism reintroduced Christianity into China with its sixteenth-century mission led by Matteo Ricci, among others. As Confucianism and Daoism traveled from China to Korea, Japan, and Southeast Asia, they encountered indigenous religions; in Southeast Asia there was a strong presence of Hinduism and Theravada Buddhism (the main form of textual Buddhism to reach China proper was Mahayana).

For purposes of discussing the Axial Age religions in the present religious situation, the focus here will be on Confucianism and Daoism to the somewhat arbitrary exclusion of the others. In the late twentieth century, with the relaxation of Communist ideology, Confucianism, Daoism, and Buddhism began serious revivals in China. Marxism itself, of course, had been promoted as something of an Axial Age religion, although sharply critical of anything "religious," by which was meant "superstitious." Christianity, too, has been growing in China, especially of the Roman Catholic and evangelical Protestant sorts.

The revival of Confucianism in the form of Neo-Confucianism in the Song dynasty continued the complex emphasis on the cultivation of humaneness and the forms of civilization that preoccupied the early Confucians.[3] Nevertheless, it also drew heavily on lessons from Daoism and Buddhism, while attempting to reject certain parts of those traditions. From Daoism it appropriated a deep metaphysical interest and vocabulary. With regard to plumbing the ontological depths of things, Zhou Dunyi, an early Neo-Confucian, asserted that the beginning of things is in nothingness, which does not need explanation.[4] From this comes fullness, and from fullness arises first yang and then yin. His text is quoted and discussed at length in *Philosophical Theology One*, Chapter 12, Section I. The background of this point lies in the Daodejing's line that the Dao that can be named is not the true Dao, but the true Dao is its mother.[5] This was fleshed out at length by Wangbi in the third century, who also developed the important Confucian distinction between substance or essence and function as discussed in Chapter 6 in connection with its Buddhist use.[6] One aspect of the philosophical significance of this general point is that what ultimately "explains" is simple and indeterminate: Anything determinate would need an explanation itself. So, the powerful ontological emphasis is on the creation of novelty in the arising of the world of changes. The novelty in part is in the creation of the present out of the past, cosmological novelty. But the ontological novelty is the creation of yin/yang changes itself from a deeper, more mysterious, "subtle," indeterminate ground.[7] From this standpoint, any appeal to a creator who is determinate, or even to the fullness of being, is not basic enough to account for the world of change. Zhou Dunyi's concept of *taiji* (The Great Ultimate) is a version of the fullness of being, and Zhou contrasts this with the more basic *wuji* (The Ultimate of Non-Being). This general point is in direct continuity with the metaphysics of the ontological act of creation in *Philosophical Theology One*, Part III. Neo-Confucians such as Zhu Xi developed elaborate cosmologies of change, involving Heavenly Principle and Earthly Material Force.[8]

Neo-Confucianism borrowed much from Buddhism as well, including the rich heritage of metaphysical debate that had begun in India among

Buddhist schools and with Hindu interlocutors, too. But the main lessons learned from Buddhism had to do with the self and with its cultivation. Roughly speaking, the Neo-Confucians derived their conceptions of selfhood from ancient Confucian sources such as the Doctrine of the Mean (Chong-Yong) and the Great Learning, however these conceptions differed from one thinker to another. They held to the general view that the central heart of the self derives from Heaven and is a capacity to appreciate things for what they are worth and to respond appropriately, with valuation involved in both perception and action. This is different from the common Yogacara Buddhist view that virtuoso consciousness simply registers things such as they are without evaluative response. The point manifests itself in the Neo-Confucian critique of Buddhism for its quietism, arguing instead that the self needs to be perfected in action, eliminating all sorts of selfishness that might distort active perception and intention. Nevertheless, the Neo-Confucians adopted the importance of meditation for personal cultivation and many of the actual Buddhist practices. Deep within the discussions among the Neo-Confucian schools has been and remains the problem of how meditation reaches to the ultimate realities of the cosmos and puts individuals in harmony with them.[9] The Buddhists, by contrast, would be slow to say that the objects of meditation are ultimate realities, although they would say that the ultimate reality discovered in meditation is that dharmas are empty (in a variety of possible senses of emptiness).

Speaking of the Neo-Confucian tradition, self-cultivation, which takes place through the studying of texts and commentaries, practical experience in administration, and advancing meditation, has two conjoined aims. One is to harmonize with ultimate reality in the ontological sense. The other is to increase skills in being more righteous, more personally whole, more humane to others, and to have more meaning in life. In the sections of this chapter to follow, the second aim will be the focus of discussion.

I. FORM/VALUE/POSSIBILITIES/OBLIGATION

The central theme of Confucianism, including Neo-Confucianism, is humaneness. As mentioned, the ontological dimension of this is to become properly attuned to the depths of existence. But what can be called the cosmological dimension, in keeping with the use of that distinction in *Philosophical Theology*, is humaneness as a trait of being in the world. To be in the world is to be under obligation, to have to work out a sense of wholeness with the components of one's life, to relate to other people, institutions, and nature beyond the human, and to find meaning in one's value-identity. Since ancient times, Confucianism has treated "Four Virtues," humanity, righteousness, propriety, and wisdom. Mencius said these arise from the "Four Beginnings": "The feeling of commiseration is the beginning of humanity; the feeling of shame and dislike is the beginning of righteousness; the feeling of deference and compliance is the beginning of propriety; and the feeling of right and wrong is the beginning of wisdom."[10]

These notions have been elaborated in countless ways in the Confucian tradition, and the strong reading given them here reflects some of the philosophy in *Philosophical Theology*. They will be correlated with the four transcendental traits of determinateness and discussed in the order established for these chapters. Chan translates the Chinese word *ren* as "humanity" or sometimes "love." It is the same word discussed here as "humaneness." In the present discussion, "humaneness" is the term for the general integrated Confucian project and "humanity" and "love" are the terms for the specific virtue lying alongside righteousness, propriety, and wisdom. There is an order to the virtues in the Chinese tradition, so that *ren* comes first, and some thinkers such as Zhu Xi argue that it not only comes first but is the source of the others.[11] The present discussion associates righteousness with possibility/obligation, humanity or love with groundedness, propriety with engaging others, and wisdom with achieving a meaningful value-identity. As will be apparent in the second section in this chapter, humanity or love is in fact the source of important dimensions of righteousness.

In the symbolic world of Confucianism, particularly Neo-Confucianism, human beings are set within a turbulent rush of processes, including natural processes such as the changes of seasons, floods and droughts, social processes such as the workings of government, military affairs, and economic changes and more personal processes having to do with family, friends, and one's own intimate matters, including emotional and physical health. These processes tend to have their own inertia, to bump into one another, to complicate one another, and to unravel. The energy or pushiness of these processes is called *qi*, which is often translated as "material force." In contrast to this is *li*, which is translated as "principle." Principle, associated with the ancient notion of Heaven, is the source of order or pattern; sometimes it is called pattern itself. Everything in the maelstrom of processes has some kind of patterned identity, but such identities are constantly shifting. So, the human situation involves the need to bring harmony to the onrush of processes, often preserving harmonies in ongoing processes such as families when the harmonies are threatened, often bringing new and unique harmonies to special situations, such as the government needs to do when the barbarians come. Pattern, order, or harmony is not limited to static instances. In fact, the underlying rhetorical metaphysics is that to be a thing is to be a change, and a change is analyzed in terms of yin/yang variations. The underlying supposition is that "things" are shifting vibratory patterns of yin/yang movements that, like waves, have frequency and amplitude. Changes result from shifts in frequency and amplitude, and such waves themselves require an environment of other changes in frequency and amplitude. The patterns of the sixty-four hexagrams in the Yijing are attempts to codify possible patterns of change. In the Neo-

Confucian cosmology, the situation of human beings is that of having to manage the maelstrom of processes and bring it to order, preserving what is good where possible and bringing new harmonies into existence. For all the moral optimism of much Confucianism, there is an underlying sense of tragedy that comes from the fact that the best harmony will be changed as novel processes are encountered. Much Confucian literature is bound up with coping with defeat.

The transcendental role of form for human beings, in Confucianism, is the situation of facing possibilities for dealing with the swirl of important processes. These possibilities all have the various values associated with the different kinds of harmonies within them. And so the sensitivity to be cultivated in a person for perceiving the worths of things accurately and responding appropriately is not to be construed in a static way, as in perceiving a person with a fixed identity. Rather it has to do with grasping who the person is in context and the value of what the person represents and is doing, and contributing to the harmonizing of the situation involved. The great emphasis in Confucianism on experience and learning how to be sensitive and effective has to do with locating where the real possibilities are and what is at stake in their differences of value.[12]

According to Mencius as previously quoted, however, the beginning of righteousness is not simply good judgment about what is at stake but a sense of shame and dislike. Righteousness is ultimately definitive of the human because it has to do with being under obligation. Failure of obligation is to be shameful, and to dislike oneself for the failure. If one has no sense of shame, one has no sense of obligation. All the Axial Age religions give ultimate importance to being under obligation. But Confucianism, more than most, associates the failure of obligation with deep shame. The Abrahamic traditions also recognize shame, but tend more to see the failure of obligation as putting one in jeopardy of divine condemnation, which turns shame into guilt. Confucianism internalizes and transforms the condemnation into shame.

Of course, many ways exist to fail obligation. Ignorance, immature reasoning, culpable lack of preparation, shortsightedness, selfish bias, greed, and other forms of failure to put oneself in the right frame for acting in the most harmonizing way are among them. The special Confucian emphasis, however, is not only on mistakes in the content of righteousness, or on failures to acquire the skills one ought to have in order to be able to act righteously, although both of these are important. The special emphasis is on commitment to fulfilling obligation itself, however short one might come up in reference to discernment and action. What is shameful is not to accept and be committed to fulfilling one's obligations as they occur. Shame in this Confucian sense is a symbol of the ultimacy of obligation that is both intensely intimate to one's self-definition and extremely transcendent with regard to the obligatoriness of the human condition.

II. COMPONENTS/GROUNDEDNESS/WHOLENESS

Deeper than the issues of shame and righteousness, although no more important for Confucianism, is the problematic of properly comporting oneself to the components of one's life. As components, Confucian worldviews emphasize family members, the social situation of one's family legacy, the economic and political aspects of the community, the stages of career that might be expected of a person relative to family roles, friends, participation in social processes, and contributions to the arts and civilization. To be a whole self is to be in proper comportment to all these things.

The fundamental Confucian insight into how to be a whole self has to do with filial piety, a notion not well understood in the West. Indeed, in degraded Confucian societies filial piety is sometimes reduced to an abusive relation in which children are rigidly controlled by and forced to care for their parents. But the insight is much more profound than its sometime abusive manifestation. Briefly put, to have humanity or love (*ren*) is to be able to raise children well. Being a good friend or an effective contributor to one's society often is understood by analogy with raising children well. What does it mean to raise children well? It means to make them virtuous, that is, to have great humanity (and righteousness, propriety, and wisdom). Therefore, a person does not really know whether her or his children are properly virtuous until it is seen how they raise their own children. The grandchildren are the test of the children. Therefore, the moral community, or what Tu Weiming calls the "fiduciary community," needs to be generations long. That community need not be a literal family of parents and children, of course. Yet the family metaphors are most powerful in the Confucian sensibility.[13]

To love a little baby is not very difficult; everyone turns their face so as to look little babies in the eyes. The chief problem with raising infants, especially newborns, is exhaustion! Small children are more complicated. Parents learn how to love through teaching skills at the right developmental stage and through teaching socialization, including the basic rituals. Basic attitudes toward other people are learned early and need parental guidance. This is particularly true with regard to socialization within the family with siblings, parents, aunts and uncles, grandparents, and so forth. Adolescence requires all sorts of new skills in parenting, learning to acknowledge the drive toward independence, encouraging it in fact, while also taking care that the adolescent children come to no harm as they step out into new roles. Adolescent children take on adult roles bit by bit, often with disastrous experimentation. For a parent to love an adolescent requires skills in loving that usually do not have to be exercised before that stage. Then children move off to their own careers and families. In Chinese peasant societies it has been common for multigenerational families to share the same home and same occupations. This is less common today in China, and Confucianism has spread broadly into modern meritocratic societies. Therefore, the means by which parents bless their children by continuing their education in virtue as they move out are more complicated than ever.

From the children's standpoint, infants hopefully learn to accept love in cuddling and nurture; small children learn to be loved by having an environment that safely allows them to develop their skills and powers, especially with regard to physical and social matters; adolescents learn to be loved by people who expect them to come to exercise responsibility without being stupid or falling into disaster; adult children learn to be loved because and by means of demonstrating their own virtue so that parents can take satisfaction in them. Filial piety is not only providing for parents in their old age: It is becoming virtuous enough to set parents free from the task of making their children virtuous. So, often, this means demonstrating one's own skills at raising children or analogous nurturing occupations.

Learning to become a person of humanity and love requires coming to terms with all the things that enter importantly into one's life. These include coming to terms with one's place in the family and with other family members. But it also includes coming to terms with one's home, or lack of it, with one's community such as it is, and with the historical and political issues that arise on one's watch. Among the components of one's life are the issues of meeting obligations, and the particular situations that define one's obligations. Also among the components are the issues of relating to others as others; in the Confucian worldview these relations are deeply channeled by ritual life. Yet another component is the task of achieving a value-identity, the Confucian virtue for which is wisdom.

With great sensitivity, Confucianism has recognized how complex and difficult it is to integrate the components of one's life with integrity. Hence, the Confucian focus on the need to cultivate oneself, not in a selfish way, but so as to be able to integrate the components of life with proper comportment.[14] Confucianism recognizes the importance of groundedness in life's components, without being reduced to the components: The self that is grounded is a difficult achievement. The tradition of Confucianism that identifies itself with Mencius sometimes seems to give the lie to the difficult project of the cultivation of the self. Mencius argued that everyone naturally has the impulses to virtue in the Four Beginnings, quoted earlier, and that these impulses would naturally flower in the virtues if they were given the chance. The orientation of Mencian moral theory has been to remove the blockages to what was taken to be the innate goodness of human nature. This stands in contrast to those who identify with Mencius's rival, Xunzi, who said that human nature is innately bad in the sense that, like infants, people are selfish unless taught otherwise.[15] In practice, however, both strains of Confucianism have emphasized the importance of learning. Learning is intellectual, with a strong emphasis on literacy. But learning is also physical, with emphases on martial arts, sports, music, calligraphy, and cooking. Moreover, because people so easily become selfish, learning has to do with emotional discernment and purification. Confucians recognize the need for learning how to be balanced and mature and would support such modern institutions as psychotherapy to help achieve this. Confucians are especially attentive to cultivating the skills of relating to other persons, to being effective in social intercourse, in accomplishing a social agenda, in learning to play and enjoy friendships; this topic will return in the next section of this chapter. Everyone has an obligation to self-cultivation, the Confucians believe, because the maelstrom components of one's own life are so very much one's own responsibility. To fulfill that obligation requires being an accomplished lover or practitioner of humanity, a process of learning that starts with good parental upbringing.

To be sure, not everyone has a good home or effective, loving parents. If Confucianism were practiced in its ideal forms for several generations, perhaps family life would improve significantly. But East Asia has been as unstable as any other area of the globe, especially in recent years. Moreover, there are extraordinary class differences there as elsewhere that lead to poverty and to the difficulties poverty has for social stability and family life. In fact, the genre of Confucius's own teachings was that of complaint against the social chaos of his time, rather like Jeremiah in the Hebrew Bible. The Confucian ideals, though attributed to the ancient sage kings, were important precisely because they were *not* exemplified in Confucius's context.

Although there have been societies that have been deeply formed by Confucian ritual, to be discussed shortly, the present religious situation is one that presents a need for Confucian humanity.[16]

III. EXISTENTIAL LOCATION/ENGAGEMENT/LOVE

The Confucian approach to others is marked by its strong emphasis on deference. Other things are to be deferred to according to the kinds of value in their own nature. The native abilities of the heart/mind are able to discern those values when they have been properly cultivated, which, as already noted, involves much learning. The discernment of the values of others applies as well to human beings, to institutions, and to nature within and beyond the human sphere.

More than the symbolic rhetoric of many religions, however, the Confucian symbolic rhetoric emphasizes the relational aspects of things and their value. Along with the whole of the Chinese tradition, nature is understood as harmonies of harmonies, with many micro-macro parallels of harmony and with much stress on the ways changes in one part of nature affect changes in other parts. What is true of nature is true of human individuals also: They are understood largely in terms of their roles in human society and in the natural order. They are not identified with those roles, however. Rather, they are identified as individuals playing the roles, with their own essential components not reduced to the conditional connections of the roles. Individuals are not identified with static identities only, such as might be determined by the roles—father, mother, younger sister, and so forth—but even more with the dynamics of playing those roles, especially playing them together, interweaving their different kinds of responsibilities.

Engaged deference to others does not lead Confucians to "love" all human beings "equally," however, as has been the ideal in some other Axial Age religions. Rather, precisely because people, as well as the rest of nature, are understood so much through their roles, they are to be loved in large part according to what is appropriate to those roles, particularly the roles that relate them to the individuals loving them. This "love with differences" means that one loves one's family members with intensities, intimacies, and responsibilities that would not be appropriate to one's love of others in the community, or others in a distant social class, or others in foreign countries. In all these cases, the basic humanity of the others is to be deferred to and cared for, but only as that humanity is parsed according to the various roles those others have, especially the roles that relate the others to the persons who are to love them.[17]

Correlative to the need to develop a loving and deeply human self is the need to engage others with appropriate kinds of humane love that help them become more loving. Because persons are identified so much in the Confucian rhetorical symbols with the roles they have, the institutions of society have a dense reality of their own, more so than for many religious cultural traditions and at least equal to the Indian notions of dharma. The institutions are made up of the interlocking sets of roles that people play with respect to one another. More than that, as conceived in the Confucian worldview, the institutions involve interacting with the roles of nature, for instance, the passage of the seasons, variants in the weather, and indeed the awesome dignity of the heavens at night. The Confucians recognize that very much of the way one engages others is determined by the social institutions that mediate the engagement. Therefore, they have thematized the importance of "administering" the institutions in which one participates. A classical role model for Confucians is the "scholar-official." The "scholar" part of that role is the continued learning involved in cultivating oneself. The "official" part is acting to minister to others through administrating some elements of the institutions that connect society. Pervasive within social institutions are administrative offices that are special roles in themselves; Confucians are encouraged to prepare themselves to hold those offices and then to seek and administer them. But even without holding some official office, one's behavior toward others is always to be nuanced by the need to attend to and care for the institutions themselves that are involved. Friendships are highly prized, for instance, which does not mean only loving one's friend in appropriate ways; it means also attending to the institutional or habitual structure of the friendship itself.

The language of roles is not quite adequate to understanding Confucian relationality in the engagement of others, especially as it takes its connotations from Western structuralist sociology and anthropology. As mentioned, the others are not only defined by the roles they play but by their own dynamic playing of them (and, of course, by activities that are not matters of role-playing). Roles should be understood, in the case of Chinese relationality, in terms of larger ritual structures. *Philosophical Theology Two*, Chapter 9, introduced the Confucian understanding of ritual, and it is appropriate to recapitulate some of that discussion.

Confucians (following principally the texts of Xunzi on this point) understand human nature to be radically underdetermined by its biology.[18] Human biology is open to being determined by a great many different cultures, alternative to one another, as in the instance of different languages, as well as ways of moving, singing, working, and so forth. Yet human nature is not natural unless it has some culture: Human beings could not have evolved with long gestation periods and childhoods without the culture of at least tribal life. And human beings cannot flourish fully without civilization that connects them with the expanse of nature, the diversity of cultures, and the arts of high culture. Therefore, the supra-biological naturalness of culture is necessary for human nature.

The Confucians analyze culture in terms of ritual, that is, learned habits that give determinate specificity to biological underdetermination and that also bear meaning. Rituals are habits that are fitted into some semiotic code. The semiotic codes are very broad, including habits for standing and moving, for gesturing meaningfully and speaking, and for leading organized social life. The codes themselves are dynamic, acquiring new habits, that is, new signs, as need arises and losing signs as the need for them disappears. The semantic and syntactical structures of codes also change as they are used in dynamic situations. Moreover, semiotic codes adapt to local circumstances. If a group has one language at some point, and the group divides into subgroups that move into new circumstances, they will develop variant languages and perhaps eventually very different languages.

The point is that every ritual habit has a meaning in terms of its semiotic code, obvious in the case with regard to the rituals of speaking, using some language as the code. Many people would not think that ways of standing are "meaningful," supposing rather that they are just physical habits. Yet they are the identity markers of given cultures, as defined by their semiotic systems. East Asians tend to stand with their feet parallel, Europeans with the toes angled out; East Asians tend to walk with their feet lowered heel-and-toe at once, like a shuffle when exaggerated, whereas Europeans put the heel down first, like the goose step when exaggerated; East Asians bend over beginning with the waist followed by the hips, whereas Europeans do the reverse. Although perhaps never being conscious of these movements being "meaningful," people can tell whether someone else is one of their group by how they stand, walk, and bend. These rituals of standing and moving might seem independent of one another. Yet in a culture they become integrated into more or less coherent styles of movement. Cultures themselves are integrated and mutually implicated sets of rituals, and rituals of rituals, and rituals of rituals of rituals. Constantly changing, cultures balance out the changes of the rituals within them as they evolve, grow, diminish, and find reinforcement or interruption.

In this perspective, the Confucian engagement with others is first and foremost a cultural engagement, with the culture itself needing administrative attention. Confucius thought his own situation was chaotic and desperately poor and unhappy because his society had insufficient rituals for maintaining family life, so necessary for learning how to be human, for maintaining government and the economy. He thus advocated the development of rituals that would make high culture possible.

Today the situation is that people necessarily engage one another across different cultures, often cultures with different values and interests and obviously with different ritual structures. What is needed today, from the Confucian perspective, is the development of new rituals that bridge cultural and civilizational differences. These rituals are necessary so that individuals in different cultures can apprehend the humanity in others and have ways to defer to them. Whereas some other religious traditions might emphasize the common dignity of all people and try to work around cultural differences, Confucians say that the common dignity of all people means that each person has a culture (often a culture that itself is in trouble) and needs to be engaged as identified through the mediation of that culture. Cross-cultural rituals are thus imperative if the engagement of the common humanity of others is to be possible.

IV. ABSOLUTE VALUE-IDENTITY

The symbols for the achievement of absolute value-identity are different in the Confucian world from those of several others of the Axial Age religions. The Abrahamic religions find their center of rhetorical gravity in symbols of standing before divine judgment. Both Buddhism and Hinduism symbolize absolute value-identity in terms of escaping the cycle of rebirth, although they interpret the escape in different ways. The principal symbols within Confucianism cluster around having a memorable life. The family rites of honoring ancestors are intimate ways of organizing approaches to absolute value-identity.

Human memory is a frail thing upon which to build a religious approach to ultimate identity. For most people across the globe, it is possible to hold in memory the generations of grandparents and great-grandparents at best. Wealthy and powerful people can build monuments that last longer. Literate classes can keep records, and the profession of the historian is ancient in many cultures. Now with photography and electronic imaging, it might be possible for ordinary people to leave memorable remains. But all memory is fragile and subject to accidental obliteration.

A memorable life is not only a function of doing and being something memorable, with lasting remains. It also is a function of the cultural operations of remembering. In Confucian culture, as in many others, the responsibility of remembering is located principally in the family, hence, the rites of honoring the ancestors. Great people can also be remembered through monuments and holidays dedicated to them. Remembering, of course, is a form of interpretation and as such is guided by the purposes and contexts of those who remember. As those purposes and contexts become ever more remote from those of the person remembered, memory loses the actual achieved value-identity of the ancestor. From the standpoint of remembering, the person remembered needs to be interpreted in terms that are meaningful to those who remember. To remember a life that means nothing to one's own person or context is very difficult and not to the point of one's own life. Yet the memory of a person's ultimate value-identity needs to defer absolutely to the meaning of that person's own context and purposes if that value-identity is to be understood as a memorable life.

To make this more complicated, part of a person's absolute value-identity includes how the person is in fact remembered in times subsequent to the person's death. Such "living memory" is part of the objective value-identity of the person and extends far beyond what the person can control. Great religious figures such as the Buddha, Jesus, or Confucius himself have an objective identity that is still alive and growing, and many people guide their lives in reference to what they imagine the great religious figures would want or advise. A memorable life includes all the strains of living memory, although the attribution of responsibility for that objective identity is complicated perhaps beyond the possibility of sorting.

Families are leaky vessels for remembering. Bloodlines can be cut short by disaster or by the failure to produce children. Sometimes it seems as if the pressure to produce children for the sake of preserving ancestral memory is very hurtful for individuals, particularly those who are homosexual, celibate, who simply choose not to marry, or cannot have children. Moreover, in a given family, each generation in descent from an ancestor has more and more ancestors to honor with remembering, and so the memory of any one ancestor is diluted. Therefore, the Confucian choice of the family as the cultural institution charged with remembering has many drawbacks. The Daoists place little stock in remembering and focus their energies for achieving absolute value-identity on longevity, hopefully immortality throughout endless time. Some theists symbolize God as having a perfect memory in which one's memorable life will never be lost; process theology makes this a metaphysical requirement for God.

Nevertheless, the intimate Confucian symbols for remembering a memorable life have important advantages in connection with the transcendent symbols. What are the transcendent symbols of absolute value-identity as a memorable life? They cluster around the Confucian notion of sincerity (*cheng*) or transparency. A memorable life is one that is understood, and the Confucian ideal of a meaningful life is one that can be understood. What is involved in having a life that can be understood?

The Confucian concept of the self is that it is a continuum of physical, cognitive, and emotional processes that reaches from the inmost heart/mind, derived from Heaven and alike in all people, to the "ten thousand" things to which the individual relates over a lifetime, which are different for everyone.[19] That continuum includes one's body, and hence its state of physical training and adeptness. It includes one's emotions that are aroused by many things and with which the person must deal, hopefully with careful cultivation and intensity. It includes the person's knowledge that is both intimately felt and shaped in the terms of the larger social and cultural semiotic structure. But then the continuum constituting the self includes all the person's perceptions, reactions, and actions, the person's enjoyments and pains, the person's playing of countless ritual roles throughout life, the person's contribution for better or worse to the community, and to the historical circumstances that occur. In an abstract sense, this is the Confucian way of expressing the achievement of value subjectively in the person and objectively in the other things affected by who the person is and what he or she does. In a concrete sense it lays out the multifarious things that give identity to a self in a lifetime of changing circumstances, perceiving and responding. The self includes the choices made under obligation, the actions by which others are engaged, shaped so often by the meanings in rituals, and the cultivated, learned skills of body, mind, and heart through which one can be grounded in the components of one's particular life.

Within this network of symbols about the self, what would an understandable life be? Ideally, it would be an understanding of all of a person's achievements as functions of the appropriate responses of the center, the heart/mind, to the accurately discerned ten thousand things of one's life. To live that way would be to live in the truth, to live ideally, no matter what the circumstances, and this is ideally understandable. What would block such transparency of response to the ten thousand things? Discernment of the natures of those things requires accurate perception, which can be achieved only by cultivating the nodes on the continuum that allow for perception; these include living in the right social institutions so that the person is not prohibited from seeing others for who they are. Response to the ten thousand things also requires a fluidity of action from the heart to the complex, relationally defined, external intended effect; many failures of cultivation can lead to distorted actions, actions that fail to achieve their intent. So, to the extent that a person fails to cultivate the means to perceive others accurately and to respond appropriately, there is a muddying of the understandable life. Of course, the blockages themselves can be understood—he hates people of other races, she failed to develop the social skill required to engage a certain person. But the pure expression of the heart/mind, the expression of Principle as the Neo-Confucians would put it, is sullied. The Confucian ideal is to live in such a way that one's heart/mind is apparent in all one does, and so that the continuum of life that constitutes the self is transparent in everything so that that heart/mind can be seen. Where that transparency is lacking, an irrationality is present that can only be noted as part of the person's identity. The root of evil, according to Confucianism, is selfishness. Selfishness leads one to misperceive the ten thousand things and to distort even one's well-intentioned actions. Selfishness consists in anything that blocks one's ability to perceive with proper appreciation and act with appropriate deference. Failure to cultivate the means for perception and action is a form of selfishness.

All lives are memorable, including the memorable failures to perceive and act well. But lives are more memorable the more their details are transparent. The Confucian hope for absolute value-identity is to achieve as transparently memorable a life as possible. This is an understanding of a life in ultimate perspective.

This discussion has focused principally on Confucianism as a resource for contemporary religious interests in engaging the transcendent and the immanent. This is only representative of the diversity of resources in the mix of Chinese religiosity.

Part II

Summary Implications

The purpose of Part II has been to read the contemporary religious situation in terms of the potential of the religious symbols of some of the Axial Age religions to function in viable sacred worldviews. An important dimension of the religious situation is that most people in the world are born into religious cultures that are identified through the central symbols of some traditional religion. Therefore, people's sacred worldviews are likely to begin with some version of the legacy of some Axial Age religion.

Part I indicated just how complex these traditional religions are, often embodying a dense history of borrowings and changes. The symbol systems in each that are prevalent now are not mere repetitions of the symbols in their founding figures; they have been interpreted and reinterpreted, sometimes in conversation with strains of other religions. Moreover, the Axial Age religions now are not unified (and likely they never were). They are divided into many "denominations" or separate traditions, sometimes competitive with one another. Different strains of emphasis are to be found within integral functioning religious communities.

The heuristic hypothesis guiding the discussions in Part II has been that each contemporary religious community finds symbols for five kinds of ultimacy. One is the ontological ultimate of the radical contingency of existence and the dependence of the world on what *Philosophical Theology One* described as the ontological act of creation. The other four are the cosmological ultimates that are transcendental traits of determinateness as such: Any world would have to contain determinate elements and thus these four cosmological ultimates, although only worlds with human beings would find them religiously interesting. The cosmological ultimates are: form, components formed, location in an existential field, and value-identity. As ultimates, these four constitute ultimate or "outermost" conditions for the existence of the world. From the human perspective, as registered in sacred worldview, these four constitute the ultimate orientations in religion, which is their engagement. Form is ultimate for religious engagement as the structure of possibilities that present alternatives for choice, possibilities that embody value. Because of form, then, and in light of the human capacity to have some control over choices and actions, an ultimate condition of human life is to live under obligation. The transcendental condition of having components presents the ultimate condition of human life of having to comport oneself to the components of one's life so as to be grounded in them with wholeness. The transcendental condition of having location in an existential field constitutes the ultimate condition of having to engage others, including both other persons and the many elements of nature. The transcendental condition of having value-identity constitutes the ultimate condition of achieving such an identity that has meaning in ultimate perspective. Underneath all of these cosmological ultimates is the ontological ultimate of contingency upon the ontological creative act, which is engaged from the standpoint of the human condition as the gratuitous, arbitrary, undeserved, and surprising ground of existence, manifest in each of the cosmological ultimates.

The chapters of Part II have surveyed several of the Axial Age religions with regard to the symbols they present in the contemporary religious situation for each of the four cosmological ultimate conditions of human life: living under obligation, the search for wholeness, engaging others, and the achievement of a meaningful value-identity. The symbols discussed have by no means been exhaustive, and frequently they have been characteristic or central to only one or a few strains within the overall Axial Age religion. In each case, an attempt has been made to indicate both ancient sources for the symbols and current interpretations of them. In each case also, an attempt has been made to elucidate the dilemma of finding symbols that are transcendent enough to refer with some faithfulness to the ultimacy in the human condition while at the same time finding symbols that are intimate enough to connect with the details of individual lives and situations. The viability of these traditional resources for contemporary sacred worldviews depends on being able to reconcile the transcendent and intimate symbols with proper contextual interpretations.

In the contemporary religious situation, sacred worldviews appropriate for the many social locations of people are likely to involve sacred canopies with symbols from one or several of the Axial Age religions. These sacred canopies need then to be integrated within the larger sacred worldviews that are appropriate to give orientation to the contents of people's lives, contents that might differ radically from one social location to another. The argument of *Philosophical Theology Three* is that these sacred canopies are theologically valid to the extent that, on the one hand, they vivify the ultimate dimensions of the entire worldview in which they are embedded and, on the other hand, they can be interpreted as true to the ultimate realities as symbolized also in the metaphysical arguments given throughout this work.

At this point we should note that the Axial Age religions are not the only sources in the contemporary religious situation for symbols of ultimacy. Religious naturalism is a variant of West Asian religions that sometimes separates itself from religious tradition as such. Secular humanism, utopianism (especially Marxism but also fascism), and devotion to free market capitalism have functioned in the contemporary situation as religions defining ultimacy and orienting life toward it.[1] Although these movements have inspired something like ultimate devotion among some people, they have not yet elaborated symbol systems that are complex enough to address the one ontological and four cosmological ultimates as boundary conditions for human life. Nevertheless, these movements might very well play important roles in the construction of viable sacred worldviews for certain positions in the present religious situation.

In addition, in several parts of the world pre–Axial Age religions are alive and well, for instance in sub-Saharan Africa, parts of Latin America, parts of India and China, and among Native Peoples of North America. Given the migrations of people across the globe, these pre–Axial Age religions show up in a variety of rich cultural mixes, as, for instance, the important role that Yoruba religion plays in some African American communities in the Americas. These religions sometimes are available for adoption by people who have been raised and cultured in Axial Age religions. So, they are important resources for various positions in the contemporary global religious situation.

Given the fact that people need sacred worldviews appropriate to their situation, no one religious tradition is likely to provide a viable sacred worldview that is wholly appropriate for a given individual. Each of the great Axial Age religions offers many different sacred worldviews today, competing with one another, and unified only to the extent that they share some of the same symbols in their sacred canopies. In light of this, it is entirely possible, and perhaps inevitable, that as people develop sacred worldviews appropriate to their situations they will combine symbols from several of the great religions in their sacred canopies, as well as symbols from secular humanism, utopianism, and the praise of freedom in capitalism, as well as from pre–Axial Age religious traditions. Such syncretism is not new, of course, but it is perhaps more viable today than in many other periods because of the close interaction of the world's religions and their sacred canopies. If symbols of ultimacy from several traditions are indeed to be made coherent, more or less, within a sacred canopy, it can only be under the conditions in which those symbols are encountered concretely.

A peculiar situation obtains today for theological elites, people who reflect on the symbols of several traditions, engage in dialogue with representatives of those traditions, and work together in a pluralistic context. It is possible in this situation to understand the symbolisms of ultimacy theoretically, examining them as various ways of engaging ultimacy, and understanding ultimacy in some philosophical terms that are more abstract and general than the principal religious symbols of ultimacy. In this way, a scholarly religious person can be deliberate about personal "investment" in symbols of ultimacy that are appropriate in a viable sacred worldview. In this way, explicitly multiple religious identities are possible, with self-conscious formations of sacred worldviews, each of which embodies several religious traditions. Even the development of a sacred worldview that embodies only one set of traditional symbols requires novelty in appropriating older worldviews to contemporary circumstances. Nothing is new in this: Religious change has been syncretistic in nearly all contexts, for instance, in the Mediterranean in the first century, India in the fifth century BCE, and China during the Song dynasty. In the present religious situation also it is possible to adopt sacred canopies from several traditions so as to have multiple religious identities. In fact, one does not have to be a scholar to appreciate the synthesis of several symbol systems into a syncretic sacred worldview: All one needs is multiple contacts. One of the purposes of *Philosophical Theology* is to advance this project of constructing appropriate, relevant, intimate, and transcendent sacred worldviews.

Part III

Normative Religion

Part III

Preliminary Remarks

Philosophical Theology Three approaches the study of religion from several angles. Part I was about the study of religion itself, culminating in the idea of the global religious situation and sacred worldviews appropriate for that. Part II was about the symbols or motifs various Axial Age religions bring to the projects of developing theologically viable sacred worldviews for the various positions in the contemporary religious situation, especially noting the issue of transcendence and intimacy. Part III is about normative claims that religion puts upon human beings because of the nature of value. Part IV will be about how human life is ultimately meaningful (or not) and how it can be ultimately rich. Each of these angles defines trajectories of analysis that cross much of the same material, illuminated in four different ways.

From the very beginning *Philosophical Theology* has asserted that nature, including human personal and social nature as well as the physical environment, bears value. In fact it bears many kinds of value. *Philosophical Theology Two* presented a preliminary analysis of this in connection with its discussion of form (*II, 1*). Form constitutes possibilities relative to ongoing processes. Relative to human processes over which we have some control, these are possibilities with different values that are options for choice. Choosing defines part of the complex value-identity of individuals. Choices made, as well as the nonhuman selective factors in actualization, constitute the complex value of actualized things, the past. This complex value includes the negative values of excluding values in possibilities that were not actualized.

Now is the time to refocus the question of the nature and objectivity of value, asking directly whether "values are real." Much modern Western philosophy says that nature is as science says, and science in principle reduces out value. Chapter 9 is a straightforward philosophical defense of the reality of value in the senses required by *Philosophical Theology*.

With the reality of value established, the subsequent chapters of this part explore three general "topics" of theology in which the nature of value places normative claims on human life: religious ethics, spirituality, and community (human membership in communities and nature). These three topics correspond roughly to the problem areas of the first three transcendental traits of determinateness as relevant to human beings. Religious ethics has to do with choices whose content comes in part from the ultimacy of obligation. Spirituality has to do with the achievement of wholeness insofar as this is an ultimate condition. Human membership in social, communal, and cultural units, and in the larger ecologies of the environment, has to do with engagement of others in the existential field. Part IV will deal with the fourth transcendental trait, the achievement of an ultimately meaningful value-identity, set in stark relief by consideration of the plausibility problem with sacred worldviews. That connects, in turn, directly with the ontological ultimate of relating directly to the radical contingency of everything on the ontological act of creation.

The rhetoric of Part III shifts to a constructive mode, setting forth a positive theology or philosophical theology. It is less concerned than Part II with justifying itself through showing how its categories interpret Axial Age religions. And it is less concerned with justifying itself through discussions of theories of religion than Part I. The aim in Part III, as well as Part IV, is to speak to the issues of how to be religious in the contemporary religious situation.

CHAPTER NINE

Value

I. DIFFERENTIAL VALUE IN A PURPOSELESS COSMOS

If the creator were to have a purpose in the creation of the cosmos, the creator would be determinate and therefore could not really be the creator of the cosmos that contains everything determinate. Something indeterminate in itself would have to create the ontological context of mutual relevance within which a purposive creator could relate to creatures, the creator itself being a creature. This austere argument was made in detail in *Philosophical Theology One*, Part III. The result is that the cosmos itself has no purpose established from beyond itself. It might have value in many senses, each of which elicits purposive human obligations, but that value does not derive from an alleged prior divine purpose, as so often expressed in theistic symbol systems.

The thought that the universe might not have a transcendent purpose has been devastating to many religious people who conclude from this that human life can have no ultimate purpose either. What lies behind this existential crisis? Most likely the crisis is one cultural fallout of the rise of modern science, which depicts nature as being without value. If nature is without value, then human life is without value, except in the dimensions that are created by the human will and projected onto nature (including human nature). If nature is without value, then something has value only in the sense that someone says it has.[1] Value is reduced to being a product of will or an emotional projection. Supposing no intrinsic value to nature, the cosmos, and human beings can have value only because some creator purposes them to have value. Value and ultimate meaning can only be the projections of a divine command, on this view. So, the rejection of divine purpose entails the loss of the last hope for human ultimate meaningfulness, the argument goes. This argument lay at the root of the existential predicament articulated so powerfully by Jean-Paul Sartre and Albert Camus in the mid-twentieth century.

Let us examine the conception of nature involved here further. Although the ideal of understanding nature in terms of mathematics goes back at least to Pythagoras and Plato in the West, this ideal did not become practical until the rise of early modern science.[2] Descartes's invention of analytic geometry allowed geometry to be combined with algebra, and, hence, with numbers and arithmetic. Newton's and Leibniz's inventions of calculus allowed volumes to be described algebraically and arithmetically. So much of what people would want to describe and understand about the things of experience seemed to be amenable to mathematical expression. Mathematics is far subtler now. But when the ancient Greeks sought to mathematize the things of experience, they had a strong sense of the grace and beauty of things, of things' various kinds of values. Aristotle, however, was sufficiently discouraged about the attempt to express the concrete worth of things in mathematical terms that he put forward instead a wholly qualitative philosophy of nature, dealing with kinds, materials, ends, and efficient causes. Some elements of Aristotelian philosophy of nature can be mathematized but only within the limits of reducing all kinds of causation to efficient causation that can be expressed in terms of mathematical measures of force. Descartes understood the point with blinding clarity: If nature is to be understood in mathematic terms, nature itself must be conceived as what is amenable to mathematical expression. So, he defined nature as corporeality, three-dimensional bodiliness that occupies and moves through space. Mind, he observed, is not corporeal, and so he defined mind as an entirely different substance from nature. In this he launched the great "mind-body problem" of Western modern philosophy, stimulating the continental phenomenological tradition on the first hand and the scientific materialist tradition on the second.

Descartes did not observe, however, that the definition of nature as material corporeality excluded the recognition of the value of natural things. Although Descartes believed that value is positive, objective, and created by God, on his theory of nature the apparent implication is that value must be a function of mind, of its will and emotions, and the beliefs that things have value must be projections onto nature.[3] John Locke expressed this point in a classical way. He said in general agreement with Descartes that the "primary qualities" of things are the material characteristics of corporeality: shape, movement, and so forth. The "secondary qualities" are the impressions of those things on the human senses, such as visual, auditory, tactile, and olfactory sensations; these are functions of human physiology, said Locke, and are not in the things of nature themselves. Values are "tertiary qualities," which is to say that they are projected onto natural things with the mind or will being active, whereas the "secondary qualities" are projected by natural things onto the mind through the activity of nature.

From the standpoint of the pragmatic semiotic theory developed throughout *Philosophical Theology*, the mathematizing moves of early modern science can easily be understood simply as the interpretation of nature in the respects in which it can be understood mathematically. There are other respects in which nature can be understood, including all those that lift up the various kinds of value involved. Chapter 1 in the present volume and *Philosophical Theology One*, Chapter 2, argue that such scientific reductionism is fruitful if its reductionist structure is understood. What a reductionist theory explains is only what the theory can construct of its representations of its subject matter, and much can be learned from this scientific approach. But the reductionist theory is only one respect in which the subject matter can be interpreted, and if that respect is taken to be the only respect that is important, the reductionist theory distorts the subject matter as directly encountered.

Much modern Western culture has assumed, as Descartes did, that nature is not what can be interpreted in a mathematizing respect (among many other interpretive respects) but rather is *only* what mathematizing can express. The influential twentieth-century Western philosopher Ludwig Wittgenstein wrote:

> All propositions are of equal value. The sense of the world must lie outside the world. In the world everything is as it is and happens as it does happen. *In* it there is no value—and if there were it would be of no value. . . . Hence also there can be no ethical propositions. . . . It is clear that ethics cannot be expressed. . . . (Ethics and aesthetics are one.)[4]

Not to put too fine a point on it, Wittgenstein at this stage in his writing had a rather narrow view of what constitutes natural facts, and most interesting things for him were not matters of fact; but this still means that, wherever value might lie, it is not in nature and we cannot learn about the values of things empirically.

Many disastrous cultural consequences followed from or were exacerbated by the modern Western separation of fact from value, including the objectification of nature so that it has no meaning or worth except for the use to which it might be put by human beings. Human beings, too, came to be considered something like machines with no intrinsic worth. Modern science did not invent the dehumanization of one's enemies, but it did provide powerful scientific rationales for that.

For religion, as mentioned earlier, the cultural conviction that nature has no intrinsic values gives rise to the following dilemma, centuries old in Western religions and emerging elsewhere now with the spread of modernization. Either nothing is intrinsically valuable and life has no meaning on its own, or something outside of the cosmos bestows value on it like a will arbitrarily defining something as valuable. Existential nihilism follows from the first horn of the dilemma. A belief in the divine command theory of purpose follows from the second. As Wittgenstein put it, "the sense of the world must lie outside the world," and some people have interpreted this to lie in a divine purpose. In various ways, religious responses of this sort have said that the world has a purpose not evident in its own nature, such as to glorify God or to give God a partner; human beings have purposes that have to do with fulfilling some divine plan for them. The definition of human beings in terms of a covenant with God in the Hebrew Bible, carried through in different ways in Jewish, Christian, and Islamic traditions, can be interpreted as God giving specific meaning and value to individual and corporate life. If it is true that a theology of divine purpose cannot be sustained, because it would make God determinate and hence not ontologically ultimate, then many religious people legitimately feel the terror of nihilism. If there is no divine will to be followed or rejected, then anything goes.

The Hebrew Bible, however, begins with quite the opposite view. Genesis 1 says that when God created the world, he saw that it was good, item by item. This is to say, the world has intrinsic characters that bear value. In the anthropomorphic story of creation, God observes this intrinsic value. By the same token, not every modern Western scientifically oriented philosopher has acceded to the view that nature is mechanical, lifeless, factual, and bearing no value. Alfred North Whitehead, perhaps the earliest truly systematic exception, argued that the substance metaphysics presupposed by modern science could not exhibit how the complicated mathematics involved in relativity theory and quantum mechanics could apply to reality. So, he asked what reality must be such that late-modern mathematical science might apply, a question similar to Descartes's. Whitehead's answer was that the causal relations imputed by science require a process cosmology in which the causal processes of change are driven by the need to attain value.[5] Although he rejected Aristotle's concept of substance, and all the other conceptions of substances developed from it, he restored something like Aristotle's sense of final cause. Anything actual, Whitehead said, is the actualization of some value. This opens the way to interpreting nature not only with respect to what can be mathematized, which is one of the starting points of Whitehead's theory, but also with respect to what can be appreciated as nature's values. For Whitehead, human beings, including their "minds," are part of nature, and so the values within human beings can be appreciated as well.

Philosophical Theology's cosmology carries on these themes from Whitehead. The cosmology itself has many crucial differences from Whitehead's, although not in the respect here mentioned. The formal theory of value developed in the next section employs many Whiteheadian categories. Even today, however, when many scientists have become conscious of the fact that the reductive character of science makes it impossible for science to register value in things even if it is there, few scientists have availed themselves of Whitehead's process-metaphysical suggestions. Therefore, it is incumbent on our argument in favor of the reality of value in anything with form to continue to examine the opposition, which we shall do in the next section.

II. THE FORMAL NATURE OF VALUE

The hypothesis about value in *Philosophical Theology* is that it is a trait of a harmony that is borne in the harmony's form. The larger hypothesis within which the value hypothesis is framed is that anything that is determinate is a harmony with form, components formed, existential location, and achieved value-identity. The following analysis shall indicate how having a form involves having a value.[6]

A form is a pattern exhibited by a plurality of components being together. The components themselves, at least partially determinate harmonies, have form. Thus, any determinate pattern is complex. "Complexity" here can be defined as containing different components, components that differ at least by their forms (as well as by their own components, existential location, and value-identity). The more different the components are from one another, the greater is the complexity.

A form is a pattern exhibiting the integration of different components each of which itself has a pattern integrating its own components (and existential location, value-identity, etc.). So also within a form a low level of patterning is the grouping of components into many subforms that are then integrated on a higher level, and again on a yet higher level, and so on, until a top level of formal unity is achieved. Thus, a hierarchy is found in forms whereby components are integrated by discrete forms that in turn are integrated into a smaller set of discrete forms, on up to a final integration that consists in a contrast in which the penultimate level of forms just fit together, each containing its own subhierarchy of forms. The top level is a definite contrast. The hierarchy of subforms within a form can be labeled "simplicity."

Complexity with minimal simplicity would be a pattern in which the components are together mostly conjunctively: *a* and *b* and *c* and *d* . . . Simplicity with minimal complexity would be a pattern of mostly homogeneous elements: The top of the internal formal hierarchy would have a form that is about the same as the next level down, which would be the same as the next level down, and so on down to the basic components that have almost the same pattern as the top. No form could be only complex with no simplicity because the level of conjunction is a higher level (minimal simplicity) than the components unharmonized. No form could be only simple or completely homogeneous because there has to be minimal diversity among components for the harmony to be determinate (essential and conditional components), with components differing at least by existential location and the slight differences in their own values that derive from the different locations.

A form has the baseline value of containing the values of the components patterned together. This thesis, of course, supposes that the components themselves have value because of their own forms, which is in general what is to be proved here. Leibniz argued that value consists in "density of being." The account here says that density of being at the baseline consists in the components with their own values, summing those values as well as the whole actualities of the components. The simplicity of a form, however, can integrate groups of components into subforms, each of which adds to the baseline value of the components in the groups. The integration level by level in the hierarchy groups components and groupings of components to make a form that contains many new forms in addition to the baseline of components. Thus, a form can add many new kinds of form, hence of value, over and above that given in the baseline, constituting an increase in density of being or value. For instance, an oil painting at its baseline of components consists of a plurality of color splotches. Some of these color splotches can be formed together to represent a frog, others a lily pad, others an insect, others a rabbit, others a fox, others a pond, others a naturalist, others a grove of trees and bushes around the pond bending a certain way. At a higher level, some splotches are formed such that the frog catches the insect with its tongue, the fox sneaks up on the rabbit, and the naturalist is watching the scene. At yet a higher level, the frog and insect are where they are because of the ecology of the pond and its surrounds. The bending of the foliage indicates a wind, the direction of which tells the fox how to sneak up on the rabbit downwind. The knowing gaze of the naturalist indicates that she understands how the ecosystem is operating. At yet a higher level, the splotches are formed so as to suggest to the viewer a literature of writings and other paintings illustrating the understanding of the human role within nature as understood through a history of naturalistic artistic representations. The top form of the painting might be something that most viewers would miss, a meaning level that requires serious erudition to recognize but an element in the painting's form that is real nonetheless.

"Elegance" can be defined as the degree of maximization of both complexity and simplicity within a form. Yet there is a tension between increasing complexity and increasing simplicity. The more different the things are that are to be brought together, the harder it is to integrate them with intermediate steps that add value. The more steps in the hierarchy of integrations, the more difficult it is to sustain different kinds of things. Elegant forms have both complexity and simplicity, the more elegant the more they have of both. But there are trade-offs, and so beginning with the same baseline components, a form might emphasize greater complexity or greater simplicity. This gives rise to different kinds of forms or values to be achieved from the same baseline components. So, there are different kinds as well as different degrees of elegance.

The previous example of the painting is biased in a crucial way. In real life, a form achieves integration by putting both complexity and simplicity at jeopardy. Eliminating components that might go into the baseline makes it easier to get the remaining ones together with some added value. Moral problems, for instance, can be solved easily simply by eliminating the interests of some of the people involved. A painter, by contrast, does not necessarily have to begin with such and such an array of paint splotches but chooses the components that fit the higher-level forms in mind. Lowering ambitions for simplicity allows more components to be together by mere conjunction if the environment allows that, but with little increase in value. Increasing elegance has its costs to complexity and to simplicity.

The more elegant the form, the more formal reality it contains, both in terms of different components and different patterns of new internal forms. As forms are the forms of harmonies, the more reality the harmonies contain. "More reality" means density of reality, not only diversity of components and not only the buildup of levels of form but both of these together. The kind and degree of density of reality is a harmony's value.

A harmony's value, however, is not only the value its form bears but also the negative value of excluding other forms (and thus values) it might have had with a different form excluded by its actual form. The next section explores the dynamics of the temporality of form, how it functions as future possibility, as present lure, and as past actuality. The point to note here is that a harmony's value is always bivalent, what its form is and what its form could have been but is not.

Why identify density of reality as described here with value? The answer is that something like this hypothesis describes what we respond to when we respond to things as valuable. The obvious and undeniable fact is that we experience things valuatively. The images that we inherit and that we construct imaginatively are formed so as to pick up on what is pragmatically important and valuable in the world to be discriminated in experience. The interpretations we make engage things in respects that are pragmatically important for our flourishing, that let us pursue our purposes and the purposive values we prize as inheritances within our cultures, and that let us inquire more deeply into what is most worth knowing and experiencing, beyond our own purposes. Our interpretations all take place within orienting theoretical constructs that present pictures or semiotic representations of contexts for objects engaged, constructs such as theories of many sorts and worldviews as analyzed in these volumes. These theoretical constructs select what is important to be integrated within them as perspectives and arrays of respects within which things are to be interpreted. In turn, our interpretive engagements with their theoretical contextualizations serve to orient us to the world normatively, guiding us toward what they represent as important and valuable to be and do.

Now it might be said that the pervasiveness of valuation is still a mere subjective projection of value on things thought to be important or valuable, not some characteristic of things. That would be fairly farfetched, however, saying that all of our experience is systematically deceived about what is interpreted to be there. Why would one suggest this to be true? Only because of another commitment to reality being only what mathematics describes: facts, not values. But the point has already been made that this argument for the mathematizing of nature is just a commitment to interpret nature only in the respects that can be mathematized. This is like a cartographer mapping only the roads in a territory, not the topology, weather, or population density. There are other respects, respects involving valuation that are almost universal in ordinary and in cultivated civilized experience in the arts, morals, politics, and the appreciation of people and nature. So, we can reject the argument that reality needs to be interpreted as fact and not value in order for mathematizing science to be true. Mathematizing science can very well be true in the respect that it maps its subject matter. But then we need a theory of valuative experience that saves the experience we have of reality being shot through with values and importances everywhere. Such a theory has been provided and shows how the experienced values of things can be taken at face value.

But is it not the case that we sometimes, even often, discover that some previous judgment about the value of something is mistaken? Our valuations are sometimes wrong, no matter how intense they seemed to be at the time. Because this is so, the values in things must be real in those things: One can be mistaken about only what is real. Or, one mark of reality is that our judgments can be mistaken about them. This point draws a crucial distinction between the values in things and the valuative experience of them. Valuative experience, in at least the four modes mentioned earlier—imagination, interpretation, theorizing, and the pursuit of responsibility—is a function of the evaluative signs at our disposal. We can discern only those aspects of value for which we have an interpretive vocabulary, although we often grope for symbols to express and allow us to engage what we encounter. The cultivation of experience itself is the process of developing the cultural and personal signs allowing for more accurate discernment of the values of things. The "hard" experiences of life include learning that we have been wrong in some of our crucial discernments. There must be something real to be wrong about.

With what philosophical theory do we understand the apprehension of value in experience? This is the problematic of aesthetics, from Plato to John Dewey in Western philosophy. Experience in its interpretive judgments unifies things aesthetically. Aesthetically, experience involves an interpretive discrimination of background and foreground in the apprehension of harmonies.[7] The background in the experience of a harmony involves two elements, triviality and vagueness. Triviality is the mere conjunction of components, where one thing does not gain added value by its relation to any other thing. At one level, the experience of a thing is of its components as unintegrated into its harmony; the limit of this is whatever is necessary to attribute these components to the harmony at all. Vagueness is the trait of a harmony by virtue of which a plurality of things is subsumed under a higher form such that the differences between the things approaches irrelevance: The plurality functions within the harmony in the guise of the higher form, as certain color splotches function as a frog in the painting. With vagueness, it is potentially possible to go back down from the vague higher form to pick out and analyze the plurality in its differentia.

Triviality and vagueness characterize the background out of which a harmony appears in experience as a foreground thing. The foreground elements of a harmony are width and narrowness. Width refers to the variety of components that are expressed in the higher levels of the harmony's hierarchy, keeping definiteness of character. The rest are dismissed as trivial or subsumed under other forms as only vaguely present. Narrowness is the dominance of the highest level of a harmony's formal hierarchy by a few simplified hierarchical structures that fit together in a definite contrast. The intensity of a thing experienced in its aesthetic dimensions is a combination of the width of things that survive in the hierarchy with the narrowness with which they are simplified in conjunction in the contrast.

This discussion of harmonies in experience calls attention to the fact that there are many different kinds of harmonies. The previous discussions in *Philosophical Theology* either have treated harmonies in the most abstract way possible as instances of determinateness or have supposed that the most important examples have been enduring harmonies such as persons with tight identity over time, or causal processes that have unifying principles through time, or historical continuities of identity. But in experience, anything experienced whatsoever, insofar as the experience itself has some form, is a harmony. The view now outside my study window is an aesthetic harmony with background elements and foreground elements and with an overall foreground contrastive character (a rather good one since it is our garden). It includes lasting things like plants, paths, and buildings in the distance. Individual harmonies including birds and insects fly into the view and then out of it. The wind causes constant shifting of things in different patterns, and the scene changes as the sun moves or I change the angle of the blinds. The mass of subatomic events is a trivial part of the background. I see plants, walks, and buildings, vaguely subsuming the plant parts a botanist would see, the parts of the paths a dog would sniff, or the illegal characteristics of the building that an inspector would fine. The more or less stable items in the garden view are massed in artistic shapes more or less (some pruning is always needed), with contrastive contours, colors, light and dark, and ready sensitivity to winds. The garden is constructed to attract birds and some insects (others are planned out). When I attend to the view, there is a determinate thisness, haecceity, to the whole view with pleasing narrowness and a ripe width of different things to notice with appreciation. That view is a harmony just as much as the bird that flies into it. Looking back at my computer screen, there is a different harmonic view, perhaps less pleasing aesthetically but none the less aesthetic in that the screen appears as a foreground against the background of the process of composition. The more elegant the view, the more valuable it is. The more discerning I am, the more I appreciate the view. The value is there in the view to be beheld.

Why should we regard this formal density of being as the nature of value? Why not just say that the hypothesis about the nature of form having hierarchies of internal forms exhibiting complexity and simplicity is good (supposing that it is) as far as it goes but is just another philosophical fact? Why say that this fact is the nature of value, with the implications of obligation that will be drawn from it? Several reasons already have been adduced: (1) It is the simplest philosophical explanation of a crucial point of the universal experience of things as having value. (2) It accords with the general agreement among philosophical and religious traditions across the globe, save the modern Western, that things have value in themselves, relative to one another, and as focused by human intentions in experience. (3) It explains in part why the modern Western tradition demurs from this consensus, the modern Western assumption that the only true knowledge of things is filtered through what can be represented in mathematical science, which eliminates the possibility that any intrinsic or relational value in things can be registered.

To be sure, Western philosophy has a strong protest tradition against the exclusion of value from nature and powerful constructive systematic accounts of value. Alfred North Whitehead analyzed this as "the Romantic reaction" in his *Science and the Modern World*. He went on to develop a technically detailed and culturally astonishing theory of value in *Process and Reality*, *Adventures of Ideas*, and *Modes of Thought*. His very late essays, "Mathematics and the Good" and "Immortality," summarize his reflections on form and value and are very close to the ideas elaborated here and in the discussions of eternity and temporality throughout *Philosophical Theology*. The classical pragmatists Charles Peirce and John Dewey also were realists regarding value in nature, for instance, in Dewey's *Art as Experience* and *Theory of Valuation*.[8] Paul Weiss, a doctoral student of Whitehead's and one of the editors of the *Collected Papers of Charles Sanders Peirce*, wrote consistently about the nature of real value throughout his long career, most systematically in *Modes of Being*. Although systematic philosophy as a genre has not been popular in dominant academic philosophic circles in the last half century, nevertheless several important systems emphasizing the importance of real value have been elaborated that are inspired by the mixture of pragmatism and process philosophy. George Allan's trilogy, *The Importances of the Past: A Meditation on the Authority of Tradition*, *The Patterns of the Present: Interpreting the Authority of Form*, and *The Realizations of the Future: An Inquiry into the Authority of Praxis*, is an important system dealing with value; the second volume gives an account of value in form that is close to that of *Philosophical Theology*. Frederick Ferré's systematic trilogy, *Being and Value*, *Knowing and Value*, and *Living and Value*, is a powerful and rich examination of value as real. Joseph Grange's systematic trilogy, *Nature: An Environmental Cosmology*, *The City: An Urban Cosmology*, and *Soul: A Cosmology*, elaborates similar themes with great aesthetic verve and phenomenological imagination and makes close connections with Chinese philosophy and with the theory of time and eternity in *Philosophical Theology*. Less systematic but equally aesthetic in inspiration are David L. Hall's *The Civilization of Experience*, *Eros and Irony*, and *The Uncertain Phoenix*. David Weissman's *Truth's Debt to Value* is an important systematic contribution that makes connection with themes in analytic philosophy. Hugh P. McDonald's two massive studies, *Radical Axiology* and *Creative Actualization*, are important twenty-first-century speculative and critical analyses of the nature and reality of value. This list could be expanded significantly with citations of scholars and followers of pragmatism and process philosophy as schools. All this is to make the point that the aesthetically oriented theory of value as resident in form being developed in *Philosophical Theology*, inspired by the interactions of pragmatism and process philosophy, has a rich contemporary context in Western philosophy, even if not one that has been much recognized by the dominant academic departments emphasizing analytic and Continental philosophy.

The hypothesis about form bearing value is illustrated abundantly by deliberation in artistic and moral experience.[9] A painter, for instance, deliberates by imaginative or actual trial, varying the colors for complexity, by putting them in this or that juxtaposition for simplicity, by creating this or that new figure within the painting, making the figures add up to new emotional, compositional, or representational entities, and so forth. In moral experience, the complexity is often set by the number and kinds of people whose interests need to be reconciled, the simplicity by the patterns of grouping the individuals and their competing interests and resources. Different scenarios are imagined with different patterns that help or harm the individuals, create new groupings or exclude groupings, leading to outcomes with greater or lesser density of being.[10] In these and other kinds of deliberations about how to make or lead to good outcomes, we commonly consider alternative ways of harmonizing a complexity of components with levels of patterns that lead to richer and more contrasting elements.

Our argument here has been that, despite the scientific representation of nature as valueless, we nevertheless experience the world as value-laden and can give a solid philosophical account of where this value in things lies: in their form.

III. THE ACTUALIZATION OF VALUE: FUTURE, PRESENT, PAST

The abstractness of the account of value in the previous section can be made a bit more concrete by relating value in form to the dynamics of temporality. *Philosophical Theology One*, Chapter 12, developed a theory of the dynamics of the three modes of time: future, present, and past, which can be summarized here. *Philosophical Theology Two*, Chapter 1, presented a preliminary theory of possibility, and the discussion here will start with a recapitulation of the latter.

The future is the form of possibilities for actualization. Its components are (a) the actualized things that must be harmonized for each date in the future, plus (b) the decision points of all the present things that determine what the future must harmonize, and (c) pure formal unity that must be schematized by (a) and (b). The future is dynamic in the sense that any given future date is relative to the date of earlier present dates in which decisions shaping the future are made. For instance, the shape of the future date of the year 2020 is one thing when 2013 is present, another when it gets to be 2014, yet another when it is 2015, and so forth. (Although adequate for the present discussion, dating by the calendar is an arbitrary measure of future moments; in real fact, the size of the future depends on the discursive character of harmonies to be realized in it.)

A future possibility relative to a given present is the form of all the possibilities that might be realized by the various contemporary decision points in the relative present. This overall future form includes the possible forms that the field of possibilities might have relative to the diverse contemporary decisions points. It also includes how that field structures possibilities relative to each decision point in the relative present, that is, what the possibilities are for each present actor or decider. In the eighteenth and nineteenth century some thinkers such as Immanuel Kant and Pierre-Simon Laplace believed or hoped or postulated that the form of the future is completely determined relative to any previous moment. But that sense of causal determinism has little to recommend it; physics and other sciences now often treat causal laws in terms of probabilities, not total determination of every change. So, at any given present, the future dates are formed with alternative possibilities that need only be consistent with one another as possible choices of selective earlier decision points. The formal way to put this is that the top-level form in the possibility is vague with respect to lower-level forms, which might be inconsistent with one another and between which a selection is made at some decision point. For a given agent, such as a human being, any future date has many alternative possibilities, some of which might be determinable by the agent insofar as they can be discerned; this is the source of freedom and responsibility as will be discussed in the next section.

Because future possibilities are harmonic forms, they have value. If a future structure allows of alternative forms for actualization, that future contains alternative values. The actualization of a future with alternative possibilities thus requires selection among which of the alternative values will be actualized and which excluded.

A present moment is an occasion within which a creative act brings about a new actual harmony. The previously actualized things are the potentials with which the creative act operates: The act creates a new actual harmony out of the past potentials by altering and integrating them so that they fit together as a new harmony.[11] The creation of novelty in a present moment is thus spontaneous relative to the past, something new over and above that past and not contained within it. The *immediate* future for that present moment is the set of possibilities whose internal alternatives can be resolved within the present moment of creative selective actualization. A *remote* future for that moment is a later date of possible values that is anticipated by a trajectory of causal processes or by a semiotic projection of how that future's alternatives should be resolved. The trajectory is like a vector of dates through which a temporally thick process leads more or less consistently from the present to an anticipated future date. A human being, for instance, might resolve the present moment by sending an email to arrange a meeting next week; the value in sending the email is not so much in the immediate future that is resolved within the present moment as it is in the remote future meeting.

The wholly determinate possibilities resolved upon in that present moment constitute a complex specific value in the form of a hierarchy as described in the previous section. The value of the creative moment is the sum of the values actualized and, negatively, those alternative values excluded. Insofar as the resolution of the immediate future values includes determining causal processes that resolve certain aspects of the remote future values, the present moment is an agent with remote future consequences. Insofar as the present is responsible for the choices that resolve the remote future, in a sense of responsibility to be defined in the next section, the present is an agent whose value includes the actualizations and exclusions of a train of values reaching into the remote future. If a present moment of creative actualization has no connections with previous or future moments that constitute an ongoing individual identity, it nevertheless has the value of selecting what it does out of the immediate and remote possibilities resolvable by its coming to be as an actuality itself. If it does have ongoing identity connections, then the moment contributes to the overall value-identity of the temporally thick identity, such as a person. In that case, the determination of remote possibilities moment by moment can take on the intentional character of a human being.

The completion of a present moment of actualization constitutes a new actual harmony that is past and that fits in determinately with the other actualizations made by contemporary present moments in the field structure of the future possibility that those contemporary present selective moments faced. The actualized harmony also fits in with the previous actual things extending into the remote past. The individualized actual harmony of a present creative and selective moment might have little integrity of its own but rather plays roles in larger structures of actualized things. Those larger structures are functions both of the solid past actualities that were potentials for the range of contemporary present moments and also of the field of immediate future possibilities for resolution in various points by the array of contemporary-with-each-other present occasions of selection.

The actual past thus bears the complex value structure of the possibilities that had been actualized in it plus the negative value structure of excluding the possibilities that were not actualized. The past consists of the vast array of actualized harmonies, interlocked, mutually conditioning each other, sometimes containing and being contained, and sometimes functioning as others to one another. The dynamism of the past is that it is always being added to, and sometimes the additions radically change the value of what had been actualized earlier. The actualized harmonies all have their values, and their values are as interrelated, intertwined, and mutually exclusive as the actual situation is.

In human experience the past in its temporal trajectory constitutes the presentationally immediate environment for present experience. We experience much of the past as remembered in memorial signs. But we experience the proximate past as the present environment taken up within an occasion of present creativity as the multiplicity of potentials for the actualization of the new present moment. The proximate past is experienced in the present with its many harmonies united by the field structure of the immediate and proximately remote future possibilities and by the very similar field structure of the proximate past itself. This is the "specious present." Human beings interpretively experience all this through the mediation of the signs in semiotic codes. We have signs that give us spatial and temporal orientation and pick up on the things that register in our sensory nervous system such as color, visual shapes, sounds, smells, and tactile feelings. Many of the harmonies in the actual world, which we apprehend in the specious present as we make decisions, are structures of human meaning. Many of the most important possibilities in the future for human beings are shaped by semiotic harmonies, and these function in choices and are actualized. Human meanings are just as much a part of the actual past as nonsemiotic physical objects. The naturalist by the pond sees the frog, insect, fox, and rabbit as present in her experience, although, of course, it takes a little time for the light to convey those sights from the things to her eyes. She also experiences as part of her present observation the difference between the frog who hunts insects by flicking his tongue at things that enter his visual field and the fox who knows he has to sneak around downwind to catch the rabbit. And as she ruminates on the literature of naturalist observation, those books from the past give her present experience an added kind of semiotic meaning.

In all this, value functions in the forms of future possibilities, in the selections of definite possibilities to actualize, and in the actualities in which those possibilities are the ones chosen. Given the vastness of the cosmos (*I, 6*) and the intensiveness of nature (*I, 7*), the value of the dynamic cosmos is complex and rich beyond human imagination, save in the most abstract of metaphysical images.

IV. OBLIGATION, RESPONSIBILITY, AND CONJOINT ACTION

This analysis of value bears upon human life in a multitude of ways. The following are most relevant to the argument here.

A field of value-laden possibilities faces a vast plurality of decision points at any one time. Most of these decision points are present creative occasions within natural processes unaffected much by human semiotic structures. Many of the decision points might be within processes of social institutions that are shaped by human semiotics but that are not themselves decision points within which human choice is exercised; human beings might have an indirect responsibility for the way these institutional decisions go. Some but not all of the decision points might include the choices of human agents, which are the ones of interest here.

Any human being at a moment of choice faces a field of future possibilities, with shifting shapes from the immediate to the remote future. That field includes possibilities that other decision points can decide, and the given individual's choices are limited by what is possible, within the field, for the other decision points, including natural, institutional, and other human deciders. This can be bafflingly complex. How often are the values resident in our possibilities dependent on what the weather is going to be, on how the traffic lights are timed, and on what others will decide to do! Human choice faces a field of alternative possibilities that are codependent on a vast number of indeterminate factors that will determine the real shape of possibilities and the values inherent in that mix.

Obligation derives from the value differentials of the various sets of alternative possibilities within the general possibility field as these alternatives are subject to human choice and control. For instance, the alternatives might make a difference to justice, or to fostering human dignity, or to caring for someone or something at risk, or to cultivating virtue. What is obligatory is that the better alternatives in these instances be actualized.

The obligation is that someone ought to do that. But who? Sometimes it is obvious that the alternatives pertain to only one agent, and so it is that agent's responsibility to fulfill the obligations involved. Much of the time, however, the obligations bear upon a multitude of possible agents, any one or few of whom might fulfill them. Whose responsibility is it in these circumstances? Much more of the time, the fulfilling of the obligations requires the cooperation or conjoint action of many human agents working together. People have to eat and the children should be educated. Whose responsibility is it to fulfill these obligations?

A distinction has been employed here between obligation and responsibility. Obligation consists in the objective character of the field of value-laden alternative possibilities as faced by human agents. All human beings are under obligation insofar as they face such value-laden alternatives and have some capacity to choose and actualize them freely. Responsibility, however, is the subjective character of the agents to be obliged in the face of value-laden alternatives. In nearly all societies there is an organized division of labor so that not every individual is responsible for all obligations. Some tend the fields while others educate the children. The subjective lineaments of responsibility are assigned by complex rituals and other structures that allow the community as a whole to face the obligations of its value-laden possibility field. Thus, a given individual might not have responsibility save for a small part of the obligations under which that individual and all the others lie.

But what happens when a society is seriously dysfunctional? Confucius lived in a time of social chaos in which the usual division of responsibilities for economic and educational matters, as well as many others, had broken down. Thomas Hobbes lived in an even worse time:

> Whatsoever therefore is consequent to a time of Warre, where every man is Enemy to every man; the same is consequent to the time, wherein men live without other security, than what their own strength, and their own invention shall furnish them withal. In such conditions, there is no place for Industry, because the fruit thereof is uncertain: and consequently no Culture of the Earth, no Navigation, nor use of the commodities that may be imported by Sea; no commodious Building; no Instruments of moving, and removing such things as require much force. No Knowledge of the face of the Earth; no account of Time; no Arts; no Letters; no Society; and which is worst of all, continuall feare, and danger of violent death; And the life of Man, solitary, poore, nasty, brutish, and short.[12]

Hobbes's philosophical understanding was that with the breakdown of the proper structures for distributing responsibilities, a state of war ensues, which for him is the "natural state" of human beings. The rational thing to do, he said, was for everyone to enter into a social contract that would construct reasonable social institutions for the handling of basic responsibilities and that includes a government with enough force to keep the peace. He was under the influence of the early modern scientific view that sought to conceive of human beings as "mechanical" and thus subject to scientific understanding. He thought then that if human beings were rational, they could be understood as always seeking their self-interest in rational ways and could be appealed to with rational argument to surrender some of their means of violent aggression to a government that would then allow them to get more of what they want under the social contract. John Locke agreed with this argument generally, although he thought that people were more rationally appetitive than aggressive and thus could be persuaded to buy in to free market capitalism in which a government guarantees the performance of contracts. Hobbes, Locke, and other social contract theorists agreed that, in a state of nature with no government, it was every man for himself (and for his women). The corollary of this is that when government breaks down and society degenerates into a state of nature, there are no obligations or responsibilities, save perhaps to oneself. Agreeing that all values are subjective human projections onto possibilities, the social contract theorists did not believe in objective obligation save that constructed by the social contract.

Philosophical Theology, by contrast, because of the objectivity of values in the nature of possibilities as such, holds that obligations to do the better with respect to value-laden alternatives obtain irrespective of the absence of social structures to distribute responsibilities. When those social structures are absent and society degenerates toward what Hobbes would call a state of nature, then each individual has the responsibility to deal with *all* the obligatory alternatives within possible reach. Instead of having no responsibilities, each individual would have responsibilities to the entire field of obligations upon which that individual's choices and actions might bear. One could not count on any one else helping and thus would be under an amazingly impossible obligation. Of course, human life is never without social structures, even when they are malfunctioning, and the pure state of nature is a literary fiction, as Hobbes himself knew. Human life in its most natural state requires a vast array of rituals, as the Confucians know. Nevertheless, when a society is dysfunctional in a certain respect, say, being caught up in racist structures, or economic oppression where the rich serve only their own interests, there might not exist structured ways of responding to the obligation to right these wrongs. The government might itself be in the thrall of racism, or of the rich. In such circumstances, the responsibility to deal with the obligations of removing racism and economic oppression reverts back to all the people. It does not disappear because the socially contracted government fails to address the obligations. It becomes the responsibility of everyone.

In the face of this, a two-sided meta-obligation should be recognized as contained within the possibility field, namely, to develop modes of conjoint action among individuals so that they can do collectively what they cannot do individually. The other side is to develop rituals of conjoint action that distribute responsibilities in efficient and rational ways. To be responsible individually is also to be responsible for working with others. To be responsible for working with others is to be responsible for building rituals and other social structures of cooperation. Because of the complexity of the value-laden possibilities that face human beings, these rituals and other social structures of cooperation find their home only in semiotically rich cultures. Thus, people are obligated to live under obligation within the context of building cultures that facilitate responsibilities. The study of ritual in *Philosophical Theology Two*, Chapter 9, is supplemented by this abstract argument requiring ritual as a means of carrying out obligated conjoint action.

This chapter has laid out a theory of value relative to human possibilities, obligation, and responsibility in very abstract fashion. The justification for this abstract presentation is to argue, once again, that value is ingredient in anything with a determinate or partly determinate character. This thesis runs against the grain of so much Western thinking affected by the fact-value dichotomy insisted upon by modern science. So, the thesis bears repeating. Throughout, the question arises about how individuals can come to understand what is possible, valuable, and obligatory. That aesthetic judgment is involved has already been argued. But the details of human knowledge of what is valuable, and how to attain it, remain to be worked out. The following three chapters come at this from different angles. Chapter 10 approaches the topic from the perspective of religious ethics, 11 from the perspective of religious virtues, and 12 from the perspective of religious companionship.

Chapter Ten

Religious Ethics

I. THE RELIGIOUS DIMENSION OF ETHICS

"Ethics" means both the practice and the study of responsible choices that address the obligations given in the value-laden possibilities under which human beings live. The word "ethics" refers back in Greek to the ethos of a community, its customs. Similarly "morals" refers back in Latin to the mores or customary habits of a community. Thinkers in the ancient Greek and Roman world called customs into question, of course. Ethics came also to mean the study of those customs, and how the customs relate to decision-making in difficult situations. The vast complexities of ethical traditions do not have to be sorted here. Nor do the complexities of comparison of those Western Greek-based philosophical traditions with parallels in South Asian, East Asian, African, and Islamic philosophies; the variety among them is rich, and the comparative issues are murky. For present purposes, the religious dimension of ethics, and its parallels, is the point of interest.

The religious dimension of ethics, as interpreted in *Philosophical Theology*, is the respects in which ethics engages ultimacy. Ultimacy has been interpreted here in terms of four cosmological ultimate realities that are transcendental traits of anything that is determinate: form, components formed in the determinate things, the location of the thing in an existential field, and its value-identity. Ultimacy also has been interpreted in terms of the ontological ultimate reality, the ontological act of creation on which the entire radically contingent cosmos rests. The "ultimacy" in these ultimates consists in their being boundary elements of reality, which is religiously interesting when translated into the boundary elements of the human world.

Thus, form itself is ultimate, because nothing could be determinate without form. What this means for human beings is that form constitutes possibilities that contain value-laden alternatives, putting people in the position of being under obligation to actualize the better options insofar as they lie under human control. Being under obligation is what is ultimate in defining the human world, whereas issues of particular obligations, and the ethical deliberation about them, are proximate (*II, 1*).

Having components formed is ultimate for any determinate thing. What this means for human beings is that each person is a long-term, discursive harmony whose needs for integration require comportment toward the important components of life. This results in an existential ideal for wholeness, coming to terms with and integrating the components, which then is a special dimension of relating to possibilities. Not only are persons harmonies of components, so are all other things. So, relating to those things includes relating to their wholeness (or lack of wholeness). This is an ultimate condition of human life, even though the particular things that are components and the problems they pose are proximate conditions (*II, 2*).

Being in an existential field with others is a universal trait of anything that is a determinate harmony; the field itself is constituted by how the determinate things relate to one another. For human beings, it is an ultimate condition to be connected with other things that are yet external to and different from oneself. Just what those other things are and the particularities of engaging them are proximate conditions, but having to be engaged itself is the ultimate condition (*II, 3*).

Achieving some identity, for better or worse, is what every determinate thing does or is, because it has the value of including its components with its form in connection with the things it engages and determines some of the values of those other things. The subjective value-identity of a thing is the value it contains within itself, and the objective value-identity is the value in other things for which it is the cause. For human beings, this ultimate condition is the value-identity of the person that gives meaning to the person's life, for better or worse. The particular components and problems of achieving an ultimately important value-identity are the proximate issues of such achievement. The ultimate condition is having to do so in the first place (*II, 4*).

The very existence of the cosmos, with such manifold things and connections as it has, is the ultimate ontological condition, depending on an ontological creative act. The proximate conditions are the various particular things that do exist. What this means for human beings is the radical dependency of their world and themselves on the creative act, which is gratuitous, arbitrary, undeserved, and surprising. This is to say, one's own existence is gratuitous, arbitrary, undeserved, and surprising, and so is that of all one cares about or disputes. Acknowledgment of this involves fundamental acceptance of being, acknowledgment of singularity, practice of humility, and of self-transcendence in awe. The proximate issues of the ontological contingency of one's life have to do with its particulars (*I, 12*).

Philosophical Theology Two detailed many ways in which these ultimate realities place conditions on human life that constitute predicaments and that are venues for ecstatic fulfillment. The topic here is how they place ultimate conditions on ethics. At a certain level, the proximate issues in the ethical response to value-laden possibilities—in the cultivation of wholeness, in engaging others well, in achieving value-identity, and getting along with the radical contingency of one's existence—are not much affected by the ultimate realities, save that they take place because those realities ultimately constitute the world. Specific issues of justice, for instance, are not different for religious and nonreligious people. Ethics is ethics irrespective of religion.

At another level, however, the recognition of the ultimate realities places an additional obligation into the possibilities that people face. The ultimate realities as conditions for human life determine that certain things ought to be valued as functions of religious engagement of ultimacy. "To value" here means what religion should cause people to prize and to search out as prize-worthy possibilities among the fields of possibilities. This sense of value is not the same as saying that the things in the environment, and their possibilities, have value as borne in their forms. It is rather to say that people develop *signs* of value that function as religious values that they seek to embody in their lives. These values add to the interpretation of the possibility fields so as to hunt out special possibilities for achieving them.

Thus, with respect to form, religion promulgates the value of justice, and the seeking of justice. With respect to components, religion promulgates the values of the dignity, beauty, and freedom of things, especially but by no means only of people. With respect to the engagement of others, religions promulgate the values of peace, care, respect, and love. With respect to the achievement of value-identity, religions promulgate the values of a virtuous and humane life. With respect to relating to the ontological act of creation, religions promulgate some version or other of acceptance of being, acknowledgement of singularity, practices of humility, and skills of self-transcendence in awe.

Because these ultimate conditions are in the nature of reality, they constitute a pull on all religions to recognize them. Without suggesting that religions respond to this pull in the same way, and continually emphasizing how the cultural systems both within and among religions are very different, it is theologically interesting to ask just how religions do relate to these philosophically expressed values. The next section shall pursue the point.

II. RELIGIOUS VALUES

The transcendental traits of determinateness obviously are interdefined because they together characterize what it means to be a determinate thing. Therefore the religious ethical values associated with them are interdefined. Yet they are responsive to the traits individually and can be expressed that way. With regard to the world's religions, these traits are elements of reality, and so the religions engage them with some symbolism or other, often with symbols that have different network contexts. One of the characteristics of the Axial Age religions is that they have the maturity to deal rather explicitly with most of the ultimate conditions, and in a variety of ways.

The religious value primarily responsive to the cosmologically ultimate human condition of constantly facing a field of possibilities with value-laden alternatives is justice and its cognates. Justice in this context means making decisions among alternative value-laden possibilities that respect the integrity of the things involved. Integrity will be defined in more detail shortly in connection with the religious values responsive to the fact of having components. This is to say, justice requires weighting the values embedded in the integrities of the things involved as very important in the construction of the decision. Negatively put, a decision is unjust to the extent that it abuses the integrity of something involved. Part of the human predicament is that sometimes no decision is possible that is wholly just; the integrity of something might be abused no matter what decision is made. Thus, part of the religious value of justice is to work for increasing the possibilities that the integrities of things might be respected.

Until the rise of ecological ethical thinking, most ethical traditions have considered human beings or, more broadly, sentient beings, to be the only things whose integrities are subject to determining justice. A human being is a complex, temporally thick, and spatially interconnected kind of harmony whose integration of important components involves intentionality and deals with the predicament of how rightly to comport the overall person's harmony to the integrities of the personal components. The integrity of a human being includes having component conditions of life that allow for integration as well as the context and fostering that provides the power and skills of intentional integration toward wholeness. Choices are unjust that abuse the abilities of people to integrate themselves intentionally or that give them such wretched conditions of life that no humane integration is possible.

One of the great advances of the Axial Age religions was to see that justice is owed to all people, not only those of one's in-group. To be sure, the practice of justice within those religions might still be heavily biased toward supporting the integrities of those within the in-group, but the ideal regarding justice is universal. The grounds for this universality were the many observations that the object of justice is anyone with the human issues of achieving wholeness or humane integration. It was during the Axial Age that such conceptions of human individuals were developed. The near universal prevalence of such maxims as the Golden Rule marks the shifting of the conception of justice from serving the in-group/out-group distinction to conceiving of all individuals as having the same issues of integrity as oneself. Justice requires respecting all individuals as deserving of support in their integrity or their search to integrate their lives with humane wholeness.

"Equality" is a value closely associated with justice, and in some ethical traditions it makes sense to say that all people should be treated equally. But what does equality mean? People are very different, with different issues of integrity. To treat them all the same would be to help some and abuse others. In many Western or modernized religious cultures, equality means something like everyone deserving an equal chance, a level playing field in matters of economic and educational dispositions. Something in this is required for respecting the integrity of all the players, but conditions are so very different it is hard to define what a level playing field might be. The Confucian tradition has recognized that different kinds of social relations make justice in the treatment of certain people different from justice in the treatment of others, all for the sake of respecting the integrities of all involved.

Another value closely allied to justice is fairness or reciprocity. This is dependent on social structures that define agreements, commitments, and what one's "due" might be. Distributive justice draws some of its motivation from fairness and reciprocity and some from equality. Retributive justice is the negative side of fairness and reciprocity, exacting penalties from people who abuse justice.

Jonathan Haidt, the social psychologist whose theory of five "moral projects" was discussed in Chapter 2, Section II, might be nonplussed by the argument of this section. As an empirical student of ethical attitudes and behavior, he believes that there are three main religious orientations. One, which he characterizes as a primary identification with a group, or a collective consciousness, places approximately equal weight on the five moral projects, giving great weight to loyalty to the group, to respect for authority and hierarchy within the group, and to the group's disgust reactions. In his latest book, *The Righteous Mind*, he adds a sixth, liberty from oppression, usually by governments or large social entities. This orientation also respects care and justice but rejects the emphasis on equality and instead ties care and justice to a sense of proportionality, depending on how much those subject to care and justice pull their own weight in and for the group. The group itself has a higher value than its members in some circumstances and surely a higher value than those who are outside the group and the structures of those other groups. The second major religious orientation for Haidt is what he calls individualism and characterizes as WEIRD: Western, educated, industrialized, rich, and democratic. These are the liberals that give great priority to care and justice but relativize loyalty, respect for authority, and disgust reactions. The third orientation he characterizes as believing in a sacred order in which purity and impurity are characteristics of a great many things and people are viewed as being in an order of sanctity relative to divinity, with issues of purity and impurity; this is a reinterpretation of the disgust reactions that gives them priority over the other four moral projects, although not rejecting those projects, because issues of sanctity override those of morals.

Because Haidt believes, with much warrant, that moral impulses have more the character of preformed intuitions than reasoned ethical conclusions, he gives equal weight to these three fundamental approaches, finding them all manifest in today's cultures. He defines morality in terms of moral systems: "Moral systems are interlocking sets of values, virtues, norms, practices, identities, institutions, technologies, and evolved psychological mechanisms that work together to suppress or regulate self-interest and make co-operative societies possible."[1] This is a functional definition that assumes that the great problem is selfishness and that its solution is whatever allows people to cooperate in a society. So, he prizes bonding as well as freedom from oppression. He treats religion as important because it emphasizes and enables social bonding and so is constrained to support the "conservative" values that promote in-group integrity.

The argument of *Philosophical Theology* has been that the five ancient moral projects—care/love, reciprocity/justice, in-group loyalty, respect for authority, and purity/impurity visceral reactions—characterize pre–Axial Age religious cultures; Axial Age cultures prioritize the first two and relativize the last three. Haidt might dismiss this as a mere liberal prejudice, representing the "conservative" culture as immature and the "liberal" one as mature. Two remarks need to be made to orient the project of *Philosophical Theology*, however, because Haidt himself represents a powerful way of thinking in the sciences.

First, in historicizing the relation between what we have called the pre–Axial Age and Axial Age ideals, we have assumed that social cohesion, efficiency, and viability are important for both. Pre–Axial Age societies obviously have already solved the problem of controlling selfishness enough for the groups to survive and flourish to a point. *Philosophical Theology* has emphasized the importance of social institutions as much as personal "selfish" interests and has defined individuality strongly in terms of social rituals that require individuation. Pre–Axial Age cultures might very well have had a stronger collective consciousness than one regarding individuals. But the Axial Age emphasis on individualism was not at the expense of a concern for coherent societies: It came rather from a sense that an individual's most important identity was in relation to ultimate principles rather than to the tribal group. *Philosophical Theology* understands the relations of individuals to groups in terms of the sharing continuum of worldviews. Therefore, the contrast between concern for the group or collective identity and individualism is wholly foreign to *Philosophical Theology's* emphasis on the superiority of Axial Age ideals and values. *Philosophical Theology* has argued that the long-term impact of Axial Age ideals in the current religious situation is to call for new forms of religious community as discussed in this volume. The bonding rituals associated with group identity such as hypnotic music and marching are not necessarily a function of religion at all. To be such, they need to be connected with ultimacy some way; otherwise they are mere political, military, or emotional bonding.[2]

Second, *Philosophical Theology* avails itself of the capacity to deal with value issues as objective matters; values lie in possibilities that can be actualized, and thence in those actualities. Although it is difficult to know these value-laden possibilities, they measure our evaluations, and religious cultures have developed elaborate discernment procedures to know them. Hence, we can reject Haidt's definition of moral systems as a definition of morality. Of course, because the enhancement of communities from local groups to high civilizations is good and prize-worthy, we should follow the advice in Haidt's definition: Find ways to regulate self-interest and make cooperation possible. But we should do a lot more as well to build high civilizations with deep human fulfillments. And the reason why Haidt's advice is good is not because it is a definition of morality, but because it serves elements of human life that have great value. This is to say, among the possibilities that we face individually and conjointly are those structures that enhance or diminish communal life, and these need to be factored in along with many other value-laden aspects of possibility if we are to take seriously the obligation under which we lie. Specifically, the decisions about elements affecting community, with the tugs of individual pursuit of self-interest and self-definition in group terms, need to be complicated by how our decisions affect all the individuals involved. In light of the latter consideration, whether individuals should be helped or harmed by decisions has to do with how the decisions affect their own integrity, not so much whether they are members of our in-group. As the Confucians have emphasized, one's responsibility to the various persons affected by actions, or conjoint actions when one acts with others, is mediated by many levels of ritualized social institutions that themselves should be affected for the better rather than the worse.

Conceptions of justice regarding human beings have developed from ancient times in all the world's Axial Age cultures, often with very different forms. Since the global colonialism of the eighteenth century, these cultural traditions have been brought into connection with one another, a process that continues today with some attempt through the United Nations and the International Court to provide common conceptions and procedures of justice insofar as that is expressed in law.

Ecological concerns have come late to global consciousness, raising the question of how to respect the integrities of things within nature that are not human, such as animals; geological structures such as oceans, mountains, and icecaps; and ecologies that combine these. Except for some animals, their integrities do not involve much intentionality or consciousness. Yet they are harmonies with such integrity as belongs to their components, form, and location. They have beauty in their own ways and value-identity with subjective and objective aspects, all as part of their integrity. Therefore it makes sense to expand the notion of justice to include respect for the integrities of nonhuman things.

The religious ethical articulation of this sense of "natural" justice is very difficult, however. Specific decisions require the selection of some form of possibility that puts the integrities of many things together, and much of nature is a system of some things using other things. Human beings as part of nature naturally use nature, which in obvious ways means not respecting integrities sometimes. The state of the discussion now is how to respect large-scale natural processes, such as energy use, local ecologies, or, as in the theology of Thomas Berry, the natural history of the Earth.[3]

The second cosmological ultimate condition is the fact that harmonies have components and need to integrate those components in ways that involve proper comportment toward them. The central religious ethical value deriving from this condition is the integrity or dignity of the human being (and perhaps in derivative ways of nonhuman natural things). Justice is acting so as to respect this integrity. "Integrity" reflects the process of the "integration" of the components of human life. "Dignity" signifies the importance of the potential of integration as well as its accomplishment. Together (though "integrity" shall include both here) they indicate something like a right to wholeness, whether or not achieved.

The meaning of integrity depends on the kinds of things that are important components of human life. To some degree the important components are functions of culture. In some cultures, to have an extended family and an hereditary place is an important component, in others not so. In some cultures, being creative is very important, while playing social roles is less so, and in other cultures vice versa. Human integrity involves the intentionality required for the project of integration into wholeness. Some traditions have associated intentionality with consciousness so that integrity consists in the possibility of purifying (in some sense or other) consciousness. Other traditions have associated intentionality with its rationality: Human beings have a special dignity because they have the capacity for rational thought (and perhaps rational action). The basic notion of dignity or integrity, however, is that human beings have the intentionality of integrating the important components of their lives with the aim of wholeness. This integrity or dignity obtains regardless of how successful one is.

The value of human integrity is felt most immediately in oneself and transferred by analogy to others. Of course, sometimes individuals hate themselves and hate the fact they possess intentionality that is charged with obtaining wholeness while coming to terms with the components of life. Clinical depression is regarded by many psychologists to take the form of turning anger against others into anger against oneself. Such self-hate itself is testimony to the value of integrity, now hated because of its difficulty. Jesus said that we should love others as we love ourselves, supposing that we do love ourselves. When we fail to love ourselves, that is a failure to respect the value of integrity, a refusal to acknowledge our own dignity.

Although the content of integrity differs in part from culture to culture, and indeed from individual to individual, it is associated in various cultures with humaneness. What is the ideal of human integration or wholeness? It includes being just, being properly engaged with others, achieving value and meaning in life, and living intentionally toward wholeness. But what these things mean depends radically on the character of one's possibilities; one's personal, social, and natural environment; one's historical place; and the particular components of one's life. A value closely associated with integrity is spiritual freedom. Not all people have much spiritual freedom. But it is an ideal that depends upon a certain kind of integration that lets one be at home with the components of life and able to act, desire, and know with a kind of abandon, a topic to be studied in the next chapter.

Actual wholeness is difficult if not impossible to achieve, especially where that means fitting the components of life into a single harmonious form. Given the demands of life's components, it is difficult to comport oneself properly to some without failing others. Often the best one can do is to achieve a balance over time, making amends later for what one fails today. Religious traditions differ with respect to how successful they believe the quest for wholeness can be. Both Hindu and Buddhist traditions rest easy with the notion that a number of individuals can be "realized" or "actualized" souls; many Christians are suspicious of that. Human integrity consists in having this task, regardless of prognosis or diagnosis of success. Simply having the task is a kind of beauty, a human glory.

The third cosmological ultimate condition for human life is the need to engage properly with the things in the existential field within which one is located. Of course, this engagement holds as well the value of justice and also the value of engaging with personal integrity. But regarding others as such, religions have thematized the values of peace-making, care, and generosity. The prime analogate of peace is the suppression or ending of war between human beings. War is a condition in which it is impossible to respect the integrities of others, although stylized ritual combat sometimes tries to make this possible. Peace-making can be generalized to be a value of nonharm far beyond the example of war among human beings.

Whereas peace-making is a somewhat negative value, meaning bringing about the cessation of war, an associated positive value is care for others. Care for human beings is derivative in part from the value of human integrity, a recognition of and respect for human dignity in others. But care is actual engagement with others, acting so as to enhance their integrity. The specifics of care depend largely on the kinds of relations one has with the relevant others. Care for family and friends is different from care for anonymous neighbors, which in turn is different from care for members of other groups, cultures, and residents of distant places. Care is shaped by institutional structures.

Peace-making is perhaps the most dramatic form of care because it intervenes to prevent obvious harm. Care also involves addressing the loneliness of others, their destitution, their suffering. However people's integrities are affected adversely by conditions, religions say that they should be engaged so as to address those conditions. Many traditions have strong codes of hospitality to strangers who are cut off from their own caring in-group.

The maximal form of care is love, which involves not only addressing the threats to another's integrity but also prizing and appreciating them for who they are, with whatever success at integration they might have, whatever status with respect to being just, with whatever they might have achieved in terms of value-identity, and with whatever roles relative to oneself in the existential field, including enmity. Love, of course, is described in various ways and has ritualized forms with varying degrees of closeness. But, in general, love is a religious ethical value that is responsive to the intrinsic value in others with whom individuals are created in the existential field of the ontological context of mutual relevance.

Generosity involves care, and sometimes peace-making, but it also is a value that calls upon people to look for ways to do good for others. It asks people to be productive themselves so that they can help others gratuitously. John Wesley, the founder of Methodism, was fond of saying that his parishioners, most of whom were lower class or lower middle class, should make as much money as they can, save as much as they can by living frugally, and give away as much money as they can. Generosity involves something like developing an attitude of cheer toward other people and a gladness in some self-sacrifice that stops short of self-sacrifice for the sake of penance.

The fourth cosmological ultimate condition of human life is the fact that each individual achieves an absolute value-identity, with both subjective and objective aspects. The religious value for this is virtue in being a human creature. Degrees of virtue exist, of course, and so the religious value is that (some) individuals become virtuosi. Religions differ significantly in how they describe the virtue of human life and the roles of virtuosity. Most religions acknowledge that the great majority of people will not be virtuosi and so set minimal levels, as it were. In the West Asian monotheisms and Daoist medieval traditions, common networks of symbols expressing absolute value-identity often employ the analogy of the courtroom, with individuals being judged on their character by God or divine bureaucrats. The judgment has to do with a level of acceptability, perhaps with remedial punishment. Those same religions, however, also have rich traditions of virtuosity that go beyond minimal acceptability. In the strains of Hinduism and Buddhism that, in their apparently opposing ways, represent absolute value-identity in terms of the extinction of determinate individual identity, "merging" with a more real reality in the former cases and simply stopping all identity in the latter, the prized virtue is whatever is required to accomplish the extinction. The underlying metaphysics for absolute value-identity, as developed in *Philosophical Theology*, is an hypothesis about identity in time and eternity (*I, 12, 13; II, 10*). That theory attempts to sort the various aspects of the religious values of humane virtue, and virtuosity, as symbolized in different religious systems.

The ontological ultimate that serves as an ultimate condition for human life is the radical contingency of the cosmos on the ontological act of creation (*I, pt. III*). That ontological act with its product, the world, has been symbolized in Axial Age religions in many ways, transcendent and intimate, as discussed throughout these volumes. Relative to human life, the world's (and one's own) radical contingency on the ontological creative act appears as gratuitous, arbitrary, undeserved, and surprising. The human grasping of these four kinds of meaning is expressed in a complex kind of gratitude, perhaps best called "ontological gratitude."

As conceived here, ontological gratitude has four dimensions of valuation, corresponding to these four kinds of meaning. With respect to the gratuitousness of creation, gratitude is the acceptance of being or existence. The scale of existence involved might be cosmic or limited more to local circumstances, indeed to one's own self. The world contains much human suffering. Job's wife recommended that he curse God and the day that he was born, his very existence and the God who gave it to him. Job did not accept that recommendation. Indeed, he accepted his (miserable) existence and demanded that God give an account of it. Many people, despite their suffering, are able to grasp the great value of all creation, especially its beauty as it appears to human beings (in optimal circumstances). These people express gratitude by the acceptance of existence in all its forms. Jonathan Edwards defined "true virtue" as "consent to being in general."[4]

With respect to the arbitrariness of creation, the value of being grateful takes on the aspect of accepting and appreciating the singularity of creation. From within creation, we can imagine a great many other ways that creation might be, different geophysical circumstances, different life forms, different historical groups, and different social positions for ourselves, being richer or poorer, high class or low, more or less intelligent, born to a dominant or oppressed group, and so forth. But the world is as it is, singular. And we are thrown into that singularity and, hence, are singular. Gratitude for our singular circumstance expresses the fact that we, like all things, are determinate with respect to other things and different from them. By contrast, gratitude for the gratuitous character of creation in the acceptance of being expresses the fact that there is the world rather than nothing at all.

Gratitude for the undeservedness of creation takes the form of a kind of ontological humility. Although every determinate thing has its own value, conditioned by the price that value exacts from other things, it is good that each thing exists. But there is no motivation in the ontological creative act to create, because the created valuable things have no reality that would justify them prior to their created existence. The theistic symbols that attribute intentionality to the creator prior to creation often represent the value in creation as the motive for the act itself, supposing that God sees that it would be a good thing to create things and then does so. But this attribution of ontologically prior intentionality cannot be sustained literally without requiring yet a deeper creator beyond the intentional creator and the other determinate creatures. So, in a very profound sense, recognition of the undeservedness of the created order requires the value of ontological humility. The religions all teach ontological humility in some form or other.

The surprisingness of the ontological creative act prompts religions to value ontological awe and wonder. Gratitude at the ontological level involves profound astonishment. Indeed, the complex character of ontological gratitude involves all four forms mixed together: consent to being, acceptance of one's singularity, humility, and awe. The religions have recognized that people who do not value this gratitude, and attempt to practice it, are somehow blind to the most important truth about life, its radical contingency on the ontological creative act, and miss out on perhaps the most profound ecstatic fulfillment. Some of the religions that personify the ontological act call this ontological gratitude a special kind of love for the act. Such love for God means, among other things, being profoundly accepting of existence and of one's singular circumstances, being humble in the face of its undeservedness, and being filled with awe and astonishment.

III. RITUAL FORMS OF NORMATIVE ACTION

Supposing that something like the account in the previous section is right, that the cosmological and ontological ultimates prompt religions to value certain very general ways of responding to possibilities in the midst of life, nevertheless, the expressions of these values depend greatly on the institutionalized or ritualized structures of human response. The values of the pursuit of justice, the respect for integrity, peace-making care, the attainment of virtue, and ontological gratitude are all meaningless without semiotic forms and meaningful social circumstances for their pursuit. Most of the time, the pursuits of those values require conjoint actions, not merely individual actions or attitudes.

Philosophical Theology approaches the understanding of institutional and social structure through the analysis of rituals. Human beings are not "natural" unless they have very basic rituals in addition to their biological endowments, and so human beings in this sense are naturally social. Chapter 12 will explore more of what it means to "belong" to ritually identified groups. Not all rituals are religious, however, only those that bear upon ultimacy.

Rituals of worship, which are most commonly identified by Western thinkers as "religious," have to do with embodying in concrete behavior the various aspects of ontological gratitude. They are directed toward the ontological creative act and serve to establish some relationships of individuals and communities to that act that indicate how the values in ontological gratitude can be acted out. The relationships depend in part on the ritualized position of the individuals. When the Chinese emperor conducted the worship ceremonies for the changing of the seasons, this expressed his position as representative of the people of the empire. When Christians attend Sunday services, they acknowledge their status as sinners and worship through pleas for forgiveness (*II, 13*).

Rituals honoring the attainment of virtue, while often seemingly only matters of communal or institutional recognition, are also religious insofar as the value of virtue itself is responsive to absolute value-identity. Allied to this are rituals honoring heroism and virtuosity, which are religious for the same reason. In addition, many societies have rituals that are directly instrumental in the attainment of virtue, rituals embodied in educational practices, in the penal system, in communal coping with disruptive people, and so forth. Most religious cultures have rituals embodied in spiritual practices that enhance virtue, as especially manifest in Confucianism. Whereas the ritual instrumentalities for the enhancement of virtue are not necessarily religious, insofar as they express the value of virtue itself, they have a religious dimension.

Rituals giving expression to care for others, particularly for peacemaking as well as care for the environment, and for generosity, are also religious insofar as they highlight the importance of care for its own sake. Most Axial Age religious traditions have both public and private rituals for fostering care, and indeed love. With the ecological movement, some religions have incorporated rituals directly related to honoring nature. Examples include the Tree-Planting movement of the Zosha Independent Christian Church of Africa, the religious celebration of Earth Day, and the recreation of a mythic "Neo-Pagan" religion of nature. The Chinese have recently adopted many of the Christian rituals about Santa Claus as part of their seasonal commercial activity. Chinese interest in intense commercial productivity long antedates free market capitalism, and the new adoption of Santa Claus might well lead to a kind of cultural consumerism that is currently criticized by religious thinkers in the West. But the subtext beneath the Chinese commercial Santa Claus rituals is the practice of being generous: Buy things in order to give them away!

Rituals fostering the appreciation of human dignity and integrity, insofar as they aim to do that for its own sake, are also religious and common among religions. They are also common among humanist movements that are "anti-religious" in the sense of rejecting organized religions and their folk symbols. Rituals honoring ancestors have the valorization of human dignity and the importance of the pursuit of integrity, if the earlier analysis of the meaning of filial piety is on the mark. All religions have rituals that are directly involved in whatever the specific tradition says is problematic in obtaining wholeness. Although religions define humaneness in many different ways, they still have ritualized behaviors for individuals and sometimes for communities that are aimed to honor human dignity as such.

This discussion is by no means adequate to indicate the complexity of religious rituals as giving expression to the great religious ethical values more or less common to the Axial Age religions. These rituals are intermixed with political, economic, and many other kinds of social rituals, and they are individuated or personalized in many ways. Moreover, the social locations within the contemporary religious situation are so diverse that the nuances of ritual behavior are both important and innumerable. Nevertheless, this discussion begins to indicate the issues of the ritual embodiment of the normative practices that are occasioned by the basic religious ethical values.

The basic religious ethical values are, among other things, signs that structure the interpretation of possibilities that involve alternative value-laden options. They cultivate, or enculturate, human beings to seek for ways of relating to the many fields of possibilities they face through life so as to enhance justice/equality/fairness and reciprocity; dignity and integrity in self and others; care, peace-making, and generosity; virtue and virtuosity; and ontological gratitude through consent to existence, acceptance of singularity, humility, and awe. Societies are organized, in part, with rituals that foster these religious values in the approach to human choice among possibilities.

IV. MINIMAL ETHICS, FREEDOM, AND LIFE ABUNDANT

Although the four cosmological ultimate conditions of human life put real pressures on religions to articulate their special values and develop ways, usually ritualized ways, of fostering them, most actions and affairs of life involve all four together. After all, the four cosmological ultimate conditions derive from the transcendental traits of harmony itself. Anything determinate bears all four traits, and everything people do involves them all. Every action involves some choice, by a more or less well-integrated agent or set of agents, usually with reference to other things and people, adding up to a contribution to the value-identity of just about everything and everyone involved. The analysis of the different clusters of religious ethical values relative to the four cosmological ultimates provides language for understanding the multiple dimensions of things in life that have ultimate dimensions at all. Similarly, hardly any part of life could fail to be a possible occasion for ontological gratitude, the religious ethical value relative to the ontological ultimate condition of contingency on the ontological act of creation.

A more general issue remains to be raised concerning religious ethics, however, applying to all its values in relevant ways. The ambiance of ethics is how to do right rather than wrong, where that difference exists. This means doing right in matters of justice; in respecting human dignity and integrity; in engaging others with care, peace-making, love, and generosity; and in the pursuit of virtue and virtuosity. For the most part, doing right means doing well enough as opposed to doing what should not be done. In practice, we most often worry about the negative, trying not to do wrong or less than we should.

Part of the reason for this is that our engagement of fields of possibilities is mediated by the signs and syntactical structures of our cultured semiotic codes. We can analyze the possibility fields only in the respects for which we have signs and interpretive habits. Of course, these signs should be improved continually and our analytical skills steadily developed so as to understand the possibilities before us. But no matter how good we are at grasping future possibilities, we need to employ cultural signs to do so, perhaps as enhanced a slight bit by the discerning poet in each of us. Ethical geniuses, including religious ethical geniuses, are able to teach new ways of thinking about future possibilities.

The cultural semiotic codes define special relationships of responsibility, as discussed in the previous chapter. So, for instance, everyone's children should be fed, but our responsibility is primarily to feed our own and those for whom we might have additional social responsibilities. We do well enough when we do that, even though some children still go hungry. We have special responsibilities for recognizing, enhancing, and perhaps mirroring the integrities or human dignity of people with whom we have long-term, multicontextual relations, such as family members, friends, and colleagues; the bar is very high for relating to the integrity of people in these relationships. The bar is somewhat lower with regard to respecting the dignity of people with whom we have casual, anonymous interactions, such as sales clerks, fellow passengers on the bus, and so forth. This bar is still significant, as the civil rights and gay rights movements have pointed out. For distant people whom we shall never meet, whom we engage as blocks of individuals united by some special characteristic, such as the strife-ridden people of a region in chaos, respect for dignity does not have to involve the norms for face-to-face interaction but rather is satisfied by working, in this instance, to alleviate the horrible conditions that are affronts to human dignity. Care for people, peace-making, generosity, and love are also structured by social relations, as discussed earlier. Similarly, the pursuit of virtue and virtuosity does not mean everyone is committed to virtuosity in every kind of virtue but only to those things salient to their existential situation. For ethics, even the pursuit of the values of religious ethics, good enough is good enough, and a passion for infinite perfection would be madness.

And yet, the infinite abundance of the world, its infinite complexity with every harmony containing an infinity of components and relating to an infinity of other things (at least vaguely and trivially), prompts something more than "good enough." Ecstatic fulfillments are frequently such prompts. The ontological act of creation creates an incomprehensible abundance of things, more things than we can identify, more than we can relate to, more than we can use, more than we can appreciate or prize. Moreover, the limits we see for ourselves are constantly being overthrown. We are more than we recognize, do more than we think, receive more than we register. In our moral limits, we judge ourselves harshly and, in many religious traditions, believe that what we deserve will determine our future, only to discover that the morrow brings more possibilities. Sometimes we symbolize this by saying that God is merciful in forgiving our sins. But, in point of fact, the superabundance of creation is a little oblivious as to morals. We have more than we deserve in immeasurable amounts. Of course, this is hard to remember when we are exhausting ourselves in some finite struggle to accomplish something difficult, or to survive a mortal illness, or cope with the death of a child. Life has all its limits. But beyond the limits there is more.

And so, part of religious ethics is to lean the slightly mad and supra-rational ladder of "more abundance" against the ambient structures of "good enough." Within religious ethics, without mitigating the fact that good enough is good enough, is the value of the impulse toward abundance: Go beyond justice to maximal improvement; beyond respect for human dignity to celebration; beyond care, peace-making, love, and generosity to swarming embrace; beyond virtue and virtuosity to a race for perfection. Of course, whereas the ontological act creates without measure (all measures being created), we finite creators create out of our limited resources, not gratuitously; create with the stereotyping of signs, not singularly; create with motives, not undeservedly; and create what is somewhat predictable, not what is absolutely surprising. Nevertheless, human creators can emulate ontological abundance to important degrees.

One reason for this is that human beings can be creative regarding possibilities. In a strict sense, as the discussion has shown so far, individuals face possibility fields that are given for them, fields whose constructions come from patterns for unifying the various actualized things and allowing for various contemporary agents to be making decisions simultaneously. Decision-making is responsive to these possibility fields. But because of the imaginative powers of intentionally shaped semiotics, individuals also can exercise creativity in reshaping possibilities. Individuals can enhance the possibilities that otherwise would be given. Human creativity consists in part in the imaginative construction of improved interpretations of possibility fields but, in larger part, in the enhancement of the possibilities themselves. Although we have the possibility of nourishing our children well, sometimes we can create the possibility of giving them really good food for their delight and the civilization of their tastes. We do well enough to honor each person's human dignity, but sometimes we can call them to an even higher dignity and integration. And so on throughout the religious values. Abundant human life can go beyond ontological gratitude, even when raised to the love of the creator, to an ecstatic devotion. This is possible because we can create such an absolute value-identity that we can escape it into the ontological creative act in ecstatic bliss. This is not an obligation, only a creative possibility for creating a special possibility.

Whereas Chapter 9 dealt with the objective conditions of value in possibilities, this chapter has dealt with some of the ways religion cultivates signs for recognizing the values most important to religions attuned to the ultimates of possibility, wholeness, engagement, value-identity, and the radical contingency of everything on the ontological act of creation. But how should we respond to what our signs can discern about the values religion most prizes? Is there anything special that religion contributes here? This is the issue of spiritual powers, to which the argument now turns.

Chapter Eleven

Spirituality

The analysis of religious ethics employed the five ultimate conditions that have been developed in this *Philosophical Theology*. But its primary orientation is to the ultimate condition of form: fields of possibilities with subaltern value-laden alternatives bearing on obligation and choice. The religious ethical values help structure human interpretations of those fields of possibilities, looking for ways within those possibilities for achieving the values. The analysis of spirituality, by contrast, is oriented to the ultimate condition of having components, comporting oneself toward them with integrity so as to achieve wholeness. It opens new dimensions of coming to understand and act upon what is valuable in life.

Spirituality is mainly about integration or the attainment of wholeness with respect to those components of life that are ultimate. In accord with the systematic analysis here, this means integration or wholeness with respect to dealing with form and possibilities; with components themselves; with others, particularly other people; with value-identity; and with the ontological act of creation upon which everything depends (*II, 2*). Of course, spirituality with regard to the ontological act of creation lies behind all the other elements of spirituality, and spiritual development of any type addresses the ontological ultimate. The particular spirituality focused on the ontological ultimate is addressed in different ways in the last two chapters of each of the volumes of *Philosophical Theology*. *One*, Chapters 15 and 16, discussed the way of mysticism in terms of the project of turning oneself into a semi-self-interpreting sign of the ontological creative act. *Two*, Chapters 15 and 16, discussed the way of participation in terms of living in concrete response to the ontological creative act. *Three*, Chapters 15 and 16, will discuss the way of cognitive orientation when the finite inadequacy of all sacred worldviews becomes apparent and living with that is a way of life. The present chapter shall focus on spirituality as oriented to the cosmological ultimates.

The inspiration for the first three parts of the model of spirituality presented here is one of Plato's several models of the soul in the Republic.[1] In that dialogue, Plato has Socrates explore three different "types of soul," the aggressive, the appetitive, and the rational types. After discussing these as different types of people, in fact, different social classes, he makes the point that every individual has all three fundamental types of soul, each of which needs to be educated or perfected, and all of which need to be harmonized in a good person. (Socrates's interlocutors, Plato's half-brothers Glaucon and Adeimantus, do not grasp that Socrates has changed premises on them from types of people to parts of soul; they are very good at following deductions from premises but not at the dialectic of examining and shifting premises themselves.) For Plato, the chief example of the aggressive type is the soldier, whose character needs to be educated by repetitive learning through martial arts, music, and dance and learning to follow ideal people. The chief example of the appetitive type is the worker, who produces things to satisfy desire; education of desire means cultivating both the right kinds of desires and ranking desires in order of importance. Virtuosi of desires can be called "saints," although Plato did not call them that. The chief example of the rational type, according to Plato, is not the theoretician, although theory and erudition are absolutely necessary for educated reason. It is rather the statesman who has to know what is possible, what is valuable in the possible, and how to achieve the good in practice.

These three types can be related to the cosmological ultimates. The wise person or sage cultivates knowledge of form and its value and how to achieve the good. The soldier or disciplined person cultivates the personal integrity that has to do with the integration of the important components of life. The saint or perfecter of desire has to do with the cultivation of engagement of others, including oneself sometimes as an other.

Plato's model needs to be supplemented with the spirituality that relates to achieving absolute value-identity, which has to do with the pursuit of excellence. Excellence is always excellence in something or other. The previous chapter discussed how religions value the cultivation of virtue in value-identity, and excellence in virtue is a kind of spiritual perfection. But excellence can be in many other things, in athletic prowess, in artistic production, performance skills, in building a family or community, making some commodity, or being a friend. In the long run, the relevant excellence for spiritual nurture is making an excellent life out of the components that happen one's way. For any individual, spirituality involves aiming at perfection in each of the areas.

The sections of this chapter explore in more detail the spiritualities of wisdom, discipline, desire, and excellence. In each section are four levels of spiritual growth that can be understood sequentially. In practice, however, the four are usually intermixed, and progress in any one leads to changes, perhaps progress, in the others.

I. WISDOM: A SPIRITUALITY OF FORM AND CHOICE

1. Wisdom begins with self-knowledge: "Know thyself," the Delphic oracle said. Because human beings are raised from the earliest moments with rituals that teach them how to move, communicate, and play social roles, never is there a moment of complete transparency of oneself to oneself. One always plays roles, presents to an audience, performs symbolic structures, and defines oneself in relation to the anticipated perceptions of others. Some people seem to get through life thinking of themselves only in these public presentations. But then, who is "oneself" really? There is no self that exists without these public relations to others. As the metaphysics of *Philosophical Theology* says, we are defined in part by the conditional components through which we relate to others. These public relations are just as necessary and intrinsic to our identity as any inward private self. We are as authentically ourselves in our public performances of identity for others as we are in private moments when we admit that performance is partly pretense. One of the great spiritual sidetracks in late modernity has been the notion sponsored by existentialists from Kierkegaard to Heidegger and Sartre that there exists a pure inward will, a true identity, that inevitably is compromised by necessary interactions with "the masses," *das Mann.* One can relate to others authentically or inauthentically, but one cannot refuse the relation to others as somehow compromising pure identity.

So, coming to know oneself is not merely a retreat to inner thoughts and passions that usually are covered up. It is also to know what our interactions with others mean, from our own standpoint and theirs. These meanings are not usually on the surface. The rise of dynamic psychology in the last century has taught us how deep, and deeply buried, our fundamental perceptions, identifications, and actions are. In contemporary spirituality the therapeutic processes of dynamic psychology are difficult to distinguish from spiritual exercises aimed at self-discovery, and much is to be learned from their combination.[2]

Self-knowledge is not limited to uncovering secret passions and memories, as in dynamic psychology and the offices of confession. It also has to do with coming to understand our place in the world, what our responsibilities are, and what the world, or its local representatives, need from us. Self-knowledge includes also how we have been hurt and inspired, forced into roles and pushed out of them. In the long run, personal identity is a maelstrom mix of given circumstances, past determinations, the accidents of our watch, special talents and limitations, aversive reactions and positive passions. None of this need be fixed in its role as a component of our lives. But it all needs to be understood.

2. This coming to self-understanding is a continuous process that is concomitant with learning to be savvy about the world, the second stage in the development of wisdom. Objective knowledge about how the world

works is important, but it is not the same thing as savvy. Savvy is what one gains from experience, coming to see the hidden or suppressed factors in social relations, how people tend to think, how institutions tend to react under varying circumstances, how the local natural environment responds to this or that human intervention or seasonal change. Savvy is what we look for in a friend or mentor when we look for advice about important life choices.

The importance of savvy for wisdom is that it is a foundation for the mental habits of treating what we know about the world as a guide to action. Knowledge is not just mirroring the world with mental representations, although interpretation with iconic reference does at least that. Knowledge also provides the discriminations that allow us to act, including the discriminations about what is worthwhile in action. We need to know the possibilities and what they are worth. Savvy is really about what goods and harms come from the way things work. Savvy, thus, includes theoretical understanding, even of the most abstract sort, because that is sometimes most helpful for discriminating among alternative value-laden possibilities. The purpose of a philosophical theology, for instance, is to contribute to savvy about how to engage ultimate realities. Perhaps the most poignant savvy is the sense for the inevitability of tragedy, especially the loss of innocence.

3. Whereas self-knowledge leads to honesty and savvy to value-discerning effectiveness, "being true," the third level of wisdom, leads to a conformation of the self to what is real. Knowledge of any sort is some kind or other of conformation of our interpretations to what they interpret. Reality is the measure of our interpretations, and our interpretations are better the more they conform to the measures. "Being true," however, is the organization of many of the more important dimensions of knowledge so that the self in some kind of holistic way is conformal to reality. Becoming true is a process of organizing one's knowledge and savvy ways so that how one lives in reference to possibilities for the actual world approaches a harmony of being fully engaged with being at ease with what is most important in life. To be true is to have depth in one's embodiment in and engagement of the world.

The chief spiritual obstacle for becoming true is egoism that causes superficiality. Interest and valuation pervade all interpretations, determining the respects in which their objects are interpreted. Good interpretations register the values of their objects so that the interests of the interpreter are well connected to what is important in the things interpreted. Egoism, however, is a trait of personality that biases interpretations in holistic ways, not necessarily leading to distortion in any particular interpretation but collectively leading to a bias so that one's orientation to the world is false to what is important in the world. It prevents depth. Because all interpretations are interested, egoism might be hard to detect. Part of the detection comes from self-knowledge. Part comes from becoming savvy about oneself. Part comes from the deliberate deconstruction of ego and the reconstruction, in its place, of a self that in its overall orientation lives true to its context, sinking deep roots, including into the ultimate dimensions.

4. The fourth level of wisdom is what many religious traditions call "enlightenment." It consists in developing something of a bifocal vision. Through the bottom lens, as it were, one sees the world in proximate perspective as the arena within which to live and act, pursing appropriate interests in regard to possibilities, wholeness, engagement, and the development of value-identity. Through the upper lens, however, one sees the world, the same world including oneself, in ultimate perspective. Religions have differed in how they articulate this. Buddhism, for instance, in some of its strains, distinguishes ordinary truth from enlightened truth, with the former corresponding to the bottom lens and the latter to the upper lens. In this regard, the enlightened lens sees everything that happens as empty, being such as it is, while the ordinary lens sees things in terms of their longtime connections and interests for practical life. True enlightenment, for the Mahayana, is to hold both visions together. Some strains of Hinduism, by contrast, distinguish the ordinary vision of "dualistic" things from a vision of the absorption of all duality into some deeper, less differentiated, unity, for instance, as in the transfiguration of Krishna into Vishnu in the Bhagavad Gita. Sometimes the monotheistic religions treat enlightenment as a glimpse of ordinary things from a God's-eye view.

The formal structure of enlightenment within this *Philosophical Theology* is the possession of signs by which a person can grasp the world as directly contingent on the ontological act of creation. This would be to see the things in the world as they are within the ontological context of mutual relevance. In a strict sense, this would be impossible because in that ontological context the essential components of the different separate things are together in ways that would be distorted by the very act of encompassing them within knowledge. The point of the impossibility of this strict sense of knowledge can itself be symbolized, however, through the development of symbols of the ontological act of creation itself. These are not only intellectual symbols, such as constructed in the metaphysics of *Philosophical Theology*, but the embodied development of the self into symbols in which the act of interpretation is the reverse of the act of creation of the interpreter. These constructions of mystical symbols, or of the mystic as an embodied symbol, are ways of mysticism (*I, 15, 16*).

II. DISCIPLINE: A SPIRITUALITY OF GROUNDEDNESS AND COMPORTMENT

The second spiritual path to be discussed here is that of discipline, obviously related to wisdom: The acquisition of wisdom requires great discipline, and wisdom is required for discipline not to be a foolish exaggeration of aggression turned against oneself. Discipline, however, relates to the ultimate spiritual condition of integration or wholeness. It involves the training of the will so as to master the centrifugal forces of the self and to build capacities for action with regard to ultimate realities. Martial imagery most often accompanies the search for the discipline of psychic integrity. Members of the Society of Jesus explicitly think of themselves as soldiers and the head of their order is called a "general." John Wesley imagined his itinerant Methodist preachers as soldiers on horseback. The Buddhist disciplines of gungfu and the Daoist disciplines of taijiquan are aimed at training the body to be ruled by the will for the sake of free action in harmony with the cosmos.[3] Perhaps the most extensive and influential exploration of the spirituality of discipline, however, is the Bhagavad Gita's depiction of the education of Arjuna, the warrior. Four levels of cultivation of spiritual discipline will be discussed here, although they overlap and play into one another and are not merely sequential.

1. The first level is to acquire an image of oneself as capable of exercising discipline. This is related to knowing oneself but is more than self-knowledge. Self-knowledge reveals what one's deep desires and fears are. One's self-image reveals how one feels oneself to be related to those desires and fears. People are shocked by the revelation of their deepest secret identity. Those deep inner forces seem to be overpowering and controlling. Many people feel themselves to be not free, to be in bondage to their most determining nature. The beginning of the cultivation of spiritual integration is the acquisition of a self-image of freedom.

The acquisition of a self-image as a free agent is part of the problem of comportment to the components that make up one's life. Discussions of this in *Philosophical Theology Two*, Chapters 2 and 6, emphasized the problematic character of comporting oneself to the quasi-independent integrities of those components, respecting their values. The opposite side of that same point is the need to comport oneself toward the components in ways that express and embody one's own freedom to integrate them. This means that among the components in one's life needs to be a developed image of oneself as a free agent. Of course, extraordinary limits exist to one's freedom: The components of life by and large are what they are and must be coped with. Sometimes they can be changed, but often the problem is just to come to terms with them. Insofar as the latter is the case, the self-image needs to acknowledge their acceptance and a willingness to deal with them. A bad self-image puts one in bondage to things that need not be bonds.

The cultivation of a self-image as a free agent begins in childhood. Many children are raised in circumstances that teach them the opposite, that they are powerless, that they are dependent on others, and that freedom would ruin the dependence. Much psychotherapy is aimed to develop, perhaps beginning at primitive levels, a sense of capable agency. Then as life's circumstances develop more and more complex levels of power, agency needs to be redefined again and again.

2. The second level in the cultivation of spiritual discipline is that of action itself. One of the most serious obstacles to developing a self-image as

a free agent is incompetence in real action. Children learn skills of acting and these skills help cultivate their sense of free agency. The martial arts are paradigmatic cases of the development of skills in action, emphasizing the united movements of thought, feeling, impulse, and body. Religions have emphasized disciplines to exercise the will's control over the body. Sometimes these have been negative in the sense that they mean to suppress bodily impulses, often sexual ones, which are taken to interfere with other spiritual development. In these instances, the body itself, with its impulses, is taken to be the enemy, or at least the field on which the good will battles with evil impulses. Peter Brown has shown that for at least some early Christians, the antipathy to the body, rejecting sex and extolling celibacy or better yet virginity, came from their sense that their very freedom depended on their being able to assert their will over their impulses.[4]

The cultivation of the actions of free agency need not be negative, however. It involves arranging and creating complexes of actions that accomplish a willed result. Agency involves social skills as well as physical skills. Social skills are not only manners but involve understanding, persuasiveness, and habits of working through the reciprocities of conjoint action. "To study" is an action that requires cultivation.

Actions are to be understood in many ways, particularly with regard to their propriety and consequences. But the spiritual discipline of action is more specific and is embodied in the advice Krishna gave to Arjuna: "To action alone hast thou a right and never at all to its fruit; let not the fruits of action be thy motive; neither let there be in thee any attachment to inaction."[5] The discipline of perfecting action involves acting for the sake of the action itself. This is not to say that one ought not also attend to motives and to the fruits that would justify the action. But it is to say that a spiritually significant action needs to be learned to be done for its own sake. To do this requires the elimination of the ego, at least in the respects bearing upon the action and its context.

3. The third level of spiritual discipline follows from the second and perhaps is implicit in it, namely, the cultivation of a detached consciousness. To be able to act without regard for the fruit of action requires detachment. Yet whether one acts at all depends on what would justify the action or would allow the impulses from which it springs to come into play. Here is a paradox. On the one hand, actions are motivated and justified by their fruit, which means one should be attached critically to the good justifications and also cultivate motivations that lead to good actions. On the other hand, one is not free to do or not do the actions unless one is detached from those motivations and able to judge justifications dispassionately.

Although most Axial Age religious traditions have disciplines for cultivating detached awareness, this is a metaphysical specialty of Buddhism. Buddhism in nearly all of its modern forms claims that there is no enduring reality in experience to which one might be attached, no goal or good that is real itself. The different Buddhist traditions give diverse and sometimes conflicting accounts of this. Psychic attachment, conscious and unconscious, is a serious metaphysical mistake that gives rise to suffering. So, the multitude of spiritual practices in Buddhism—meditation, chanting, the round of monastic life—provides many avenues for the cultivation of detached awareness. Although most Buddhists would express this as the dropping away of the self, it can also be understood as a peculiar level of integration of the self in which the self can recognize things for what they are and not project attachments onto them.

4. The fourth level of spiritual discipline seems to be the opposite of the third, namely, the capacity of total devotion. Just as a soldier ideally is willing to give everything, including life, for the battle, so the self can become sufficiently disciplined to give itself away for its cause, the relevant ultimate reality. The bhakti strains in many religious traditions emphasize devotion, often under the self-understanding of love. Love, in this instance, means being able to give oneself wholly to the ultimate reality beloved, to God, the Buddha of the Western Lands, or whatever. But who is sufficiently self-possessed to be able to give oneself away? Only the hero of discipline who is organized, among other ways, by a self-image of freedom, who is skilled at doing what is willed, and who is detached enough from ego and self-interest so as to be able to give or withhold devotion. Love without such discipline can be a sloppy, unskilled, empty gesture with a lot of feeling but little engagement of the whole self.

III. DESIRE: A SPIRITUALITY OF EXISTENTIAL LOCATION

The spirituality of perfecting desire is commonly associated with saintliness in many traditions. Of course, it cannot be separated from other dimensions of spiritual development, and its demarcation as a model on its own is somewhat arbitrary. Confucius said, "At seventy I could follow my heart's desire without transgressing moral principles."[6] But this supposes that by then he had the wisdom to know the moral principles and the disciplined integration of character to follow them in habitual, instinctual ways. Nevertheless, the special spirituality of perfecting desires can be understood in something of its own terms. The reason for this is that the spirituality of desire is the principal spiritual address to otherness, to others. It is the dimension of spirituality that most closely engages other things within the existential field. Insofar as things are engaged by desire, the structure of desire is an important determinant of the character of the existential field.

The spirituality of the perfection of desire has four discernible though intermixed levels: the cultivation of desire itself, the cultivation of love, the cultivation of power, and the cultivation "of consent to being in general," to use Edwards's phrase.

1. The cultivation of desire itself is important because much of the time people want things because their culture says to want them, not because of any

fine passion for them. Some of the things people desire give them pleasure, such as sex and good food, so that there is a quick feedback reinforcement of the desire; but this need not lead to purifying and focusing the desire, only to repetitive behavior. Under ordinary circumstances, desire is a function of what people bring to the engagement of others, which, of course, is part of the valuative elements in all interpretation.

But the true perfection of desire is rooted most significantly in the desirable characters of the things desired. Elementary normative conditions for engagement are that people be aware of and appreciative of others. Every creature, as a harmony, has some value, and authentic engagement involves discovering what that value is and appreciating it. Most situations of desire involve needs on the part of the desiring person, but true desire cannot be limited to that. People need a sustaining, nurturing natural environment and desire this for their own sakes. But when they learn to discern the beauty of their natural habitat, they desire it for some of its intrinsic desirability and can act through time to sustain and enhance it. People need institutions for the education of children and desire them for their children's sake; but when they learn to discern the beauty of good education, they desire the educational institutions for their own sake and work to help their children take advantage of them. People need friends for sharing and the overcoming of loneliness and desire them as part of their own happiness; when they learn to discern the beauty in their friends, however, they desire their friends in the form of reveling in and prospering their friends. People need lovers for the sake of satisfying sexual impulses and, only slightly more generally, carrying on families; as they learn to discern their lovers' true beauty, they desire them for their own sakes, for the sake of their lovers' satisfaction.

So, the elementary stage of perfecting desires is to go beyond desire as need to desire as a passion for things because of the goodness or beauty in the things. "Passion" is the operative word here, because it connotes being moved by the thing desired rather than merely seeking out the thing desired due to some internal need or cultural predisposition. Passionate desire is rare and requires cultivation.

This might seem in direct conflict with the Buddhist attack on attachments and, perhaps to a lesser degree, with the other South Asian religions' wariness about commitment to things that pass away so quickly in time. True, for many people in those traditions, and for many people in other traditions who have been harmed by disastrous desires, a kind of passionless life might seem ideal. But there is a significant difference between an attachment to what is not real, the Buddhist complaint, and desire for things with value such as it is. Most Buddhists have no complaints about delighting in what is real, which is a part of *pratitya-samutpada*.

2. The spiritual discipline of perfecting love has been discussed extensively in *Philosophical Theology Two*, especially Chapters 3 and 7. In many respects love is merely the intensification of desire to an heroic power. But

the tipping point between intense desire and love is when the center of attention shifts from the relation of the desired object with the lover to the loved object's own perspective on the world. In this case the lover puts the loved object in the position of that whose interest determines the lover's actions. One of the common marks of this is when the lover is willing to sacrifice something important for the beloved, whether the beloved is a natural environment or a person. The sacrifice of one's life very often is a mark of the move beyond desire to love.

An added dimension to the spirituality of love is to shift from centering attention on the beloved alone to attention to the beloved as a creature of the ontological creative act. In this perspective, the other is loved because of its place in the ontological context of mutual relevance, however that might be symbolized. This kind of love is a communion of the lover and the beloved because both are equally real together and separately in that ontological context of mutual relevance. When love has been cultivated to have the deep symbols for this kind of engagement, the willingness of the lover to be sacrificed for the good of the beloved subtly transforms itself into a willingness to give up the beloved as desired. This kind of love, approaching that of the creative act itself, is strangely dispassionate in its compassion.

3. Yet another level in the spiritual perfection of desire is the cultivation of the coordination of desires and loves into power. For most people, making their desires compatible with one another is a struggle. Many of life's most profound dilemmas consist in incompatible desires and loving commitments. Part of spirituality is to become wise enough to set priorities and disciplined enough to hold oneself to them. Beyond the issues of compatibility, however, is the possibility of coordination, of compounding desires so that the pursuit of some feeds the pursuit of others. The possibility structure of coordination of desires is a hierarchy such that the coordination of desires on one level makes possible desires on another level that when coordinated make possible desires on much higher levels. Saints have loves most people cannot imagine. In a simple way, we can understand how loving several people allows for loving a circle of friendship on top of the individual relations, which makes it possible in a society of such circles to love the society, which with its arts and culture makes it possible to love a civilization. The higher-level objects of love can be viewed abstractly, as when we think intellectually about a civilization and are derisive of shallow people who love their civilization more than they love any individual. On the other hand, if the embodied signs and acts of loving individuals deeply and passionately are carried up into loving the circle of friends, and are not diminished by vagueness, and the circles are held concretely in the society one loves, and the society remains vivid in the civilization, then the love of the civilization carries with it all the power of the loves that make it up. Such a love is an extraordinarily elegant harmony of passions.

Having desires is a kind of power, and having coordinated desires is having greater power. A saint who can love a civilization without losing the power of loves for individuals, and institutions of individuals, has a very great power. This kind of intensely elegant power of passion is fierce and not always well directed. In some Western mythology, for instance, in John Milton's *Paradise Lost*, Satan is the very best of the angels, with the greatest power, and yet was misdirected to become the very worst.

4. The fourth kind of spiritual perfection of desire is the addition of the ontological ultimate condition to the passions, selflessness, and coordination of desire so that all those thing are means of loving the ontological act of creation with its created world. All these dimensions of desire are engaged interpretations with embodied signs. The semiotic system of most of these signs is not verbal but actual bodily life—the actions, feelings, and habitual organizations of a human life through time in a complex, semiotically significant environment. The ontological context of mutual relevance is not a determinate thing over and above all the created things within it: It is the act by which those things are created together. To think about it is not all that difficult; any philosophical theologian can do it. But to engage it with all one's heart, with one's body, feelings, emotions, and life patterns, requires the development or acquisition of special, integrative, embodied signs that constitute the lover as a sign that engages the ontological act. This is the mystic's task, to become a sign that intends the creator, a sign that is identical with the mystic's being created, at least in some respects.

IV. EXCELLENCE: A SPIRITUALITY OF VALUE-IDENTITY

Whereas the wisdom dimension of spirituality relates to form, the disciplined dimension to components, and the desiring dimension to others in the existential field, the spirituality of excellence relates to absolute value-identity. It, too, can be analyzed on four levels, coordinated with the other dimensions. The first is the acquisition of personal excellence, whose model might be the athlete. The second is the perfection of the contribution of one's excellence to the world. The third is commitment to both objective and subjective excellence as one's identity in ultimate perspective. The fourth is the abandonment of identification with that personal and public excellence and acceptance of the value of the whole.

1. The acquisition of personal excellence is, among other things, a form of spiritual perfection. Without it, people can get by doing what they do well enough. Many people do very little well and achieve seriously subpar value-identity. Doing well enough is the parallel in spirituality to the minimal moral achievement in religious ethics (*III, 10, iv*). Doing something excellently is more than is commonly expected for most human beings in most cultures.

Excellence at many activities has a utilitarian value. Being an excellent driver leads to safety in driving; being an excellent pianist might provide for a good living as an entertainer; being an excellent parent leads to more fortunate children. Perhaps the most common motive for excellence is the achievement of the fruits of excellence. The spiritual side of excellence, however, is excellence for its own sake. This is because excellence is the ideal for human beings in respect to the ultimate condition of value-identity.

Paul Weiss has argued that part of the meaning of "sport" is that athletes pursue excellence for its own sake, in a rather pure way, and that as such athletes are a kind of representative of all people in respect of excellence.[7] He pointed out that while there are many kinds of excellences, excellence is somewhat showcased and highlighted in sport. Like most kinds of excellence, athletic prowess requires vast amounts of training and preparation. Yet on the field or in the pool or pulling across the water, the excellence lies in the particular performance itself with no excuses or larger context than the event. One either performs excellently or one does not. The team either performs excellently or it does not. In competitive sports the goal is to win. Sometimes that is a utilitarian sense of victory, where winning means something besides the excellence of the performance. Sometimes, as in running races, winning is merely the standard by which to measure excellence. But with regard to excellence itself, the most excellent athletes sometimes do not win, and sometimes winning is merely the by-product of excellence. The excellence is in the performance itself, in the moment from beginning to end and no more. In this respect, sport is a good paradigm for excellence in some aspect of life. It requires preparation, discipline, the acquisition of skills, and many other things, but it consists in the performance of that which is excellent. Performing artists such as musicians, actors, and dancers are much like athletes in this regard, also good paradigms or representatives of human excellence.

2. Personal excellence might or might not make a positive contribution to the world. Given the effort that goes into athletic or artistic performance, often the most its public contribution amounts to is entertainment. But there are kinds of excellence that have to do with making contributions to others. Ultimate personal identity has two domains, the value achieved in the harmonies that make up a person, called subjective value-identity, and the value contributed to other things that those other things integrate with their own essential components, called objective value-identity (*II, 4*). The spiritual pursuit of personal excellence leans in the former direction and the pursuit of excellent public contributions leans toward the latter.

Three rough classes of public endeavors for spiritual excellence can be distinguished, although they are closely interconnected. The first is the excellence of dealing well with people and being a good influence on them. Most parents begin with high commitment to excellence in raising their children and some become truly excellent. Similarly with friendships and collegiality. There are some people whose excellence at personal relations simply light up a room.

The second is excellence in dealing with the institutions of personal and social life, serving others through attending to the proper cultivation and administration of institutions. Obvious institutions that need cultivating are academic and economic ones. Some people attain truly excellent skills at caring for institutions, and for individuals through the institutions, who are not particularly excellent at face-to-face relationships. Institutional leaders of excellence are often not admired as easily as people excellent at face-to-face contributions to individuals precisely because they have to blunt and sometimes distort themselves, or seem inauthentic in individual encounters, in order to work for the greater good of the institution. Nevertheless, it is possible to aspire to spiritual excellence in the care of institutions and to recognize it in others.

3. The third kind of public excellence is in relation to nature, caring for the environment, learning to harmonize with nature, healing its wounds, being sensitive to its harmonic and causal patterns that are not particularly important on the surface for human affairs. Some farmers are like that, and travelers, and naturalists. Myriad ways exist in which individuals can attain to excellence in relating to nature so that nature is improved by what they do and how they live their lives.

A person's absolute value-identity consists in the value the person achieves subjectively within his or her own life and objectively in the things the person affects, contributing value to them that they integrate in their own essential ways. Excellence in the ways these are combined in a life is an ultimate spiritual goal, the achievement of which is very difficult. The third level of spiritual excellence is devoted to achieving excellence as a person in this value-identity. This level cannot be a spiritual perfection if it would mean compromising one's attention to excellence in making public contributions or in personal forms of achievement. That would be a strange kind of selfishness. Rather it is an integration of the personal and public sides in ways that can symbolize a whole-self-and-its-effects and attempt to make that an excellent thing. Religions have various symbols for this integration, perhaps the best being that of the truly humane person as characterized by the Confucian tradition. In the symbolism of the Western monotheisms, this is the ultimate identity that a person brings to God, the identity that stands under judgment, and an important aspect of spiritual perfection is making this ultimate identity as excellent as possible.

The excellence of absolute value-identity is easy to miss because it so easily decomposes into its two domains, the subjective and the objective. Excellence in personal integration or wholeness is akin to personal excellences: The athlete is akin to the soldier who was the model for disciplined integration. Excellence in objective contributions is akin to public contributions, to heroism and leadership. Excellence in the absolute value-identity that unites them both is hard to discern.

The reason for the difficulty is that there can exist no standpoint, such as value in the given individual or value in another, that embraces the subjective and objective domains. Only the ontological context of mutual relevance holds together those two sides, because they exist in things that are mutually determining but still other to one another. Paradoxical as it seems, a person's absolute value-identity is not a character of that person per se because it is not limited to the person's own harmony. The heart of human sociality is that our value-identity includes what we do to other things, which is part of their character. So, to discern a person's absolute value-identity, we need symbols that move indirectly through the ontological context of mutual relevance to embrace the elements of value-identity that are in things other than the person as well as in the person, both of which make up the person's own value-identity. Our ultimate and true self is not only the harmony we make of the components of our lives, which are then internal to us, but includes also the value-identities that we cause in other things. In the terms of the Western monotheisms, the self exists only in God, not in any harmony of oneself that has first-person token reference in relation to other-person token references. Yet, the individual harmony has much of the responsibility for how others are affected by its human choices. Therefore, it is possible to strive for excellence in that absolute value-identity that is not merely a part of oneself.

4. The fourth level of excellence is the converse of the third. The ultimate value identity we achieve willy-nilly and that, through spiritual development, we can make excellent, exists not in any individual but only in the ontological context of mutual relevance. Therefore, it is a perfection of excellence to abandon our concerns for our own excellence in ultimate identity and revel with satisfaction in the absolute value-identity of the whole creation. This abandonment does not mean that we strive to make excellent some values beyond our own absolute value-identity, which would be impossible, a matter that ipso-facto would merely extend our own absolute value-identity. Nor does the abandonment mean that we should not also press for the excellence of our own positive absolute value-identity. Rather, it means excellence in relinquishing concern for our own value-identity so as to accept it as being only part of the larger value-identity of the creation. In light of this excellence, we can accept our own limitations, failures of achievement, and death, with equanimity and joy. The value-identity of the creation as a whole, whatever that turns out to be, is enough. As several religious traditions put it, salvation comes only when one abandons the concern for salvation. This is a perfection of nonattachment. It is a perfection of identification with the ontological act of creation, which is as close to any thing as it is to oneself and, in fact, is close to all only as they are together.

Here is the most important paradox of personal identity. On the one hand, we are what we make of ourselves, our subjective mode of value-identity. On the other, we are how we affect other things, the objective mode. These are absolutely particular and definitive of personal identity. But beyond both is the identity of the ontological act of creation itself that is the fullness of each individual's personal reality. Except insofar as we recognize our identification with the whole act of creation, whatever that might entail now unimaginable to us, we do not grasp who we really are. Put the other way, the ontological act of creation is our true and only absolute identity. We are not dissolved to indeterminate merging. Our very haecceity is the ontological act itself.

Such spiritual insights made concrete are only for mystical adepts. The quotidian analogue of this is the endeavor to identify ourselves through spiritual companionship, the topic of the next chapter. Spirituality has been treated in this chapter as an individual affair, emphasizing that its themes are those of a person's integration of the components of that individual's life. Yet it is a commonplace that we come to know and relate to ourselves with whatever sagacity, discipline, saintliness, and excellence we can master only through interactions with others. Self-differentiation from others is a long, complex process with much give and take, learning to see ourselves through the eyes of others and learning to peer through the eyes of others only through learning to use our own. Therefore, the discussion of spirituality as if it were merely a matter of well-grounded wholeness is incomplete by itself. Perhaps it is even misleading if it suggests that companionship in religion is not integral. Therefore, spiritual companionship is important to understand as relating to each of the dimensions of spirituality discussed in this chapter.

Chapter Twelve

Religious Companionship

Spiritual companionship is that part of religious companionship that is focused on individual spiritual growth. Religious life of the individual involves much more than just spiritual growth in the sense discussed in the previous chapter. It involves all aspects of attaining and celebrating ecstatic fulfillments and coping with the ultimate predicaments of human life. Nearly all aspects of religion involve individuals relating with others: We are all harmonies that include close relations with others among our defining components, and those others have lives of their own not to be reduced to their roles in our lives. Therefore, religious companionship, more inclusive that spiritual companionship, is a topic on its own.

Philosophical Theology Two, Part IV, probed the issues of religious participation from the angle of how individuals gain access to religion's resources for engaging ultimacy, especially with regard to predicaments and ecstatic fulfillments. These resources lie principally, although surely not exclusively, in religious communities, which were analyzed in terms of rituals, commitment, faithful engagement of others, and the concrete inhabitation of worldview shared in part with others. Now many of those same issues can be revisited under the topic of what it means to gain a community of religious companions. In this chapter we shall take religious communities to be communities of religious, including spiritual, companions. The theme of religious companionship relates to the fundamental condition of being with others in an existential field and being oneself in part because of that.

The question of whether and how to belong to a religious community is extraordinarily complicated today, more so than in most periods of the past, for several reasons. First, it seemed clearer in the past what a religious community is, namely, an authoritative religious tradition with local branches in which individuals participate. The chapters of Part I indicate several senses in which this kind of community-belonging is problematic, as will be spelled out further on (*III, 13, 14*). Second, anthropology and sociology offered methodological models for describing and sometimes explaining communities but now find it difficult to identify what is religious about them. Third, our pluralistic society offers many options for religious communal participation and membership, so that the authority of a natal community is challenged. Fourth, most established religious communities are now challenged both by new ideas and experiences to which they are ill oriented and by corruptions in their own ethical practices.

On the other hand, religious practices are complicated and need to be learned. The achievement of any kind of in-depth relation to something ultimate requires cultivation. Cultivation is sustained and enhanced by companionship. Companionship is particularly important when it comes to being critical about one's religious practices and spiritual developments. One becomes oneself through engaging others, most helpfully as companions.

How then can we understand religious communities, and participation and membership in them, insofar as they are the substance of companionship? The place to begin is with a philosophical definition of some of the contours of affiliation in terms of the cosmology and semiotic theory of *Philosophical Theology*. These categories and the distinctions among them are functions of the philosophical theory under development here and should not be understood to involve the rejection of categories developed for different purposes by the social sciences. Nevertheless, the following discussions elaborating philosophical categories for understanding religious communities might seem strange to thinkers accustomed to social science approaches. Their worth lies in the eventual usefulness of the distinctions they bring to the fore and how these relate to other systematic matters of philosophical theology.

Before undertaking that inquiry, however, a distinction should be drawn between the theological and religious problematic of finding authentic religious communities to which one can belong, communities that embody engagements of ultimacy, and the social and political problematic of finding social groups that embody ultimate dimensions of social life. Churches and other religious communities serve some of these social functions. For instance, celebrations of birth, marriage, and death need some social venue in which people can gather who are not necessarily in the same religious community with a shared sacred worldview. When a person dies, for instance, Christians and Jews, Buddhists and Hindus, might want to attend the funeral, which is shaped by a particular worship practice in a particular sacred worldview but made open to all for the purpose of the funeral. The rituals involved celebrate the life of the person, even though perhaps none of the people attending the funeral would participate in the larger ritual life of that social religious community for the sake of their own religious life. The religious dimension of social organizations is an important topic on its own but not the topic of what makes for an authentic religious community, our topic here.

I. SEMIOTIC SPACE

The natural space of physical and imaginative existential fields is the broadest context within which human beings are affiliated with things. We are members of nature, and all our other affiliations and memberships take place within that. The social space of human interactions takes place within natural space. But human beings relate to things in nature that are not necessarily within the social space. Although no one has denied that social interactions take place within the connections of nature, it has not always been clear that the nonsocial relations of people to nature and nonsocial natural objects are ultimately, that is, religiously, important. Often in the past the outer boundaries of what is religiously important have been set by social relations, for instance, relations between peoples, including semiotically meaningful relations with God or gods. Now we are becoming aware of the ultimate significance of individuals', groups', and indeed the human species' relations and obligations to the larger stretch of nature.

Within the space of nature lies social space, the space created by human interactions in which people give one another semiotically charged conditional components. The social space, strictly speaking, includes all human interactions. What is significant about human interactions is that all human beings have semiotic systems so that, to them, their actions and interactions are meaningful. But in social space there does not have to be a common semiotic system, only the recognition that all the parties have semiotic systems. Sometimes social encounters involve clashes among different semiotic systems, as when the Native Americans first met the European colonizers. The initial interactions were meaningful to all parties, interpreted within their own systems. But it took time before enough common signs were developed, with common syntax and semantics, for the social space to be inscribed with a common semiotic space.

Semiotic space is the field created by the interplay of symbolic networks within a semiotic system. A semiotic space need not be consistent and coherent in its varied symbolic networks and their various syntactical and semantic structures. It might contain several such networks, connecting them with some slippage, like the semiotic system of a person who knows several languages and translates back and forth among them, using different ones to engage different matters of life. Most of human society on Earth shares a vague semiotic system that allows for meaningful interactions among their separate symbolic networks, the only exceptions being isolated tribes who are affected by the human actions of others but have no semiotically meaningful interactions with them.

Cultures are symbolic networks that are embodied within groups of people that provide the semiotic detail necessary for the main parts of life. Cultures are embodied by being taught, mainly through the teaching of ritual, including the rituals of language. Cultures are also learned and unlearned in the life of the groups, with much human adaptability and creativity making cultures dynamic intensifications of larger semiotic systems. When a group interacts with another group with a different culture, they share in an overall semiotic system that is intensified in each of their ways. To discern how two cultures connected within a larger semiotic system differ, and what things they share through the larger system, is an empirical matter. The opportunities to study this are much greater when investigators play down the separate narratives each culture might have that seem to exaggerate their independence.

Cultures are always somewhat vague with respect to actual meaningful interpretive engagements. Each interpretation particularizes or intensifies the symbols carried in the culture. A given culture also is vague with respect to different specifications of it inside itself. For instance, in a sharply class-oriented society, such as the caste system that has obtained in various guises in India, the overall culture distinguishes and relates the castes functionally while each caste has its own culture with regard to such things as work, diet, marriage expectations, ritual practices, and so forth. The subcultures within a larger culture might be antagonistic to one another or to the perceived larger culture. Within a group there may be many levels of culture, with the higher being vague with respect to the specifications of them lower down.

One among many semiotic elements in a culture is a vague worldview that provides orientation for other cultural things in the various domains. Each subculture in the larger culture has a worldview more specific to itself, oriented to its own specific domains that might differ from the domains of the other subcultures. Each group in the subculture, and each individual in the group, specifies worldviews to the particular domains of their own lives. Worldviews can cut across cultures, serving to orient the several cultures in which an individual might participate. A given individual's worldview, however, might fail to provide orientation for some culture in which the person participates, in which case that participation is relatively meaningless in comparison with the person's other cultures.

A community is a group united by the stated or unstated authority of a worldview that defines and orients the community's various functions, values, and purposes. It might be a multicultural community. The community's worldview is somewhat vague with respect to how individuals within the community form their own worldviews.

To draw a distinction that has great importance in the study of religious communities, a person can be said to *participate* in a community when the person adopts and lives with the community's uniting worldview, in the group of people holding the worldview. The person can be said to be a *member* of the community when the person explicitly affirms participation *and is accepted by others* in the community according to some measure of acceptance. Sometimes the measure of acceptance is an affirmation on the part of the members that the community is an in-group and that membership in it excludes memberships in certain other communities. In the case of religious communities, some require a form of exclusive membership and others do not.

Individuals participate in many communities. Perhaps in certain historical periods or in groups of a very small scale, individuals could be in one community only, whose worldview embraced common membership and included all the domains of the individual's life. In the present situation, however, most individuals participate in many groups and many communities. One of the complexities of developing a worldview adequate for an individual is that it needs to provide orientation across groups and communities.

II. RELIGIOUS COMMUNITY DEFINED

Some of these categories can now be applied to the understanding of religious communities. The following analysis does not pretend to limn out everything that has been called a religious community. A very great many kinds of things have been called religious communities, from highly regulated monastic "total institutions" to the sophisticated elite educational camaraderie of the Confucian literati.[1] Religious communities have been defined in opposition to larger political, economic, and culturally unified communities and also identified with nations and their governments, as in the case of Islam in some periods.[2]

Nevertheless, no fair phenomenological way exists to identify religious communities in distinction from or relation to other kinds of communities with which they might overlap, for instance, familial, political, or economic ones. The only fair way to identify religious communities is by means of the philosophical definition of religion, which is stipulative and finds its justification in the sense it makes of philosophical considerations, empirical considerations for understanding religious movements, and considerations of experience. The definition of religion in *Philosophical Theology* is: *human engagement of ultimacy expressed in cognitive articulations, existential responses to ultimacy that give ultimate definition to the individual and community, and patterns of life and ritual in the face of ultimacy*. What makes a community religious, according to this definition, is that it is united by a worldview that facilitates the engagement of ultimacy in these ways.

This is to say, a community is a religious community if it has an authoritative worldview containing a sacred canopy through which ultimate things can be engaged in cognitive terms, in patterns of community life, and in ways that give ultimate existential definition to individuals and sometimes to the communities themselves. A community might have a sacred canopy and thus employ religious symbols but not facilitate the engagement of ultimate matters with the sacred canopy. This would not be a religious community, although it might appear that way because of the presence of the sacred canopy. Most social scientists would take this to be a religious community because of the sacred canopy. A community might have a sacred worldview through which some people in the group might engage ultimate matters but which lacks the authority to engage all people in the group with ultimacy, either directly or through participation in patterns such as rituals that do engage ultimacy (*III, 13, 14*). In this instance, the community would not be a religious community, but, by virtue of its sacred worldview, some individuals within it would be religiously engaged. A sacred worldview not only has a sacred canopy but might very well articulate how elements in the sacred canopy relate to some or all of the domains of life oriented by the worldview, giving them ultimate dimensions. A worldview that does not relate the sacred canopy to much else can serve to unify a religious community, but one that exists only in the domains affected by the ultimacy in the sacred canopy. This is to say, the group that constitutes the religious community might share very little about life that is religious, perhaps only their ceremonial worship. The importance of this descriptive point lies in the prevalence of "conservative" religious groups that segregate their religious commitments from scientific and other forms of participation in a more secular culture that rejects their sacred canopy.

A religious community might involve people from several different cultures. What unites it as a religious community is a sacred worldview that is authoritative vaguely for all within it; but then each culture within the community would have a more specific sacred worldview, specifying the sacred canopy of the whole in ways that make sense of the domains of life special to its own culture. Each culture itself might have subcultures, with subspecializations of sacred worldviews, and so forth, down to individuals who have individuated sacred worldviews. For instance, suppose that the religious community of worshippers of Krishna/Vishnu takes the Bhagavad Gita as the main source of symbols for the ultimate and as an authoritative text. In a vague sense, all worshippers of Vishnu are part of a religious community defined by that, although some also might be part of the community defined by worship of Shiva, with the latter dominant in their lives. There are many competing schools of Vaishnavism, each with its own specification of the Vaishnavite sacred worldview, and thus each with its own interpretation, perhaps in a commentarial tradition, of the Bhagavad Gita, although differing about the authority of other sacred sources about Vishnu. The schools themselves have an evolving history and therefore evolving differences within their sacred worldviews. People live out the lives of these traditional schools in local settings, local in both time and geography, each specifying and modifying the sacred Vaishnavite worldview. Individuals in each place further specify the sacred worldview. Thus, there is a vast, historically dynamic nest of levels of vagueness and specificity defining the levels of religious community to which a Vaishnavite might belong.

For thinkers whose primary image of religious communities is a local face-to-face one, such as congregations or small religiously homogeneous villages, the vaguer levels of religious community might seem to be less real. The reality of a religious community, however, has to do with how it existentially defines the identity of the individuals who belong to it. What is existentially defining comes from the sacred canopy, and this might be specified down to triviality at the particular local level. For instance, in the Roman Catholic and Anglican churches, the most important religious community is that connected with the Eucharist. No matter what parish church an individual attends, perhaps a different one each week, the heart of the religious community is through participation in the Eucharist and what that stands for. The local variants, parish by parish, might not count for much, and the individual might not get much religious nourishment from any one local situation besides its embodying the celebration of the mass. On the other hand, the Roman Catholic Church in some of its official teachings attempts to say that the most existentially identifying thing about membership in it is defined by the very vague level of the unity of the church as acknowledging the authority of the pope, the bishop of Rome. What makes the Eucharist effective, according to these teachings, is the celebrant and his congregation being in communion with the bishop of Rome. And yet many Roman Catholics accept the connection of the Eucharist with the pope as an incidental matter and disregard official papal and other top-down church teachings on many issues of theology and morals: What counts for them as their religious community is the celebration of the mass itself everywhere.

Participation in a religious community as defined here to some degree and in some forms constitutes the existential identity of the participants through the ways the community facilitates engagement of ultimacy. *Philosophical Theology* argues that there are five related ultimates: an ontological one, namely, the radical contingency of the cosmos on the ontological act of creation; and four cosmological ones, namely, the ultimacy of form/possibility/obligation, the ultimacy of components and comportment toward them in wholeness, the ultimacy of existential location and the engagement of others, and the ultimacy of value-identity and the meaning of life. An individual's ultimate existential identity involves relating to all five of these in one way or another. The individual's most real religious community or communities are those with sacred worldviews through which those five ultimates are engaged. For an individual to belong to different religious communities for relating to different ultimates is quite possible.

"Worship" is the shorthand term in these volumes to indicate how individuals in community most directly engage the ontological act of creation and their own contingency. That term, however, carries connotations of public ritual that might obscure other forms of "worshipful" engagement of the ontological act of creation. To engage that, symbols for it must be devised and internalized, which is often the work of mystics of various sorts. Mystical meditation needs to be considered a form of worship for the word "worship" to be clear here. The religious community of mystics might never involve face-to-face meetings, communicating rather through literatures crossing times, cultures, and even "named" religions such as Hinduism, Christianity, or Cabbalistic Judaism. Not all people who are religious necessarily engage the ontological act of creation, though by definition they must engage some ultimate reality, and the ultimate realities are connected.

Every determinate thing created by the ontological act has the four transcendental traits that define the four cosmological ultimate conditions for human existence. One of these, obligation, is very important for all the major Axial Age religions, and how individuals define themselves in respect of standing under obligation depends on their participation in a religious community whose sacred canopy does that. If an individual relates to standing under obligation through a sacred canopy shared with no one else (if such a thing were possible), that person would be in a community of one; the same is true with respect to the other ultimates. Individuals also can (but need not) define themselves existentially by how they relate to their own wholeness, understood in terms of comportment to the important components of their lives. The religious community through which they do this, learning its discipline, is the real one for them in this respect. Similarly, individuals can (but need not) identify themselves existentially by how they take up the tasks of engaging others, and the religious community through whose sacred worldview they do that is the real one for them in this respect, whatever its level of vagueness and specificity. Likewise with absolute value-identity: If individuals define themselves existentially in relation to this, the religious community through whose sacred worldview they do this is the real one for them.

The Axial Age religions each have evolved in such ways as to offer symbols of ultimacy and vague sacred worldviews so that one sacred worldview defines a religious community that engages its participants in all respects of ultimacy. The complexity of these religions comes in part from having to relate to all these ultimate realities in some integrated fashion. But in the present religious situation, these traditions are fragmented in their authority for many people, and thus the communities defined by their sacred canopies can work as religious communities only in part, perhaps providing worship of the ontological act of creation and a commitment to standing under obligation but no ultimacy for wholeness or engaging nasty others. Some people find no traditional religion, that is, a community defined by a traditional sacred worldview, provides the symbols by which they can engage ultimacy in any of its dimensions in existentially identifying ways.

III. CRITICAL BELONGING

The two previous sections have focused on the nature of religious communities; this section and the following focus on the nature of belonging. The unity of a religious community is its sacred worldview, and thus participation in the community involves adoption of that sacred worldview and specifying it so that it orients the particulars of one's own life. *Philosophical Theology One*, Chapter 4, Section IV, distinguished three existential continua that characterize holding to a worldview, in this case a sacred worldview, one with a sacred canopy that relates to at least some of the other domains of life. These continua are "sharing," "comprehensiveness," and "intensity."

Sharing in a sacred worldview and the community it defines runs along a continuum from minimal to maximal sharing. A Christian, for instance, can share with all other Christians some kind of commitment to Jesus and very little else. The emphasis on Jesus in the Christian's sacred canopy can be through reference to the New Testament depictions of him, although the interpretations of those depictions might not be shared. Other aspects of the Christian sacred canopy, however, might not be shared, for instance, the issues surrounding the concept of the Trinity, or creation, or models of God, or belief in atonement, or resurrection. Then, beyond the sacred canopy, the Christian's sacred worldview might have domains that are not shared with others who do share the sacred canopy. The situations of Christians across the globe are so varied that no one sacred worldview could be shared by all, for it would fail to orient what is differently important for them. Nevertheless, for some Christians (and the same is true for members of other named traditions), the identification is with such a vague Christian sacred worldview that sharing is maximal. Most people are in between the minimal and maximal points on the sharing continuum.

A special complication regarding sharing is that most religious communities have sacred worldviews that tolerate internal disagreement. On one level, this is just the recognition that the sacred canopy can be made intimate to radically different social locations only through symbols that are different from one another, perhaps even contradictory in some respects. On another level, this is the recognition that disagreement about some of the meanings of ultimacy in the shared sacred worldview is itself part of the worldview. For instance, it is fairly common within many Christian communities today to recognize it to be a debatable question whether Jesus's love ethic regarding the engagement of others trumps the justice demand that the weak be protected; the outcome of the debate can produce a pacifist or a military response to hostile invasion. Pacifists and those promoting armed defense recognize their disagreement but do not take that disagreement to mean they have different sacred worldviews; the shared sacred worldview embraces that difference. On the other hand, even where certain disagreements are built in to sacred worldviews, there are pressures to define the limits of disagreement, saying what commitments are necessary.

Comprehensiveness is a continuum regarding how much of life is oriented by a sacred worldview. For some religious communities, the defining sacred worldview is rather limited to matters pertaining to the sacred canopy with very little impact of the sacred canopy on other domains within the worldview. For most practical purposes, such religious communities look fairly secular in most aspects of life. At the other end of the continuum are sacred worldviews in which many if not all aspects of life are determined one way or another by the sacred canopy. For very religious people, most of life is affected by its ultimate dimensions as determined through the sacred canopy. For minimally religious people, equally committed to their sacred worldview, only certain few circumscribed affairs of life are ultimately important. Religious communities exist for people all along the continuum of comprehensiveness.

Intensity is the continuum of degrees of commitment by individuals to religious communities defined by sacred worldviews, ranging from minimal and perhaps fitful commitment to wholehearted and all-consuming commitment, with many stops in between. For many people, the intensity of their commitment to a religious community varies with their stage of life (*I, 4; II, 14, 15*). Variance in intensity registers in the different domains of life oriented by the sacred worldview: Sometimes those domains are oriented by the sacred worldview in great detail, and at other times the orientation comes from many other things, including other worldviews.

Some religious communities have structural organizations such that commitment includes being accepted in an organizational way, for instance, adoption into membership, acceptance into more select and demanding units of the organization such as monastic orders, and the like. Commitment, this is to say, means a willingness to accept the authority of the organization to grant membership, and the willingness to do whatever is necessary to obtain that grant.

But it should be remembered that not all religious communities have structural organizations. A community is religious for an individual if it is a group unified by a sacred worldview through participation in which the individual existentially is identified in respect of one, several, or all of the five ultimate realities. Thus, it is possible for an individual to have one or more religious communities that cut across several organizations. The organizations might present themselves as religious communities and function that way for some people, for instance, those belonging to organized churches or monastic communities. But a given individual might find only certain aspects of it, and certain members within it, as parts of the individual's own religious community. In such a circumstance the organization itself is not the individual's religious community, although it might well be a social or political community in which the individual participates in social or political respects. Whether the social aspects of the organized community overlap the religious aspects for a given individual depends on whether the sacred worldview of the organization is the same, with only variations in specificity, as the sacred worldview of the individual by virtue of which existential self-identification with regard to ultimacy is made. For some people, the social life of an organized church community is prized for its own sake while they find their own real religious community elsewhere.

For a great many people in the contemporary religious situation, especially those in modernizing pluralistic circumstances, the religious tradition of their birth or native culture provides most of the symbols of ultimacy in what turns out to be their sacred canopy, at least in vague form. People born Jewish will have Jewish symbols of ultimacy, while those born Shaivite will have those of Shiva. Many people in these circumstances also use their tradition's offices of worship in which to express their ultimate gratitude for existence. But in other respects they no longer live amid a social group of people shaped by their traditional sacred worldview. They live in circumstances to which that traditional sacred worldview is largely irrelevant or does not provide orientation. And they might reject the traditional authority of the sacred worldview (while still using the traditional symbols of ultimacy), which turns the community defined by the traditional sacred worldview into a social or political but not a religious community for them. If people like this are to find a religious community, it will be through combining communal elements that fit within a sacred worldview that works for them with respect to self-identification relative to ultimacy.

The issue of authority is especially complicated in modernity across diverse locations in the religious situation. For some people, a sacred worldview can have authority because it was taught to them early on, with the same authority as knowing how to stand or to signal respect, and nothing arises to challenge it; these people are little affected by modernity. For other people, a sacred worldview has authority because they will to grant it authority. That willing might have any number of motivations, perhaps changing over a lifetime. It might come as a defensive response to an attack on the plausibility of one's native and assumed religious community. It might come through a conversion to a new religious community and sacred worldview, overthrowing what previously had been accepted as authoritative. It might come as the result of due deliberation on the sacred worldview that one wants to make authoritative to orient life. In all these instances, the sacred worldview has authority because the individual grants it authority.

For some people, the sacred worldview has such revelatory force regarding some or all of the ultimate matters that granting it authority is a natural or easy act of will. That is, it would be stupid not to will it to be authoritative. This position is difficult to sustain in the modern world, however, because it is now apparent that all sacred worldviews need interpretation, and the interpretation needs to survive the issues of plausibility (*III, 13, 14*). Rather, the theologically defensible justification of granting authority to a sacred worldview so as to define one's ultimate dimensions of life through its community is that the sacred worldview can demonstrate its plausibility.

Plausibility by itself does not entail commitment. Given the variety of religious options and the baffling complexity of life, commitment to a religious community requires an act of faith, which is to say, an act of will to give the religious community's sacred worldview authority.

Why would one make that kind of faith commitment, granting authority to a sacred worldview, especially in this confusing age? The answer is, because of the utilitarian value of a religious community in the concrete shaping of a religious life. *Philosophical Theology Two*, Part II, detailed many ways in which religion offers remedies to the multitude of dimensions of human predicament. Theses remedies are extremely difficult to access without participation in some religious community (or several religious communities) that holds them. By the same token, as *Philosophical Theology Two*, Part III, argued, the many forms of ultimately defining ecstatic fulfillments need articulation and common celebration through communities of companions. Granting authority to a religious community and its sacred worldview is not the same as finding self-identity in the ultimate respects. It is, rather, accepting or adopting the community as the means by which one might find that existential identity. Or, put more dynamically, one adopts and grants authority to a religious community because of the hope it can be the parent handing down the remedies to the human predicament, the vessel as it were; because of the need for companions in the many dimensions of religious life; and because the community might be the means to offer what one learns to others. One can hope also that a religious community can be a means to expressing the terrors and joys of ecstatic religious fulfillment, something to be much celebrated and rehearsed in memory and anticipation.

IV. ULTIMATE BELONGING

Belonging to a religious community is a utilitarian means to obtaining proper relations to what is ultimate. Thus, a person's identity as belonging to a religious community at most can be a penultimate sense of identity. To the extent that a religious community is rightly endowed and the person's participation is full and intense, the community's mediation of ultimacy in its symbols and the practices shaped by those symbols can be transparent. In this instance, there would be little difference between the community's penultimate sense of identification for the individual and reality's ultimate sense of existential identification. For many people in traditional circumstances, living the life of a religious community is all there is with regard to their relating to ultimacy. On the other hand, many people's participation in their religious community is fitful at best and sometimes problematic. Moreover, even if those communities are constructed by the individual who stitches together the many separately derived elements into a unique sacred worldview with new religious connections with other people, religious communities are usually very broken vessels for containing religious resources, for companioning, and for receiving one's contributions.[3]

A special complication forces the distinction between the penultimate belonging appropriate to a religious community and the ultimate belonging appropriate to one's created status. A religious community is an in-group, distinguished from other people who are not part of it, who do not share its sacred canopy, and who are not regarded as companions in the community. The more effective the religious community in shaping the lives of its members through the ultimate dimensions of more and more domains, the more special that community is. To be seriously religious means deep participation in the religious life of the community, even if that community is a stitched-together group of people from many different social groups, including different religious traditions. The deeper the participation and mutual collaboration, the more set apart the religious community, the more it is an in-group.

The paradox is that, common to the heirs of the Axial Age revolution, the function of the in-group is to relate everyone to the gratuitous, arbitrary, undeserved, and surprising ontological act of creation, to the obligation of justice to all people, to everyone's need for ultimate wholeness, to the engagement of everything in creation as deserving creatures, and to everyone's need for absolute value-identity. All this is to say, the religious in-group at its best is the utilitarian community to train and exercise its members in commitments to universal gratitude, justice, wholeness, care, and meaningfulness. Moreover, the religious community is committed to working with people outside itself to hold and live by these universal commitments to ultimacy. So, the very point of the religious community is to deny ultimacy to itself! Because its utilitarian function is so great in the promotion of proper human orientation to ultimacy, a religious community should be loved and nurtured as such. But belonging to the community is only proximately, if sometimes penultimately, important.

Ultimate belonging is what human beings have in relation to creation and to its ultimate conditions. More ultimately important than belonging to a religious community is belonging to a created world of determinate (or partially determinate) beings. This means we belong to a world that, because of form, gives us value-laden possibilities and the obligation to choose well among them. We belong to a world in which everyone has age-relative tasks of obtaining some kind of personal wholeness through proper comportment with the components of that person. We belong to a world in which we owe deference and respect to everything created with us in the existential field. Most of this world is a vast expanse of nature far beyond any human social register, and we are becoming aware of the difference the human species, with its social organizations, makes to nature. We belong to a world in which we and everything else achieves some value-identity, and in the case of human beings this means finding a meaningful life in ultimate perspective. Most of all we belong to a world of gratuitous, arbitrary, undeserved, and surprising creation, the recognition of which evokes awe and gratitude.

Whereas human beings belong to religious communities by joining them and willing to accept their authority, human beings also *belong* to creation whether recognized or not. Therefore, ultimate belonging is a matter of revelation, of waking up to what human beings are created to be. When recognized, this belonging to the ultimate realities of creation relativizes, and at the same time justifies, belonging to religious communities.

How can we know when we have taken our ultimate belonging to be to the act of creation unless we have companions who help us see it?

Part III

Summary Implications

Part III, "Normative Religion," has put forward positive philosophical/theological categories for understanding four important components of religious life. First, it presented in Chapter 9 a philosophical account of value as objectively real. The thesis was presented and defended that form itself bears value: That anything that has form has value, that to be determinate in any way is to have form, that to be is to be determinate (*I, 9*), and therefore to be is to be valuable. Value in temporal things was analyzed as a function of form in *possibilities*. Possibilities sometimes contain alternatives for actualization, which means they contain alternative possible values. Present moments involve selection among possibilities, actualizing some and excluding others. The actual includes the values selected, and it also has the value of excluding the values denied (*II, 1*).

An implication of this theory of value relative to human choice is that religion has an interest in providing interpretive categories for assessing future possibilities, categories that facilitate discerning analysis and also conjoint action to actualize values. Religious ethics, the topic of Chapter 10, thus articulates basic values as interpretive categories and fosters reflection on moral problems in light of these values. By and large, the various Axial Age religions have something like the same values for interpreting the classes of future possibilities that bear upon choice itself, human dignity, care of others, and human meaningfulness, as well as responses to creation.

Another implication of the theory of value is that the achievement of wholeness involves spiritual development, the topic of Chapter 11. Four dimensions of spiritual development were analyzed, the cultivation of wisdom, of discipline, of loving, and of excellence. Spiritual models of these include the sage, the soldier, the saint, and the virtuoso.

Being religious itself often, although not always, involves belonging to a religious community for the sake of companionship. Chapter 12 analyzed religious communities in terms of layers of association defined by semiotic structures of meaning. A religious community is a group that might cut across several cultures and that is unified by a sacred worldview in terms of which its members can achieve existential self-definition relative to ultimate realities and ultimate dimensions of experience. Most traditional religious communities are also social groups with a religious self-identification. But in the present pluralistic religious situation, many individuals treat the traditional communities as nonreligious social or cultural groups and develop their own religious communities with individuals and other groups that can be united by the sacred worldview that seems most plausible to them. Individuals can be committed to these religious communities by ceding them authority to shape their lives in ways relating to ultimacy. But ultimate belonging is not to the religious communities that facilitate our relations with ultimate reality, rather, it is to the creation itself that is constituted by the ontological creative act and that exhibits ultimate conditions of form, components, existential location, and value-identity in every creature.

The upshot of the discussion of community and religious belonging is that new models are required, different from those typical in apologetics and in the history, sociology, and anthropology of religion. These models have been supplied in the cumulative discussions of worldview beginning with the first chapter of *Philosophical Theology One.*

Chapter 10 focused on religion's orientation to possibilities and obligations, Chapter 11 on religion's orientation to the components of the human self and its wholeness, and Chapter 12 on religion's orientation to others to be engaged religiously, in religious communities. What about religion's ultimate search for meaning? This is the topic of Part IV.

Part IV

Religionless Religion

Part IV

Preliminary Remarks

Our argument so far has led to an appreciation of religion as intense involvement in the world as the venue for engaging ultimacy. But the argument has not escaped the repeated notice that sacred worldviews are difficult to find and problematic when found. This point undergirds our final approach to meaning and the confrontation with the radical contingency of the ontological act of creation.

Real religion kicks in when religion breaks down. This is an ancient religious truth. For instance, the Rg Vedic "Hymn of Creation":

1. Non-being then existed not nor being:
There was no air, nor sky that is beyond it.
What was concealed? Wherein? In whose protection?
And was there deep unfathomable water?
2. Death then existed not nor life immortal;
Of neither night nor day was any token.
By its inherent force the One breathed windless:
No other thing than that beyond existed.
3. Darkness there was at first by darkness hidden;
Without distinctive marks, this all was water.
That which, becoming, by the void was covered
That One by force of heat came into being.
4. Desire entered the One in the beginning:
It was the earliest seed, of thought the product.
The sages searching in their hearts with wisdom,
Found out the bond of being in non-being.
5. Their ray extended light across the darkness:
But was the One above or was it under?
Creative force was there, and fertile power:
Below was energy, above was impulse.

6. Who knows for certain? Who shall here declare it?
Whence was it born, and whence came this creation?
The gods were born after this world's creation:
Then who can know from whence it has arisen?
7. None knoweth whence creation has arisen;
And whether he has or has not produced it:
He who surveys it in the highest heaven,
He only knows, or haply he may know not.[1]

The deep religious traditions all have had forms of apophatic theology, the explicit recognition that the truth they are trying to express is beyond their means of expression.[2] Significant thinkers in the traditions also have known that this becomes a crisis when something happens for which their best ideas are inadequate, perhaps on a personal scale when death and suffering can never quite be domesticated by a sacred worldview, or on a social scale when one's people is destroyed, or on a cosmic scale when the flood comes or the world looks to end. Scholars such as Peter Berger, when he wrote *The Sacred Canopy* in the mid-twentieth century, worried that religion itself was collapsing into secularism under the conditions of modernity, a thesis made famous by Max Weber. But that kind of collapse was nothing new. Religions have been coping with it for millennia. The twentieth-century religious situation resolved itself into a vast efflorescence of new and evangelical religions around the world and a renewed recognition that religion is alive and vital when some of its traditional forms are not.

But a paradox lies in all of this. The truth of religions' various expressions of apophasis—the inadequacy of their sacred canopies—is a kataphatic claim. If this claim is true, that the canopies ultimately are inadequate to symbolize ultimate reality, then this claim itself is in jeopardy. A simple way to say this is that sacred canopies and the worldviews to which they give sacred dimensions are at best hypotheses about reality. As hypotheses, they are fallible and surely, in fact, are inadequate to the fullness of ultimate reality.

The simplicity of this fallibilism, however, disguises the ontological predicament. The religious function of a sacred worldview is to provide an authoritative orientation for the important dimensions of life, especially in times of crisis. The pragmatists know that we live by our hypotheses, not questioning them until some reason for questioning arises.[3] Once a hypothesis is questioned, however, particularly one as large and globally orienting as a sacred worldview, it loses its orienting authority. How then do we live regarding orientation toward ultimate matters? We live on the cusp of orientation.

Ultimacy is defined in *Philosophical Theology* in terms of finite/infinite contrasts (*I, 1, ii*). Living adequately within a sacred worldview, we are oriented directly or indirectly by the finite side of the contrasts. With respect to the finite, we take the radically contingent world as given, the possibilities with alternative values as given, the tasks of integration as given, the existential field with others as given, and the achievement of cumulative value-identity as given. The infinity in these finite/infinite contrasts is felt as a kind of mystery infecting the finite side. When we live inadequately within a sacred worldview, on the cusp of its authority, the infinite side takes equal place with the finite side. We live with the negation as well as the affirmation of ultimate reality as contained in any articulation.

How is all this to be understood (noting the irony of the fallibility of this understanding)? The first approach is to study the plausibility of sacred canopies, the topic of Chapter 13. The second, and parasitic, is to study how sacred worldviews become implausible, thematizing the issues of authority and its loss, the topic of Chapter 14. The third is to explore the depths of the ontological predicament when living on the cusp of a sacred worldview's authority, Chapter 15. The fourth is to reflect on the practice of being religious when religion itself breaks down, Chapter 16.

Chapter Thirteen

The Plausibility of Sacred Worldviews

We can begin the analysis of the plausibility of sacred worldviews by recalling the distinction between worldviews, sacred canopies, and sacred worldviews (*I, 1, 4; II, 16; III, 4, 12*). *Worldviews* are assemblages of symbols that provide orientation for the various domains of life. They provide orientation for things that exist or take place in those domains, giving them meaning; sometimes they provide further orientation by relating domains to one another. Worldviews differ from one another in the domains for which they provide orientation and in the ways they relate, or fail to relate, various domains to one another. They also differ in the kinds of connecting themes employed to relate domains, for instance, narrative, political, scientific, or metaphysical. *Sacred canopies* are parts of some worldviews that consist of symbols or symbolic networks (including theories) that provide orientation toward what is taken to be ultimate. Not all worldviews have sacred canopies. Ultimate realities have been analyzed here as finite/infinite contrasts, and the symbols within sacred canopies enable engagements with finite/infinite contrasts. In some worldviews, the domain of the sacred is related to some or all other domains, thus articulating ultimate dimensions within those other domains. A *sacred worldview* is one in which the sacred canopy is related to all or nearly all of the other domains so that everything is oriented in part to ultimacy.

Philosophical Theology Two, Chapter 16, argued that the inhabitation of a sacred worldview is important for engaging the remedies religion offers for human predicaments. To the extent a worldview contains important domains of life that are not connected with a sacred canopy, a person cannot bring the religious remedies to bear except quite indirectly. Although worldviews are contingent matters that vary considerably, *Two* throughout argued that the five elements of ultimate reality *can* be related to just about every domain: the ultimacy of obligation that comes from having possibilities for decision of different value, the ultimacy of integration of the components of one's life with a sense of grounded wholeness, the ultimacy of engaging things that are other and yet connected through one's social location, the ultimacy of achieving value-identity, and the ultimacy of the radical contingency of everything determinate. Therefore, sacred worldviews are possible, and the great religious traditions have developed versions of them that have been adapted for various circumstances by their communities and individual members.

But how can we tell which sacred worldviews are plausible for the contemporary religious situation? As long as one is in a culture that takes a sacred worldview for granted, this is not an issue. Yet people have struggled for millennia with the plausibility of sacred worldviews that are no longer taken for granted. In what does the plausibility of sacred worldviews consist? Four answers will be explored here. The first is that plausibility involves consistency of several sorts. Second, plausibility requires that the sacred worldview be applicable to the various kinds of ultimate human predicaments. Third, plausibility requires that the sacred worldview sustain the tension between transcendence and intimacy in its symbols of ultimacy and of the ultimate dimensions of things (*I, 6, 7*). Fourth, plausibility requires that the sacred worldview be authoritative in some sense, not only plausible as an hypothesis but authoritative for orienting one's approach to fallibility.

I. CONSISTENCY WITH KNOWLEDGE

Plausibility first of all requires consistency within the sacred canopy, that is, among the various symbols systems that enable the engagement of ultimates, the finite/infinite contrasts defining the boundary conditions of the world. But what does consistency mean in this circumstance? It does not necessarily mean logical consistency because sometimes the symbol systems that address ultimacy are so diverse and wild that they cannot be expressed in the well-formed formulas necessary for the application of logical analysis. The symbol systems addressing the ultimacy of obligation might have nothing on the same scale as the symbol systems addressing integration and wholeness, or as the symbol systems addressing engagement, or those addressing the achievement of ultimately important value-identity, let alone those addressing the radical contingency of the ontological creative act.

Consider, for instance, the Christian sacrifice imagery surrounding Jesus, imagery that was prominent from the earliest layers of Christian development in the New Testament, as in the Eucharistic rites, and long before symbols of Trinitarian divinity were developed. Generally, the sacrifice images function to engage the ultimate predicament of failure of obligation, which is imagined as deep impurity that prevents people from approaching God or causes them to be cast away from God. The background imagery in early Christianity is the Levitical sacrifice system in which the people's ritual impurity, which would keep them from approaching God or participating in the ritual worship, is cleansed by the performance of various animal and grain sacrifices. In the

Christian Eucharistic rite, Jesus is quoted as saying that the cup of wine is a new covenant in his blood, thus interpreting his bloody death in reference to the old covenant in which Moses sacrificed oxen and splashed half of their blood on the altar and half on the people to ratify the Sinai covenant.[1] Jesus himself was called the Lamb of God who takes away the sins of the world, a reference to the Levitical atonement right in which the sins of the people and the priest are laid on a lamb or goat who is then sent out in the wilderness to be devoured by demons (hence, the term "scapegoat").[2] But Jesus was also called the paschal lamb, in reference to the Passover remembrance of the Israelites in Egypt who smeared lamb or goat's blood over their doors to prevent God from killing their firstborn when God was killing all the other firstborn in Egypt.[3] The paschal lamb has nothing to do with sins, only with averting death. Christians also interpreted Jesus as the redemption sacrifice, in the symbol system within which people's souls were given over to Satan because of their sins and God had to redeem them with something extremely valuable, that is, his own son's life; but Satan was tricked, because he could not keep Jesus. These three symbol systems of sacrifice are not logically consistent (*I, 3, i*).

Are they coherent thematically, if not consistent logically? Whereas consistency means lack of logical contradiction, coherence means that one requires the others for its own meaning. Only partly can they be said to be coherent. Although the atonement and paschal sacrifice imageries were developed in a period when the Israelites did not believe in life much beyond death, that is, no immortality or resurrection, by the time of Jesus many Jews, particularly Hellenized ones, did have a hope to escape death. But, the weight of sin is so great, some early Christians feared, that people would die because of it. Hence, the atonement sacrifice to remove sin was coupled with the paschal sacrifice to escape death, even though the symbol systems are very different. By Jesus's time, also, Judaism had been much affected by Zoroastrian dualism in which the good divine forces are in contention with malign supernatural forces, giving a powerful negative role to Satan.[4] In this circumstance, lying underneath much of Paul's theology, human beings as sinners are pawns in the war games between God and Satan, and Jesus's redemption of human beings is a divine victory to be culminated by Jesus's bringing of all saved souls up into heaven, something a little (but not much) like the Levitical sacrifice bringing the purified people back into the presence of God.[5] By the time the sacred canopy of (some of) the Jews included a conception of immortality, some place for bad souls had to be imagined for the afterlife, that is, a hell ruled over by Satan and his minions, as an alternative to God's heaven. There is a little thematic coherence among these symbol systems, although not much.

On the other hand, these symbol systems, inconsistent and incoherent as they might be, do resonate together. Failure to take obligation seriously is crippling and must be fixed, hence, the atonement imagery. This is a matter of life and death, hence, the paschal imagery. It is also a matter of the ultimacy of the difference between good and evil, hence, the God-Satan dualism. It is a matter of the ultimate meaning of human life, hence, the heaven-hell symbolism. Because of the extraordinary complexity of the predicaments associated with obligation, symbols that address one part of it set off different symbols addressing related parts, even when the symbols themselves suppose different intellectual and existential contexts. Interestingly, nearly every other religious tradition is also deeply involved with sacrifice symbolism and rituals. There is a reason in reality why this is so, namely, the ultimate impurity that arises within the human predicament of obligation.

Jesus, of course, was not interpreted symbolically only in terms of the obligation nexus of ultimacy. He was interpreted as a healer and shepherd, bringing people to physical and spiritual health and organizing the ideal harmony of society to include feeding and healing the people. He was interpreted in terms of his ethic of love as a way of engaging other people. He was interpreted as both promising and leading a way to God as one's absolute value-identity. He was interpreted as the firstborn image of the invisible (that is, beyond determinateness) God.[6] Each of these great domains of human predicament was addressed with Christian symbol systems, often without much logical consistency or thematic coherence but with resonance. A sacred canopy, to be plausible, needs at least significant resonance.

Consistency of a different sort is required across all the domains of a worldview, in order for the worldview (as opposed only to its sacred canopy) to be plausible. Again, this is not likely to be logical consistency because the domains of a worldview are difficult if not impossible to bring into a single language of well-formed formulas. But where the worldview is formulated in well-formed formulas, logical inconsistency is a serious blow to plausibility. Those attempting to form a "scientific" worldview are most likely to attempt logical consistency. And yet scientific language is still very far from being able to articulate and connect with aesthetic and moral domains. A scientific image of the world might be able to provide an overall orientation for many domains, but it falls into radical incoherence when it denies the possibility of orienting domains of aesthetic, moral, and often existential concern. Most worldviews find consistency not in logic, or thematic coherence, but in resonance with a few basic themes. As the next chapter will argue (if it needs any argument!), to find any worldview with connection to the very many important domains in complex late-modern life with much consistency is extremely difficult.

A third place where the plausibility of sacred worldviews needs consistency is in the applicability of the symbols of the sacred canopy to the symbols of cultural life. The world of the Mediterranean in the first century was deeply committed, in most of its many cultures, to the symbolism of sacrifice. The Christians shaped the vaguely common sacrifice culture around Jesus. Twenty-first-century Africans might have a sacrifice culture similar to the ancient Mediterranean world and so can adopt the first-century Christian symbols with some ease and little sense for the need for demythologizing.[7] But twenty-first-century Europeans and Americans are very far from a sacrifice culture. How could a bad situation be improved by killing something else? they ask. This notion of sacrifice makes little cultural sense in modern and late-modern cultures. Contemporary Enlightenment and post-Enlightenment Christians (and this applies somewhat similarly to most modernized religions) have to struggle to appreciate what the bloody language of the atonement was all about. Therefore, the consistency required to make a set of ancient symbolic systems functional for a contemporary sacred canopy must come from intensive reinterpretation of the old symbols into meanings that connect with contemporary culture. The attainment of this kind of consistency was the goal of the demythologizing movement in twentieth-century Christian and Jewish theology. But theology has always engaged in this kind of transformative interpretation of religious symbols to a new context. The better this is done, the better a traditional sacred canopy can function with plausibility.

A fourth form of consistency required for the plausibility of a sacred worldview is the consistent articulation of ultimate dimensions across all the domains of the worldview. To have the consistency of resonance within the sacred canopy of symbols of ultimacy is hard enough. To have those symbols of ultimacy interpreted so as to have robust significance within contemporary culture is even harder. To develop enough consistency across the worldview so as to allow the different domains of life to be oriented to one another is hard. But to make their ultimate dimensions articulate for orienting daily life is very difficult indeed. People who live in a scientifically naive fundamentalist sacred canopy can live in a worldview that also is scientifically shaped so long as the domains are segregated; to be a fundamentalist scientist or engineer is possible by means of cognitive dissociation. But the ultimacy of the fundamentalist sacred canopy cannot be brought to bear on the domains of life oriented by the scientific parts of the worldview, and the worldview is radically inconsistent. Recognition of this is one of the motives of fundamentalist attacks on science. When ultimate crises arise, the worldview becomes implausible or dysfunctional.

II. APPROPRIATENESS FOR PREDICAMENTS AND ECSTATIC FULFILLMENTS

This last point leads to another dimension of the plausibility of sacred worldviews, namely, how well they deal with the array of human predicaments and ecstatic fulfillments, a general problem for the plausibility of worldviews, sacred or otherwise. Although worldviews are constantly modified as they are used, in an important sense they are antecedent to the events and things to which they provide orientation. A common difficulty with any traditional worldview is that it is ready to orient things that no longer happen or conditions that no longer obtain. Moreover, the arising conditions and the events that are newly important might not find any orientation in a traditional worldview. "Traditional" here does not have to mean a deep culture: The worldview that spoke effectively to the circumstances of one's youth might be dithering and silent about the circumstances of one's old age.

The concern here is with sacred worldviews. The first point to note is that the structure of a worldview's orientation of a domain of affairs is internally complex, with multiple substructures that might or might not be connected in a consistent orientation. Consider eating lunch. This act is part of the ongoing metabolic health of the diner and is to be oriented in part by the role this particular lunch plays relative to other meals and other occasions of nourishment. The act is also part of the larger field of energy needs the person has because of what he or she has been and will be doing, which in turn is part of the larger social shape of the person's life, which in turn is part of a pattern of larger social activities involving other people, and so on. The symbolic representation of each of these "implications" is something like a stack of ever-broader conditions, for example, this lunch as part of a larger diet as part of larger issues of nourishment, or this lunch as part of the person's energy needs, which are part of the person's overall activity, which is part of the social activities of which the person is a part. Much of orientation is the placing of things, events, matters, among other things, in such stacks. Most worldviews have orienting elements that symbolically bring these two "stacks" together so that nourishment and social energy needs are oriented to one another. Most worldviews also have orienting stacks for lunch that place it in stacks articulating social rituals, such as when to have lunch, with whom, and what to eat, which are themselves part of the larger issues of family and social relations. In some of these worldviews, the orienting stacks for nourishment and energy expenditure are oriented to the social ritual stacks, and in other worldviews they are not, so that the social rituals inadvertently can lead to a bad diet. Some sacred worldviews have orienting stacks such that eating lunch is an occasion to say grace and give thanks for the food, which itself is under a stack of considerations concerning the ultimacy of everyday acts as related to a sacred canopy. Eating lunch can also be oriented under a stack of considerations about the economics of the food, its cost, the conditions of its availability, the conditions under which the food comes to exist and gets to the local market, and so forth. Not many common worldviews have much depth of orientation in these matters, although reflective thinkers can point out the causal nexuses involved and say that the economic stack of orientations should be more articulate in the cultural worldview at hand. They can point out that it should also be oriented with regard to the stack of ritual observances in the ultimate dimension of eating, as well as to the stacks of orientations regarding energy use and personal nourishment.

The orientation structure of the domain of eating lunch thus has what might be called vertical and horizontal potential connections. Each stack of orienting symbolic systems has a vertical order of inclusion. The stacks themselves can have horizontal connections. The heuristic image of vertical and horizontal connections is too rigid, of course, to describe the incredibly intricate interweaving of symbolic systems. Too many diagonal lines of connection and looping connections between higher and lower levels in the interrelated stacks would have to be tracked. But it is apparent through these connections how eating lunch might be oriented in a sufficiently rich worldview to the act of harvesting a crop, which might in turn be oriented to an act of defending territory by military means, which might be oriented to an act of legislation in a government, which might be oriented to a religious system that gives legitimacy to the government as well as to the warrior as well as to the festal harvest as well as to the grace said by the person at lunch. All of these in turn might relate to symbolic systems interpreting the peoples' place in cosmic history and in the natural environment. And in turn these might be traced through the symbols of a sacred canopy to ultimate conditions of obligation, wholeness, engagement, value-identity, and sheer dependence on the ontological creative act.

All of these potential connections are based on causal connections that have symbolic expressions. The causal connections need symbolic expression because the worldview itself is a system of symbols. The causal connections are extremely important for the plausibility of a worldview. A given worldview might impute causal connections that are not real. This is not necessarily a problem unless something comes up with respect to which that causal connection is supposed to hold but does not. If, for instance, a worldview says that dancing a certain way in a drought will produce rain, and no amount of skillful dancing produces rain, the plausibility of the worldview will be strained. Other explanations might be invoked to cover the lack of causal connection, such as that the people have offended the gods who were supposed to bring rain in response to the dance. But that kind of assertion of explanatory extra-causal connections has its limits with regard to plausibility.

The Jewish interpretation of the people of Israel as the Chosen People of God contained some fairly explicit symbolized causal connections, namely, that if the people kept the covenant, God would give them prosperity in the land that had been claimed by the Canaanites. When the Israelites had difficulty taking possession of the land, it was blamed on their failure to keep the covenant. When the Assyrians, and then the Babylonians, destroyed the political nations of Israel and Judah, the great prophets attempted to blame this on the people's failure to keep the covenant. But this was strained, because the people seemed to have done too little to merit the devastation of the country. For all the promises about faithfulness and divine protection, the nation of Israel has occupied and controlled its land only for a few centuries beginning with the time of David, a few more centuries as a vassal of Greek and Roman overlords, and now less than a century under the protection of the North Atlantic powers. For many Jewish thinkers, the Nazi holocaust simply could not be explained away as somehow deserved for failure to keep the covenant, and they repudiated the causal connections asserted in the covenant. Christian assertions of causal connections between the resurrection of Jesus and the establishment of a wholly just society have suffered similar counterevidence. Paul expected Jesus to return and finish the job within Paul's own lifetime. Then the excuse was made that a day in the divine life is like a thousand years of human time, but that causal explanation wore thin. The world seems no more just now than it was in Jesus's time and has often been more unjust. So, the eschatological elements of Christianity have come to seem more and more implausible to many, while others live in continued eschatological hope. Similarly, Muslim expectations that the rigorous pursuit of Islamizing the world would lead to victory, because everything that happens is caused by the divine will, have led to problems of symbolic causation. That belief was plausible when Islam in fact was conquering the world. But when the Islamic world caved in to the European colonial powers, it was hard for many Muslims to swallow that this was God's will, and the causal symbolic network became less plausible. The humbling of China by those European colonial powers produced a similar shock to certain of the causal assumptions of the Chinese worldview.

These illustrations of the failure of imputed symbolic causal connections in large-scale, culture-wide worldviews are widely known. But nearly all individuals, with far more personalized worldviews, have known the shock of finding that some important expected causal connections, expressed in the orientations by which everyday affairs are understood, simply do not hold. Our interest here is with the sacred worldviews, and the point is that the sacred worldviews are plausible in part to the extent that their complex orienting structures articulate causal structures that turn out to be real and do not assert causal structures that turn out to be lacking.

In one sense, then, a worldview is plausible to the extent that it articulates a web of genuine causal connections or at least does not articulate causal connections that turn out to be false. In another sense, however, a worldview is plausible to the extent that it offers orientation in the first place to things that seem important on their face. Many things happen in life that have little if any meaning beyond their own characters: They receive no orientation from the worldviews at hand. When these things seem to be important, or disruptive, or painful, people seek meaning for them by orienting them in some worldview. The worldviews at hand suffer in plausibility when they cannot make sense of what happens.

Often the new things that seem meaningless come from changes in conditions. For instance, when for economic reasons people in rural conditions with extended families move to the more isolated and anonymous life of the city, perhaps being mobile in a job market that takes them from place to place, the anonymity of life seems meaningless. The old worldview that gave meaning to the individual in an extended family has nothing to offer for the new conditions, except perhaps lament for the passing of the good old days. A new worldview for orienting social identity through life's developments is needed. The migrations of people, the fortunes of war, changing climate, and a host of other "accidents" can render old worldviews implausible because they simply provide little or no orientation in the new conditions. Changes in personal life circumstances can have a similar effect.

One of the advantages of a richly textured sacred worldview is that the sacred elements point to relatively transcendent conditions that are likely not to be affected by changes in local circumstances. This is to say, many sacred canopies are adept at accounting for changes in social organization, migrations, the fortunes of war, and even changing climate. Nevertheless, the transcendence easy for sacred orientation carries its own liability for the plausibility of sacred worldviews, as we see in the next section.

III. SUSTAINING INTIMACY AND TRANSCENDENCE IN SYMBOLS

The plausibility of sacred worldviews depends very much on sustaining the tension between the transcendence in the symbols of ultimacy and the intimacy that makes them relevant to the orientation of the various domains of life. *Philosophical Theology One*, Chapters 6 and 7, as well as in *Three*, Chapters 5 through 8, discussed the needs for both transcendence and intimacy. In respect of plausibility, the symbols of ultimacy need to be thoroughly transcendent because challenges to plausibility easily take the form of showing that what is represented as ultimate in fact is proximate and perhaps a distortion of its ultimate background. *Philosophical Theology* argues that there are five irreducible domains of ultimacy based on the metaphysics of determinate being. To repeat them, these are (1) the possession of form, which means for human beings the facing of alternate possibilities of differing value, (2) the possession of components, which means for human beings the issues of comporting the whole toward the integrities of the components, (3) the possession of existential location, which means for human beings the issues of engagement with others as others yet intimate in mutual definition, (4) the possession of absolute value-identity, which means for human beings the achievement of meaning before the ultimate, and (5) the radical contingency of all of the aforementioned ultimate conditions on the ontological creative act, which means for human beings all the issues of being creatures of gratuitous, arbitrary, undeserved, and surprising existence.

As expressed in the sacred canopy itself, and in the dimensions of ultimacy that a sacred worldview articulates for various mundane domains, the sacred canopy is plausible to the extent that it preserves connection with the five finite/infinite contrasts involved. The complexity of this task is not to be overestimated, because each of these contrasts can be symbolized only through a variety of interlocked approaches.

For instance, the ultimate boundary area of obligation requires the symbolic articulation of the situation of facing possibilities with alternative realizations, alternatives with structures that yield different kinds and degrees of value. The possibility field must be interpreted as affording opportunities for human influence. Subtle symbolic accounts need to register that the actualization of one alternative includes within the actual result the exclusion of the alternative values that might have been actualized. The symbolic accounts need to articulate how the choosers define their own identity by the choices they make, as well as the values in their choices. The accounts need to articulate conjoint actions, and the differential results for the identities of the individuals and of the social group that binds them in conjoint action. The accounts need to articulate the problems of coming to understand the possible alternatives and how to achieve them and what to do about the fact that possibilities themselves can be articulated only in the respects in which a person's culture has appropriate signs. The accounts need to discriminate the kinds of guilt that result from failures of obligation. Most of all, and most difficult to track, the symbolic accounts need to be able to distinguish the proximate affairs of specific choices among possibilities from the ultimate affairs of responding to the choices as matters of obligation. Proximate guilts have to do with bad choices. Ultimate guilts have to do with subversions of obligation as such. Sacred worldviews need symbols of ultimacy relative to possibilities that keep the distinctions alive between proximate and ultimate guilts.

Similarly, the ultimate boundary condition of having components needs to find in a sacred worldview the ability to symbolize the important components of human life, taking into account not only local affairs but also the components as defined by the other ultimate boundary areas. The worldview needs also to symbolize the various interrelated senses of self or wholeness in a human harmony so as to articulate how those senses can be diversely comported to the various components. The failures with regard to addressing the predicament of proper comportment need to be articulated in their various consequences and in their self-defeating modes. Most important, the worldview as sacred needs to articulate the distinction between proximate failures of proper comportment in grounded wholeness and the ultimate failure to address comportment and grounded wholeness itself.

Likewise, with regard to the ultimacy of engagement, a sacred worldview needs to be able to symbolize the important kinds of things to be engaged, including individuals, social institutions, and nature in a broader sense. It needs to articulate the senses of otherness involved and the senses of existential mutuality as exhibited in the existential field. As with the other ultimate boundary areas, it needs to distinguish between proximate successes and failures of engagement and the ultimate commitments to or withdrawal from engagement itself.

With regard to the ultimacy of achieving a value-identity, a sacred worldview needs symbols to articulate all the ways in which a person holds value subjectively within the person's own harmony, as well as the ways in which a person objectively affects or even effects values that are parts of other harmonies, including other persons, social institutions, and undomesticated nature. A sacred worldview needs to symbolize important distinctions between the value-identity a person just accumulates through existential involvement in life and those aspects of value-identity that are the person's own responsibilities. And in all of this, if the worldview is to be plausible as a sacred worldview articulating the ultimate, distinctions need to be symbolized between the proximate achievements of value-identity and the ultimate predicament of facing absolute value-identity as such.

Finally, a sacred worldview is plausible to the extent it can symbolize the radical contingency of the world and the power of the ontological act of creation in which the mutual togetherness of the multitude of things exists. Although many finite things might seem to "explain" the existence of the radically contingent manifold of determinate things, those finite things themselves must be recognized as created and their transcendence given voice. Otherwise, that pervasive sense of contingency, for which the subjective form in human experience includes gratuitousness, arbitrariness, undeservedness, and utter surprise, will not be recognized and the plain non-ultimacy of proximate finitude will ruin the sacredness of the worldview. In all these instances, as expressed in the vast variety of religious symbolic structures articulating the vertical and horizontal connections of orientation in a worldview, a failure to tie the symbols to a system that registers transcendent ultimacy threatens the plausibility of the sacred worldview.

Nevertheless, an opposite and competing requirement for plausibility exerts its pressures on a sacred worldview. In each of its domains, the symbols of ultimacy need to be given such intimate expression that they can relate to the particular circumstances in which individuals and groups have predicaments. Respecting the proper pressures for transcendence, sacred worldviews can succumb to the temptations to employ only such transcendent symbols as are immune to the critical tractions of concrete life. Yet those symbols do not actually orient the particulars of life to ultimacy unless they can engage life's intimate details. Therefore, interpretive chains must be included within sacred worldviews that connect the distinctions just mentioned concerning the five ultimate places of life's boundary conditions with individual circumstances.

For instance, everyone betrays friends on occasion, say, by slighting them in a social situation in favor of attending to someone else. Proximately considered, this is something people regularly deal with, trying to make amends, to repair the breach in friendship, and to cope with the situations and pressures that cause a particular betrayal in the first place. This is just part of life. But, in addition, any such betrayal is an ultimate failure of obligation to the friend, something of ultimate significance. Although it would be foolish, indeed pathological perhaps, to give ultimate significance to a single incident of slight, still that incident lies within the overall ultimacy of moral obligation, and it needs to be interpreted in terms of what it means for the individual's relation to ultimate obligation. Not to have some interpretive chain that relates the proximate incident to the ultimate context of obligation would be to admit a false disruption of the chain of conditions behind the incident leading to the ultimate conditions defining obligation as such. The incident would be peculiarly meaningless in terms of some of the ultimate conditions of life. So, the worldview needs to include symbolic resources for connecting each morally freighted action to the ultimate conditions of obligation.

So also with regard to components. Knowing that one should comport oneself with all the forms of proper comportment to the important components of life so as to be a whole self is not immediately connected with how to relate to the problems of one's diet, or lifestyle, or slighting of a friend. The slighting of a friend is not only a predicament of failure on grounds of obligation: It is also a predicament of one's wholeness as a friend of others. So, a sacred worldview needs interpretive symbols to relate each of the issues of comportment to the transcendent ultimate matter of being an integrated, well-grounded, whole self. The components have their own integrities that need to be registered within one's wholeness, and this is a universal ultimate condition. How can a particular issue be interpreted in this regard, not just in its own proximate terms but in its ultimate terms? The sacred worldview needs to provide interpretive procedures and symbols to do this.

The same is true with regard to the ultimate grounds for engaging others as other and yet intimately connected. The proximate issues of engagement can be oriented in many proximate ways, such as discussed in the previous section. But each issue also has an ultimate dimension that needs to be interpreted in the case of the proximate issue. The ultimate dimension of engagement needs to be registered in each case of engagement that involves the human predicament. So, Confucians present interpretive rituals that symbolize different forms of engaged human relations as ultimately important for individuation. Christians say that each person should be loved, and that this applies to loving enemies, as interpreted in the parable of the Good Samaritan.

With regard to achieving absolute value-identity, that lofty condition needs to be interpreted in terms of the singularity of a person's life, allowing the person to come to terms with the details of existence, the idiosyncrasies, the bland commonalities, the particular histories, and intimate subjective feelings of pride, contempt, aversion, and passion. Without interpretive chains that can allow a person to identify her or his own specifics in light of the ultimacies of individual value-identity, the transcendent conditions are not intimate enough to orient the person in the worldview, and the worldview itself suffers in plausibility.

The tension between transcendence and intimacy in sacred worldviews shows that worldviews are not merely static symbol systems. Rather, they also involve symbols for keying in processes of interpretation. No sacred worldview would contain the interpretive chains ready-made for making the transcendent references to ultimacy in the various predicament areas intimate to the address of those predicaments. But the sacred worldviews need to articulate the need and perhaps procedures for interpreting the transcendent to the intimate. Some religious traditions include within their worldviews expressions of the institutions of spiritual formation and guidance. This is particularly true of those traditions that put the role of the guru in a dominant place. Other traditions have substituted roles for psychotherapy, or existential self-analysis. To the extent that sacred worldviews do not recognize the need for interpretation of the transcendent ultimacies in terms of the intimate conditions, they lack a crucial element of plausibility.

IV. AUTHORITY IN ORIENTATION

Another element of plausibility is the authority of the sacred worldview. So long as the sacred worldview is simply the presumed, habituated, background collection of orientations, its authority is unproblematic and consists simply in the fact that it is in use. But when the worldview is questioned, or even brought to consciousness as a somewhat connected set of orientations, the function of authority in plausibility is raised.

Hardly ever are worldviews contemplated as wholes. Most people are aware of areas of their worldview when they are relevant to orienting something at hand and would think about the scope, coherence, and validity of the worldview as a whole only under special circumstances. Nevertheless, just because of the more or less tight connections among the various domains of a worldview, all of a worldview has some kind of authority attached to it. The subtle problem for analysis is that whatever authorizes different domains might be different in each case. In a worldview with serious disconnections between the sacred canopy and various occupational domains, say, which are oriented by powerful symbols of a scientific worldview, that which gives authority to the scientific domains is different from that which gives authority to the more directly religious ones. What gives authority to the domains of life involving domesticity might be family tradition, while that which gives authority to the domains of politics might be the philosophy of a particularly charismatic high school teacher. In this sense there usually exists a plurality of domains each with different sources of authority, say, scientific culture, biblical fundamentalism, family tradition, influential political philosophies. If any one of these is challenged and rejected, the others might stand. A scientist, for instance, might become persuaded by theological creationism and give up the authority of science even for those domains of life that practice science; or the person might lose the fundamentalist faith; or the person might come to perceive the family domestic traditions as distinctly dysfunctional, or change basic political philosophies. The other authorizing elements, governing other domains, might not be much affected.

Nevertheless, because worldviews orient domains to one another, as well as the various items within each domain, more unifying senses of authority are also involved. The connections among domains (or the worldview's representation that there is no connection, as in the case of people who keep their religion and science strictly separate), themselves need authority. Nothing is to say that all the orienting connections among the domains need to be authorized by the same thing. A variety of thematic types of connections might exist among select domains in life, perhaps several types making connections (perhaps inconsistently) across the same domains. But each of those thematic types needs to be authoritative and might have its own kind of authorization.

What is meant by authorization? Something makes a worldview, or a stretch of a worldview, authoritative. Many different kinds of things can give such authority. Cultural prestige is perhaps the most common; in late-modern society, the scientific enterprise itself has great cultural prestige whereas religion does not; in other societies, religion has more prestige than science. Charismatic personalities can give rise to the authority of worldviews or stretches of domains of worldviews with which they are associated. Sometimes, antiquity of tradition gives authority; other times, successful novelty in points of view gives authority. Sometimes, the very richness of a text, such as the Vedas or the Bible, and the plurality of fruitful ways in which it can be interpreted, in David Tracy's sense of the "classic," gives authority to worldviews that claim those texts.[8] In respect to sacred canopies in worldviews, and in their bearings on other domains, authority sometimes derives from expressions of revelation that seem compelling. When claims to revelation are challenged, sometimes their authorizing force is diminished.

These remarks have pointed up some of the objective characters of authority in sacred worldviews, things that make the worldviews, or at least significant stretches of their connected domains, seem authoritatively compelling. The subjective side of authority is just as important, however: The authoritativeness of the worldview must be accepted as such. Sometimes that acceptance of authority is continuous with its objective compulsion. But, sometimes, a worldview is not authoritative except insofar as a person accepts it as authoritative.

Particularly is this true with regard to sacred worldviews. Protestant Christian fideism is perhaps an extreme case but illustrative. In this religious construction, one chooses membership in Christianity and that choice means the acceptance of some Christian sacred worldview as authoritative. In cases where belonging to a religion is a matter of choice and of commitment to live by that choice, part of the choice is the granting of authority to the associated sacred worldview. Though not an extreme fideist, Augustine "converted" to Christianity by putting on a Christian worldview like putting on the garments of a responsible adult.[9] This worldview became authoritative for him, whereas before it had been only an option. To be sure, he modified the worldview in which he invested himself in public ways like no one before or since. But it was authoritative for him because he willed it to be.

Contemporary global society is much like Augustine's Mediterranean world. Any inherited worldview is likely to be placed alongside other sacred worldviews so that even the matter of carrying on one's inheritance involves at least a modicum of choice to do so in the face of options. But with the world changing as fast as it is, the domains of life are under constant revision and new ones are arising. Hardly any worldview can be inherited from a generation ago without change, which means at least a slightly new affirmation of its authority. So, part of living in a situation in which oriented meaning is sought is the ongoing subjective work of affirming the authority of a worldview or some stretch of one. Regarding sacred worldviews, the commitments perhaps made in adolescence need steady, if minor, revision and reaffirmation. Part of a person's absolute value-identity is the cumulative revisions and affirmations of the authority of the worldview by which life is oriented. For those people who are seriously religious and strive to achieve a dense inhabitation of a sacred worldview, the subjective affirmation of the authority of the worldview is a matter of ultimacy.

We need to raise a final problem with authority here for exploration in subsequent chapters. Regardless of what kind of authority is affirmed for a sacred worldview, its logical status is that of an hypothesis that is fallible. A sacred worldview is a large-scale, variously coherent, hypothesis for engaging reality for the purpose of orienting the affairs of life. That the sacred worldview is fallible does not mean that it is wrong, although surely all worldviews can be improved. But it does mean that it might be wrong. The more one understands one's sacred worldview, the more its authority, as well as its specific and overall orienting functions, are perceived as vulnerable to correction. The subjective side of affirming authority needs to cope with the recognition of fallibility. Otherwise, the plausibility of the sacred worldview is weakened.

This chapter has analyzed in general terms some of the conditions for the plausibility of a sacred worldview. To be plausible, a sacred worldview needs important kinds of consistency, appropriateness for orienting the actual affairs of life, successful ways of balancing transcendence and intimacy in symbolizing ultimacy in the various dimensions of life, and objective authority subjectively affirmed. The next chapter makes these general terms concrete by discussing plausibility and implausibility in current situations.

Chapter Fourteen

The Implausibility of Sacred Worldviews

The positive purpose of this chapter is to lay down some conditions for the development of an adequate sacred worldview (*III, 4*). The negative purpose of the present chapter is to discuss some of the serious difficulties for traditional sacred worldviews occasioned by the contemporary situation. Its order follows that of Chapter 13. With regard to issues of consistency, it will focus on the challenges of science and scientific worldviews for sacred canopies; Chapter 1 in this volume presented positive elements of a scientific sacred worldview. With regard to issues of appropriateness, the chapter will focus on the challenges of a global society; in Chapter 2, we saw a positive conception of Axial Age religion for the contemporary global society. With regard to issues of transcendence and intimacy in symbolizing ultimacy, the present chapter focuses on the challenges of a purposeless cosmos for a symbol system that handles ultimacy (*III, 9*); Chapter 4 developed this positively for contemporarily plausible systems of normative, historical religious sacred worldviews. With regard to issues of authority, the present chapter focuses on the challenges of fallibility that will be developed in existential terms in Chapter 15.

I. CONSISTENCY AND SCIENCE

The great challenge to traditional sacred worldviews in this late-modern or postmodern period is science. The picture of the cosmos that is being filled in with such critical empirical success by the sciences is radically different from the pictures of the cosmos that were current at the time of the formation of the great world religions. This is true for the ancient cultures of East Asia, West Asia, and South Asia, diverse as their ancient world pictures were. First, scientific physics and astronomy upended the traditional world pictures, and then evolutionary biology and now biochemistry are making the ancient world pictures seem even more dated.

The great European philosophers who were involved in the development of modern science recognized this challenge of conflicting world pictures to traditional sacred worldviews. Descartes, Hobbes, Locke, Spinoza, Leibniz, Hume, Kant, Hegel, and others were careful to articulate the emerging scientific world picture in conjunction with astonishingly imaginative new conceptions of God as the ultimate in their Christian or Jewish sacred canopies, and all tried to articulate a consistent, new sacred worldview. Spinoza developed the rudiments of a sophisticated theory of hermeneutics that directly addressed what should be done with the old world picture in order to carry on a (Jewish, in his case) sacred canopy consistent with science as he understood it. The demythologization movement in twentieth-century Christianity also attempted to respond to this challenge.

The first kind of consistency in sacred worldviews challenged by science is consistency within the sacred canopy domain. The fundamental challenge is that any determinate thing depicted as ultimate needs to be explained by science or something consistent with science. For, if it is determinate, it needs explanation in terms of that with respect to which it is determinate and in terms of why it exists at all. This is a devastating criticism of all those sacred canopies that depict God as ultimate and yet as having a nature, such as personhood, potential agency apart from creation, and goodness in any determinate sense. Science points out that these determinate characteristics are all to be understood in terms of causal developments, for instance, the development of personhood through relations with others, defining potential agency in terms of others to be acted upon with antecedent resources, and so forth. Any determinate God would have to be explained in terms of things that are not God, which runs counter to most claims about ultimacy and divine aseity.

By contrast, the conception of God as the otherwise indeterminate ontological act of creation is completely consistent with science. Anything determinate is created, according to this notion of *Philosophical Theology*, and thus can be understood and explained by science so far as science is able. Nothing in the notion of creating *ex nihilo* conflicts with a scientific claim that everything determinate is to be understood in terms of other determinate conditions: The respects in which things are determinate are to be understood in terms of conditional components working through the existential field. The conceptions of form, components, existential location, and value-identity are also claimed to be ultimate in *Philosophical Theology*. Insofar as they are determinate, they are determinate with respect to one another within the concept of harmony, and the hypothesis about determinateness itself as harmony conflicts with nothing scientific. Science itself must presuppose that some hypothesis about determinateness is possible in order to formulate any concepts of explanation. The existence of the ultimates of form, components, existential location, and value-identity is explained by the ontological creative act, although in a dialectical way: For anything to exist at all, it needs to be determinate, and so determinateness is ultimate in the sense that, if there is to be anything, it has to have the transcendental traits of harmony.

But the conception of an ontological act of creation is very far from many conceptions of God as a personal agent who both creates and acts within the created world. These are the conceptions that have widespread acceptance today among theistic religions and that determine many people's worldviews in those religions. They, alas, are not consistent with science, which tends to render them implausible. Conceptions of the ultimate based on metaphors of consciousness and emergence do not have this difficulty with science because they contain inner apophatic notions that push toward indeterminacy. Pure consciousness is not determinate—Brahman without qualities—neither is the spontaneous source from which all things with properties emerge.

The second area of consistency challenged by science is that bridging the domains of a sacred worldview, especially bridging across the connections of the sacred canopy with any other domains. Most traditional sacred canopies are expressed in terms of ancient world pictures. Many other domains in contemporary life are expressed in terms of scientific world pictures. A sacred worldview might be consistent if the sacred and scientific domains are kept wholly apart. But how can that be? To gaze up and see outer space and not heaven is difficult, and so is the opposite, seeing heaven and not outer space. But most difficult for the consistency of total segregation of stretches of a sacred worldview is the fact that those stretches cannot be oriented to one another. And so the sacred worldview does not give any meaning to one side in terms of the others.

This is particularly difficult for the third area of consistency, which is the need of the symbols of ultimacy in the sacred canopy to bear on the other domains in the worldview. A worldview with a sacred canopy that does not bear on the other important domains is hardly a sacred worldview. Yet the symbols of ultimacy in the sacred canopy are not relevant for much of life at all unless they can be significant elements in the orientation of each important mundane domain. If the culture of that domain is radically discontinuous with the symbolic structure of the ultimate elements, then a radical inconsistency will make the sacred worldview implausible and ineffective as well. So, how can the ancient elements in the sacred worldview be interpreted within the worldview so as to relate to contemporary ways of thinking? The sacred worldviews that do not incorporate this serious interpretive function will be implausible. More of the problems of interpretation will be discussed in Section III in this chapter.

Perhaps the most important kind of consistency question for sacred worldviews is that by which the many important mundane domains are reshaped by connections with the sacred canopy. To have consistent symbols of ultimacy in the sacred canopy as interpreted through science is one thing. To have consistency in symbols that connect the many domains within a worldview is another. It is yet another thing to have consistency between the symbols of the sacred canopy and the various cultural expressions of the other important domains. At this point, many people who live richly developed contemporary cultural lives simply give up on sacred canopies in their worldview.

Nevertheless, the challenge to make explicit the connected representations of ultimate dimensions in many different domains remains. The ideological domain of thinking respectfully about everyone is contradicted by a domain that says respect is limited to those in a culture like one's own. The domain of finding ultimate meaning in befriending certain people who have betrayed and demeaned one sometimes is cut off from befriending people who are one's explicit and active enemies. The domain of engaging nature in conservational ways is sometimes cut off from engaging nature that immanently will kill you or destroy your place. The domain of finding meaning in one's absolute value-identity might be focused on elements in the values of others that one might control; but this is different and sometimes alien from the aspects of value in others that are beyond one's control.

This last point leads to the final one in this section: What is consistency in a sacred worldview insofar as individuals' absolute value-identity is formed? This is perhaps the most difficult question of consistency of all. At the first level is the problem of learning how to conceive one's value identity in terms of others, when the others turn out to be much different from what one expected. This point will be expressed in many contexts to come.

At the second level is the recognition that much modern science supposes that some neutral overarching perspective exists from which all things can be seen in their proper connections and disconnections. But this scientific supposition is false. Every perspective for judgment is particular, however generalized. Furthermore, there can exist no concrete perspective from which the differences among essential components of really different things are represented together (*I, 13; II, 4*). Some finite perspective is always presupposed and that finite perspective reduces the essential elements of the other to components of the perspective. So, at the third level, consistency is gained only by finding ways to get any finite context of comparison of ultimately real things (with their separate essential components) to deconstruct. The only solution to this existential problem of sacred worldviews is the cultural acceptance of any finite domain as what it is, described, however, as something created and thus related to the ultimates of radical contingency, form, components, existential location, and value-identity. This is the ontological context of mutual relevance: To preserve respect for mutually engaged otherness requires representing the things and oneself as together in the ontological context of mutual relevance, with some symbols or other for this ontological context. In this context, things are together with their separate essential components. Only in this context can we formulate the respect due to each other. But there is no finite perspective on this ontological togetherness within that context; all finite perspectives are limited to cosmological togetherness except through symbols of the ontological act itself.

II. APPROPRIATENESS FOR A GLOBAL SOCIETY

The plausibility of a worldview depends in part on its being appropriate to the conditions of life to which it aims to provide orientation (*III, 13, ii*). Appropriateness includes being applicable to the conditions and also being adequate in the sense of addressing the conditions.

The contemporary conditions for a plausible sacred canopy for all but the most isolated individuals include social location in a global society that is knit together in various ways by new technologies of communication, travel, and business. A useful distinction is to be drawn at this point between society and culture.[1] A society is defined by the lines of causation of social interaction, and hardly anyone today is exempt from being caught up in causal patterns that involve nearly everyone else. These patterns include economic, military, political, intellectual, artistic, and scientific matters, and many forms of communication; they also include effects on the environment caused in one place and affecting other places, perhaps the whole globe, as in the case of global warming. Any social form with which people and institutions in a society interact is part of that society by virtue of the causal interaction. A culture, by contrast, is a system of meanings that has identity in part through its various distinctions from the meaning systems of other cultures. People have a common culture precisely at those points where it might be possible for them to have different cultures, where the meaning systems agree in fact although they might not agree.

To be sure, the contours of the meaning systems defining cultures are subject to much debate. Sometimes cultures are understood in very broad terms as, for instance, Samuel Huntington did in his *The Clash of Civilizations and the Remaking of World Order*. Other times cultures are understood in micro-analytic terms, as when the culture of one family is compared with those of its neighbors. Anthropologists began the modern social scientific understanding of culture with the analysis of relatively isolated tribal cultures whose meaning systems developed from within, as it were, in contrast to cultures that define themselves in part by distinction from other cultures.

The relevant sense of culture for the present discussion is that provided by a sacred worldview. We live in a global society but have many different sacred worldviews, each of which in part defines a religious culture. To say that the different worldviews correspond to different religions is tempting, and for shorthand purposes this is sometimes satisfactory. So, there are Buddhist, Confucian, Christian, Daoist, Hindu, Jewish, Muslim, and secular sacred worldviews. But, of course, many mutually contradicting variants have been developed within each one of these, and each variant has mutually contradicting subvariants arising from local conditions, and each individual individuates the local sacred worldview in ways different from everyone else. Moreover, in actual religious life many crossovers exist among the top-down named religious traditions so that a given local community's actual sacred worldview might not be named accurately by the larger tradition designation; individuals are far more syncretistic, particularly in a religiously pluralistic situation.

The last several chapters (and *II, 16*) have elaborated the point that serious engagement of ultimacy requires richly inhabiting a sacred worldview, which includes involvement with the practices associated with it. The sacred worldview orients not only more or less direct engagements with ultimacy, as in worship and ritual, but also the indirect engagements relative to the ultimate dimensions of otherwise mundane domains of life. The previous section sketched some of the ways in which a sacred worldview, to be plausible, must consistently orient many concrete affairs together regarding ultimacy. So, the sacred worldview needs to be particular enough to orient a given individual's life, particular also in most instances to orient a social group's life in ultimate matters. Given the differences among both individuals and communities, sacred worldviews, in order to be plausible, need to be particular and different from one another when they work to orient significantly different lives.

So, traditional sacred worldviews have in nearly all instances defined themselves in distinction from, often in opposition to, alternative sacred worldviews and developed their particularities through those oppositions. Good historical reasons lie behind this opposition, of course. Most religious traditions originate in opposition or transformation of some previous tradition. The result, however, is that concrete life within a traditional sacred worldview is distinctive over against the concrete life of alternatives, and in that lies its particularities. Some common elements obtain, as when both Buddhists and Hindus meditate in a cross-legged yoga posture, assuming that posture to align the spine with natural energies although meditating to quite different purposes; Christians, Jews, and Muslims pray in different postures from one another and from the South Asians but with the common assumption that their postures are forms of prostration before God as a king. The point is that the rich inhabitation of a sacred worldview most likely needs some concrete form of meditation. Given today's religious pluralism in most of the world, to sit cross-legged on some occasions, to kneel on others, to daven on yet others, and sometimes to meditate while playing taijiquan, is possible. Yet the more diverse the forms practiced by any one person, the less likely any will be practiced with the seriousness of an adept, and fascination with such diversity sometimes leads to serious investment in none. Serious inhabitation of a sacred worldview requires definite particularity in the worldview and the practices it orients. One has to be a something, not an anything, in religious matters.

How then can inhabitation of a sacred worldview avoid an in-group mentality that is destructive of engagements with people outside the culture of one's sacred worldview? The ultimate conditions of obligation demand that individuals treat others with justice, regardless of whether the others belong to one's in-group. Engagement of others requires respecting their own essential subjectivities while also respecting their connections, which in this case means different religious cultures.

The history of religions has exhibited enormous conflicts based on bigotry and hostility toward out-groups and their members. The evil of this has been recognized in principle since the arising of the Axial Age religions, but the practice has too often been plainly contradictory to the universality of justice and care. The last century has witnessed a great flourishing of interfaith dialogue, perhaps best symbolized as inaugurated by the 1893 World Parliament of Religions in Chicago. One cumulative result of that dialogue, or its very many particular dialogues, has been recognition among the religious elites that all religions have paths to what they take to be ultimate, even when the ultimate is articulated diversely.[2] In some circumstances, the elite leaders of different traditions can practice their particular ways next to one another. Nevertheless, the elites are usually not representative of the rank and file of their own communities. Evangelical Christians, for instance, often believe that evangelical Christianity is the only real engagement of ultimacy and that the others are potential enemies unless they can be converted; some Roman Catholics and Muslims feel the same way.

But the social practice or ritual of mutual toleration of alternative intense inhabitations of different sacred worldviews, though a great advance on bigotry and hostility, is inadequate by itself. How can one respect a practitioner of a very different religious culture, defined by a different sacred worldview, without appreciating that other's worldview from within? And how can one come to appreciate that other's sacred worldview from within without practicing it to some degree, dwelling within that other sacred worldview in the intimacies of daily life? The evangelical Christian has a serious point: To tolerate someone else's religion as merely different is to not care much about that person. Therefore, care for the other means either converting that person to one's own sacred worldview for engaging ultimacy or coming to know that other's ways of engaging ultimacy through some serious degree of participation from the inside.

In our global society, the plausibility of a sacred worldview requires both particularity and openness to knowing others with alternative sacred worldviews (including most secular worldviews that define ultimacy in anti-traditional terms). Knowing those others, so as to respect them with care and justice, entails inhabiting their own sacred worldviews to some degree. Therefore, one's own sacred worldview is plausible, in part, to the extent that it registers alternative sacred worldviews and orients one's own practices within those alternatives required for coming to respect those who live according to them. Contemporary sacred worldviews suffer in plausibility to the extent that they are not particular enough for orienting concrete life, and also to the extent that they do not embrace the alternative sacred worldviews within themselves. For, to the degree they fail in the latter, they fail to articulate engaging others with justice and care. Most traditional sacred worldviews are struggling to develop ways to embrace their alternatives and internalize them. To embrace the alternatives is not, as such, to say that the alternatives are valid, only that they are the sacred worldviews of others who need to be treated with justice and care. The embrace of the alternatives is to internalize them to the point where the empirical issues of validity can be addressed, just as one addresses those issues with regard to one's own sacred worldview.

The reason this internalizing of other sacred worldviews within one's own is so important is that one's sacred worldview needs to be appropriate to the ultimate predicaments of life and to offer its remedies. These ultimate predicaments include the obligations to relate to people with commitments to other sacred worldviews (or to none); the issues of self-integration with grounded wholeness when this includes integrating across conflicting internalized worldviews; issues of engaging others with respect, justice, and love; and issues of achieving an absolute value-identity that includes the value one contributes to others who might be in conflict about ultimacy with oneself. If one's sacred worldview does not address these issues forced by the causal interactions of a global society that require engagements across such conflict, it is not plausible as appropriate for the human predicament as concretely expressed.

III. TRANSCENDENCE AND INTIMACY IN A PURPOSELESS COSMOS

Traditional sacred canopies generally exhibit a peculiar dual consciousness. On the one hand, they elaborate forms that allow human life to be contained within the wild cosmos by domesticating the ultimate, and, on the other hand, they have their apophatic moments when they symbolize the very breakdown of those domestic limitations. Many West Asian sacred canopies, and some South Asian ones, represent the cosmos to be created with a purpose for human life within it, such that the events that seem destructive of human life still can be reconciled to that divine purpose. East Asian sacred canopies often represent the ultimate as giving a central place to human life, as in the Confucian motto about the human completing Heaven and Earth; Greek and Roman Paganism is close to this type. Many South Asian sacred canopies, found in Hinduism and Buddhism, represent the ultimate purpose of life to be escape from time's flow, with various understandings of how one's real self (or lack of one) is defined in relation to the ultimate. All of these sacred canopies provide containment for human life and allow for the development of sacred worldviews within which that containment can be lived out.

But late-modern science has painted world pictures that are incompatible with most of those domesticated representations of ultimacy. The size and age of the cosmos, when grasped by some symbolic means or other, make it wholly implausible to think of the human race as the center of the universe, the purpose for which all else is made. However miraculous in complexity and potential excellence, human beings are not a microcosm of the universe. However important they are to us, human history and affairs are but flotsam on the gaseous sea of natural processes. However containing the projects of liberation from the conditions of time and change might be, including the obligations of compassion for suffering, those projects amount to no more than what individuals can achieve, no more or less. However intricate and coordinated the human design, fitted into a precious and fragile environment for human habitation, all this comes from the blind causal processes of evolution.

The cosmos is so vast that the human place is but an accident, of short duration at that, in cosmic history. The values that are achieved in human civilization and individual lives are simply what they are. The only purposes are those of human beings. Life has no meaning beyond the meaning contained within itself, in its enjoyments and histories. The scientific world picture says, on the one hand, that the cosmos is utterly wild and undomesticated and, on the other hand, that it works according to powers that are not scaled to purposeful human life. While sacred (or non-sacred worldviews) might deny this stark scientific picture of the universe, this picture describes the lives people live, more or less well. Many things happen, in defiance of some traditional sacred worldviews, to reinforce this picture, and the science is becoming well-enough known in popular terms that people come to recognize and accept the scientific world picture in times of crisis. Sacred worldviews that attempt to domesticate cosmic wildness lose plausibility. The world cannot be seriously conceived to be a kingdom ruled over by a divine king; nor are human responsibilities to be limited to the obedience of a vassal.

The result is pressure to make the symbols of ultimacy in sacred canopies more and more transcendent (*I, 6*). To develop transcendent symbols of the ultimate in ways compatible with the blind wildness of the cosmos is quite possible. The symbols of an ultimate ontological act of creation giving rise to determinate things with the ultimate traits of form, components, existential location, and value-identity are examples of a sacred canopy that is compatible with the scientific world picture. Nevertheless, symbols of ultimacy transcendent enough to resonate with the scientific world picture can lack the intimacy for many people necessary to allow the ultimate to be relevant to the mundane domains of life in a sacred worldview. How can there be ultimate dimensions of life's matters when the symbols of ultimacy are so undomesticated?

Plausibility in a sacred worldview today requires sustaining the tension between transcendent symbols of ultimacy and symbols of ultimacy sufficiently intimate to allow the worldview to orient the concrete affairs of life. This is not a new problem. Thomas Aquinas, for instance, knew from philosophical arguments that God should be conceived in ways wholly transcending the determinate world and did so with his idea of the pure, simple, infinite Act of To Be, a notion of actuality developed from Aristotle's metaphysics of act and potency. Yet Thomas knew also that this transcendent sense of God was useless for orienting people's daily lives if it could not in turn be symbolized with intimate symbols; for him, those of the Bible. So, he developed an elaborate theory of analogy according to which the infinite Act of To Be could be symbolized in analogy with finite human virtues and powers, eventually as a divine agent who could act in history. Thomas's theory was that all the finite acts of determinate things are delimitations of the infinite act in God, so that God could possess finite determinate traits, such as goodness and rationality, albeit in infinite form. Thomas could avail himself of biblical materials, therefore, but with the tacit understanding that he was speaking only analogically, and those biblical materials provided the intimate symbols needed to orient Christian life. Of course, Thomas's doctrine of analogy fails. If finite traits are infinite in God, they are indeterminate, not like their finite versions, not different from one another, not even different from nothing, and the biblical symbols of finite divine character cannot be applied to God. Nevertheless, Thomas was right that the transcendent symbols of ultimacy, metaphysical in his case (and in that of *Philosophical Theology*), need to be interpretable with symbols of intimacy.

The theology of symbolic engagement developed in *Philosophical Theology* addresses the questions of intimate symbols for that which is known also to be radically transcendent with its theory of reference. Specifically, the difference between iconic and indexical reference is crucial. An intimate iconic reference, filled with the domesticated symbols that accord a central human place in the universe and transcendent purpose to life, might very well be false, given the transcendence of ultimate reality. But that supposed iconic likeness might very well be true when the reference is indexical. Living within a sacred worldview whose domestic symbols of ultimate dimensions are iconically false might still be authentic if their indexical reference carries across what is transcendently ultimately valuable, for instance, getting on with the responsibilities of one's watch. Whether it does so in given cases is an empirical matter to be examined with regard to the functioning of the sacred worldview.

The plausibility of a contemporary sacred worldview therefore depends in part on its being able to employ intimate symbols of ultimacy, perhaps in themselves incompatible with the scientific world picture, so that they do carry across what is true about ultimacy, as understood in terms of the transcendent symbols, without allowing false implications to be drawn from their domestic forms. For personalistic symbols of ultimacy, common in biblical monotheisms and many forms of Hinduism, the greatest challenge comes from theodicy. If God is imagined as a good, controlling, omnipotent agent, how are humanly catastrophic tsunamis possible? The transcendent understanding of God as an ontological act of creation reinforces the symbol of God as omnipotent; nothing happens that is not part of the creative act. Therefore, the sacred worldview would have to give up any claim that God is an agent with a good character. Intimacy in the monotheistic symbols systems often requires people to image God as an agent who listens to prayer. That is indexically correct when it comes to orienting prayer to be the honest expression of the heart; but it is indexically false if it leads to expectations that God hears and answers prayers, resulting in radical disorientation when prayers are not answered. The point also holds with sacred worldviews deriving from other traditional symbol systems than the personifying ones: The symbols of intimacy are false and literally implausible when they conflict with the scientific world picture, but they might be true and authentic if their indexical use leads to grasping the ultimate realities in their true worth and significance.

Striking proper balances between transcendence and intimacy in sacred worldviews relative to the scientific world picture is extraordinarily difficult. Many, though by no means all, individuals who are self-conscious about the scientific world picture despair of transforming a traditional sacred worldview or developing a new one that embodies the intimate symbols necessary for the orientation of concrete life. This issue is vastly complicated by the worldview continuum of symbols that stretches from the sophisticated ones that might be vetted by considerations of the sort expressed here to symbols active in folk culture. The folk culture symbols of intimacy so often are radically false if referred iconically, and a determination of their possible indexical authenticity requires many steps of interpretation.

IV. AUTHORITY, FALLIBILITY, AND CONTAINMENT

To speak of sacred worldviews as plausible or implausible is not only to make an historical or sociological comment about their religious function, although it is at least that. More important, the consideration of the plausibility and implausibility of sacred worldviews acknowledges them to be hypotheses. Hypotheses are fallible. They might in fact be so reinforced by internal helpfulness and external evidence that they can be taken for granted. We can *assume* them to be proved. But they are still hypotheses that guide engagements and might be mistaken. In point of fact, the self-conscious regard of sacred worldviews as hypotheses for orientation leads to attempts to improve them.

If a sacred worldview is to be plausible today, it needs to acknowledge its fallibility on its own terms. This is nothing new. Nearly every theologically rich tradition has had its apophatic moments. Even the most metaphysically sharp theologians have recognized that their best concepts are not good enough to express the ultimate. Some, such as Nagarjuna, have used their sharpest concepts to prove the very point that all concepts are inadequate to ultimate reality. Yet something special attends the pragmatic claim that theologies and sacred worldviews are hypotheses and for this reason fallible.

To understand what is special about the fallible hypothesis form of apophatic theology, a brief review of the pragmatic epistemology underlying

Philosophical Theology is in order (see also *1, 2, 3*). Charles Peirce asked whether there is any such thing as an intuitive cognition, by which he meant a cognition that immediately receives its object (a use of the term "intuition" that comes from Kant).[3] If there were, we would not know it to be such except by a subsequent judgment that itself would be either a fallible inference or an intuition, and so on. He concluded that there are no direct intuitions, only inferences or interpretations of given objects, and illustrated this with many examples from perception, showing perception to be inferential. Inference proceeds according to rules that are hypotheses about how things connect, and these hypotheses become habituated so that we just automatically interpret the world according to them most of the time. This is to say, through the hypotheses that are formulated in our semiotic systems and habituated into our engagements of the world, we learn to perceive the world. Perception, Peirce argued is an inferential, hypothetical matter. *Philosophical Theology* has developed the view that, through theology and religious practice, we come to perceive the ultimate, albeit through fallible hypotheses. Sacred worldviews are among the media of the perception of ultimacy.

Sometimes, however, our perceptions are confused, blocked, distorted, or absent when they should be present and we do not know what to believe. Here is where inquiry begins. The best way to fix belief, Peirce argued, is to call up the hypothetical character of our habits of thought, including perception, and check them out.[4] Is there reason to doubt any relevant hypothesis? Can any relevant hypothesis be improved? Of course, we cannot doubt all of our hypotheses at once. In fact, most of them must be true enough for us to get along, and to get along so well that we suspect that certain of them are questionable. Are there any beliefs that are not in the form of hypotheses? No. Regardless of how well-proven an hypothesis is, regardless of how immediately certain it seems to consciousness, it still has the form of an hypothesis. This includes sacred worldviews.

The special thing about the pragmatic interpretation of sacred worldviews as fallible hypotheses is that they are more plausible the more they make themselves vulnerable to correction. As we have seen throughout *Philosophical Theology*, this means that they should make themselves vulnerable to correction from philosophical criticisms of as many sorts as possible, from a careful internalizing and criticism of as many different religious traditions as possible, building always on comparative theology, from attending to the findings of as many sciences as bear upon religious matters and from constant inquiry into the consequences of living on the basis of the sacred canopy. The plausibility of a sacred worldview is immediately threatened by any refusal of vulnerability, by a refusal to take philosophical criticism seriously, by a refusal to engage the meaning and truth of alternative theologies and sacred worldviews, by any neglect or rejection of scientific inquiry, by any inattention to the significance of consequences of living according to the sacred worldview. Any attempt to entrench a sacred worldview against criticism weakens its plausibility.

Furthermore, plausibility in a sacred worldview requires the active seeking out of correction because we know that sacred worldviews are crafted from antecedent worldviews that indeed employed all the defenses of invulnerability. Sacred worldviews often have demonized their alternatives and so were blinded from learning from them. They have taken on fideistic forms that reject the relevance of philosophical criticism and so remained in their contradictions. They have claimed that the sciences are irrelevant to revealed truth and so do not understand very well the religious life they orient. They have rejected the lessons of the fruits of their beliefs and so have blundered along dealing hurts and harms. When it comes to reaching out for the lessons of vulnerability, the history of sacred worldviews and the religious communities oriented by them is filled with obstinate refusals to learn. Contemporary sacred worldviews vying for plausibility are heirs to this frustrating history. And so our contemporary sacred worldviews need to be aggressive in making themselves vulnerable to correction.

But what does this do to their authority? How can the sacred worldviews, especially their sacred canopies engaging ultimacy, be authoritative for the serious religious life when their very plausibility involves their commitment to vulnerability and transformation? What objective factor could authorize an hypothetical sacred worldview? What subjective commitment to its authority would be possible? The factors constituting authority discussed in Chapter 13, Section IV, do not sit well with hypothetical authority.

Nevertheless, implausibility is even more devastating to the authority of sacred worldviews than their mere hypothetical status. Therefore, the objective condition that most authorizes a sacred canopy is its very vulnerability to correction. That sacred worldview is most authoritative that has been vetted through as many avenues of correction as possible. Moreover, if the sacred worldview contains within itself procedures for its own improvement as improvements become possible, then it is all the more authoritative.

The subjective affirmation of the authority of the sacred worldview similarly rests on a commitment to vulnerability to correction, and willingness to modify one's orientations as they are corrected. To have this commitment and willingness is extremely difficult. For instance, it would imply that one's participation in a ritual, such as the Christian Sunday morning service discussed in *Philosophical Theology Two*, Chapter 9, would be conditional upon being able to give an interpretation of its iconically false (the ultimate is not a king) liturgical affirmations that allows them to be indexically true. If such an interpretation cannot be given, then one's participation might be qualified, perhaps even abandoned. Problems such as these should not be given an overly cognitive interpretation. The indexical quality of the liturgical references would have to be judged in terms of the function of the ritual in the life of the community; perhaps those rituals in fact lead people to be more personally responsible and less like vassals. Nevertheless, commitment to vulnerability and willingness to change are hard to sustain when engaged in the ultimately important task of achieving absolute value-identity. Whereas it is common to hope for certainty upon which to commit one's life, vulnerability calls one to hope for correction upon which to commit one's life. Anything less is a blow to plausibility.

This chapter and the previous have discussed the conditions for the plausibility of sacred worldviews and the problems faced in maintaining plausibility with authority. *Philosophical Theology* has attempted to provide such a plausible sacred worldview, at least in an outline that might be filled in by people in different positions in the global religious situation. The question remains, however, of the existential situation when the apparently best and most authoritative sacred worldview implodes. The following two chapters address this question.

CHAPTER FIFTEEN

Imploding Worldviews and Ontological Predicaments

I. COSMOLOGICAL AND ONTOLOGICAL BOUNDARY CONDITIONS

The introduction to *Philosophical Theology Two* sketched a distinction between the cosmological and ontological dimensions of ultimate human predicament. The cosmological dimensions are those that derive from the character of human existence in the cosmos. Of course, life is filled with predicaments, but our interest in *Philosophical Theology* is on those that derive from ultimate characters of human existence because ultimacy is what defines religion.

Philosophical Theology One, Part III, elaborated the thesis that the ultimate characters or traits of the cosmos come from the nature of determinateness itself. The thesis is that to be determinate at all, no matter what kind of world this turns out to be or what it contains, is to be a harmony that is determinate (even if also partly indeterminate) with respect to other harmonies. Any harmony has form, components integrated with the form, existential location relative to other harmonies, and the value-identity of getting these components together with this form in this existential location relative to others. Furthermore, to have different harmonies together as mutually determining yet genuinely other to one another requires a context that is not itself a cosmological condition, not another harmony. The dialectic argues that this ontological context of mutual relevance is an ontological act of creating all determinate harmonies that itself is sheer making, with no nature except what comes to be in the creating of the cosmos. Thus, the ultimate conditions for there being any kind of world for human beings are these: form, components, existential location, value-identity, and the radical contingency of determinateness as such on an ontological act of creation.

These ultimate conditions for there being any determinate world at all of any sort are analyzed in *Two* in terms of the boundary conditions they constitute for human beings, the cosmological boundary conditions and their predicaments. They are, in summary, first, that form as an ultimate condition bears upon human life insofar as people face possibilities with alternative possible outcomes that have differences in value. Value is a function of formal ways of putting formed contents together. Because some of these value-differentiated alternatives are subject to human control, people are defined, ultimately, by the fact that they can make things better or worse, actualizing these values and excluding those, or the other way around. Thus, people are under obligation to choose the better, to live with the results responsibly, and to a host of other elements of the ultimate boundary condition of living under obligation. Second, because human beings have many important components in their lives, they ultimately are grounded, or not grounded, in those components by how they comport themselves toward them and live under the ultimate condition of needing not only formal unity but wholeness with respect to their comportment. Third, because human beings relate to genuinely other things, and find their existential location by how they do so in the existential field constituted by these interconnections with other things, they face the ultimate boundary condition of the need to engage those others with respect for both their interconnections and their otherness that is beyond the connections. Fourth, because human beings do make up their value-identities in some measure by their own free choices, an ultimate boundary condition of life is to achieve a value-identity that is who the people are in ultimate perspective, including in that identity not only the components and forms of their own ongoing temporal identity but also their effects in other things. Fifth, because of the radical contingency of the entire cosmos, human beings face the ultimate issues of being and nonbeing, life and death. Predicament complexes around obligation, wholeness, engagement, ultimate identity, and being/nonbeing have been articulated in many different ways by the world's religions, all of which respond somehow to these ultimate conditions of cosmological predicament. Religion as such needs to articulate and negotiate the predicaments of these ultimate conditions.

Similarly, the ecstatic fulfillments of religion are also understood in *Two* in terms of the cosmological ultimates as well as the ontological ultimate. Ecstatic meaning in time and ecstatic life in eternity are shaped by the cosmological ultimates of choice relative to possibilities and integral life in all time's modes. Fulfillment in ecstatic love of others in the existential field is possible only through love of the ontological act of creation and its product, which is gratuitous, arbitrary, undeserved, and surprising. Fulfillment in ecstatic freedom finds ultimate meaning in the release from the quest for meaning and identification with the ontological act of creation as sheer love, however that is symbolized.

The ultimate cosmological predicaments and ecstatic fulfillments cannot be articulated and negotiated without sacred worldviews. Worldviews need to be sacred in the sense of including sacred canopies that articulate the ultimate conditions. Sacred worldviews also need to be plausible in the sense that they articulate how the important domains of life, to which they should give orientation, are affected by the ultimate predicaments of obligation, grounded wholeness, engagement, value-identity, and being/nonbeing. The previous two chapters have discussed some of the ways by which this articulation needs to be accomplished and how difficult it is to do so.

A radically different sense of human predicament, an ontological predicament, occurs when one's sacred worldview becomes implausible, breaks down, and ceases to provide orientation. This might be because its sacred canopy is rent in some serious way. Or it might be because some or all of the patterns of integration within the worldview that orient one domain to another become implausible. It might be because the ultimate conditions cannot be symbolized in sufficiently intimate ways to orient important domains of life. Or it might be because the sacred worldview loses its authority to orient. Most often, these breakdowns occur because of some crisis that simply cannot be given orientation with the worldview.

Existential implosions of worldviews can disorient any seeming step forward and drive people back onto something lost in the imploded sacred worldview with a passion like absolute faith. Consider the sacred worldview of Islam that includes from almost the beginning the ultimate symbol system that whatever happens is the will of Allah. This worldview was positively reinforced historically and psychologically so long as Islam was in ascendency, even though dissention surrounded the Muslim leadership from the time of the living memory of Mohammed. The sacred worldview survived the internecine wars among Islamic factions and nations, resetting itself with the victors. But when the Ottoman Empire and most of the rest of Islam caved under to the Western colonial powers, that sacred worldview imploded: Who could admit that the total defeat and humiliation of Islam is the will of Allah? What was the way forward? To modernize Islam as fast as possible at the invitation of and on the model of modern Christian Europe? Or to reassert a fundamentalist version of Islam backed by violence and absolute faith that whatever they did was the will of Allah? The backward move shames the cosmopolitan moderation of civilized Islam.[1]

Or consider the Jewish worldview that Israel is God's Chosen People, interpreted in many ways over the century, all of which imploded with the Holocaust. What orientation remained for a way forward? Abandoning identity as the Chosen People? Abandoning belief in God? Recurring to the ancient myth of Chosenness by driving the "Canaanites" off the land to establish a Jewish state that would be impregnable because of its military power? Alas, the Jewish vow never to forget the Holocaust is in stark dissonance with the Palestinian vow never to forget their right of return to their homes and that of their parents that interprets Israel to represent the Western humiliation of Islam.

Or consider the plight of Christian evangelicals, believing that God acts in the world to reward the faithful with success (in heaven if not on earth) and to punish those who do not accept Jesus Christ, whose worldview was undermined by scientific demonstrations that the Bible is neither historically nor scientifically true. What to do? To retreat into fundamentalism in the face of scientific evidence against their worldview? Or to abandon the entire worldview of the benevolent Christian-friendly God who rules affairs like a king in favor of atheistic secularism, or, even more radically, in favor of Christian liberalism?

The examples of the existential implosion of worldviews could be multiplied. Consider the collapse of the Marxist worldview that gave ultimacy to the transformation of society according to a few broad generalizations about class analysis and ownership of the means of production. The revolutionary imposition of that worldview on actual societies reduced wealth and exacerbated the problems of the distribution. Consider the implosion of the Chinese worldview that China is the cultural center of the world under the impact of defeats by Western powers, by the Japanese, and then by a Western philosophy, Marxism.

Of course, all these existential implosions are enormously more complicated and complex than indicated here. Moreover, smaller groups and individuals go through existential implosions of more local worldviews that are just as fierce. The result is the same, however: loss of ultimate meaning.

This is the ontological predicament, loss of ultimate meaning or orientation. Religions' grand sacred worldviews provide a wealth of ways of articulating obligation and dealing with guilt, of overcoming disintegration and finding wholeness, of engaging without final estrangement, and of achieving value-identity that is acceptable in ultimate perspective even when miserable. They even provide many ways of coping with life and death, being and nonbeing. But when those sacred worldviews are broken, the result is no orientation for any of those dimensions of cosmological predicament. The result is meaninglessness.

The ontological predicament, over and above the cosmological, is to cope with the peculiar kind of meaninglessness that results from the implosion of sacred worldviews and the loss of their orientation of both ultimate and proximate matters. In an important sense to be explored, this is where *religions* as fragile and fallible cultural expressions of engagements of ultimacy yield to *religion*, which engages ultimacy through seeking plausible expressions. When the sacred worldviews implode, the deepest part of religion comes to the fore. In their various ways, religions as cultural constructions have recognized this in their embrace, however hesitant and unhappy, of apophatic theology.

II. APOPHASIS AND KATAPHASIS

Apophatic theology is the negative move that says that the positive theological claims at hand fall short of the mark: No conceptions adequately determine ultimate reality. Nearly every religious tradition with a long history of literate reflection has apophatic theological moments. Neo-Platonism, which was extremely influential within Christianity and Islam, and fairly influential within Judaism, is redolent with apophatic theology because the One is beyond the Dyad and, hence, beyond any conceptual determination. Mystics such as Meister Eckhart and Jacob Boehme, and more recently Nicolas Berdyaev, represent apophatic theology with their interests in cosmogony, the arising of God from the abyss of nonbeing, paralleling the opposite plunge of the mystic from the world into that abyss.[2] Many forms of Hinduism treat rational thought as but a ladder to reach the realization of that which is beyond conceptualization, Advaita Vedanta being the best known in the West.[3] The great Chinese classic, the Daodejing, begins with the line, "The Tao (Way) that can be told of is not the eternal Tao; the name that can be named is not the eternal name. The Nameless is the origin of Heaven and Earth; the named is the mother of all things."[4]

Apophatic theology is not merely the admission that all conceptualities fall short. Pragmatic fallibilism says this universal shortfall is true of any interpretive engagement whatsoever, although trivial in most cases: Despite falling short of complete knowledge, most of our interpretations are quite adequate for most of life. Apophatic theology says that some positive theological assertions, or symbolic engagements, are mistaken. Apophatic theology negates some positive or kataphatic theology. In the implosion of sacred worldviews, apophatic theology is not engaged unless certain critical areas of those worldviews are negated. In some instances of implosion, the implosion merely can be denied by holding on to certain parts deemed essential with fundamentalist fervor; or the implosion can be merely accepted like falling into terminal illness. Apophatic theology, however, addresses the implosion with deliberate negation.

Duns Scotus was among the most important thinkers dealing with apophatic and kataphatic theology to point out that no negation can be made except on the basis of some affirmation that calls for it.[5] He had in mind, among other things, Thomas Aquinas's claim that God is good, beautiful, actual, and so forth only by analogy with human goodness, beauty, and finite actuality. Thomas would have to know something about God that is not analogous in order to know that knowledge of God is only analogous to knowledge of human beings. Thomas did, of course, claim to know that God is the infinite Act of To Be, although this still leaves a quandary about the distance between divine infinity and finite determinate virtues: Is there anything left of the meaningfulness of goodness, beauty, and actuality in God (*I, 9, iii*)? Scotus's real concern was with Thomas's claim that *being* itself is analogous, that God *is* divine infinity in a different sense from that in which a finite thing *is* its nature. Scotus concluded that being itself is univocal, not analogous: Because God *is* infinite in the same sense of *is* that a finite thing *is* its finite nature, we can know God to be infinite.

Theology cannot be wholly apophatic, therefore. The negation in apophasis must have some justification in kataphasis. Kataphatic theology is the engagement of ultimacy with the positive interpretive symbols functioning as hypotheses about ultimate reality and the ultimate dimensions of things. The theology involved in the critical development of sacred worldviews, especially their sacred canopies, is kataphatic. Kataphatic theology works by engaging ultimacy discriminately according the symbolic theological hypotheses involved. Apophatic theology, in its turn, is also an attempt to engage ultimacy but through the denial of something positive: Instead of saying that God is personal, the apophatic move would be to say that God is not personal, which is a way of engaging God. Apophatic theology is not a rejection all theological engagement of the ultimate in favor of disengagement. Rather, it is a rejection of certain kataphatic theology as too limiting for the ultimate. Admission of the implosion of a sacred worldview is a kataphatic ground for apophatic denial.

Apophatic and kataphatic theology necessarily go hand in hand. Kataphatic theologians sometimes reject apophatic negation because it seems to be the denial of whatever truth there is in the positive statements, especially in those statements that are well-formed formulas, such as doctrines that are used in argument. Nevertheless, most kataphatic theologians would admit that, while their positive interpretations are true rather than their denials, they do not contain the whole truth. Apophatic theologians need kataphatic theology in order to justify their negation.

What happens, then, when sacred worldviews lose their plausibility? It would seem to be a victory for apophatic theology. This would be the case in those instances in which the sacred worldview becomes implausible because it is based on too small a truth and a larger truth becomes apparent. A Daoist sacred worldview based on the view that the Dao is mellow and harmonious becomes implausible when it becomes apparent that the Dao is wild, especially in relation to matters of the human scale. The apophatic theology rejects the mellow Dao by the kataphatic evidence of lack of domesticated harmony in the Dao. Wildness is not so much a positive characteristic but a perceived absence of humanizing limits. If Daoist thinkers go on to embrace a cosmology that articulates natural movement in ways unscaled to human affairs, wildness can become a positive—that is, a new kataphatic—affirmation. Or a monotheistic theology based on a symbolizing of ultimate reality as a cosmically scaled just king who rewards the good and punishes the evil can become implausible in the face of overwhelming evidence that the world is not run justly, the standard problem of theodicy. An apophatic response would be to reject the symbols of God as a just king, prominent as they are in biblical texts, and the rejection would be based on the kataphatic observations of the unjust character of the world. The apophatic theologian might go on to develop a larger conception of God that embraces the injustice in natural and social processes, which would be a kataphatic construction, justified as a better hypothesis than the just king symbols.

Philosophical Theology One, Part III, gave a kataphatic dialectical argument to the effect that determinate things would not be possible without being created as related-but-other-than-one-another by an ontological act of creation. That ontological act cannot be determinate in any way except as the result of creating the determinate things of the world. Otherwise, a deeper ontological creative act would be needed to connect the determinate act with the determinate things it creates. The result of this kataphatic argument is a powerful apophatic argument for rejecting any determinate character apart from creation for the ontological act, which is the most ultimate reality. That act cannot be conceived as a person with intentions, or as a principle that by nature is good, or as the fullness of being; nor can it be conceived as some analogue of human consciousness, or some wellspring from which things emerge. Any characterization of the ontological act must be done strictly in terms of what it creates: It is the creator of this world. The only truly ultimate characteristics are those deriving from the creation of determinateness as such, and they are traits of determinate being or harmonies: form, components, existential location, and value-identity (*I, 15, 16; II, pt. I*). Given this metaphysical foundation, *Philosophical Theology* is deeply apophatic and rejects the symbols of a great many religious strains.

Yet this metaphysically developed theology, dialectically kataphatic and negatively apophatic, is extremely "transcendent," indeed ascetic.[6] How can it include symbols of sufficient intimacy to provide orientation in a sacred worldview, particularly to the domains of mundane life that seem far from any metaphysically expressed sacred canopy? The answer we have developed has two steps that need to be taken together. One is to point out that every domain of life involves the facing of alternative possibilities with different values and therefore obligatoriness insofar as people affect the outcome, every domain involves comportment toward the components of life, every domain involves engaging others, and every domain contributes to the achievement of value-identity. Thus, every domain has an ultimate dimension, in fact, four ultimate dimensions, of the cosmological sort. On top of that, every domain in itself and in its connections with others is radically contingent, which is also an ultimate dimension, the ontological one. But how can these five dimensions be symbolized so as to make a difference to the ways the mundane (and sacred!) domains are oriented? The metaphysics is likely to be significant only for metaphysical adepts whose number is not large. The second step, therefore, is the symbolization of the dimensions of ultimacy in religious terms that involve intimacy. The great traditional religions have elaborate symbols for these, as we have seen, and these symbols can be employed as controlled in their interpretations by the metaphysical side of the theology. The mutual contestations and borrowings of the great traditions frequently have produced new symbols, or new interpretive practices. The events of the age produce new symbols of immediate intimacy, as Bultmann appreciated about existentialism.

New cultural media such as film and internet communications develop new kinds of symbols, all of which can be interpreted within the guidance of philosophical theology. So, in principle sacred worldviews can be developed that indeed do exhibit the ascetic negative theology that accompanies the metaphysical argument given here.

The fact, however, is that these sacred worldviews have not been developed, and the sacred worldviews associated with most large cultural and religious traditions are under threat of implausibility, the reasons for which were discussed in the previous chapter. The sacred worldviews of antitraditional or secular movements are also under threat of implausibility. The sacred canopy of *Philosophical Theology* is not easily embodied in any sacred worldview. Even if it is true philosophically, can it be an orienting worldview that gives meaning to the important domains of life?

III. THE DESPERATION OF MEANING-MAKING

When a sacred worldview implodes and there is no ready substitute, no orientation exists concerning what to do, at least no orientation at the level of the imploded sacred worldview. Although local orientations might remain in place, the orientations that frame the meaning systems for the overall frame of life are gone, especially those for the meaning systems of the sacred canopy. In these circumstances the local affairs of life seem chaotic and without meaning. Without meaning, there is little hope and despair drives people to seek meaning, usually meaning of the sort that was lost with the implosion of their sacred worldview. This point needs to be examined in detail, because it can easily lead to the hostile claim that religious meanings are false fictions made up to relieve people of despair and the terror of chaos. A rather direct correlation lies between this point and the discussion of ultimate concern in *Philosophical Theology One*, Chapter 5.

To be sure, some people have little or no ultimate concern. Their response to the implosion of a cultural sacred worldview is simply not to respond. They seek no more meaning in their lives that is given locally in various mundane domains with minimal orientation. Perhaps they can survive all their lives like this, with nothing out of the ordinary, no tragedy, suffering, or special empowerments to prompt them to seek more meaning. But most people do live with an orientation to ultimate meanings that might not even be noticed until it implodes or slowly vanishes, leaving the blahs. In this case, what they seek most are new orientations to what is ultimate that are expressed in sufficiently intimate symbols that they can prioritize the things in their lives. The question of prioritization becomes more acute the more the plausibility of the sacred worldview seems in doubt.

A second common response to the implosion of a worldview that we noted earlier is to invest some part or version of it with reinstated authority and hold to it in a fideistic fashion. This is to say, it is given unquestionable status regardless of what might have made the sacred worldview implausible in the first place. That status is reinvested with authority and held tenaciously. The power in this response is that life is given a new set of priorities through the defense of the unquestionable status of whatever is left of the worldview. In fact, however, the set of orientations within the recovered part of the worldview might not be very important anymore. Christian and Muslim fundamentalisms, for instance, both embrace sacred worldviews that preach peace and love, and yet both are defended with a prioritizing of life that in extreme though common cases includes bellicosity and hatred. The new prioritizing comes not from the content of the fundamentalist reduction and absolutizing of elements of the otherwise imploded worldviews as much as from the defense of the unquestioned status given them against those who might attack. The vigor of the defense is often greatest when directed at those who have declared the sacred worldview itself to be implausible. The fundamentalist response is often accompanied by a feeling of being embattled.

Two principal problems undermine this response. One is that whatever corroded the sacred worldview in the first place is likely again to wear down its defense in reduced form in the long run. The other is that the defense of a fundamentalist form of the sacred worldview is likely not to be about engaging ultimacy but about finding something to which to be ultimately committed that is not recognized as ultimate because the original sacred worldview symbolizing ultimacy has imploded. This can take the form of defending a particular political movement, culture, or way of life for its own sake and not because it is a way of inhabiting a sacred worldview. Ultimate commitment to something genuinely not ultimate is demonic, as Tillich would say.

A third kind of response to the implosion of a sacred worldview is to embrace the despair and accept a deep skepticism. This is a definite way of prioritizing the domains of life relative to ultimacy: the claim that no ultimate prioritizing is possible. Unlike the first response, based on little or no ultimate concern in the first place, this despairing skepticism is deeply affected by an ultimate concern seeking ultimate priorities. But no ultimate reality or ultimate dimensions of mundane domains of life are to be found in the wake of an imploded sacred worldview, and the disappointment is itself a peculiar kind of prioritizing. Sometimes the despairing skepticism becomes sublimated into a form of the first response, the having of no ultimate concerns. Sometimes despairing skepticism becomes entwined with fundamentalist absolutism in a dance of alternation, flipping from one side to the other, fanaticism and despair.

Sometimes despairing skepticism takes the form, Camus-like, of an ultimate commitment to what are recognized as non-ultimate projects in ethics, social reform, art, literature, or other domains of endeavor. Or, as Frank Sinatra is said to have remarked, referring to bourbon, "Whatever gets you through the night!" If the mundane domains of life have no ultimate dimensions, they still might present the possibility of achieving proximate goods. The despairing skeptic can be committed to the relief of suffering, the management of family and friendship, the living of a decent life, without ever finding anything ultimate in these things. This positive kind of life is associated with some practical and nonphilosophical strains of stoicism, and it is possible when all that is left of a sacred worldview is its non-sacred elements, and then only given such coherent orientation as necessary to be able to get along. Despairing skepticism can be a kind of non-sacred secularism that deals conscientiously with issues of obligation, wholeness, engagement, and value-identity, perhaps even radical contingency, without seeing any ultimacy in these things. This contrasts with the kind of secularism often associated with modern humanism that rejects traditional forms of sacred canopies, especially their authority, but still is oriented by the ultimacy in the boundary conditions defining the world of mundane domains.[7]

A fourth kind of response to the implosion of a sacred worldview is to recognize that it is only an hypothesis, as argued in the previous chapter, and to launch into the task of finding a better one. This is not an uncommon response. Most late-modern people find that their adolescent sacred worldviews implode to some degree when they get to college and hunt for more sophisticated ones. Although to think of the process of maturation as incremental is tempting because easily domesticated, for many people it is a matter of lurching from one sacred worldview to another, sometimes not merely replacing the earlier with the later but emotionally rejecting the earlier. Sometimes the process of finding a superior sacred worldview is long and takes detours through the apathetic, fundamentalist, and despairing skeptical roads. For some individuals life bears a rather large number of these life-shaking implosions and quests for new, more satisfying sacred worldviews.

The process of questing for an improved sacred worldview should not be viewed only from the subjective psychological perspective of the patient of implosion, however. In most instances, the reasons for implausibility in sacred worldviews are objective. They concern real matters of various kinds of inconsistency, inappropriateness of the worldview to the particulars of life, failures to hold in tension the symbols of transcendence with those of intimacy, and collapses of authority, among other reasons for implausibility. Thus, while late-modern cultures might offer a number of sacred worldviews that can be ranked in order of sophistication and so discovered serially in the personal process of maturation, there might be no culturally articulated sacred worldview that in fact is adequate to particular circumstances.

The distinction between pressures for transcendence and those for intimacy in symbols of ultimacy points up two versions of this inadequacy, both of which might function at once. On the one hand, the pressures for transcendence push the symbols of ultimate reality away from all representations that would give it determinateness, which would in turn require something more ultimate to ground and explain the determinate. The argument in *Philosophical Theology* is that the ultimate boundary conditions in determinateness—form, components, existential location, and value-identity—themselves require and result from an ontological act of creation that is itself indeterminate apart from creating. No sacred worldview will be plausible in this age that cannot envision the act of creation as transcendent enough to create the vast cosmos and infinitely dense web of nature (*I, 6, 7*). In fact, the ontological creative act must be conceived as creative of form, of multiplicity to be formed, of existential fields of multiply-formed things, and value-identity, and, hence, in itself apart from creating the ontological creative act can have no form, multiplicity, location, value, or other identity.

On the other hand, to be plausible and thus capable of orienting contemporary life, a sacred worldview has to find ways to interpret the rigor of the transcendent symbols of ultimacy into intimate symbols. These symbols might be those of traditional religions but only as interpreted so as to be consistent with the transcendent ones. As remarked earlier, it is extremely difficult to interpret the symbols of the great traditions so as to be consistent with the pressures for transcendence without making them impotent as intimately able to orient life's particulars. So, great "poetry" is needed in many fields to accomplish this interpretive connection. A plausible sacred worldview needs to embody both the transcendent and intimate forms of symbols, interpretively connected, in order to have the kinds of consistency, appropriateness, and authority required. This is difficult indeed and remains always an unfinished task.

This difficulty is compounded by the fact that not all, in fact only a very few, seekers after adequate sacred worldviews in response to serious implosions are likely to be able to grasp worldviews with much sophistication. The discussions in *Philosophical Theology One*, Chapter 4, pointed out that on the sophistication–popular culture continuum, the practical affairs of life in most instances lie in the middle and thus are not addressed by the super-sophisticated symbols of transcendence and subtle reinterpretations of symbols of intimacy.

IV. TERROR OF THE INFINITE

So, the situation is that, realistically speaking, no practical sacred worldview is within easy reach that is plausible in ways that most worldviews are not. The existential situation, of course, might not be as sweeping as the previous sections of this chapter have suggested. The logical status of sacred worldviews is that they are complex hypotheses, in fact hypotheses of hypotheses of hypotheses, more or less well grounded. Those that implode because of one kind of implausibility or another are not well grounded and cease to function. Nevertheless, as Peirce pointed out, we do not doubt everything at once. Some subhypotheses in the sacred worldview, for instance, direct symbols of ultimate reality, might lose their plausibility because of representing too much determinateness in the ground of determinateness itself, while the symbols for the ultimacy of obligation, wholeness, engagement, and value-identity remain more or less intact; this happens to people much affected by science. Or the symbols of ultimacy in obligation might collapse, while those of wholeness and contingency remain intact. And so on.

Therefore, the task of repairing the imploded sacred worldview is nearly always a piecemeal endeavor. If the implausible elements are basic to the overall structure of the sacred canopy, the things that hold steady might not provide much overall comfort during the piecemeal repair. But there is some continuity. Moreover, the things to correct in the imploding sacred worldview are only the things for which there is reason to doubt. Although cracks in a worldview tend to cascade like a landslide, perhaps not everything needs to be corrected, and specific things can be worked on, specific symbolic references, specific problems of interpretation. Yet the repairs are difficult and nonobvious. When they appear, they are revelatory, although their revelatory status might be difficult to recognize because of the different places occupied on the continuum between sophisticated and folk culture symbols. Nevertheless, if one bears in mind that hypotheses are improved by being amended and corrected with new forms, new openness to evidence, and steadfast commitments to vulnerability, one can have hope.

Another qualification to the sweeping challenge of the implosion of implausible sacred worldviews in our late-modern cultures is that it is only individuals who hold to, and can lose, sacred worldviews. The sacred worldviews are cast in the symbols of the larger culture, of course, and the dynamics of groups can be understood in part in terms of the vicissitudes of the worldviews for the group as a whole. Not for a second should the social nature of the semiotic structures of worldviews be forgotten. Nevertheless, the group is made up of the socially interactive actions of the individuals. Each individual engages life, especially its ultimate dimensions, in ways peculiar to the individual version and form of appropriation of the sacred worldviews presented by the culture. As has been noted, the social context for most individuals today offers many candidate worldviews, and the actual functioning sacred worldview of any person is unique to that person. The implosion of any sacred worldview takes a form unique to that person. Much of the authority that an individual invests in a worldview, or divests when it implodes, can derive from larger social attitudes about authority; when the group loses confidence in a sacred worldview or a significant part of it, the individual fails to be reinforced in the investment of authority. Conversely, when an individual loses faith, the pressures of the group can re-instill authority. Nevertheless, group pressures only go so far, especially for mature individuals. Whether the sacred worldview is comprehensive in its orientation of the person's life, and whether it is held with much intensity, makes a difference to the existential significance of its implosion. This qualifies the rather sweeping discussions of the existential significance of imploding sacred worldviews in the contemporary religious situation (or in any religious situation, because this is not the only age of imploding sacred worldviews).

Nevertheless, whether viewed as a social matter or an individual matter, sacred worldviews are hypotheses. Most traditional sacred worldviews have represented themselves as having an authority more absolute than that of more or less well-confirmed hypotheses, an authority of some kind of revelation. But whether or not the hypothetical character of sacred worldviews is recognized, that is their logical status. The best kind of authority a sacred worldview can have is that appropriate to hypotheses, namely, that it makes itself vulnerable to correction and remains unscathed.

This leaves the religious situation, then, in the following state. For most late-modern people, the best sacred worldviews available have difficulty with their plausibility, are under reconstruction, and offer little orientation about what to do other than to commend the process of inquiry in this precarious situation of imploded or potentially imploding sacred worldviews. "Process of inquiry" sounds too thin, although it is the language natural to dealing with dicey hypotheses. "Desperate search for meaning" better conveys the existential force of the situation. But this is itself an orientation, the orientation at the deepest heart of religious life.

The ontological symbolic engagement of ultimacy is a process of religious quest that is itself something like a finite/infinite contrast. The finite side is the concrete process of dealing with shaky, perhaps imploded, sacred worldviews and attempting to improve them to adequate plausibility. This is theological work that is undertaken in sophisticated ways by professional theologians and intellectual adepts. But it is undertaken in existential ways that are just as fierce by people all across the spectrum of sophistication. The finite side is always partial, incomplete, fallible, and probably self-conscious about some of its own limitations.

The infinite side of the ontological symbolic engagement of ultimacy is terror at the chaos that looms in the shadow of its hypothetical status and felt limitations. What if the sacred worldview at hand is implausible and irreparable? What if the repairs that work today fail tomorrow? The feeling tone of the ontological symbolic engagement of ultimacy is a contrast of the process of inquiry (the desperate search for meaning) itself, on the finite side, and the terror of the chaos of what would be if all hypotheses fail, on the infinite side. Desperate search is joined with terror about the arbitrariness and limitations of all searches in a felt finite/infinite contrast.

The depths of apophatic theology lie in this contrast with the kataphatic processes of theological inquiry addressing the search for effectively plausible sacred worldviews. The most important positive affirmation that allows for the negation embodied in the terror is the recognition of the hypothetical status of even the best symbolic engagements of ultimacy. The most important negation is the chaos that would obtain were the symbolic engagements to fail to provide ultimate orientations. No wonder the mystics devoted to negative theology were held in suspicion by the majority of religious people: Who likes to live with terror? Every time the terror is domesticated by some significant progress in improving sacred canopies, it seems the terror breaks out again. So it is that religious people live most deeply in this contrast between the finite and infinite sides of ultimacy.

With regard to ultimate concerns, the broad middle of the continuum between little or no ultimate concern and truly ultimate concern is occupied by people engaged with ultimacy for the sake of prioritizing their lives. They look to some sacred canopy to provide orientation to what is ultimate. Perhaps they change their lives in concrete ways so as to be better prioritized. Sometimes people with deep ultimate concern change their lives drastically, perhaps abandoning many of the domains of life for a monastic existence or for an existence devoted exclusively to service to others with no thought for themselves. But so long as they engage the ultimate in order to prioritize their lives, even to exclusive devotion, they have only penultimate concern in a strict sense. The project of prioritizing their lives compromises the ultimacy that they engage.

The most ultimate concern is to abandon the issues of prioritizing their lives and just engage the ultimate with the best symbols available. This ultimate form of ultimate concern is the embrace of the finite/infinite task of the search for ultimate meaning with its feeling tone of effort and terror in tight contrast. The matters of prioritizing life are abandoned with respect to their ultimacy. Although every life has its priorities, they need not be ultimately important. A life devoted to the religious quest at this deep ontological level has to have some order to it, though many examples exist of religious seekers who renounce ordinary ways of ordering life. Perhaps the theological way that embraces the feeling tone of the finite/infinite contrast of desperate inquiry and chaos can be lived under the aegis of an order of life that looks unexceptional. Kierkegaard's knight of faith looks no different from ordinary people.

Wesley J. Wildman addresses this issue by arguing that the apophatic leading of people through the implosion of those worldviews that can sustain religious communities means that the efforts to sustain such communities cannot tolerate apophatic theology up front, and that the place for apophasis is on the underside of religious communities.[8] He is right that religious communities have often exiled their apophatic prophets when their worldview comes under pressure. But Wildman's argument supposes that the apophatic dialectic is taken by the community to be employed as a kataphatic hypothesis that, viewed that way, undermines the community. Rather, the apophatic dialectic is employed to save the grounds of the community when its kataphatic sacred worldview implodes. This radical "saving of the community," however, is what many do not want, for it means that the community needs to acknowledge that its own prioritizations of life are transcended and the religious community is merely a proximate concern, not a religiously ultimate one. Religious communities have ultimate dimensions but are not themselves ultimate, and this is shown by the work of apophatic dialectic when the organizing sacred worldviews implode.

The burden of the argument of *Philosophical Theology Three* regarding religious communities is that the old model of face-to-face ethnic or geographical communities cannot be sustained. New senses of community need to be developed that recognize, on the one hand, the universality of the claims of love and justice and, on the other hand, the highly particularized needs of individuals to find others with whom they can be religious companions. The old senses of community have limited application. The full reach of the Axial Age revolution is to require communities whose scope and identity is not just reflective of the universalizing powers of empire but of the globalizing power of the human condition.

The deepest ontological remedy for the brokenness of the human condition in its ultimate predicaments is to abandon the search for salvation in the sense that turns on prioritizing life in any ultimately important way. Most of the great religions have recognized this paradoxical situation. If one is struggling to attain salvation, one has not found it, and the concern for salvation itself is part of the problem. Buddhism in nearly all of its forms is most direct about this. Attachment to the task of overcoming suffering means continued suffering, however ultimate that task is represented to be. The bodhisattva's vow to nurture all sentient beings to enlightenment is paradoxical because all have it already.

The cosmological predicaments, and the religious remedies for them, indeed deal with ultimacy, as found in form, components, existential location, value-identity, and the radical contingency of all that on the ontological creative act. The engagement of ultimacy in these dimensions, however expressed in religions' terms, can be genuine and true engagement. There is no way of dealing with the ultimate dimensions of all the mundane domains of life without something like this complex of engagements of ultimacy in at least these five forms. But none of these engagements is itself as ultimately deep as the ontological engagement that copes with the fallible finitude of all sacred canopies, and their ongoing need for greater plausibility, as felt in conjunction with ontological terror.

Chapter 15 of *Philosophical Theology One* dealt with how to engage the ultimates through thinking them in the metaphysical terms of the ontological theory developed in that volume. The present chapter deals with how to surmount the need to repair the ontological human predicament by engaging in the process of theological search for meaning under the uncertain conditions of fallibility. With what are we left? On the one hand we have the state of the inquiry such as it is, with its problems and possible ways forward but also with its limitations and no guarantee of being able to succeed past the remains of imploded sacred worldviews. There is just the task of inquiry such as it is to which ultimately concerned theologians can give themselves. On the other hand is the terror to which those theologians also necessarily give themselves. Can these be balanced? Can the terror be set aside for an hour so as to work productively on the inquiry? Can the work be set aside so as to feel the terror at the chaos that gives the inquiry its importance? That these questions cannot be answered is part of the feeling tone of the finite/infinite contrast in the ontological engagement of the ultimate. Another way to put this is what Krishna said to Arjuna: You have a right to the action—the work of searching for more adequate symbols for engagement—but not to its fruits, a guarantee that something adequate is to be found. This is the human predicament at its ontological depths and religion's remedy, shadowed though it be. Religion's ontological symbolic engagement of ultimate reality lives on the cusp of effort and terror, the point where effort ceases and falls into terror and where terror becomes effort to orient itself.

Chapter Sixteen

Ontological Salvation and Ecstatic Fulfillment

How is it possible to live on the cusp between the desperate effort to achieve appropriate ultimate orientation and the terror of the chaos that makes that effort significant? The engagement of ontological ultimate reality raises this question when it is accompanied by the felt recognition of the fallibility, limitation, and internal apophatic negation of the best of human symbols of ultimacy and their orienting sacred worldviews. The answer to be elaborated here can be called "ontological faith." Faith is meant here in a deeper sense than the kinds of faith relative to the cosmological predicaments discussed in *Philosophical Theology Two*, Chapters 13 and 15. Ontological faith includes them as necessary ingredients, however, just as the ontological symbolic engagement of ultimacy in the ontological predicament and ecstatic fulfillment includes participation in the cosmologically defined predicaments and their remedies, fallible and challenged in their plausibility as they might be, and their forms of ecstatic fulfillment. Paul Tillich described ontological faith as "the courage to be."[1]

Ontological faith is the courage to live on the cusp of the work of symbolic engagement of ultimacy and the terror of the chaos felt in the recognition of the inadequacy of the symbols, the point where both are visible and felt in a contrast, and where any movement in one leads to the other. This courage takes four forms and requires all together. They are: the courage to accept mystery, the courage to accept fragmentation, the courage to accept rejection and death, and the courage to accept a world without oneself. These are explored in the sections of this chapter. They correspond roughly to the finite/infinite contrasts of form, components harmonized, existential realities, and value-identity. Living with courage in each of these domains is an ecstatic fulfillment.

I. THE DAO CANNOT BE NAMED[2]

The courage to accept mystery acknowledges that no sacred canopy (including a philosophical theology) and no sacred worldview ever adequately names ultimate reality. Guided by what symbols they have, people engage ultimate reality as still mysterious.

In a sense, everything is mysterious because nothing can be engaged in all possible respects. Always there is something left uninterpreted in even the simplest, most common, ordinary, and familiar things. We can speak of this sense of mystery as cosmological and acknowledge its depths especially with regard to the mystery of other human beings.

Ontological faith involves something more than this level of mystery, however. It is the courage to accept the gratuitous, arbitrary, undeserved, and surprising fact that there is form at all, something nameable. Human beings might never be able to articulate the nature of form in a perfectly adequate way, and in *Two*, Chapter 1, we reflected on some of the complexities of form's bearing on human life as possibility, carrying value, and bestowing obligation. This is a cosmological limitation. The ontological limitation is that form itself is contingent, and the engagement of this fact embraces the terror of what would be if there were no form. That there is form at all, anything formed, anything bearing value because of its form, is a mystery that is felt in form's contingent and ultimate nature as a finite/infinite contrast. Heidegger raised "the ontological question" in a profound way in his discussion of the "thrownness" of *Dasein*, the arbitrary fact that a human being is just located in position. But his way was not profound enough, because the arbitrariness attends not so much to human thrownness but to the thrownness of the entire cosmological context of form, components, existential location, and value-identity into which human beings are thrown. Heidegger's limitation came from starting phenomenologically from *Dasein* rather than from human beings as harmonies of harmonies within harmonies, which are constituted with the transcendentals of form, components, existential location, and value-identity and intrinsically require other things.

From the standpoint of efforts to develop an adequate sacred worldview to orient life, the problem is to get the right account for the form of the ontological foundations of the world, developing the hypothesis that names the ultimate so that it can be engaged. *Philosophical Theology* has argued throughout that the best hypothesis for a plausible sacred canopy is the theory of the ontological creative act that creates all determinate things. This hypothesis has been defended with a dialectical argument about what determinate things need in order to be determinate. The strength of the argument is that the topic of determinateness is so very basic, framed through the problem of the one and the many, and presupposed as needing an account in discussions of every other topic. Of course, the argument has to be logical, but logic itself presupposes determinateness in the principle that "*a* does not equal non-*a*," and, hence, depends philosophically on their being an account of determinateness. Nevertheless, all this, however basic, is still a discursive, fallible, construction of philosophical ideas. It is never expressed adequately and doubtless someday will be amended or rejected for good reason. The metaphysics at the heart of *Philosophical Theology* is at best a plausible hypothesis, for now and as compared with alternatives. What it cannot say well is a limitation of this cosmological effort to name ultimate reality.

But what it does say well is that ultimate reality is ontologically mysterious because form itself is contingent on that which is nothing more than the arbitrary act of creation. The hypothesis of the ontological act of creation "justifies" the acknowledgment of the fact that ultimate reality has to be named as significantly unnamable because of the infinite side of the finite/infinite contrast of form. Perhaps the intellectual understanding of this brings some comfort to the ultimate search for meaning.

But the existential feel of the mystery embraces also the terror of form's arbitrariness. "Terror" is not an entirely satisfactory word here. From an ordinary human standpoint, the possibility that there would be no formed possibilities, that everything slides to chaos, is terrifying. This is worse (though perhaps not much worse) than simply being unable to figure out what the possibilities are. But the mystery in the contingency of form itself is located in the ontological predicament, the predicament engaged fully only when one has abandoned the penultimate concern of engaging the ultimate so as to prioritize and orient one's life. At this point, when one is ultimately concerned rightly to engage ultimate reality in itself and for its sake rather than one's own, perhaps the terror turns to awe. The ontological mystery of form is not so much about the order one might lose, terrible though that might be. Rather, it is about the awesomeness of the gratuitous, arbitrary, undeserved, and surprising fact of form in determinate existence.

Why then does facing mystery in this sense require ontological faith? Why does symbolic engagement of the ultimate shot through with awe have something problematic about it that calls for courage? The answer is that facing this awesome mystery makes wholly ambiguous one's own standing as engaging interpreter. Because the mystery bears the radical contingency of form, it casts the contingency of the context of engagement itself into something like a finite/infinite contrast. The human interpreter involved in ontological symbolic engagement of ultimate reality's mystery does not bear the security of a nontrivial existential location: The interpreter is not at the center of anything. The interpreter's location, although, of course, always obtaining, is trivial because the ontological engagement leaves any orientation to that position behind to engage the mystery. Ontological faith, this dimension of the courage to be, is needed to hold on to the mysterious ultimate itself as the only significant orientation. Consider the experience of the anonymous rower recounted in *Philosophical Theology One*, Chapter 16, Section I.[3] Wholly disoriented with regard to time and place, choking, weeping, groaning, crying out, the rower had to exercise astonishing faith to hold on to the experience of "power, insignificance, exhilaration, dread. . . . The infinite abyss had taken me up, and I was all the world, and I was nothing. All words fall away." The rower could hold on to that experience only with the utmost courage, bearing up the loss of self. And to seek that experience again and again, as he did, requires the ontological faith that the experience itself is its own reality, both its fearsomeness and its fascination. That experience, as we saw in *Philosophical Theology One*, became a sign for holding the ontological act of creation in bodily form so that the ultimate can be perceived (*I, 16, i*). What is perceived is not the ultimate reality as formed but as the arbitrary, gratuitous, undeserved, surprising existence of determinate (formed) existence itself.

II. "TO ACTION ALONE HAST THOU A RIGHT AND NEVER AT ALL TO ITS FRUIT"[4]

Among the components of our lives are many projects. Some are small and make up the texture of everyday life; others are larger, such as shaping a career, making a particular significant difference to one's community; carrying out a friendship or marriage; accomplishing something of a political, artistic, or philosophical nature. Many such projects are actually accomplished with a satisfying finish. But many more are not. We live fragmentary lives in many respects.

Consider Arjuna, to whom Krishna addressed the words in this section's title. About to lead his forces into battle, he sees many of his friends, teachers, and relatives among the enemy. How can he make war on them? How can he break the relationships he has with them? Krishna tells him (although it is more complex than this) that Arjuna has no right to those relationships beyond what he has already enjoyed, no right to victory in the battle, only the right to do what his duty is at the time, to fight. This is an epitome of dharma as duty.

Or consider Jesus, represented in the Christian New Testament as a would-be healer, teacher, and prophetic renewer of his religion. Yet those he healed often did not reciprocate with gratitude. His disciples were particularly dense about understanding his message, especially according to Mark's account. His critical revitalization of Second Temple Judaism was nipped in the bud, he was arrested on charges irrelevant to his own purposes, and he was executed at a young age. Although he could say "it is finished" with regard to his dying, and perhaps to a much larger redemptive purpose (according to some of his interpreters), hardly anything else was finished. He lived an extremely fragmented life. Buddhists have teased Christians about the fact that Jesus did not live long enough to organize his religious movement very well, resulting in many divergent and often contradictory traditions. The Buddha, by contrast, lived to be eighty and organized a complex set of monastic and other institutions with rather clear lines of authority and succession (although over time it seems to have become as denominationally diverse as Christianity).

Nearly everyone is involved in projects that are important components of their lives of which they can accomplish only fragments. Sometimes the projects are taken up by others. Sometimes they simply are dropped. Sometimes they are prevented by opposition. Sometimes attention is merely diverted to other things. This is a fact about complex human life, and for every person it poses problems about how to be comported to these fragments. Would it not be happy if the wholeness of human life would include the completion of its important projects? Alas, what wholeness is possible has to be found in the integration of life's fragments. A large part of maturation is learning to bear up with the fragments of life, both small and tragic, and to move on. A healthy soul finds integration among the fragments.

Living on the cusp of the work to provide true orientation to life in a sacred canopy and the terror of recognizing the chaos of what would be the case if there were no ultimate reality providing orientation involves more than grounding oneself with wholeness in the fragmentary components of life. The recognition of the multiplicity of components as an ultimate finite/infinite contrast, being a transcendental trait of determinateness itself, includes the recognition of its contingency. There need be no components, which would mean that there would be no harmonious life. There is no necessity in having components to which to be comported, no parts to be made whole. What one has, given the facts of life, is simply the components that are given among the facts. These are fragments.

The spiritual significance of this is not only that one can learn to live with the fragments, but also that one has the right only to them and not to their potential completion. This point is central to all kinds of Buddhism. In fact, in the Buddha's Fourfold Noble Truths, the cause of suffering is said to be attachments to things as if they were more than such as they appear in experience. Release from suffering involves becoming detached from those expectations that one has a right to what is more than immediately present. Some forms of Buddhism, especially the Madhyamaka, go so far as to say that there is no own-being whatsoever in things, no lastingness of entities, no real futures for what seem to be ongoing projects.[5] Surely most people do not only see the world in terms of what is actually real but also in terms of their expectations. So, when something happens to destroy their expectations, they view the reality as a fragment of something larger to which they had been related.

Disappointment that life is fragmentary can lead to resignation. Arjuna was slumped in his chariot with debilitating resignation that he could not complete his action as a warrior without fragmenting his relations with those about whom he cared. But resignation is not a way of engaging the ultimacy of the components of life as a finite/infinite contrast. The ontological engagement of ultimacy in the finite/infinite contrast of fragmentary components of life requires being able to see those components for what they are and comport oneself toward them as components of oneself, such as they are. In some forms of Buddhism, true vision is to see things such as they are. Suchness is the immediate reality of things without compromise by memories of past identity or expectations of future fulfillments. Poets can cause us to see just what is there to be seen, and all of reality seems to be contracted in that.

Learning to see the fragments for what they are and nothing more, but still as components of life, is not enough to embrace them in their limitations. To embrace their limitations, a deeper courage is called for. For, the embrace of those fragmented components needs to be a commitment to hold them and let them define oneself. They are the components of one's own life, and that life is nothing more than how one comports oneself toward them in integrating them.

The terror of the fragmentary is that the fragments are all there is as the contents of one's life. How can one commit oneself to battle or to teaching dull Galileans if that is all there is? Why go on when nothing lasts and most likely one cannot finish? In the face of the mere arising and falling of dharmas, why put out the effort? Why not simply give in to despair? Does there not have to be fruit that justifies the wholehearted effort that one's projects need if they are to be the content of one's life?

No, the ontological situation is that we get only what we get. If there has to be a payoff, then resignation and despair are appropriate interpretive symbolic responses to the finite/infinite contrasts of the components of life. But the fruits of one's efforts often are not seen. Some efforts bear no fruit. Yet if one does not embrace the work, fragmented though it is, then one has not comported oneself toward those components of life.

The radical contingency of the components of life is realistically faced with a feeling tone that grasps the infinite as well as finite side. The finite side of the components is whatever they determinately are. The infinite side is that this is all they are, and even that is a surprise. Ontological faith is necessary to embrace the radical limitations of the fragmentariness of existence.

III. "LOVE YOUR ENEMIES"

Jesus's imperative in the Sermon on the Mount to love one's enemies[6] is an implication of the Axial Age conviction that all people should be loved, not only those in one's in-group. But it is more than that. To love one's enemies is to love those who presumably reject one's love and, possibly, one's very being. Considered in the context of the ultimacy of having existential location and of the boundary condition of engaging others in awareness, appreciation, courage, and love, loving enemies requires the courage to sustain intentionally loving engagement when engagement itself is rejected. Enemies usually do not want one to engage them in love. To do so, ultimately considered, requires ontological faith.

Like having form, which consists in realized possibilities, and like having wholeness of self, which consists in being well grounded in the components of one's life, having existential location in a world with which one should be engaged with care for other things is simply a given component of existence. As determinate things, people are harmonies of which these, plus having value-identity, are transcendental traits. Being engaged with others is simply an ultimate existential condition of existence, including human existence. The cosmological human predicament with respect to engagement is how to do it so as to respect the things engaged, all creatures of the ontological creative act. The question is not whether to be engaged but how to do it well without withdrawing in denial and, when failing, how to reestablish connection.

The radical contingency of determinate reality, however, means that the ultimate condition of existential location in a field with other things to engage is radically contingent. No unconditional necessity exists for people to be existentially located and so engaged. Of course, if there are to be determinate things, they must be mutually engaged with one another so as to be determinate with respect to one another: This mutual determination constitutes the existential field itself. And if there are to be determinate things, they must be harmonies of components with form, and so forth. But the radical contingency of determinate reality means that no unconditional necessity exists for there to be determinate reality at all. That the determinate world exists at all, is gratuitous, arbitrary, undeserved, and surprising.

Living on the cusp between the best we can do to symbolize ultimate reality and the terror of the chaos that would obtain if there were no ultimate reality to symbolize, recognition of the radical contingency of engagement with others gives the question of continued engagement an ontological depth. It is one thing, the cosmological predicament, to fail to engage properly and to retreat into oneself. It is another thing, the ontological predicament, to find engagement itself challenged. Enemies rejecting one's loving engagement are paradigms of the rejection of engagement as such.

Courage in the face of the cosmological predicament is the courage not to retreat into oneself but to stay engaged. Courage in the face of the ontological predicament is the courage to affirm existence as such, both of self and others. But why should that be a problem? To understand the vicissitudes of engagement is not difficult. Failure and loss, the temptation to withdraw into oneself, the faith needed to stay engaged, are all comprehensible. Moreover, loving enemies, even when they reject the love, sometimes can have the effect of bringing them around, of enticing them to accept the love, of becoming friends rather than enemies. But loving enemies to make them friends does not get any extra credit, according to Jesus in the statement from which the title of this section comes: Everybody loves their friends. It takes a divine-like love to hold on to enemies that are truly in enmity.

But why should we love enemies when that love should not be contingent on hope that they might become friends? The answer is that they should be loved because they are creatures with value-identity. Just as the ontological act of creation is the giving of existence to the entire determinate world, with the value thereby achieved, so human engagements with the other things created (and themselves, too) should be appropriately appreciative and respectful of the value-identity of those other things. This is so even if those other things are enemies out to kill you, earthquakes to crush you, germs to sicken you, or an array of natural processes that will wear you down to dust. The cosmological predicaments of engagement have to do with needing to engage well so as to bring about the best results that lie within human power. The ontological predicament of engagement is to engage so as to exist with others, requiring the affirmation of those others regardless of their helps or harms to oneself.

When one's sacred worldview that orients the vicissitudes and salvations of the cosmological predicaments of engagement implodes, or is called into question, or is in process of being amended, or is recognized as at best a vulnerable hypothesis, and one is on the cusp of having no orientation about the most ultimate of matters, the affirmation of engagement as a condition of existence is a matter of ontological faith. The ontological faith is the courage to affirm existentially located existence itself.

This does not necessarily mean some vast metaphysical experience of existence as such. It means rather simply the engagement of those things that come up on one's watch as a way of affirming existence.

IV. THIS IS NOT THE ONLY TIME OR PLACE

Living on the cusp of the struggle to find the meaning of ultimate things has implications for achieving absolute value-identity. The value-identity a person achieves has two locations (*II, 4*). One is in the person's own life as that is embodied through the course of time in getting the components of life harmonized with the life's evolving forms through the existential locations involved. This is the subjective location of value-identity. The other is the effects of the person's life on the value-identities of other things, integrated into their own harmonies, with the influences transformed in various ways through things other than the person. This "objective location" is actually multiple locations, in other people, in institutions, histories, local and distant human affairs, and in the wider natural environment. The value-identity a person achieves in other things is just as much part of the person's absolute value-identity as that which is achieved within the person.

Although the locus of the subjective value-identity is the person's own harmony, understanding this in terms of the person's own eternal identity (*I, 12*), no determinate perspective exists from which the multiplicity of objective value achievements (for better or worse) can be located. Each of those influences is integrated into the harmonies in which it is resident. But the harmonies are ontologically together only in the ontological context of mutual relevance, that is, as the mutually conditioning termini of the ontological creative act. Therefore, it is only in the ultimate reality of the ontological creative act that a person has absolute value-identity. In fact, even the eternal identity of the persons is not located solely within time but only in the eternal and immense ontological creative act that holds times and places together.

Living on the cusp thus gives the feeling tone of gratuitousness, arbitrariness, undeservedness, and surprise to the very predicament of achieving an absolute value-identity, because that ontological creative act has no necessity in it. Like the existence of form, or of being well grounded in components, or existential location, having absolute value-identity is radically contingent. When the sacred worldview is on the cusp of appearing or dissolving, living on that cusp requires ontological faith. For, it involves the recognition that there might not have been any absolute value-identity, for oneself or anything else. Ontological faith is required in this circumstance to seize the possibilities, components, and connections of life and achieve a value-identity anyway. Theists might feel the intimacy of this in the following way: Not only might there not be any soul to be brought under judgment, there might not be any judge.

The practical implication of this is the difficulty of blessing a world without oneself in it. Extensive as one's objective value influences might be, they are miniscule in the extensive sweep of things, the vast cosmos within which the whole of human evolution is but a blip. Intensive as one's subjective value influences might be, the meaningful human shape of them quickly falls away, and one's life is significant mainly for the metabolic processes of the Earthly ecosystem. The point is an ancient one. The author of the biblical Ecclesiastes wrote:

> For every thing there is a season, and a time for every matter
>   under heaven:
> A time to be born, and a time to die;
> A time to plant, and a time to pluck up what is planted;
> A time to kill, and a time to heal;
> A time to break down, and a time to build up;
> A time to weep, and a time to laugh;
> A time to mourn, and a time to dance;
> A time to throw away stones, and a time to gather stones
>   together;
> A time to embrace, and a time to refrain from embracing;
> A time to seek, and a time to lose;
> A time to keep, and a time to throw away;
> A time to tear, and a time to sew;
> A time to keep silence, and a time to speak;
> A time to love, and a time to hate;
> A time for war, and a time for peace.[7]

"Vanity of vanities," concluded Ecclesiastes. But what would he have said had he realized that most of the times and places in cosmic history were impossibilities for any of the things he mentioned? Even the most expansive sense of a person's absolute value-identity is but a small part of the vast cosmos. From most points of view, the absolute value-identity of the entire human race, not to mention any given individual, is at best what the poet W. H. Auden calls an "ironic point of light," an "affirming flame."[8]

Death is not only a natural process, although it needs to be accepted as that. Death is also an emblem of the gratuitous, arbitrary, undeserved, and surprising contingency of the whole of determinate existence. With one's own death, the existence of the cosmos goes out for one's consciousness. But the existence of the cosmos does not go out for the perspectives that follow, nor for the perspective of the ontological context of mutual relevance. To grasp this, and to affirm a world in which one no longer exists, is an act of ontological faith. Ontological faith affirms commitment to the details of one's life at the cusp where the questioning of the ultimate meaning of existence is felt with an equally strong feeling for the chaos that would be if it were not for the ontological creative act. Ontological faith is the perceptive grasp and total affirmation of the radical contingency of ultimate reality.

Is ontological faith a function of the great traditional religions? Most of them do deal with the fallibility of their own teachings and what to do about that. Nevertheless, ontological faith is not contained within the religions in any way that can be expressed adequately in a sacred worldview. Rather, it is a function of religion itself, the struggle to engage ultimate reality in its many dimensions and to find the symbols for doing so. Religion is the actual engagement, not the expression of the engagement in symbols alone.

Living with ontological faith is the ecstatic fulfillment of religionless religion. Religion is religionless when the inhabitation of sacred worldviews is of proximate and not ultimate importance. Religionless religion might in fact involve the explicit rejection of all sacred worldviews and their putative authority. Nevertheless religionless religion is still religion because it is the engagement of the ultimate realities with ontological faith, in whatever symbols that faith is framed. Because ordinary traditional symbols might be employed, religionless religion in some instance might look very much like plain religion. Then again, the symbols religionless religion can employ might be wholly different from those of any traditional religion.

The existential difference between religionless religion and plain religion is in the way the symbols of the engagements of the ultimates are referred. Religionless religion holds all of its significant symbols to be true as indexically, not iconically, connecting the interpreter to the ultimate realities, basically, to the ontological creative act with its determinate cosmic product. There might be some valid iconic reference, especially at the most abstract transcendent level. But religionless religion has its reality in the individual becoming a self-interpreting sign of the ontological creative act, which is to be a particular kind of creature. It is to be a creature ecstatically fulfilled in being created with the singular, eternal, gratuitous, arbitrary, surprising, and undeserved creation of all. For the ecstatic fulfillment of ontological faith, the ontological act of creation is not the object of the engagement of ultimates but, in some profound semiotic switch, the subject. The deepest ecstatic fulfillment is to feel oneself to be part of the ontological act eternally creating, a timeless song, an infinite dance, in one's own time and place.

Part IV

Summary Implications

Part IV of this volume has asked about the dimensions of the human predicament and ecstatic fulfillment that arise when sacred canopies are rent, with the consequence that in various ways the sacred worldviews within which they help orient human life become implausible. How can religion provide orientation toward ultimate matters when the plausibility of its orienting worldviews is in question? This is the ontological predicament, to be distinguished from the cosmological predicaments of human life that are articulated within sacred canopies and the worldviews containing them. It is also the venue for the deepest ontological ecstatic fulfillment.

Chapter 13 explored this question with an analysis of the plausibility conditions for sacred worldviews. Four main types were singled out: consistency, appropriateness for the situation, a balance of transcendent and intimate symbolizations, and authority. Obviously, these conditions for plausibility overlap and interpenetrate. Chapter 14 then discussed important aspects of the contemporary situation that challenge the plausibility of each of these types of conditions. The consistency of traditional sacred worldviews is challenged by modern science; their appropriateness for contemporary life is challenged by the fact that we live in a global society; sustaining both transcendent symbols and intimate ones sufficient for effective orientation is challenged by recognition of the purposelessness of the cosmos (among other factors); and the authority of sacred worldviews is challenged by the recognition that sacred worldviews are fallible hypotheses, and often hypotheses under stress.

Chapter 15 drew out the distinction between cosmological and ontological boundary conditions that was made in the introduction to *Philosophical Theology Two*, filling in the argument that developed in the intervening chapters. Then it pulled together the logical implications of the interdependence of apophatic and kataphatic theology in bringing the theory of symbolic engagement to a new level. The interpretive elements of symbolic engagements are hypothetical and, when the hypotheses are shown to be wanting in serious ways, the engagement itself is affected. The ontological predicament is how to live with the engagement of ultimate matters when one is also apophatically negating the orienting powers of the sacred world-view guiding the engagement. Caught on that cusp, ontological faith is to continue the engagement despite the powerful feeling of the finite/infinite contrasts of radical contingency.

Chapter 16 drew practical implications of ontological faith by examining the radical contingency of the four ultimate conditions of determinateness, as these appear in human experience; form, components formed, existential location, and value-identity. These dimensions of the ontological predicament are knowing/not knowing, being a self/nonself, being engaged/not being engaged, and achieving value-identity/registering no worth. All of these are versions of being/nonbeing. Ontological faith is the courage to affirm the being side in every instance: proceeding with the question to understand ultimate reality with improved hypotheses, coming to terms with having to bring to harmony the mere fragments that are components of life, staying the course with the engagements of one's watch, and accepting the finite value-identity that is only a small part of the value-identity of creation lodged in the ontological creative act.

This volume of *Philosophical Theology* began with reflections on the study of religion itself and ends with spiritual ruminations. Both are proper parts of philosophical theology, however different they seem in cognitive genre. In between, Part II was a study of how some of the major Axial Age religions alive today can contribute theologically acute symbols for the present religious situation, diverse as that is and requiring different contributions in different contexts. The chief issue regarding theologically acute symbols is how the transcendent symbols that do justice to ultimacy can be kept in appropriate interpretive connection with symbols intimate enough to relate to the diverse sacred worldviews that are appropriate in the religious situation. Following that discussion, Part III raised issues of the normative concerns of religion, understood theologically. It presented in a formal way the theory of value in possibilities that we have reflected on piecemeal throughout *Philosophical Theology*. Then, in respect to the ultimate trait of form/possibilities/obligation, it discussed religious ethics, commenting on the ways in which reality causes religious life to develop values for interpreting possibilities. In respect to the ultimate trait of comporting toward components of life, it discusses spirituality as a deliberate concern for developing wholeness with regard to the ultimates of form, components, engaging others, and absolute value-identity. In respect to the ultimate trait of engaging others in the existential field, it discusses the nature of membership, indeed companionship, in religious communities according to several important senses of belonging.

Both this volume and *Philosophical Theology Two* are organized around certain important philosophical ideas introduced in *Philosophical Theology One*.

The first is the set of metaphysical ideas having to do with what it is to be determinate. These ideas interpret determinateness as harmony, and any harmony has four metaphysical traits: form, components formed, existential location, and absolute value-identity. These four traits constitute the cosmological ultimate realities to be found as boundary conditions for anything whatsoever. Many chapters in these volumes have been organized into four sections reflecting some aspect of the four cosmological ultimates.

The second philosophical idea is that determinate things must be plural and can only be together with their essential and conditional components insofar as they are created by an ontological act of creation. The created things are together in the ontological context of mutual relevance that is the termination of the ontological creative act. This act, it has been argued, is the ontological ultimate, that which is symbolized in certain respects in various religions as God, Brahman, Shiva, Emptiness or Buddha-mind, the Dao, Heaven, Vacuity, and so forth.

The third philosophical idea is the understanding of temporal life within the context of the eternity of the ontological act of creation. Eternity is the togetherness of the modes of time—past, present, and future—and space (or whatever the complicated relations among these things turn out to be). That togetherness cannot be temporal. The logic of eternity means that all the moments of creation are together as past, as present, and as future, all modes in dynamic interaction. Within time, location is always at a spontaneous present. Within eternity, all the times of a person's life are real and together and are related to all other things with respect to which they are determinate. Eternal life is more concrete than temporal life, though not so vivid as in the spontaneity of consciousness.

The fourth philosophical idea is the semiotic theory of symbolic engagement, elaborated out of pragmatism. The theory of signs has particularly important elements regarding reference, which can be iconic, indexical, and conventional. Many religious symbols are indexically true but not iconically true. An important distinction is operative between the extension of a sign in an interpretation, meaning its syntax and semantics within a semiotic system, and the intention of a sign when it and its extension are used to engage some reality. Only actual intentional interpretations are true or false of real objects.

The fifth philosophical idea is that the semiotics of many religious symbols is affected by people engaging what are real ultimate realities. Because these realities are ultimate and form the boundaries of the humanly meaningful world, every theology needs to engage them in some way. Among the most important realities is the need for symbols of ultimacy to address the transcendent character of ultimacy while being intimately available to relate the ultimate to the mundane domains of life. This emphasis on theology in actual practice needing to cope with religiously important realities is the opposite approach to the study of religious symbols from phenomenology. Phenomenology presumes that the phenomena are identifiable for analysis, and then inevitably it is criticized for importing culturally laden categories that distort the phenomena. In *Philosophical Theology*, philosophical ideas are used to define the phenomena, which then can be studied within the parameters of the definitions. The philosophical definitions are to be justified by philosophical reasons as well as by their general heuristic helpfulness in organizing inquiry.

A sixth philosophical idea has been the conception of ultimacy or ultimate reality in terms of the boundary conditions for the world, which Peter Berger calls a "sacred canopy." *Philosophical Theology* has elaborated the notion of sacred canopies in many dimensions throughout these volumes and in particular with reference to how they function in larger worldviews according to which people find orientation for the ordinary things that take place. Sacred worldviews are necessary for anyone to find intense participation in religion, intense enough to respond to the human predicaments.

A seventh philosophical idea, following from the preceding, is that a certain kind of transcendent human ecstatic fulfillment is obtainable by engaging the ultimate in religious symbols that have the effect, over the long haul, of transforming people themselves into self-interpreting symbols of ultimacy. Spiritual adepts do this in extraordinary ways that are not easily domesticated in traditional religious symbols. But even ordinary people in ordinary ways of life can find themselves blessed by an ultimate beauty and goodness that is not much diminished by intractable predicaments.

An eighth philosophical idea is that religious worldviews generally say that something is broken in the human condition and needs to be fixed. *Philosophical Theology Two* analyzed brokenness and its repair with regard to relations to form/possibility/obligation, to components of one's life, to engagements of other things in the existential field, and to the achievement of absolute value-identity. *Philosophical Theology Three* has argued that worldviews need to be relevant to particular situations and that the religious situation today has many particular situations within it. Therefore, no one sacred worldview can fit all. Religious pluralism is necessary in the sense that different sacred worldviews are required to orient different contexts. What all theologically viable sacred worldviews should have in common, however, is a readiness to symbolize the important aspects of the ontological ultimate and the four cosmological ultimates.

A ninth philosophical idea is that religion *is human engagement of ultimacy expressed in cognitive articulations, existential responses to ultimacy that give ultimate definition to the individual and community, and patterns of life and ritual in the face of ultimacy*, to quote from the introduction to *Philosophical Theology One*. These volumes have elaborated the required theories of ultimacy, of cognitive articulations, of communal patterns of life in the face of ultimacy, and of many defining existential responses to ultimacy. Perhaps the justifying usefulness of this definition of religion has been spelled out sufficiently to make a contribution to theological inquiry.

Three pervasive themes have been developed through the cumulative arguments of the three volumes.

One is that ultimate reality is to be conceived in a pluralistic way, with an ontological creative act that is otherwise indeterminate creating anything that is determinate; whatever determinate things are created, they have as transcendental ultimate conditions: form, components, existential location creating mutual existential fields, and value-identity. This theme is radical on two counts: It forces the recognition that all determinate religious symbols of ontological ultimacy are broken, iconically false and only possibly indexically true, and it provides a thematic matrix for organizing most other dimensions of religion conceived as engaging ultimacy. A crucial consequence of this theme is the claim regarding religion that it develops as an engagement with the real characters of ultimate reality, something with which every culture needs to cope, and thus is not merely a social construction, even though its symbols are all socially constructed through the engagements with ultimacy.

The second theme is that human engagements with ultimacy interweave two forms, coping with ultimate predicaments and enjoying ecstatic fulfillments. Usually one of these has been emphasized to the exclusion or diminishment of the other. But both are important and are to be understood as conjoined in the five ultimates. The ultimates provide the ultimate boundary conditions that constitute the predicaments. They also provide the diverse venues for engaging the ontological creative act in ecstatic fulfillment of human meaning and value.

The third theme takes the form of calling for a radical reconsideration of the communal aspect of religion. The concept of sacred worldviews has been employed to interpret the ways in which people share or do not share in their engagements with ultimacy. The sharing of worldviews is a matter of the scope of who shares, of the scope of what the worldviews orient, and of the intensity of involvement of individuals in these worldviews. The approach thus diminishes the importance, for the study of *religion*, of groups named by social communities, especially ethnic communities, and of traditions named by the labels of religious membership. Given the diversity and complicated affiliations and interactions in a global society, the worldview approach is more realistic to people's actual issues of engaging ultimacy than the approaches that start with communal definitions. At some distant point in the primeval human past, religion might have been associated especially with the devices of human bonding, employing hypnotic rituals of togetherness. By the time of the Axial Age revolution, however, complex community organizations already were in place and that revolution expanded the scope of who counts in the religious community in ultimate senses. By our own time, the need for religious community is different from the need for social bonding as such and is structured by the needs for engaging ultimacy in our time.

These three themes constitute a significant new approach to the understanding of religion and present a theology with considerable novelty, even though no idea is wholly new. The length of this study, seeming sometimes tedious, and the reworking of the same ideas from many angles, seeming sometimes repetitive, have been aimed to produce a new vision of religion centered on these themes, a vision made persuasive by making it seem familiar.

Notes

PREFACE

1. See Whitehead, *Religion in the Making*, p. 17; quoted in *II, introduction, i.*

2. The theory of truth employed in *Philosophical Theology* says that it is the carryover of what is valuable or important from the object into the interpretation in the respect in which the signs involved stand for the object and as mediated by the biology, culture, semiotic systems, and purposes of the interpreter and the interpreter's community. See *I, 2, 3*, and Neville, *Recovery of the Measure*, Part 1.

3. The author's mentor from undergraduate days onward, Smith died in 2009. For his arguments about philosophy and theology, see his *Reason and God*, especially Chapters 7–13.

4. See Rorty's introduction to his edited book by that name.

5. See the writings of William M. Sullivan on the "professions." His central work is *Work and Integrity: The Crisis and Promise of Professionalism in America*; his *Reconstructing Public Philosophy* deals more particularly with philosophy.

6. See Bonhoeffer's *Letters and Papers from Prison*, for instance, Number 137 to Eberhard Bethge. See also the editor, John W. De Gruchy's, introduction, which is helpful on the theme of "religionless Christianity."

7. See Karl Barth's *On Religion: The Revelation of God as the Sublimation of Religion*.

8. See Tillich's *The Protestant Era* and, most especially, the whole of Volume 3 of his *Systematic Theology*.

9. See not only his *The Secular City* but also the later *Religion in the Secular City*.

10. On the varieties of responses within Islam to modernization and the creation of Muslim identity, see Andrew Rippin's *Muslims: The Religious Beliefs and Practices*, Chapters 9–17, especially the last chapter.

11. See Edward Said's *Orientalism* and Talal Asad's *Genealogies of Religion: Discipline and Reasons of Power in Christianity and Islam*.

12. See Talal Asad's *Formations of the Secular*.

13. See Michael Hogue's discussion of the Western orientation of religious naturalism in his *The Promise of Religious Naturalism*, especially Chapters 1–2.

14. The distinction between supernaturalism and supranaturalism is made by Paul Tillich at the beginning of his *Systematic Theology*, Volume 2. "Supernaturalism" is belief in disembodied intentional agents. "Supranaturalism" is belief in a being (or beings) extending or existing beyond the natural realm, such as a creating God; supranaturalism would not include concepts of the Neo-Platonic One or Thomistic Act of To Be or Hindu Brahman, which are not thought of as beings. See Wesley J. Wildman's analysis of this in his *Science and Religious Anthropology*, Chapter 2.

15. See Wesley J. Wildman, *Religious Philosophy as Multidisciplinary Comparative Inquiry*, especially Chapter 6. See also Neville, *On the Scope and Truth of Theology*.

16. On the issues of indexical and iconic reference regarding the truth of symbols, see *I, 2, 3*; *I, 2*, also deals with reductionism, as does *III, 1*.

INTRODUCTION

1. Barth, *The Doctrine of the Word of God, Church Dogmatics*, Volume 1, Part 1, p. 1.

2. Tillich, *Systematic Theology*, Volume 1, p. 3.

3. Zizioulis, *Being as Communion*, p. 15.

4. See his *The Silence of God: The Answer of the Buddha*, for instance.

5. In point of fact, most theologies even of the confessional mode are elitist in much this sense. Christians, for instance, who embody their religious lives in popular religious forms rarely read Tillich, or even Barth, surely not Rahner or Zizioulis.

6. See Wildman, "Neville's Systematic Theology of Symbolic Engagement," for the criticism that the theology is too austere, and his "The Ambiguous Heritage and Perpetual Promise of Liberal Theology" for the analysis of liberalism.

7. See Whitehead, *Religion in the Making*, p. 17.

8. See Neville, *Ritual and Deference*, Chapter 3, and *Normative Cultures*, Chapter 7.

9. See the more nearly complete argument in Neville, *Recovery of the Measure*, Chapters 3–4.

10. For a recent study of this with comparisons to the Confucian tradition, see Warren G. Frisina's *The Unity of Knowledge and Action: Toward a Nonrepresentational Theory of Knowledge*.

11. See Justus Buchler, *Nature and Judgment* and *The Main of Light*.

12. See Wesley J. Wildman's essay "The Significance of the Evolution of Religious Belief and Behavior for Religious Studies and Theology," for a critical analysis of potential distortions in several of these explanatory approaches to religion on the models of natural science.

13. Discussed and cited in *I, introduction, i*.

14. Karen Armstrong, *The Great Transformation*, pp. xv–xvi.

15. See his masterful *Comparative Theology: Deep Learning across Religious Borders*.

CHAPTER ONE. SCIENCE, AND CULTURE

1. See, for instance, the debates about these issues detailed in David Sloan Wilson's *Darwin's Cathedral*.

2. For thinkers who believe that religion is not genetically adaptive, see Steven Pinker, "The Evolutionary Psychology of Religion"; Lee A. Kirkpatrick, "Religion

Is Not an Adaptation"; or Richard Dawkins, *The God Delusion*. Of course, the issue often has to do with what they count as religion.

3. For a careful discussion of genetic adaptations, exaptations, and spandrels, with a review of the literature regarding religion as an evolutionary product, see Wesley J. Wildman, "The Significance of the Evolution of Religious Belief and Behavior."

4. See, for instance, Roy Rappaport, *Ritual and Religion in the Making of Humanity*.

5. See Neville, *Normative Cultures*, Chapter 7.

6. See McNamara's *Neuroscience of Religious Experience*.

7. See Wildman's "The Significance of Evolution for Religious Beliefs and Behavior for Religious Studies and Theology." His far more comprehensive review of evolution and religion is his *Science and Religious Anthropology*, Chapters 3–8.

8. For a good expository summary of cognitive science and evolutionary theory as explaining religion, see Todd Tremlin's *Minds and Gods: The Cognitive Foundations of Religion*. For an excellent selection of different, sometimes competing, points of view within the field, see Patrick McNamara, editor, *Where God and Science Meet*, Volume 1, *Evolution, Genes, and the Religious Brain*.

9. See his *Religion Explained: The Evolutionary Origins of Religious Thought*, p. 5, for this and the following points about Boyer's approach.

10. Cognitive scientists and evolutionary biologists are not the only groups of inquirers who define religion in terms of supernatural agents. Nancy Frankenberry and most of her very sophisticated philosophical colleagues in her edited volume *Radical Interpretation in Religion* do the same. See the discussion of her book in *I, preface*.

11. Justin Barrett is a Calvin College conservative Christian. Richard Dawkins and Daniel Dennett, in attacking religion on the grounds that cognitive science shows it to be an illusion and that history shows it to be harmful, attack Christianity as the paradigmatic religion. Most religious studies scholars are highly suspicious of taking Christianity to be the paradigmatic religion.

12. Ilkka Pyysiainen, in *Supernatural Agents: Why We Believe in Souls, Gods, and Buddhas*, takes pains to point out that Buddhism believes in supernatural agents, arguing that the Buddha himself was ascribed a kind of supernatural status. But, the Buddha is not ultimate in Buddhism and was important for teaching just that dharma.

13. See Barbara Herrnstein Smith's *Natural Reflections: Human Cognition at the Nexus of Science and Religion*, Chapter 3, a study of Scott Atran's theory.

14. See Wesley J. Wildman's "The Significance of the Evolution of Religious Belief and Behavior for Religious Studies and Theology" for a much more expansive critique and assessment of the cognitive science of religion than given here.

15. See Nathaniel Barrett's "Toward an Alternative Evolutionary Theory of Religion: Looking Past Computational Evolutionary Psychology to a Wider Field of Possibilities." See also the response to this article by Justin Barrett and his colleagues, Jeffrey P. Schloss and Michael J. Murray, "Looking Past vs. Overlooking Cognitive-Evolutionary Accounts of Religion: A Response to Nathaniel Barrett," which misses the point of Nathaniel Barrett's criticism of the computer model. See Nathaniel Barrett's response to their response, "What Are the Constraints of Computational Theory? A Reply to Schloss, Barrett, and Murray."

16. See McNamara's *The Neuroscience of Religious Experience*.

17. Some critics would say that political science and economics departments are at fault for not paying more attention to the impact of religion on the problems they study.

18. As noted earlier, two of the cognitive scientists building theories based on evolutionary biology discussed in the previous section, Pascal Boyer and Scott Atran, are anthropologists; Justin Barrett is a psychologist. "Cognitive science" is a label applied to the disciplines of anthropologists, sociologists, psychologists, evolutionary biologists, and neuroscientists who are interested in developing explanations of topics in their fields through some version or other of a modular theory of mental/neural structures.

19. See the systematic study of religious experience opening itself to the questions of validity in Wesley J. Wildman's *Religious and Spiritual Experiences*, especially Chapter 5.

20. For a sharp exposition of these critical questions, see Kathryn Tanner's *Theories of Culture*, Chapters 1–3. See also *I, 4*, for the discussion of the existential continuum for relating to worldviews, another approach to the questions of culture reflecting a postmodern perspective.

21. For a historical introduction to queer theory and a discussion of the major players, see Annamarie Jagose's *Queer Theory*, especially Chapters 7–8.

22. Kant, in fact, used the word "phenomenon" to apply to the social or transcendental mental construct only, in distinction from the thing in itself that was studied.

23. Agassiz's argument was part of his larger scientific view that different species of animals were associated with different regions of the globe and that there were successive kinds of these species in each region. He thought there was no evidence that any material force in these species could create the intelligibly related different successive species and so claimed that God must create each species in each place in each era according to an intelligent divine plan: Each new species in time, and each apparently related species in a different region, was created specifically by God according to that plan. Africans, thus, were different in origin and, if inferior, were created that way. He did say that there was a unity of the human race across regions that consisted in their common obligation to moral life, even though there was no unity in origins. In this he stood against his contemporary biblicists, who wanted to trace all human beings to Adam and Eve. Nevertheless, his work was used by people who wanted to insist on the general inferiority of Africans, and his authority as a scientist gave them authority. See Jon H. Roberts's "Louis Agassiz on Scientific Method, Polygenism, and Transmutation: A Reassessment."

24. See Richard von Krafft-Ebing, *Psychopathia Sexualis*, the introduction by Ernest Van Den Haag, for a discussion of the emerging medical model in Krafft-Ebing's work and the field more generally. On the Roman Catholic position regarding homosexuality, see Thomas C. Fox's *Sexuality and Catholicism*, Chapter 5.

25. Chandler Burr notes:

> Lesbians were forced to submit to hysterectomies and estrogen injections, although it became clear that neither of these had any effect on their sexual orientation. Gay men were subjected to similar abuses. *Changing Our Minds* [a documentary film by James Harrison, 1992] incorporates a film clip from the late 1940s, now slightly muddy, of a young gay man undergoing a transorbital lobotomy. We see a small device like an

> ice pick inserted through the eye socket, above the eyeball and into the brain. The pick is moved back and forth, reducing the prefrontal lobe to a hemorrhaging pulp. Harrison's documentary also includes a grainy black-and-white clip from a 1950s educational film produced by the U.S. Navy. A gay man lies in a hospital bed. Doctors strap him down and attach electrodes to his head. "We're going to help you get better," says a male voice in the background. When the power is turned on, the body of the gay man jerks violently, and he begins to scream. Doctors also tried castration and various kinds of aversion therapy. None of these could be shown to change the sexual orientation of the people involved.

See Burr in Jeffrey S. Siker's *Homosexuality in the Church: Both Sides of the Debate*, p. 118.

26. See Burr, *Homosexuality in the Church*, p. 119.

27. On Tylor and Frazer, a good analytical criticism is to be found in Daniel L. Pals's *Eight Theories of Religion*, Chapter 1.

28. See Edmund Husserl, *Ideas*, especially Chapter 3.

29. For this discussion of phenomenology of religion, I am indebted to Gavin Flood's learned and reflective study *Beyond Phenomenology: Rethinking the Study of Religion*. For a study of Eliade that defends him against the charge of unwonted theology and also connects him with the metaphysics of *Philosophical Theology* (in an earlier version, Neville, *God the Creator*), see John R. Mason, *Reading and Responding to Mircea Eliade's "History of Religious Ideas."*

30. Flood, *Beyond Phenomenology*, pp. 8–9.

31. Flood, *Beyond Phenomenology*, p. 15.

32. See Blum's "Retrieving Phenomenology of Religion as a Method for Religious Studies."

33. For an analysis of how intentionality can arise out of the naturalistic metaphysics and cosmology affirmed in *Philosophical Theology*, see Neville, *Recovery of the Measure*, especially Chapter 13, dealing with the computer analogy.

34. Robert N. McCauley in *Why Religion Is Natural and Science Is Not* works very hard to understand a complicated sign that involves so many dimensions of interpretation going on all at once, because he starts by taking seriously the assumption in some dominant cognitive science that each interpretation is a small unit, such as a computer function, that is connected inferentially with all the other elements in the apparently unified interpretive experience. Had he started with a semiotic theory of the Peircean sort, such as is developed here, he would have had an easier time.

35. The complexity of what needs an account is far greater than indicated here. Intentional engagement has at least four modes: imagination, interpretation, theorizing, and the pursuit of responsibility. Each of these modes has distinct ways of valuing, such that "truth" is the carryover of what is valuable from the intended object into the interpreter. For a technical theory of imagination, indicating what neuroscience needs to be able to account for, see Neville, *Reconstruction of Thinking*, Part 2. For an equally technical account of intentionality in interpretation, set in the context of a philosophical cosmology, see Neville, *Recovery of the Measure*. For an account that presents the same challenge regarding theorizing and the pursuit of responsibility, see Neville, *Normative Cultures*, Parts 1 and 2, respectively.

36. In the *Critique of Pure Reason*, Kant analyzed this as "transcendental illusion."

CHAPTER TWO. AXIAL AGE RELIGION

1. The principal locus of Jaspers's idea of the Axial Age is his *The Origin and Goal of History*. This was a relatively late work for him (1949 in German, 1953 in the English translation). He seems not to have regarded the idea of the Axial Age as all that important. In the Library of Living Philosophers volume, *The Philosophy of Karl Jaspers*, which was published in 1957, there is no article on the topic. He does not include the idea in his "Philosophical Autobiography" at the beginning of the volume, nor does the phrase appear in the glossary of terms peculiar to his philosophy or in the index to the volume. In the "Philosophical Autobiography" he does have these two paragraphs about how to think about world history:

> In contradistinction to the great encyclopedias as collections of materials, which are achieved by the teamwork of many and which certainly are indispensable and meritorious,—an over-all view, attempted by the philosophizing of a single person, must set its task quite differently: not to know everything, not to give completeness of material, but a concise description of the fundamental modes of the historical conception, constantly illustrated by significant examples; —to arouse the mind to a sense of historical wholeness, of hierarchical order and of greatness, and of the few singularly great men; —to find orientation in what is essential in a given period, in a given problem, in the forces that effect the thinking; —to gain intuitive insight into the great historical independent origins in China, India, in Asia Minor and in the Occident; —to make perceptible the historical itself in distinction from the abstractly universal.
>
> The work on the world history of philosophy, with which I am at present occupied, intensified the consciousness which, since my occupation with Chinese philosophy in the 'thirties, had become self-evident, but which formulated itself only later: we are on the road from the evening-glow of European philosophy to the dawn of world philosophy. On this road all of us individuals will be left. But it will go on into a future which, in addition to the most terrible, also shows the brightest possibilities. (pp. 83–84)

2. Tribal, pre–Axial Age religion flourishes on the grandest scale in Africa. See Jacob Olupona's *African Spirituality* for a seriously thorough treatment of a contemporary pre–Axial Age set of religious cultures. Of course, in Africa the tribal religions have been in interaction with Jewish, Christian, and Muslim sources for centuries.

3. The account here is highly generalized, which is satisfactory for present purposes but obscures many fascinating variations in detail. See Karen Armstrong's *The Great Transformation* for a narrative description of the evolution of tribal religions into the various Axial Age religions. See Robert Bellah's *Religion in Human Evolution* for a more detailed, interdisciplinary account.

4. See Jonathan Haidt, "The New Synthesis in Moral Psychology" and "The Emotional Dog and Its Rational Tail: A Social Intuitionist Approach to Moral Judgment." Haidt holds that these moral projects determine us to approach moral situations with predetermined "intuitions" about what to do, for which we subsequently

develop rational justifications. See Wesley J. Wildman's discussion of this in *Religious and Spiritual Experiences*, Chapter 6. Haidt has developed a systematic popular presentation of his theory of moral intuition in his recent *The Righteous Mind: Why Good People Are Divided by Politics and Religion*. In this book he exchanges the language of moral projects for that of "foundations" for morality. He also downplays the early evolutionary venue for the development of the foundations and adds a fifth moral foundation, the pursuit of liberty in the face of oppression, that has arisen in more recent history.

5. See David Sloan Wilson's *Darwin's Cathedral*, Chapter 1, for an account of hunter-gatherer societies that represents them as nonhierarchical. His main point is that the group has strongly enforced mores that serve to pressure members to behave in ways that benefit the group, not just self-interest. The relation of individuals to the group moral expectations illustrates the claim made in the text about the authority of the in-group.

6. Gore Vidal's novel *Creation* is the story of a Persian diplomat who is the grandson of Zoroaster and travels to China, where he meets Confucius, and to India, where he meets the Buddha, settling in Athens at the end of his life, where a stonemason named Socrates works on his wall. Though fiction, the meetings are plausible.

7. "All under heaven" is a slogan in Chinese culture roughly equivalent in one respect to the Chinese slogan "the ten thousand things." But it is not equivalent precisely in the respect that it collects the ten thousand things under the unity of heaven. See John H. Berthrong, *All Under Heaven*, for a fascinating deliberate expansion of what the ancient Chinese would have included under heaven to a conceptual East-West dialogue.

8. See Michael J. Puett's *To Become a God: Cosmology, Sacrifice, and Self-Divinization in Early China*.

9. See Daniel Boyarin, *Border Lines*, for a description of the vast diversity among Christian and Jewish communities in the early centuries, a diversity so complex that Christians and Jews were hard to distinguish. For an account of the establishment of orthodoxy, see Philip Jenkins's, *Jesus Wars*.

10. See Samuel Huntington, *The Clash of World Civilizations*.

11. See James Davison Hunter, *Culture Wars*.

12. See, for instance, Haidt's article "The New Synthesis in Moral Psychology" and his *The Righteous Mind*. In the latter he refines his earlier categories. He calls the moral "projects" "foundations" and accounts for preferences on the basis of deep social-intellectual commitments. The "liberals" who give great weight to the care and fairness foundations tend to be individualists and are WEIRD (Western, educated, industrialized, rich, and democratic, p. 96) and stand opposed to people who identify first with the group and, therefore, give great weight to the loyalty and respect for authority foundations. In contrast to both the individualistic and collectivistic cultures, he cites religious cultures that see the world as sanctified, or polluted; he ascribes disgust reactions to people who view the world as sanctified (or in need of sanctification). He also claims that a new moral foundation has arisen, liberty/oppression, that views the world in terms of oppressive forces that would threaten liberty, which then becomes the most important value to espouse. Although he recognizes the ancient evolutionary advantage of collectivist ethics, he does not give an historical account that says that the Axial Age responded to universal elements by favoring the care and fairness foundations as applied universally and that this is resisted by pre–Axial Age tribalism that privileges group loyalty, respect for authority, a sense of sacred pollutants, and a late capitalist sense that we deserve what we have. The historical dimension is important

for *Philosophical Theology*. *Philosophical Theology* deals with what Haidt characterizes as sacred religious orientations emphasizing purity in terms with its analysis of worldviews on the continuum of sacred and profane: Just how much of the mundane domains of life given orientation within a worldview is related to the sacred canopy part of that worldview? If very much of life is given a sacred dimension, then the worldview approaches what Haidt sees as an overwhelming concern for purity, so that people might think that burning the flag in protest to a government policy is blasphemous.

13. Legend has it that Jesus's disciple Thomas took Christianity to India, and if that legend is literally false, it represents a real historical movement for early Indian Christianity. On the Portuguese suppression of Mar Thoma, Nestorian, Christianity, see Samuel Hugh Moffett's *A History of Christianity in Asia*, Volume 2, Chapter 1. See also Charles Corn's *The Scents of Eden: A History of the Spice Trade*.

14. This observation is made about popular religion in China. But there have been sophisticated amalgams of the "three schools." See Judith Berling, *The Syncretic Religion of Lin Chao-en*.

15. See John H. Berthrong, *The Divine Deli: Religious Identity in the North American Cultural Mosaic*. His most detailed discussion of connections between Confucianism and Christianity is in his *All Under Heaven: Transforming Paradigms in Confucian-Christian Dialogue*. See also his discussion of Boston Confucianism: Many Boston Confucians, including this author, are also Christians, a certain sort of Confucian and a certain sort of Christian.

16. See Philip Jenkins, *The Lost History of Christianity*, especially Chapter 4, for an alternative view of Muslim attitudes toward Christianity during certain important periods.

17. This evolution is intended concretely here to refer, among other manifestations, to the author's Comparative Religious Ideas Project with its reports, edited by Neville, *The Human Condition*, *Ultimate Realities*, and *Religious Truth*. The project of *Philosophical Theology* arises from this comparative base of the main Axial Age religions.

CHAPTER THREE. THEOLOGY AND THE RELIGIOUS SITUATION

1. This point is argued at greater length and more directly in Neville, *On the Scope and Truth of Theology*.

2. For a comprehensive study of the original parsing of political and theological authority in Islam, see Patricia Crone's *God's Rule: Government and Islam*. For studies of the situation in contemporary Islam, see Said Amir Arjomand, editor, *Authority and Political Culture in Shi'ism*.

3. See James Miller's *Daoism: A Short Introduction*, and then his study of one textual school, *The Way of Highest Clarity*.

4. On theology and ritual in Hinduism, see Francis X. Clooney, S.J., *Thinking Ritually*. There is debate about whether the Hindu renouncer traditions were offshoots of Brahmanical householder piety or were outside influences that came to be integrated with householder Hinduism. See Gavin Flood, *An Introduction to Hinduism*, Chapter 4, and Patrick Olivelle, "The Renouncer Tradition."

5. Karl Barth was the premier confessional Protestant Christian theologian of the twentieth century. See his *Anselm: Fides Quaerens Intellectum (Faith in Search of Understanding)*.

6. George Lindbeck is a leading figure in ecumenical and interfaith dialogue, representing confessional Protestant (Lutheran in his case) theology. See his *The Nature of Doctrine*, especially Chapters 1 and 3. The Yale School is a confessional theology that offers a deep interpretation of the nature of a religious community. Francis X. Clooney, S.J., is careful always to present himself as a confessional theologian, a Roman Catholic thoroughly committed to his Catholic faith however willing he is to expand it and learn about it through comparisons with other religions.

7. Rowan Williams, *On Christian Theology*, pp. xiii ff. See Neville, *On the Scope and Truth of Theology*, Chapter 1, for an extended discussion of confessional theology and of Williams's theory (and David Tracy's).

8. Rowan Williams, *On Christian Theology*, p. xiii. Italics in the original.

9. Although Williams illustrates this point with the theology of Hans Urs von Balthasar, the work of Karl Barth is an equally good illustration. The power in his telling of what he takes to be the Christian narrative is in its aesthetic beauty and persuasiveness.

10. Williams, *On Christian Theology*, xiv.

11. He is speaking as a Christian here, but the point holds for any theological tradition that begins with the celebration of its own symbols and their practices.

12. Williams, *On Christian Theology*.

13. See David Tracy, *The Analogical Imagination: Christian Theology and the Culture of Pluralism*, especially Chapters 1–2.

14. Williams, *On Christian Theology*, p. xvi.

15. The career of Friedrich Schleiermacher, the great founder of liberal Protestant theology, is a case in point. His early, 1799, *On Religion: Speeches to Its Cultured Despisers*, appealed to direct experience and positioned itself so as not to have to appeal to the specific trappings of Christian practice. His later and magisterial *The Christian Faith* required that the experience of absolute dependence always be embedded in religious culture for any significant meaningfulness.

16. For some of the wilder uses of Jesus as a symbol for various dimensions of ultimacy, see Neville, *Symbols of Jesus*. For a more comprehensive account, see Roger Haight, S.J., *Jesus: Symbol of God*.

17. On this, see Sachiko Murata, William C. Chittick, and Tu Weiming, *The Sage Learning of Liu Zhi*. Liu was a Chinese Muslim who wrote extensively about Islam in Confucian terms and whose work is now of interest in Persia, where it is being translated into Arabic. Here the point is to show the continuity of Islam and Confucianism in the most transcendent matters.

18. See Christopher Key Chapple, *Yoga and the Luminous*. Chapple shows that yoga practice, and some of the ideology, was common to many forms of Hinduism, Buddhism, and Jainism.

19. See Stephen C. Angle's *Sagehood: The Contemporary Significance of Neo-Confucian Philosophy*, especially Chapters 7–9.

20. Paul Tillich, *The Religious Situation*. See also the translator's preface to this volume by H. Richard Niebuhr, which is an excellent introduction to Tillich's early thought.

21. See Werner Schuessler's "Tillich's Life and Works."

22. From the table of contents.

23. See Tillich's *Theology of Culture*. In 1919 he had published a lecture entitled "On the Idea of a Theology of Culture." See also Jean Richard, "Tillich's Analysis of the Spiritual Situation of His Time(s)."

CHAPTER FOUR. A VIABLE SACRED CANOPY

1. The points in this paragraph owe much to the inspiration of Robert S. Corrington. See especially his *Nature's Religion* and *Ecstatic Naturalism: Signs of the World.*

2. For a recent selection of approaches to this question, see John F. Wippel, editor, *The Ultimate Why Question: Why Is There Anything at All Rather than Nothing Whatsoever?*

3. These are three of Hopkins's most famous and popular poems, printed in many collections of his works and anthologies of poetry. They are quoted here from *The Poems of Gerard Manley Hopkins*, edited by W. H. Gardner and N. H. MacKenzie, "Pied Beauty" on pp. 69–70, "The Windhover" on p. 69, and "God's Grandeur" on p. 66.

4. Hopkins studied Duns Scotus beginning when he was twenty-eight and developed his poetic theory of "inscape" as a parallel to Scotus's theory of haecceity or "thisness."

5. This was the main theme of his early *The Religious Situation* and it echoed through all his works, especially the *Systematic Theology*.

6. See Martin E. Marty and R. Scott Appleby, editors, *Fundamentalisms Observed*, for very serious essays about fundamentalism in different parts of the world associated with Christianity, Judaism, Islam, Hinduism, Sikhism, Buddhism, Confucianism, and Japanese religion. They make the point about defensiveness.

7. The Methodist movement in America during the nineteenth and twentieth centuries founded many dozens of colleges and a significant number of universities because of the conviction derived from John Wesley that spiritual growth, "sanctification," requires increasing sophistication.

PART II. PRELIMINARY REMARKS

1. See Diamond's *Guns, Germs, and Steel*, p. 14. "Cargo" meant post–Stone Age material goods and technologies.

2. See Laurenti Magesa, *African Religion: The Moral Traditions of Abundant Life*, pp. 18–28. This book is a fine summary of African religion taken as a whole.

3. Edited by Jacob K. Olupona, *African Spirituality: Forms, Meanings, and Expressions* contains important essays by a wide range of scholars of African religion. The first essay, by Dominique Zahan, "Some Reflections on African Spirituality," is an excellent summary of the theological cosmology of African religion.

4. This is the important thesis of Lamin Sanneh's *Translating the Message: The Missionary Impact on Culture*. Sanneh's is perhaps the most important study of the way religions change as they move from culture to culture.

5. Kwame Bediako, *Christianity in Africa: The Renewal of a Non-Western Religion.*

CHAPTER FIVE. ABRAHAMIC RELIGIONS

1. The Ten Commandments, for instance, assert that Yahweh should be placed first by the Israelites among the Gods available to them, which included those of Egypt and Canaan. The Sinai Covenant was to bind Israel and Yahweh together in contrast to other possible religious allegiances the people of Israel might have. The process of covenantal and ethnic purification stressed by Ezra and Nehemiah upon

the return of the Jewish elite from the Babylonian exile was a strong move to reassert the in-group integrity of the people strictly sworn to Yahweh.

2. See David B. Burrell, CSC, "Creation," in Tim Winter, editor, *The Cambridge Companion to Classical Islamic Theology*, Chapter 7, for a concise history and categorization of Islamic theological treatments of creation, also with reference to Islamic philosophy. See also Oliver Leaman's *A Brief Introduction to Islamic Philosophy*, Chapters 2, 4, and 5, for a focus on philosophical approaches to the unity of God and the divine work of creation. Theology and philosophy often have been sharply distinguished in Islamic thought and sometimes have not cohabited easily.

3. On Neo-Platonism in Islam, see Syed Nomanul Haq's *Names, Natures, and Things: The Alchemist Jabir ibn Hayyan and His "Kitab al-Ahjar" (Book of Stones)*. For general introductions on the topic, see Majid Fakhry's *A History of Islamic Philosophy*, Chapter 1, and Oliver Leaman's *A Brief Introduction to Islamic Philosophy*, Chapters 1–2.

4. See Jon Levenson's *Creation and the Persistence of Evil* and also the claim within contemporary process theology that God influences the form of the world but does not create the world from nothing; God is dependent on the world and vice versa.

5. See S. Nomanul Haq, "The Human Condition in Islam: Sharia and Obligation," especially pp. 162–163, for an interpretation of the Muslim view. See Anthony J. Saldarini and Joseph Kanofsky, "Religious Dimensions of the Human Condition in Judaism: Wrestling with God in an Imperfect World," for Jewish interpretations. See Paula Fredriksen and Tina Shepardson, "Embodiment and Redemption: The Human Condition in Ancient Christianity," for early Christian views. These essays were written in collaboration with one another in the Comparative Religious Ideas Project.

6. See Michael Zank's "Jewish Ethics in a Modern World" for an analysis of a variety of Jewish positions and the reasons for them.

7. On these complicated issues, see Nicholas de Lange and Miri Freud-Kandel, editors, *Modern Judaism*, Chapters 6–9, 15–17, and 27–29.

8. On the point of cultural participation in Christianity, see Neville, *Symbols of Jesus*, pp. 240–242.

9. See Robert L. Wilken, *The Land Called Holy: Palestine in Christian History and Thought*, for a fascinating study of Christian and Jewish attitudes toward that territory as they developed through history.

10. See Anthony J. Saldarini and Joseph Kanofsky, "Religious Dimensions of the Human Condition in Judaism: Wrestling with God in an Imperfect World."

11. Romans 7:15, NRSV. For an imaginative theological elaboration of this contradiction, see Thomas J. J. Altizer, *History as Apocalypse*.

12. The most influential of these is Lynn White, an historian of Western medieval technology. See his "The Historical Roots of our Ecological Crisis." White's emphasis is mainly on Christianity because of its predominance in the development of modern technology that objectifies nature as subject to human domination.

13. See, for instance, Berry's *The Great Work: Our Way into the Future*.

14. See the collection edited by Mary Evelyn Tucker and John Berthrong, *Confucianism and Ecology: The Interrelation of Heaven, Earth, and Humans*. See also the collection edited by James E. Miller, N. J. Girardot, and Liu Xianogan, *Daoism and Ecology: Ways within a Cosmic Landscape*.

15. See the collection edited by Mary Evelyn Tucker and John Grim, *Hinduism and Ecology: The Intersection of Earth, Sky, and Water*. See also her collection edited

with Duncan Ryuken Williams, *Buddhism and Ecology: The Interconnection of Dharma and Deeds.*

16. Luke 10:29–37.

17. See S. Nomanul Haq, "Ultimate Reality: Islam" and "The Human Condition in Islam: Sharia and Obligation."

18. A point stressed by Patricia Crone in *God's Rule: Government and Islam.*

CHAPTER SIX. BUDDHISM

1. The central "Questions of King Milinda" are readily available, for instance, in Radhakrishnan and Moore, editors, *A Source Book in Indian Philosophy*, pp. 281–284.

2. See "Beginningless Ignorance: A Buddhist View of the Human Condition," by Malcolm David Eckel with John J. Thatamanil, p. 52. Eckel's text gives the sources.

3. See, for instance, Malcolm David Eckel's *Bhaviveka and His Buddhist Opponents* for a detailed analysis of critical differences between Mahayana schools as expressed in Bhaviveka's debate form.

4. On Nagarjuna, including a translation of key texts, see Frederick J. Streng's *Emptiness: A Study in Religious Meaning.*

5. For a more detailed account, see Eckel and Thatamanil, "Beginningless Ignorance."

6. Eckel, *Bhaviveka*, p. 87. See also Eckel's *To See the Buddha*: Note the vision imagery.

7. See Eckel's discussion in "Beginningless Ignorance," p. 53. The relevant text of the "Questions of King Milinda" is in Radhakrishnan and Moore, editors, *A Source Book in Indian Philosophy*, pp. 281–84.

8. See Frederick J. Streng's *Emptiness.*

9. See Kirk MacGregor's *A Comparative Study of Adjustments to Social Catastrophes in Christianity and Buddhism* for a historical analysis of shifts in popularity from forms of Buddhism making strong claims on virtuosity of meditation to forms of Pure Land in which all action comes from Amida Buddha and little or nothing is required from the devotee.

10. For a clear discussion of some of the varieties of steps in Buddhist practice, see Sung Bae Park's *Buddhist Faith and Sudden Enlightenment*, especially Chapter 10. Hua-yen practice, for instance, is organized in fifty two stages.

11. In Radhakrishnan and Moore, editors, *A Source Book in Indian Philosophy*, p. 275.

12. See John Powers's *A Bull of a Man: Images of Masculinity, Sex, and the Body in Indian Buddhism.* This is a fascinating study, even if Powers's postmodern enthusiasms for gender issues suggests some disconnection from the issues of consciousness.

13. Park, *Buddhist Faith*, p. 1. See also Park's *One Korean's Approach to Buddhism: The Mom/Momjit Paradigm.*

14. The *ti-yong* construction was formulated as a philosophical conception perhaps first by Wang-bi. See Chan, editor, *A Source Book in Chinese Philosophy*, pp. 322–323.

15. Park, *Buddhist Faith*, p. 19.

16. Chinul, quoted in Park, *Buddhist Faith*, pp. 19–20.

17. Park himself represents the Yogacara tradition. For a Madhyamaka account of the distinction between conventional truth and ultimate truth, see Malcolm David Eckel's *Jnanagarbha's Commentary on the Distinction between the Two Truths.*

18. Park, *Buddhist Faith*, Chapters 16, 17, and conclusion.

19. See Mary Evelyn Tucker and Duncan Ryuken Williams, *Buddhism and Ecology: The Interconnection of Dharma and Deeds*, for discussions of Buddhist compassion for the nonsentient environment.

20. See Winston Leyland, editor, *Queer Dharma: Voices of Gay Buddhists*, Volumes 1–2, for many accounts of this phenomenon. For powerful representations of the failures of religious communities and the development of new kinds of communities among gay people in the face of the AIDS crisis, see Paul Monette's *Last Watch of the Night* and Andrew Sullivan's *Love Undetectable: Notes on Friendship, Sex, and Survival.*

21. See, for instance, Keiji Nishitani, *Religion and Nothingness.*

22. See *The Lotus Sutra*, translation by Gene Reeves, p. 279.

23. *The Lotus Sutra*, Reeves translation, p. 55.

CHAPTER SEVEN. HINDUISM

1. See Gauri Viswanathan's "Colonialism and the Construction of Hinduism" and David Smith's "Orientalism and Hinduism."

2. See Gavin Flood's fascinating account of the return of Hinduism to India in his *Introduction to Hinduism*, Chapter 11.

3. See Patrick Olivelle's "The Renouncer Tradition."

4. See Christopher Key Chapple's *Yoga and the Luminous: Patanjali's Spiritual Path to Freedom.*

5. The account of Abhinavagupta's theology here draws heavily on Paul Eduardo Muller-Ortega's *The Triadic Heart of Siva.*

6. See Muller-Ortega, *The Triadic Heart of Siva*, Chapter 5.

7. See Muller-Ortega, *The Triadic Heart of Siva*, p. 114 and Chapter 6.

8. Muller-Ortega, *The Triadic Heart of Siva*, p.114.

9. Muller-Ortega, *The Triadic Heart of Siva*, p. 106.

10. Flood, *Introduction to Hinduism*, p. 52. His quotation, "the ritualistic order of Vedic Sacrifice," is from J. C. Hesterman's *The Inner Conflict of Tradition: An Essay in Indian Ritual, Kingship, and Society* (Chicago, IL: University of Chicago Press, 1985), p. 3.

11. In the contemporary scholarly consciousness in the West, Hindu metaphysics generally has eclipsed Hindu ethics. A good counterweight is the fine study by Harold Coward, Julius J. Lipner, and Katherine K. Young, *Hindu Ethics: Purity, Abortion, and Euthanasia.*

12. For essays on the ecological sensibilities of Hinduism, see Mary Evelyn Tucker and John Grim, editors, *Hinduism and Ecology: The Intersection of Earth, Sky, and Water.*

13. Bhagavad Gita 12:2–7, Radhakrishnan translation in Radhakrishnan and Moore, editors, *A Source Book in Indian Philosophy.*

14. Bhagavad Gita 10:32–34, Radhakrishnan translation in Radhakrishnan and Moore, editors, *A Source Book in Indian Philosophy.*

15. Bhagavad Gita 12:13–20, Radhakrishnan translation in Radhakrishnan and Moore, editors, *A Source Book in Indian Philosophy.*

16. For the details of this account of the history of the Vedic Upanishads, see Brian Black's *The Character of the Self in Ancient India*, especially, for the dating issues, the introduction. As early Upanishads, Black analyzes the Brhadaranyaka, Chandogya, Kausitaki, Taittiriya, and Aitareya Upanishads. Among the later ones are the Kena, Katha, Isha, and Svetashvatara Upanishads.

17. On Ramanuja, see John Braisted Carman's *The Theology of Ramanuja: An Essay in Interreligious Understanding.*

18. On Shankara and these questions of superimposition and identity, see John Thatamanil's *The Immanent Divine.*

CHAPTER EIGHT. CHINESE RELIGION

1. Livia Kohn argues that Chinese religions should be considered as a whole, from which Confucianism, Daoism, shamanism, and Sinicized Buddhism are practical abstractions. See her "Chinese Religion."

2. See Martin Palmer, *The Jesus Sutras: Rediscovering the Lost Scrolls of Taoist Christianity.*

3. See the recent set of scholarly studies of Neo-Confucian philosophy in John Makeham, editor, *Dao Companion to Neo-Confucian Philosophy.*

4. See his "An Explanation of the Diagram of the Great Ultimate" in Chan, editor, *A Source Book in Chinese Philosophy*, Chapter 28. Much of this is quoted in *I, 12, i.*

5. There are many translations of the Daodejing. See, for instance, Wing-tsit Chan's in his *Source Book*, Chapter 7, p. 139, for this passage.

6. For Wangbi's text, see Chan, editor, *Source Book*, Chapter 19.

7. For further discussion of the Daoist texts, including Wangbi's, see Neville, *Ritual and Deference*, Chapter 4.

8. This point has been a particular focus of the work of John Berthrong in the context of comparisons with Western notions of change. See his *Transformations of the Confucian Way*, Chapters 4–5; *Concerning Creativity*, especially Chapter 5; and *Expanding Process.*

9. See the excellent account of the education of the Confucian sage to perceive the ultimacy of harmony and the concrete harmonies that order the cosmos in Stephen C. Angle's *Sagehood*, Chapters 4, 6–9.

10. Mencius, 2A:6. Wing-tsit Chan translation in Chan, editor, *A Source Book in Chinese Philosophy*, p. 65.

11. See Zhu Xi's "A Treatise on *Jen* (*Ren*)," in Chan, editor, *Source Book*, pp. 593–597.

12. This is a major theme traced in Angle's *Sagehood.*

13. See Tu Weiming, *Centrality and Commonality*, especially Chapter 3.

14. See Tu Weiming, *Humanity and Self-Cultivation.*

15. See Edward J. Machle, *Nature and Heaven in the Xunzi.*

16. On the deep connection between ritual and humaneness (*li* and *ren*) in Confucianism, see Herbert Fingarette's *Confucius: The Secular as Sacred.*

17. See, for instance, Chan's comments on Moism, which advocated universal and equal love, in his *Source Book*, p. 211, in which he discusses the Confucian "love with differences."

18. See Xunzi's "Discourse on Nature" in *Xunzi*, Volume 3, Chapter 17; an earlier translation is in Chan, editor, *A Source Book in Chinese Philosophy*, Chapter 6. See the discussion in Machle's *Heaven and Nature in the Xunzi.*

19. This is an interpretation of the Confucian classic, the Doctrine of the Mean (Chong-yong). See Chan, editor, *Source Book*, Chapter 5.

SUMMARY IMPLICATIONS

1. See John E. Smith's *Quasi-Religions.*

CHAPTER NINE. VALUE

1. For a materialist attempt to derive meaning for human life within a valueless cosmos, see Owen Flanagan's *The Really Hard Problem: Meaning in a Material World.*

2. For a classic analysis, see E. A. Burtt, *The Metaphysical Foundations of Modern Science.* For a more elaborate account of this point, see Neville, *Reconstruction of Thinking*, Chapter 1.

3. See Descartes's Reply to Objections VI, in *Philosophical Works of Descartes, Vol. 2.*

> For it is self-contradictory that the will of God should not have been from eternity indifferent to all that has come to pass or that ever will occur, because we can form no conception of anything good or true, of anything to be believed or to be performed or to be omitted, the idea of which existed in the divine understanding before God's will determined Him so to act as to bring it to pass. Nor do I speak of priority of time; I mean that it was not even in the order, or in nature, or in reasoned relation, as they say [in the schools], so that the idea of good impelled God to choose one thing rather than another. Thus, to illustrate, God did not will to create the world in time because he saw that it would be better thus than if he created it from all eternity; nor did he will the three angles of a triangle to be equal to two right angles because he knew that they could not be otherwise. On the contrary, because he worked to create the world in time it is for that reason better than if he had created it from all eternity; and it is because he willed the three angles of a triangle to be necessarily equal to two right angles that this is true and cannot be otherwise; and so in other cases. . . . Thus that supreme indifference in God is the supreme proof of his omnipotence. (p. 248)

4. Ludwig Wittgenstein, *Tractatus Logico-Philosophicus*, p. 183, Paragraphs 6.4–6.421.

5. He argued this in different ways in *Science and the Modern World*, *Process and Reality*, and *Adventures of Ideas.*

6. The analysis summarizes and expands the discussion in *II, 1*, which in turn is an expansion of the hypothesis about determinateness and harmony in *I, 10.* The theory of value elaborated here needs to be approached from many different angles.

7. For the sources of the following analysis, see Whitehead's *Process and Reality*, pp. 110–112, and Neville, *Reconstruction of Thinking*, pp. 164–166.

8. For a study of Peirce's approach to value, given that Peirce did not write about it in a systematic fashion, see Douglas R. Anderson's *Creativity and the Philosophy of C. S. Peirce.*

9. For an expansive analysis of this illustration, see John Dewey's *Art as Experience.*

10. On the use of imagination in moral and aesthetic deliberation about alternatives, see John Dewey's early *Human Nature and Conduct.*

11. This is the general idea behind Whitehead's conception of actual occasions. The differences between the theory in *Philosophical Theology* and Whitehead's *Process and Reality* are developed in Neville, *Recovery of the Measure*, Divisions 2 and 3.

12. Thomas Hobbes, *Leviathan*, pp. 103–104.

CHAPTER TEN. RELIGIOUS ETHICS

1. *The Righteous Mind*, p. 270.

2. See Haidt's *The Righteous Mind*, Chapters 10 and 11, where he associates religion with the bonding of a "hive," claiming that it is a team sport. Rituals from primeval times to contemporary rock concerts have sometimes produced strong feelings of collective bonding, but whether they are religiously significant rather than merely socially or politically significant, depends on whether and how they bear on ultimacy.

3. See Thomas Berry, *The Great Work.*

4. See Jonathan Edwards, *The Nature of True Virtue.*

CHAPTER ELEVEN. SPIRITUALITY

1. This point is developed at length in Neville, *Soldier, Sage, Saint*, Chapter 1; that book is summarized and augmented in the first three sections of this chapter.

2. On the interaction of dynamic psychological and more traditional processes of spiritual development, see Don S. Browning's *Reviving Christian Humanism: The New Conversation on Spirituality, Theology, and Psychology.*

3. See Michael Raposa's *Meditation and the Martial Arts.*

4. See Peter Brown, "Bodies and Minds: Sexuality and Renunciation in Early Christianity."

5. Bhagavad Gita 2:47, in Radhakrishnan and Moore, editors, *A Source Book in Indian Philosophy*, p. 110.

6. Analects 2:4, in Chan, editor, *A Source Book in Chinese Philosophy*, p. 22.

7. See Paul Weiss, *Sport: A Philosophic Inquiry*, Chapter 1, especially p. 17, where he writes, "Athletes are excellence in the guise of men."

CHAPTER TWELVE. RELIGIOUS COMPANIONSHIP

1. On "total institutions," see Erving Goffman's *Relations in Public.*

2. See, for instance, H. Richard Niebuhr's *Christ and Culture* and Patricia Crone's *God's Rule.*

3. See James M. Gustafson's *Treasure in Earthen Vessels: The Church as a Human Community* for a classical study of this point in reference to Christian communities.

PART IV. PRELIMINARY REMARKS

1. "Hymn of Creation" from the Rg Veda, Book 10, Number 129, translated by A. A. Macdonell, in Radhakrishnan and Moore, editors, *A Source Book in Indian Philosophy*, pp. 23–24. This hymn dates from at least 500 BCE and perhaps has roots a thousand years before that.

2. Some of these are reviewed in *I, 6,* in connection with pressures toward transcendence in symbols of ultimacy.

3. For Peirce's views from early in his career, see *The Essential Peirce,* Volume 1, Chapters 2–4, 6–7. For Dewey, see *Essays in Experimental Logic.*

CHAPTER THIRTEEN. THE PLAUSIBILITY OF SACRED WORLDVIEWS

1. On the biblical expressions of the Christian Eucharistic rite, see 1 Corinthians 11:23–26 and parallels in the passion stories in Mark, Matthew, and Luke. On the Israelite "old covenant," see Exodus 24:3–8. The old covenant involved animal sacrifice, whereas the new covenant involved symbolic human sacrifice and cannibalism.

2. On the Levitical rite of Atonement, see Leviticus 16. On Jesus as the Lamb of God who takes away the sins of the world, see John 1:29.

3. See Exodus 12 for the story of the Passover lamb.

4. See, for instance, the Book of Daniel in the Hebrew Bible and the Book of Revelation in the New Testament.

5. See Paul's discussion of Jesus raising people into the heavens at the Last Judgment in 1 Thessalonians 4–5.

6. See the discussion in Colossians 1. The prologue to the Gospel of John makes a similar point in saying that Jesus is the incarnation of the logos.

7. See Laurenti Magesa, *African Religion,* pp. 201–209.

8. See David Tracy's *The Analogical Imagination,* Chapters 3–5.

9. See Augustine's *Confessions,* Book 8. For a fine analysis, see Carl G. Vaught's *Encounters with God in Augustine's "Confessions": Books VII–IX,* Chapter 2.

CHAPTER FOURTEEN. THE IMPLAUSIBILITY OF SACRED WORLDVIEWS

1. The distinction between society and culture is elaborated at greater length in Neville, *Religion in Late Modernity,* Chapter 7.

2. This point is not a commitment to the metaphor of the ultimate being one mountaintop with many different paths up to it.

3. See his paper "Questions Concerning Certain Capacities Claimed for Man," in *The Collected Papers of Charles Sanders Peirce,* Volume 5, pp. 135–155, and in *The Essential Peirce,* Volume 1, Chapter 2.

4. See his essay "The Fixation of Belief," in *The Collected Papers of Charles Sanders Peirce,* Volume 5, pp. 223–247, and in *The Essential Peirce,* Volume 1, Chapter 7.

CHAPTER FIFTEEN. IMPLODING WORLDVIEWS AND ONTOLOGICAL PREDICAMENT

1. See the discussions in Andrew Rippin's *Muslims,* Parts 5–6.

2. See Berdyaev's *The Beginning and the End.*

3. Vedanta is not the only such Hindu tradition, however. See, for instance, the Kashmir Shaivism as explained by Paul Eduardo Muller-Ortega in his *The Triadic Heart of Siva.*

4. Translated by Wing-tsit Chan in his *A Source Book in Chinese Philosophy*, p. 139.

5. See Scotus's *Philosophical Writings*, p. 15.

6. For a careful and thorough theological analysis of this point about the ascetic character of the theory of ontological creation, see Wesley J. Wildman's "Neville's Systematic Theology of Symbolic Engagement." Wildman despairs of the usefulness of this theology for any but a few; if this is so, they are the ones to whom appeal is made for the truth of the theology of *Philosophical Theology*.

7. See John E. Smith's *Quasi-Religions*, Chapter 2.

8. See Wildman's "The Ambiguous Heritage and Perpetual Promise of Liberal Theology."

CHAPTER SIXTEEN. ONTOLOGICAL SALVATION AND ECSTATIC FULFILLMENT

1. In his *The Courage to Be*, Tillich discussed several senses in which human beings are threatened by nonbeing and require faith as the courage to overcome them. *Philosophical Theology* provides a somewhat different analysis of the ontological predicament, although one deeply indebted to Tillich. Tillich's version of the phrase used here, "living on the cusp," was "living on the boundary." See his book, *On the Boundary: An Autobiographical Sketch*.

2. The full opening stanza of the Daodejing, quoted in part in the previous chapter, in the standard version used by Wangbi, goes as follows (in Wing-tsit Chan's translation, p. 139):

> The Tao (Way) that can be told of is not the eternal Tao;
> The name that can be named is not the eternal name.
> The Nameless is the origin of Heaven and Earth;
> The Named is the mother of all things.
> Therefore let there always be non-being so we may see their subtlety [mystery],
> And let there always be being so that we may see their outcome.
> The two are the same,
> But after they are produced, they have different names.
> They both may be called deep and profound [mysterious].
> Deeper and more profound,
> The door of all subtleties!

The word Chan translates as "subtlety," *miao*, also means "mystery." The word he translates as "profound," *hsuan*, also means "mysterious."

3. I am about to describe an experience I had while rowing one night on Lake Washington. Understand, in reading it, that this sort of "thing" would occasionally happen to me. The history of my life has been an ongoing attempt to understand and to reproduce this experience. Attempting to symbolize this experience, as well as repeating the experience itself, are endeavors that have given my life meaning.

I was preparing for the 2000 Olympics in Seattle. If, where, and when I wanted to row, I rowed. My life was utterly monastic; everything I did was organized around rowing. I knew exactly how many hours my body needed to rest before I could work out again, and so I would sometimes work out at night, as my physical cycle would prompt a workout at two, or three, or four in the morning. No drinking, no social life, just the rhythm of my training, the rhythm of the boat, the rhythm of my breathing, year after year after year.

It was time to practice. It was around two in the morning, late spring, and it had been warm in Seattle, so the night air was just right for rowing. My boat was very fine, 28 feet long, 18 inches wide, fiberglass, about 29 pounds, an object with great aesthetic appeal. Sitting in it, I am about eight inches off the water, with but the needle-like bow of the boat reminding me that I am not somehow myself, floating over the water. And at night, the boat is difficult to see, and my eyes look far over the water; sweat and fatigue blur my vision.

I'm alone. I head out, through Portage Bay, through Union Bay, and into the massive and uncharacteristically still expanse of Lake Washington. I've pulled my rowing gear off and am naked now, which is how I row whenever I can get away with it. Not a boat around, most of the houses on shore dark and, in any case, far, far away. And everything is okay because I'm all breath now, and rhythm, and my eyes half shut, but in no way sleepy: focused, concentrating, relaxed. And I row.

And I row, and there is *nothing* of my life in this place, there is nothing in this place, and I've forgotten myself; my consciousness is mixing with the darkness and I become unsure of where I am and where I am not. The dark water and the dark sky hide the horizon and the whole world is colored deep gray-black. I have no sense of direction, as a man lost at sea without land to teach him his position. Time is an endless instant, meaningless.

In this place that is my floating breath, in an emptiness without any center or limit, I am beset, if I can use that word, by the utterly overwhelming weight of infinite blackness around me. I am filled with an intensity of feeling that is agonizing, a feeling too intense for me to contain. The sense of it is all things at once: power, insignificance, exhilaration, dread.

And on I row, choking, fascinated, and afraid. It quickly becomes more than I can bear, and I find myself weeping, and groaning, and crying out. I am madness, my sense of exhilaration beyond measure, my fear of annihilation a welcome relief and yet a dread to me, a sense of omnipotence that was not for any body to have to hold. The infinite abyss had taken me up, and I was all the world, and I was nothing. All words fall away.

I stop rowing sometime later. Was it five minutes? Twenty? I am crying now, just crying. Not sad, but wrung out. Crying because it helps soothe the aching in me; and I am grateful that it is over. The row home was forgettable. Dulled and numb, I don't think as much as peek around the corner of the memory my body still holds. I return home and am ill at ease for the rest of the night and confused and worried the next day as I struggled to symbolize and make finite what had happened. I feel unhinged, and overwhelmed, and yet utterly, passionately alive.

4. This is Krishna's remark to Arjuna in the Bhagavad Gita, 2:47. The whole verse is this: "To action alone hast thou a right and never at all to its fruit; let not the fruits of action be thy motive; neither let there be in thee any attachment to inaction." Translated by S. Radhakrishnan, in Radhakrishnan and Moore, editors, *A Source Book in Indian Philosophy*, p. 110.

5. For instance, in the sixth and seventh centuries, especially in South India and the Ganges basin, intellectual debate among Buddhists and between Buddhists and

non-Buddhist schools reached a culture of great precision. See Malcolm David Eckel's translation of and commentary on one of the most important and encyclopedic of these Buddhist thinkers, Bhaviveka, in Eckel's *Bhaviveka and His Buddhist Opponents*. Bhaviveka's text, *The Heart of the Middle Way*, contains three chapters about his own position, then two chapters on his opponents among the Buddhists, and finally four chapters on non-Buddhist schools, the Samkhya, Vaishesika, Vedanta, and Mimamsa. Eckel translates the two chapters on the Buddhist schools, which differ from one another and from Bhaviveka about the nature of reality.

6. Jesus's remark in the Sermon on the Mount. The full text of that pericope at Matthew 5:43–45 is:

> You have heard that it was said, "You shall love your neighbor and hate your enemy." But I say to you, Love your enemies and pray for those who persecute you, so that you may be children of your Father in heaven; for he makes his sun rise on the evil and on the good, and sends rain on the righteous and on the unrighteous.

7. Ecclesiastes 3:1–8.

8. See Auden's poem, "September 1, 1939," in his *Selected Poems*, pp. 95–97; the quoted lines are on p. 97.

Bibliography

Altizer, Thomas Jefferson Jackson. *The New Apocalypse: The Radical Christian Vision of William Blake*. East Lansing, MI: Michigan State University Press, 1967.

———. *The Self-Embodiment of God*. New York, NY: Harper & Row, 1977.

———. *History as Apocalypse*. Albany, NY: State University of New York Press, 1985.

———. *Genesis and Apocalypse: A Theological Voyage Toward Authentic Christianity*. Louisville, KY: Westminster/John Knox Press, 1990.

Anderson, Douglas R. *Creativity and the Philosophy of C. S. Peirce*. Dordrecht: Martinus Nijhoff, 1987.

Anderson, James F., translator and editor. *An Introduction to the Metaphysics of St. Thomas Aquinas*. Chicago, IL: Henry Regnery, 1953.

Angle, Stephen C. *Sagehood: The Contemporary Significance of Neo-Confucian Philosophy*. Oxford, UK: Oxford University Press, 2009.

Aquinas, Thomas. *Summa Theologiae*. Latin-English edition. Volume 1, *Prima Pars*, Q. 1–64; Volume 2, *Prima Pars*, Q. 65–119. Scotts Valley, CA: Createspace, NovAntiqua, 2008.

———. *An Introduction to the Metaphysics of St. Thomas Aquinas*. Translated and edited by James F. Anderson. Chicago, IL: Henry Regnery, 1953.

Arjomand, Said Amir, editor. *Authority and Political Culture in Shi'ism*. Albany, NY: State University of New York Press, 1988.

Armstrong, Karen. *The Great Transformation: The Beginning of Our Religious Traditions*. New York, NY: Random House, 2006.

Asad, Talal. *Genealogies of Religion: Discipline and Reasons of Power in Christianity and Islam*. Baltimore, MD: Johns Hopkins University Press, 1993.

———. *Formations of the Secular: Christianity, Islam, Modernity*. Stanford, CA: Stanford University Press, 2003.

Atran, Scott. *In Gods We Trust: The Evolutionary Landscape of Religion*. Oxford, UK: Oxford University Press, 2002.

Auden, W. H. *Selected Poems*. Selected and edited by Edward Mendelson. Expanded edition. New York, NY: Random House, 2007.

Barrett, Justin L. *Why Would Anyone Believe in God?* Walnut Creek, CA: AltaMira Press, 2004.

———, with Jeffrey P. Schloss and Michael J. Murray. "Looking Past vs. Overlooking Cognitive-Evolutionary Accounts of Religion: A Response to Nathaniel Barrett." *Journal of the American Academy of Religion* 78/3 (September 2010), 622–628.

Barrett, Nathaniel F. "Toward an Alternative Evolutionary Theory of Religion: Looking Past Computational Evolutionary Psychology to a Wider Field of Possibilities." *Journal of the American Academy of Religion* 78/3 (September 2010), 583–621.

———. "What Are the Constraints of Computational Theory? A Reply to Schloss, Barrett, and Murray." *Journal of the American Academy of Religion* 78/3 (September 2010), 629–632.

Barth, Karl. *The Doctrine of the Word of God, Church Dogmatics*, Volume 1, Part 1. Translated by G. T. Thomson. Edinburgh, UK: T&T Clark, 1936.

———. *Anselm: Fides Quaerens Intellectum (Faith in Search of Understanding)*. Translated by Ian W. Robertson. Cleveland, OH: World Publishing, 1962.

———. *On Religion: The Revelation of God as the Sublimation of Religion*. Translated with an introduction by Garrett Green. London, UK: T&T Clark, 2006. Paragraph 17 of the *Church Dogmatics*, 1.2.

Bediako, Kwame. *Christianity in Africa: The Renewal of a Non-Western Religion*. Edinburgh, UK: Edinburgh University Press, 1995; Maryknoll, NY: Orbis, 1997.

Bellah, Robert N. *Religion in Human Evolution: From the Paleolithic to the Axial Age*. Cambridge, MA: Harvard University Press, 2011.

Berdyaev, Nicolas. *The Beginning and the End*. Translated by R. M. French. New York, NY: Harper Torchbooks, 1957.

Berger, Peter L. *The Sacred Canopy: Elements of a Sociological Theory of Religion*. Garden City, NY: Doubleday, 1967.

———. *A Far Glory: The Quest for Faith in an Age of Credulity*. New York, NY: Doubleday, 1992.

———, with Thomas Luckmann. *The Social Construction of Reality: A Treatise in the Sociology of Knowledge*. Garden City, NY: Doubleday, 1966.Berling, Judith. *The Syncretic Religion of Lin Chao-en*. New York, NY: Columbia University Press, 1980.

Berry, Thomas. *The Great Work: Our Way into the Future*. New York, NY: Belltower/Crown, 1999.

Berthrong, John H. *All Under Heaven: Transforming Paradigms in Confucian-Christian Dialogue*. Albany, NY: State University of New York Press, 1994.

———. *Concerning Creativity: A Comparison of Chu His, Whitehead, and Neville*. Albany, NY: State University of New York Press, 1998.

———. *Transformations of the Confucian Way*. Boulder, CO: Westview Press, 1998.

———. *The Divine Deli: Religious Identity in the North American Cultural Mosaic*. Maryknoll, NY: Orbis Books, 1999.

———. "Boston Confucianism: The Third Wave of Global Confucianism." *Journal of Ecumenical Studies* xv/1–2 (Winter–Spring 2003), 26–47.

———. *Expanding Process: Exploring Philosophical and Theological Transformations in Chia and the West*. Albany, NY: State University of New York Press, 2008.

———, and Evelyn Nagai Berthrong. *Confucianism: A Short Introduction*. Oxford, UK: Oneworld, 2000.

———, and Mary Evelyn Tucker, editors. *Confucianism and Ecology: The Interrelation of Heaven, Earth, and Humans*. Cambridge, MA: Harvard University Press/Harvard Center for the Study of World Religions, 1998.

———, Liu Shu-hsien, and Leonard Swidler. "Contemporary Confucianism and Western Culture." *Journal of Ecumenical Studies* xv/1–2 (Winter–Spring 2003), 26–47.

Black, Brian. *The Character of the Self in Ancient India: Priests, Kings, and Women in the Early Upaniṣads*. Albany, NY: State University of New York Press, 2007.

Blum, Jason N. "Retrieving Phenomenology of Religion as a Method for Religious Studies." *Journal of the American Academy of Religion* 80/4 (December 2012), 1025–1048.

Bonhoeffer, Dietrich. *Letters and Papers from Prison*. Edited by Christian Gremmels, Eberhard Bethge, Renate Bethge, and Ilse Toedt; English edition edited by John W. De Gruchy. Translated by Isabel Best, Lisa E. Dahill, Reinhard Krauss, and Lancy Lukens; "After Ten Years" translated by Barbara and Martin Rumscheidt; Supplementary material translated by Douglas W. Stott. Minneapolis, MN: Fortress Press, 2009.

Boyarin, Daniel. *A Radical Jew: Paul and the Politics of Identity*. Berkeley, CA: University of California Press, 1994.

———. *Border Lines: The Partition of Judeo-Christianity*. Philadelphia, PA: University of Pennsylvania Press, 2004.

———. *Socrates and the Fat Rabbis*. Chicago, IL: University of Chicago Press, 2009.

Boyer, Pascal. *Religion Explained: The Evolutionary Origins of Religious Thought*. New York, NY: Basic Books, 2001.Brockington, John. "The Sanskrit Epics." In Gavin Flood, editor, *The Blackwell Companion to Hinduism*, Chapter 5.

Brown, Peter. "Bodies and Minds: Sexuality and Renunciation in Early Christianity." In David M. Halperin, John J. Winkler, and Froma I. Zeitlin, editors, *Before Sexuality: The Construction of Erotic Experience in the Ancient Greek World*, 479–493. Princeton, NJ: Princeton University Press, 1990.

Browning, Don S. *Reviving Christian Humanism: The New Conversation on Spirituality, Theology, and Psychology*. Minneapolis, MN: Fortress Press, 2010.

Brumbaugh, Robert S. *Unreality and Time*. Albany, NY: State University of New York Press, 1984.

Buchler, Justus. *Nature and Judgment*. New York: Columbia University Press, 1955.

———. *The Main of Light: On the Concept of Poetry*. New York: Oxford University Press, 1974.

Burrell, David B., CSC. "Creation." In Tim Winter, editor, *The Cambridge Companion to Classical Islamic Theology*, Chapter 7.

Burtt, E. A. *The Metaphysical Foundations of Modern Science*. Garden City, NY: Doubleday Anchor, 1954; first edition, 1924, second revised edition, 1932.

Capps, Walter H. *Religious Studies: The Making of a Discipline*. Minneapolis, MN: Fortress Press, 1995.

Carman, John Braisted. *The Theology of Ramanuja: An Essay in Interreligious Understanding*. New Haven, CT: Yale University Press, 1974.

Chan, Wing-tsit, editor and compiler. *A Source Book in Chinese Philosophy*. Princeton, NJ: Princeton University Press, 1963.

Chapple, Christopher Key. *Yoga and the Luminous: Patanjali's Spiritual Path to Freedom*. Albany, NY: State University of New York Press, 2008.

Chittick, William C. *The Sufi Path of Love: The Spiritual Teachings of Rumi*. Albany, NY: State University of New York Press, 1983.

———. *The Sufi Path of Knowledge: Ibn al-'Arabi's Metaphysics of Imagination*. Albany, NY: State University of New York Press, 1989.

———. *Faith and Practice of Islam: Three Thirteenth-Century Sufi Texts*. Albany, NY: State University of New York Press, 1992.

———. *Imaginal Worlds: Ibn al-'Arabi and the Problem of Religious Diversity*. Albany, NY: State University of New York Press, 1994.

———. *The Self-Disclosure of God: Principles of Ibn al-'Arabi's Cosmology*. Lahore, PK: Suhail Academy, 2000.

———. *The Heart of Islamic Philosophy: The Quest for Self-Knowledge in the Teachings of Afdal al-Din Kashani*. Lahore, PK: Suhail Academy, 2004.

———. *Ibn 'Arabi: Heir to the Prophets*. Lahore, PK: Suhail Academy, 2007.

Clooney, Francis X., S.J. *Thinking Ritually: Rediscovering the Purva Mimamsa of Jaimini*. Vienna, AU: De Nobili Research Library, 1990.

———. *Comparative Theology: Deep Learning across Religious Borders*. Oxford, UK: Wiley-Blackwell, 2009.

Collins, Randall. *The Sociology of Philosophies: A Global Theory of Intellectual Change*. Cambridge, MA, and London, UK: Harvard University Press, 1998.

Corn, Charles. *The Scents of Eden: A History of the Spice Trade*. New York, NY: Kodansha America, 1998.

Corrington, Robert S. *Nature and Spirit: An Essay in Ecstatic Naturalism*. New York, NY: Fordham University Press, 1992.

———. *An Introduction to C. S. Peirce: Philosopher, Semiotician, and Ecstatic Naturalist*. Lanham, MD: Rowman & Littlefield, 1993.

———. *A Semiotic Theory of Theology and Philosophy*. Cambridge, UK: Cambridge University Press, 2000.

———. *Ecstatic Naturalism: Signs of the World*. Bloomington, IN: Indiana University Press, 1994.

———. *Nature's Self: Our Journey from Origin to Spirit*. Lanham, MD: Rowman & Littlefield, 1996.

———. *Nature's Religion*. Foreword by Robert Cummings Neville. Lanham, MD: Rowman & Littlefield, 1997.

Coward, Harold G., Julius J. Lipner, and Katherine K. Young. *Hindu Ethics: Purity, Abortion, and Euthanasia*. Albany, NY: State University of New York Press, 1989.

Cox, Harvey. *The Secular City: Secularization and Urbanization in Theological Perspective*. New York, NY: Macmillan, 1965.

———. *Religion in the Secular City: Toward a Postmodern Theology*. New York, NY: Simon & Schuster, 1984.

Crone, Patricia. *God's Rule: Government and Islam: Six Centuries of Medieval Islamic Political Thought*. New York, NY: Columbia University Press, 2004.

Crosby, Donald A. *A Religion of Nature*. Albany, NY: State University of New York Press, 2002.

———. *Living with Ambiguity: Religious Naturalism and the Menace of Evil*. Albany, NY: State University of New York Press, 2008.

Dawkins, Richard. *The God Delusion*. Boston, MA: Mariner/Houghton Mifflin, 2006; paperback edition with a new preface, 2008.

Deacon, Terrence W. *The Symbolic Species: The Co-Evolution of Language and the Brain*. New York, NY: W. W. Norton, 1997.

De Lange, Nicholas, and Miri Freud-Kandel, editors. *Modern Judaism*. Oxford, UK: Oxford University Press, 2005.

Descartes, René. *Philosophical Works of Descartes*. Translated by Elizabeth S. Haldane and G. R. T. Ross. In two volumes. New York, NY: Dover, 1966.

Dewey, John. *Democracy and Education. John Dewey: The Middle Works, 1899–1924, Volume 9, 1916*. Edited by Jo Ann Boydston. Carbondale, IL: Southern Illinois University Press, 1980. Original edition, New York, NY: Macmillan, 1916.

———. *Essays in Experimental Logic*. Chicago, IL: University of Chicago Press, 1916.

———. *Human Nature and Conduct: An Introduction to Social Psychology*. New York, NY: Henry Holt, 1922.

———. *Experience and Nature. John Dewey: The Later Works, 1925–1953, Volume 1: 1925*. Edited by Jo Ann Boydston, with an introduction by Sidney Hook. Carbondale, IL: Southern Illinois University Press, 1987. Original edition, New York, NY: Minton, Balch, 1934.

———. *Art as Experience. John Dewey: The Later Works, 1925–1953, Volume 10: 1934*. Edited by Jo Ann Boydston, with an introduction by Abraham Kaplan. Carbondale, IL: Southern Illinois University Press, 1987. Original edition, New York, NY: Minton, Balch, 1934.

———. *Theory of Valuation*. In *International Encyclopedia of Unified Science* 2/4. Chicago, IL: University of Chicago Press, 1939.

Diamond, Jared. *Guns, Germs, and Steel: The Fates of Human Societies*. New York, NY: Norton, 1997.

Durkheim, Emile. *The Elementary Forms of the Religious Life*. Translated from the French by Joseph Ward Swain. New York, NY: The Free Press, 1965; original edition, George Allen & Unwin, 1915.

Eagleton, Terry. *Literary Theory: An Introduction*. Minneapolis, MN: University of Minnesota Press, 1983.

Eastman, Timothy E., and Hank Keeton, editors. *Physics and Whitehead: Quantum, Process, and Experience*. Albany, NY: State University of New York Press, 2004.

Eckel, Malcolm David. *Jnanagarbha's Commentary on the Distinction between the Two Truths: An Eighth-Century Handbook of Madhyamaka Philosophy*. Albany, NY: State University of New York Press, 1987.

———. *To See the Buddha: A Philosopher's Quest for the Meaning of Emptiness*. New York, NY: HarperCollins, 1992.

———. *Bhaviveka and His Buddhist Opponents*. Cambridge, MA: Department of Sanskrit and Indian Studies, Harvard University, Harvard University Press, 2008.

———, and John J. Thatamanil. "Cooking the Last Fruit of Nihilism: Buddhist Approaches to Ultimate Reality." In Robert Cummings Neville, editor, *Ultimate Realities*, Chapter 6.

———, and John J. Thatamanil. "Beginningless Ignorance: A Buddhist View of the Human Condition." In Robert Cummings Neville, editor, *The Human Condition*, Chapter 3.

———, and John J. Thatamanil. "With Great Noise and Mighty Whirlpools the Ganges Flowed Backwards." In Robert Cummings Neville, editor, *Religious Truth*, Chapter 3.

Edelglass, William, and Jay L. Garfield, editors. *Buddhist Philosophy: Essential Readings*. Oxford, UK: Oxford University Press, 2009.

Edwards, Jonathan. *The Nature of True Virtue*. In Paul Ramsey, editor, *Jonathan Edwards: Ethical Writings*. New Haven, CT: Yale University Press, 1989. Volume 8 in *The Works of Jonathan Edwards*, general editor John E. Smith.

Eliade, Mircea. *The Sacred and the Profane*. Translated by Willard R. Trask. New York, NY: Harper & Row, 1959.

———. *Patterns in Comparative Religion*. Translated by Rosemary Sheed. New York, NY: Meridian Books, 1963; original French edition, 1949.

Fakhry, Majid. *A History of Islamic Philosophy*. Third edition. New York, NY: Columbia University Press, 2004.

Fingarette, Herbert. *Confucius: The Secular as Sacred*. New York, NY: Harper & Row, 1972.

Flanagan, Owen. *The Really Hard Problem: Meaning in a Material World*. Cambridge, MA: MIT Press, 2007.

Flood, Gavin. *An Introduction to Hinduism*. Cambridge, UK: Cambridge University Press, 1996.

———. *Beyond Phenomenology: Rethinking the Study of Religion*. London, UK: Cassell, 1999.

———, editor. *The Blackwell Companion to Hinduism*. Oxford, UK: Blackwell, 2003.

Foucault, Michel. *The Order of Things: An Archaeology of the Human Sciences*. New York, NY: Random House, 1970.

———. *The Use of Pleasure: The History of Sexuality, Volume Two*. Translated by Robert Hurley. New York, NY: Random House, 1985.

Fox, Thomas C. *Sexuality and Catholicism*. New York, NY: George Braziller, 1995.

Frankenberry, Nancy K., editor. *Radical Interpretation in Religion*. Cambridge, UK: Cambridge University Press, 2002.

Frazer, J. G. *The Golden Bough: A Study in Magic and Religion*. Third edition, in twelve volumes. London, UK: Macmillan, 1911–1915.

Fredriksen, Paula, and Tina Shepardson. "Embodiment and Redemption: The Human Condition in Ancient Christianity." In Robert Cummings Neville, editor, *The Human Condition*, Chapter 6.

Frei, Hans W. *Types of Christian Theology*. Edited by George Hunsinger and William C. Placher. New Haven, CT: Yale University Press, 1992.

Frisina, Warren G. *The Unity of Knowledge and Action: Toward a Nonrepresentational Theory of Knowledge*. Albany, NY: State University of New York Press, 2002.

Gadamer, Hans-Georg. *Truth and Method*. New York, NY: Sheed & Ward, 1975; original edition, 1960.

Goffman, Erving. *Relations in Public*. New York, NY: Basic Books, 1971.

Golding, William. *The Lord of the Flies*. New York, NY: Capricorn, 1959.

Goodenough, Ursula. *The Sacred Depths of Nature*. Oxford, UK: Oxford University Press, 1998.

Gustafson, James M. *Treasure in Earthen Vessels: The Church as a Human Community*. New York, NY: Harper & Brothers, 1961.

Haidt, Jonathan. "The Emotional Dog and Its Rational Tail: A Social Intuitionist Approach to Moral Judgment." *Psychological Review* 108/4 (2001), 814–834.

———. *The Happiness Hypothesis: Finding Modern Truth in Ancient Wisdom*. New York, NY: Basic Books, 2006.

———. "The New Synthesis in Moral Psychology." *Science* 316 (May 18, 2007), 998–1002.

———. *The Righteous Mind: Why Good People Are Divided by Politics and Religion*. New York, NY: Pantheon, 2012.

Haight, Roger, S.J. *Jesus: Symbol of God*. Maryknoll, NY: Orbis Books, 1999.

Haq, S. Nomanul. *Names, Natures, and Things: The Alchemist Jabir ibn Hayyan and His "Kitab al-Ahjar" (Book of Stones)*. Foreword by David E. Pingree. Boston, MA: Kluwer Academic Publishers, 1993.

———. "The Human Condition in Islam: Sharia and Obligation." In Robert Cummings Neville, editor, *The Human Condition*, Chapter 7, 156–174.

———. "Ultimate Reality: Islam." In Robert Cummings Neville, editor, *Ultimate Realities,* Chapter 4.

Hardwick, Charley D. *Events of Grace: Naturalism, Existentialism, and Theology*. Cambridge, UK: Cambridge University Press, 1996.

Harper, Charles L., Jr., editor. *Spiritual Information: 100 Perspectives on Science and Religion: Essays in Honor of Sir John Templeton's 90th Birthday.* Philadelphia, PA: Templeton Foundation Press, 2005.

Harvey, Van A. *The Historian and the Believer: The Morality of Historical Knowledge and Christian Belief.* New York, NY: Macmillan, 1966.

Hegel, Georg Wilhelm Friedrich. *The Phenomenology of Mind*. Translated by J. B. Baillie. Second edition revised. New York, NY: Macmillan, 1949.

———. *Lectures on the Philosophy of Religion, Together with a Work on the Proofs of the Existence of God*. In three volumes. Translated from the second German edition by E. B. Speirs and J. Burdon Sanderson. New York, NY: Humanities Press, 1962.

Heidegger, Martin. *Being and Time*. Translated by John Macquarrie and Edward Robinson. London, UK: SCM Press, 1962.

Heltzel, Peter G., and Amos Yong, editors. *Theology in Global Context: Essays in Honor of Robert Cummings Neville.* New York, NY, and London, UK: T&T Clark, 2004.

———. *Jesus and Justice: Evangelicals, Race, and American Politics*. Foreword by Mark A. Noll. New Haven, CT: Yale University Press, 2009.

Hobbes, Thomas. *Leviathan*. Introduction by A. D. Lindsay. New York, NY: E. P. Dutton, 1950. Original edition, 1651.

Hogue, Michael S. *The Tangled Bank: Toward an Ecotheological Ethics of Responsible Participation*. Princeton Theological Monograph Series 89. Eugene, OR: Pickwick Publications, 2008.

———. *The Promise of Religious Naturalism*. Lanham, MD: Rowman & Littlefield, 2010.

Hoopes, James, editor. *Peirce on Signs: Writings on Semiotic by Charles Sanders Peirce.* Chapel Hill, NC: University of North Carolina Press, 1991.

Hopkins, Gerard Manley, S. J. *The Poems of Gerard Manley Hopkins*. Edited by W. H. Gardner and N. H. MacKenzie. Fourth edition. Oxford, UK: Oxford University Press, 1967.

Hunter, James Davison. *Culture Wars: The Struggle to Define America*. New York, NY: Basic Books/HarperCollins, 1991.

Huntington, Samuel P. *The Clash of Civilizations and the Remaking of World Order*. New York, NY: Simon & Schuster, 1996.

Husserl, Edmund. *Ideas: General Introduction to Pure Phenomenology*. Translated by W. R. Boyce Gibson. New York, NY: Macmillan, 1931.

Jackelen, Antje. *Time and Eternity: The Question of Time in Church, Science, and Theology*. Translated from the German by Barbara Harshaw. Philadelphia, PA: Templeton Foundation Press, 2005.

Jagose, Annamarie. *Queer Theory: An Introduction*. New York, NY: New York University Press, 1996.

James, William. *"Essays in Radical Empiricism" and "A Pluralistic Universe."* Edited by Ralph Barton Perry. New York, NY: Longmans Green, 1942; original edition of *Essays in Radical Empiricism*, 1912; original edition of *A Pluralistic Universe*, 1909.

Jaspers, Karl. *The Origin and Goal of History*. Translated by Michael Bullock. New Haven, CT: Yale University Press, 1953. Original edition, *Vom Ursprung und Ziel der Geschichte*. Zurich: Artemis, 1949.

———. *The Philosophy of Karl Jaspers*. Edited by Paul Arthur Schilpp. The Library of Living Philosophers. New York: Tudor, 1957.

Jenkins, Philip. *The Lost History of Christianity: The Thousand-Year Golden Age of the Church in the Middle East, Africa, and Asia—and How It Died*. New York, NY: HarperCollins, 2008.

———. *Jesus Wars: How Four Patriarchs, Three Queens, and Two Emperors Decided What Christians Would Believe for the Next 1,500 Years*. New York, NY: HarperCollins, 2010.

Johnson, Mark. *The Body in the Mind: The Bodily Basis of Meaning, Imagination, and Reason*. Chicago, IL: University of Chicago Press, 1987.

Kakol, Peter Paul. *Emptiness and Becoming: Integrating Madhyamika Buddhism and Process Philosophy*. Foreword by Robert C. Neville and preamble by Purushottama Bilimoria. New Delhi, India: D. K. Printworld, 2009.

Kant, Immanuel. *Critique of Pure Reason*. Translated by Norman Kemp Smith. London, UK: Macmillan, 1929. Original German first edition, Riga: Johann Friedrich Hartknoch, 1781; second edition, 1787.

Keeton, Hank, and Timothy E. Eastman, editors. *Physics and Whitehead: Quantum, Process, and Experience*. Albany, NY: State University of New York Press, 2004.

Kierkegaard, Søren. *Purity of Heart Is to Will One Thing: Spiritual Preparation for the Office of Confession*. Translated by Douglas V. Steere. New York, NY: Harper & Brothers, 1938.

———. *"Fear and Trembling" and "The Sickness unto Death."* Translated by Walter Lowrie. Princeton, NJ: Princeton University Press, 1941. Reprint edition, Garden City, NY: Doubleday, 1955.

Kirkpatrick, Lee A. "Religion Is Not an Adaptation." In Patrick McNamara, editor, *Where God and Science Meet*, Volume 1, Chapter 8.

Kohn, Livia. *Seven Steps to the Tao: Sima Chengzhen's* Zuowanglun. Monumenta Serica Monograph Series 20. Nettetal, DT: Steyler Verlag—Wort und Werk, 1987.

———. *Taoist Mystical Philosophy: The Scripture of the Western Ascension*. Albany, NY: State University of New York Press, 1991.

———. *Early Chinese Mysticism: Philosophy and Soteriology in the Taoist Tradition*. Princeton, NJ: Princeton University Press, 1992.

———. "Chinese Religion." In Robert Cummings Neville, editor, *The Human Condition*, Chapter 2.

———. *Chinese Healing Exercises: The Tradition of Daoyin*. Honolulu, HI: University of Hawaii Press, 2008.

———, editor, in cooperation with Yoshinobu Sakade. *Taoist Meditation and Longevity Techniques*. Ann Arbor, MI: Center for Chinese Studies/The University of Michigan, 1989.

Krafft-Ebing, Baron Richard von. *Psychopathia Sexualis: A Medico-Forensic Study*. Translated by Harry E. Wedeck, with an introduction by Ernest Van Den Haag. New York: G. P. Putnam's Sons, 1965. Original Latin edition, 1886.

Lakoff, George. *Women, Fire, and Dangerous Things: What Categories Reveal about the Mind*. Chicago, IL: University of Chicago Press, 1987.

———, and Mark Johnson. *Metaphors We Live By*. Chicago, IL: University of Chicago Press, 1980.

———, and Mark Johnson. *Philosophy in the Flesh: The Embodied Mind and Its Challenge to Western Thought*. New York, NY: Basic Books, 1999.

Lang, Bernhard, and Colleen McDannell. *Heaven: A History*. New Haven, CT: Yale University Press, 1988.

Leaman, Oliver. *A Brief Introduction to Islamic Philosophy*. Cambridge, UK: Blackwell/Polity, 1999.

Lerro, Bruce. *From Earth Spirits to Sky Gods: The Socioecological Origins of Monotheism, Individualism, and Hyperabstract Reasoning from the Stone Age to the Axial Iron Age*. Lanham, MD: Lexington Books, 2000.

Levenson, Jon D. *Creation and the Persistence of Evil: The Jewish Drama of Divine Omnipotence*. New York: Harper & Row, 1988.

Leyland, Winston, editor. *Queer Dharma: Voices of Gay Buddhists*. In two volumes. San Francisco, CA: Gay Sunshine Press, 1998 and 2000, respectively.

Lindbeck, George A. *The Nature of Doctrine: Religion and Theology in a Postliberal Age*. Philadelphia, PA: Westminster Press, 1984.*Lotus Sutra, The*. Translation and introduction by Gene Reeves. Boston, MA: Wisdom Publications, 2008.

McCauley, Robert N. *Why Religion Is Natural and Science Is Not*. New York, NY: Oxford University Press, 2011.

McDannell, Colleen, and Bernhard Lang. *Heaven: A History*. New Haven, CT: Yale University Press, 1988.

MacGregor, Kirk R. *A Comparative Study of Adjustments to Social Catastrophes in Christianity and Buddhism: The Black Death in Europe and the Kamakura Takeover in Japan as Causes of Religious Reform*. Lewiston, NY: Edwin Mellen Press, 2011.

Machle, Edward J. *Nature and Heaven in the Xunzi: A Study of the "Tien Lun."* Albany, NY: State University of New York Press, 1993.

McNamara, Patrick, editor. *Where God and Science Meet: How Brain and Evolutionary Studies Alter Our Understanding of Religion*. Volume 1: *Evolution, Genes, and the Religious Brain*. Volume 2: *The Neurology of Religious Experience*. Volume 3: *The Psychology of Religious Experience*. Westport, CT, London, UK: Praeger, 2006.

———. *Neuroscience of Religious Experience*. New York, NY, and Cambridge, UK: Cambridge University Press, 2009.

Magesa, Laurenti. *African Religion: The Moral Traditions of Abundant Life*. Maryknoll, NY: Orbis, 1997.

Makeham, John, editor. *Dao Companion to Neo-Confucian Philosophy*. Dordrecht: Springer, 2011.

Manning, Russell Re, editor. *The Cambridge Companion to Paul Tillich*. Cambridge, UK: Cambridge University Press, 2009.

Marion, Jean-Luc. *Reduction and Givenness: Investigations of Husserl, Heidegger, and Phenomenology*. Translated by Thomas A Carlson. Evanston, IL: Northwestern University Press, 1998.

———. *Being Given: Toward a Phenomenology of Givenness*. Translated by Jeffrey L. Kosky. Stanford, CA: Stanford University Press, 2002.

Marty, Martin E., and R. Scott Appleby, editors. *Fundamentalism Observed*. Chicago, IL: University of Chicago Press, 1991.

Mason, John R. *Reading and Responding to Mircea Eliade's "History of Religious Ideas."* Lewiston, NY: Edwin Mellen Press, 1993.

Masuzawa, Tomoko. *The Invention of World Religions: Or, How European Universalism Was Preserved in the Language of Pluralism*. Chicago, IL: University of Chicago Press, 2005.

Miller, James E. *Daoism: A Short Introduction*. Oxford, UK: Oneworld, 2003.

———. *The Way of Highest Clarity: Nature, Vision, and Revelation in Medieval China*. Magdalena, NM: Three Pines Press, 2008.

———, N. J. Girardot, and Liu Xianogan, editors. *Daoism and Ecology: Ways within a Cosmic Landscape*. Cambridge, MA: Harvard University Press, 2001.

Moffett, Samuel Hugh. *A History of Christianity in Asia. Volume I: Beginnings to 1500.* San Francisco, CA: HarperSanFrancisco, 1992. *Volume II: 1500–1900.* Maryknoll, NY: Orbis Books, 2005.

Monette, Paul. *Last Watch of the Night: Essays Too Personal and Otherwise*. New York, NY: Harcourt Brace, 1994.

Moores, D. J., editor. *Wild Poets of Ecstasy: An Anthology of Ecstatic Verse*. Nevada City, CA: Pelican Pond, 2011.

Muller-Ortega, Paul Eduardo. *The Triadic Heart of Siva: Kaula Tantricism of Abhinavagupta in the Non-Dual Shaivism of Kashmir.* Albany, NY: State University of New York Press, 1989.

Murata, Sachiko. *The Dao of Islam: A Sourcebook on Gender Relationships in Islamic Thought.* Foreword by Annemarie Schimmel. Lahore, PK: Suhail Academy, 2001.

———, William C. Chittick, and Tu Weiming. *The Sage Learning of Liu Zhi: Islamic Thought in Confucian Terms.* Foreword by Seyyed Hossein Nasr. Cambridge, MA: Harvard University Press, 2009.

Nagarjuna. See Frederick J. Streng's *Emptiness.*

Neville, Robert Cummings. *God the Creator: On the Transcendence and Presence of God.* Chicago, IL: University of Chicago Press, 1968; reprint with a new introduction, Albany, NY: State University of New York Press, 1992.

———. *Soldier, Sage, Saint.* New York, NY: Fordham University Press, 1978.

———. *Reconstruction of Thinking.* Volume 1 of *Axiology of Thinking*. Albany, NY: State University of New York Press, 1981.

———. *Recovery of the Measure.* Volume 2 of *Axiology of Thinking*. Albany, NY: State University of New York Press, 1989.

———. *Normative Cultures*. Volume 3 of *Axiology of Thinking*. Albany, NY: State University of New York Press, 1995.

———. *The Truth of Broken Symbols*. Albany, NY: State University of New York Press, 1996.

———. *Boston Confucianism: Portable Tradition in the Late-Modern World*. Albany, NY: State University of New York Press, 2000.

———. *Symbols of Jesus: A Christology of Symbolic Engagement*. Cambridge, UK: Cambridge University Press, 2001.

———. *Religion in Late Modernity.* Albany, NY: State University of New York Press, 2002.

———. *On the Scope and Truth of Theology: Theology as Symbolic Engagement.* New York, NY, and London, UK: T&T Clark, 2006.

———. *Ritual and Deference: Extending Chinese Philosophy in a Comparative Context.* Albany, NY: State University of New York Press, 2008.

———. *Realism in Religion: A Pragmatist's Perspective*. Albany, NY: State University of New York Press, 2009.

———, editor. *The Human Condition: A Volume in the Comparative Religious Ideas Project*. Foreword by Peter L. Berger. Albany, NY: State University of New York Press, 2001.

———, editor. *Ultimate Realities: A Volume in the Comparative Religious Ideas Project*. Foreword by Tu Weiming. Albany, NY: State University of New York Press, 2001.

———, editor. *Religious Truth: A Volume in the Comparative Religious Ideas Project*. Foreword by Jonathan Z. Smith. Albany, NY: State University of New York Press, 2001.

Newberg, Andrew B. *Principles of Neurotheology*. Farnham, UK: Ashgate, 2010.

Niebuhr, H. Richard. *Christ and Culture*. New York, NY: Harper & Brothers, 1951.

Nishitani, Keiji. *Religion and Nothingness*. Translated with an introduction by Jan Van Bragt and a foreword by Winston L. King. Berkeley, CA: University of California Press, 1982.

Olivelle, Patrick. "The Renouncer Tradition." In Gavin Flood, editor, *The Blackwell Companion to Hinduism*, Chapter 12.

Olupona, Jacob K, editor. *African Spirituality: Forms, Meanings and Expressions*. Volume 3 of *World Spirituality: An Encyclopedic History of the Religious Quest*. New York, NY: Herder and Herder/Crossroad, 2000.

Orsi, Robert A. *Between Heaven and Earth: The Religious Worlds People Make and the Scholars Who Study Them*. Princeton, NJ: Princeton University Press, 2005.

Otto, Rudolf. *The Idea of the Holy: An Inquiry into the Non-Rational Factor in the Idea of the Divine, and Its Relation to the Rational*. Translated by John W. Harvey. Fourth impression, revised with additions. Oxford, UK: Oxford University Press, 1926; first edition, 1916.

Palmer, Martin, Eva Wong, Tjaling Halbertsma, Zhao Xiao Min, Li Rong Rong, and James Palmer. *The Jesus Sutras: Rediscovering the Lost Scrolls of Taoist Christianity*. New York, NY: Ballantine, 2001.

Pals, Daniel L. *Eight Theories of Religion*. Second edition. Oxford, UK: Oxford University Press, 2006. The first edition lacked the study of Max Weber and so was entitled *Seven Theories of Religion*.

Panikkar, Raimundo. *The Silence of God: The Answer of the Buddha*. Translated from the Italian by Robert R. Barr. Maryknoll, NY: Orbis Books, 1989.

Park, Sung Bae. *Buddhist Faith and Sudden Enlightenment*. Albany, NY: State University of New York Press, 1983.

———. *One Korean's Approach to Buddhism: The Mom/Momjit Paradigm*. Albany, NY: State University of New York Press, 2009.

Peirce, Charles Sanders. *The Collected Papers of Charles Sanders Peirce*. Edited by Charles Hartshorne and Paul Weiss, Volumes 1–6, and by Arthur Burks, Volumes 7–8. Cambridge, MA: Harvard University Press, 1931, 1932, 1933, 1933, 1934, 1935, 1958, 1958, respectively.

———. *The Essential Peirce: Selected Philosophical Writings: Volume 1 (1867–1893) and Volume 2 (1893–1913)*. Edited by Nathan Houser and Christian Kloesel, Volume 1, and by the Peirce Edition Project, Volume 2. Bloomington, IN: Indiana University Press, 1992 and 1998, respectively.

Pinker, Steven. *The Blank Slate: The Modern Denial of Human Nature*. New York, NY: Viking, 2002.

———. "The Evolutionary Psychology of Religion." In Patrick McNamara, editor, *Where God and Science Meet*, Volume 1, Chapter 1.

Plato. *Republic.* Translated by Paul Shorey. In Edith Hamilton and Huntington Cairns, editors, *The Collected Dialogues of Plato, Including the Letters.* New York, NY: Pantheon Books, 1961.

Powers, John. *A Bull of a Man: Images of Masculinity, Sex, and the Body in Indian Buddhism.* Cambridge, MA: Harvard University Press, 2009.

Puett, Michael J. *To Become a God: Cosmology, Sacrifice, and Self-Divinization in Early China.* Cambridge, MA: Harvard-Yenching Institute/Harvard University Press, 2002.

Pyysiainen, Ilkka. *Supernatural Agents: Why We Believe in Souls, Gods, and Buddhas.* Oxford, UK: Oxford University Press, 2009.

Radhakrishnan, Sarvepalli, and Charles A. Moore, editors. *A Source Book in Indian Philosophy.* Princeton, NJ: Princeton University Press, 1957.

Rahner, Karl. *Foundations of Christian Faith: An Introduction to the Idea of Christianity.* Translated by William V. Dych. New York, NY: Crossroad, 1989.

Raposa, Michael L. *Peirce's Philosophy of Religion.* Peirce Studies Number 5. Bloomington, IN: Indiana University Press, 1989.

———. *Meditation and the Martial Arts.* Charlottesville, VA: University of Virginia Press, 2003.

Rappaport, Roy A. *Ritual and Religion in the Making of Humanity.* Cambridge, UK: Cambridge University Press, 1999.

Richard, Jean. "Tillich's Analysis of the Spiritual Situation of His Time(s)." In Russell Re Manning, editor, *The Cambridge Companion to Paul Tillich*, Chapter 8.

Richardson, Robert D. *William James: In the Maelstrom of American Modernism.* Boston, MA: Houghton Mifflin, 2006.

Ricoeur, Paul. *The Symbolism of Evil.* Translated from the French by Emerson Buchanan. Boston, MA: Beacon Press, 1967.

———. *The Conflict of Interpretations: Essays in Hermeneutics.* Edited by Don Ihde. Evanston, IL: Northwestern University Press, 1974.

———. *Time and Narrative.* Volume 1. Translated by Kathleen McLaughlin and David Pellauer. Chicago, IL: University of Chicago Press, 1984.

———. *Fallible Man.* Revised translation by Charles A. Kelbley, introduction by Walter J. Lowe. New York, NY: Fordham University Press, 1986; original edition, 1960, original translation, 1965.

Rippin, Andrew. *Muslims: Their Religious Beliefs and Practices.* Third edition. London, UK: Routledge, 2005.

Roberts, Jon H. "Louis Agassiz on Scientific Method, Polygenism, and Transmutation: A Reassessment." *Almagest: International Journal for the History of Scientific Ideas* 2 (2011), 77–99.

Rorty, Richard. *The Linguistic Turn: Recent Essays in Philosophical Method.* Chicago, IL: University of Chicago Press, 1967.

———. *Philosophy and the Mirror of Nature.* Princeton, NJ: Princeton University Press, 1979.

———. *Consequences of Pragmatism.* Minneapolis, MN: University of Minnesota Press, 1982.

———. *Achieving Our Country: Leftist Thought in Twentieth-Century America.* Cambridge, MA: Harvard University Press, 1998.

Roy, Louis, O.P. *Transcendent Experiences: Phenomenology and Critique.* Toronto: University of Toronto Press, 2001.

Rue, Loyal. *Amythia: Crisis in the Natural History of Western Culture.* Tuscaloosa, AL: University of Alabama Press. 1989.

———. *Everybody's Story: Wising Up to the Epic of Evolution.* Albany, NY: State University of New York Press, 2000.

———. *Religion Is Not about God.* New Brunswick, NJ: Rutgers University Press, 2005.

Said, Edward W. *Beginnings: Intention and Method.* New York, NY: Basic Books, 1975.

———. *Orientalism.* New York, NY: Random House, 1978.

———. *Culture and Imperialism.* New York, NY: Alfred A. Knopf, 1993.

Saldarini, Anthony J., and Joseph Kanofsky. "To Practice Together Truth and Humility, Justice and Law, Love of Merciful Kindness and Modest Behavior." In Robert Cummings Neville, editor, *Religious Truth,* Chapter 4.

———, and Joseph Kanofsky. "Religious Dimensions of the Human Condition in Judaism: Wrestling with God in an Imperfect World." In Robert Cummings Neville, editor, *The Human Condition,* Chapter 5.

Sanneh, Lamin. *Translating the Message: The Missionary Impact on Culture.* Revised and expanded edition. Maryknoll, NY: Orbis, 2009.

Schleiermacher, Friedrich. *On Religion: Speeches to Its Cultured Despisers.* Translated by John Oman with an introduction by Rudolf Otto. New York, NY: Harper & Brothers, 1958; this translation is of the third edition, somewhat changed from the original 1799 edition.

———. *The Christian Faith.* Translation of the second German edition by H. R. Mackintosh and J. S. Stewart. Edinburgh, UK: T&T Clark, 1928.

Schuessler, Werner. "Tillich's Life and Works." In Russell Re Manning, *The Cambridge Companion to Paul Tillich,* Chapter 1.

Scotus, John Duns. *Philosophical Writings.* Translated and edited by Allan Wolter, O.F.M. New York, NY: Thomas Nelson & Sons, 1962.

Short, T. L. *Peirce's Theory of Signs.* Cambridge, UK: Cambridge University Press, 2007.

Siker, Jeffrey S., editor. *Homosexuality in the Church: Both Sides of the Debate.* Louisville, KY: Westminster/John Knox Press, 1994.

Sizgorich, Thomas. *Violence and Belief in Late Antiquity.* Philadelphia, PA: University of Pennsylvania Press, 2009.

Smith, Barbara Herrnstein. *Natural Reflections: Human Cognition at the Nexus of Science and Religion.* New Haven, CT: Yale University Press, 2009.

Smith, David. "Orientalism and Hinduism." In Gavin Flood, editor, *The Blackwell Companion to Hinduism,* Chapter 2.

Smith, John E. *Reason and God: Encounters of Philosophy and Religion.* New Haven, CT: Yale University Press, 1961.

———. *The Spirit of American Philosophy.* New York, NY: Oxford University Press, 1963.

———. *Purpose and Thought: The Meaning of Pragmatism.* New Haven, CT: Yale University Press, 1978.

———. *Quasi-Religions: Humanism, Marxism, and Nationalism.* New York, NY: St. Martin's Press, 1994.

Stausberg, Michael. *Contemporary Theories of Religion: A Critical Companion.* London, UK: Routledge, 2009.

Stone, Jerome A. *Religious Naturalism Today: The Rebirth of a Forgotten Alternative.* Albany, NY: State University of New York Press, 2008.

Streng, Frederick J. *Emptiness: A Study in Religious Meaning: A Depth Study of the Philosopher Nagarjuna and His Interpretation of Ultimate Reality: Including Translations of Nagarjuna's "Fundamentals of the Middle Way" and "Averting the Arguments."* Nashville, TN: Abingdon Press, 1967.

Sullivan, Andrew. *Love Undetectable: Notes on Friendship, Sex, and Survival.* New York, NY: Random House, 1998.

Sullivan, William M. *Reconstructing Public Philosophy.* Berkeley, CA: University of California Press, 1986.

———. *Work and Integrity: The Crisis and Promise of Professionalism in America.* New York: NY: HarperCollins, 1995.

Tanner, Kathryn. *Theories of Culture: A New Agenda for Theology.* Minneapolis, MN: Fortress Press, 1997.

Taves, Ann. *Religious Experience Reconsidered: A Building-Block Approach to the Study of Religion and Other Special Things.* Princeton, NJ: Princeton University Press, 2009.

Taylor, Mark C. *After God.* Chicago, IL: University of Chicago Press, 2007.

Thatamanil, John J. *The Immanent Divine: God, Creation, and the Human Predicament: An East-West Conversation.* Minneapolis, MN: Fortress Press, 2006.

Tillich, Paul. *The Religious Situation.* Translated by H. Richard Niebuhr. New York, NY: Henry Holt, 1932. Living Age edition, New York, NY: Meridian, 1956.

———. *Systematic Theology.* Volume 1, Volume 2, Volume 3. Chicago, IL: University of Chicago Press, 1951, 1957, 1963, respectively.

———. *The Courage to Be.* New Haven, CT: Yale University Press, 1952.

———. *The Protestant Era.* Abridged edition. Translated by James Luther Adams. Chicago, IL: University of Chicago Press, 1957.

———. *Theology of Culture.* Edited by Robert C. Kimball. New York, NY: Oxford University Press, 1959.

———. *On the Boundary: An Autobiographical Sketch.* New York, NY: Charles Scribner's Sons, 1966.

Toulmin, Stephen. *The Uses of Argument.* Cambridge, UK: Cambridge University Press, 1958.

———. *Human Understanding: The Collective Use and Evolution of Concepts.* Princeton, NJ: Princeton University Press, 1972.

Tracy, David. *The Analogical Imagination: Christian Theology and the Culture of Pluralism.* New York, NY: Crossroad, 1981.

Tremlin, Todd. *Minds and Gods: The Cognitive Foundations of Religion.* Foreword by E. Thomas Lawson. Oxford, UK: Oxford University Press, 2006.

Tu, Weiming. *Centrality and Commonality: An Essay on Confucian Religiousness.* A revised and enlarged edition of *Centrality and Commonality: An Essay on Chung-yung.* Albany, NY: State University of New York Press, 1989.

———. *Humanity and Self-Cultivation: Essays in Confucian Thought.* Reprint edition with a new foreword by Robert Cummings Neville. Boston, MA: Cheng & Tsui, 1998.

Tucker, Mary Evelyn, and John H. Berthrong, editors. *Confucianism and Ecology: The Interrelation of Heaven, Earth, and Humans.* Cambridge, MA: Center for the Study of World Religions and Harvard University Press, 1998.

———, and John Grim, editors. *Worldviews and Ecology.* Maryknoll, NY: Orbis, 1994.

———, and Duncan Ryuken Williams, editors. *Buddhism and Ecology: The Interconnection of Dharma and Deeds.* Cambridge, MA: Harvard University Press, 1997.

———, and John Grim, editors. *Hinduism and Ecology: The Intersection of Earth, Sky, and Water*. Cambridge, MA: Harvard University Press, 2000.

Tylor, Edward Burnett. *Primitive Culture: Researches into the Development of Mythology, Philosophy, Religion, Language, Art, and Custom*. Fourth edition, revised, in two volumes. London, UK: John Murray, 1903; original edition, 1871.

Van der Leeuw, G. *Religion in Essence and Manifestation*. Two volumes. Edited by Hans H. Penner. Translated by J. E. Turner. New York, NY: Harper, 1963.

Vaught, Carl G. *The Journey toward God in Augustine's "Confessions": Books I–VI*. Albany, NY: State University of New York Press, 2003.

———. *Encounters with God in Augustine's "Confessions": Books VII–IX*. Albany, NY: State University of New York Press, 2004.

Vidal, Gore. *Creation: A Novel*. New York, NY: Random House, 1981.

Viswanathan, Gauri. "Colonialism and the Construction of Hinduism." In Gavin Flood, editor. *The Blackwell Companion to Hinduism*, Chapter 1.

Weiss, Paul. *Sport: A Philosophic Inquiry*. Carbondale, IL: Southern Illinois University Press, 1969.

White, Lynn. "The Historical Roots of Our Ecological Crisis." *Science* 155 (March 10, 1967), 1203–1212.

Whitehead, Alfred North. *Science and the Modern World*. New York, NY: Macmillan, 1925.

———. *Religion in the Making*. New York, NY: Macmillan, 1926.

———. *Adventures of Ideas*. New York, NY: Macmillan, 1933.

———. *The Function of Reason*. Princeton, NJ: Princeton University Press, 1929; reprint edition, Boston, MA: Beacon, 1958.

———. *Process and Reality: An Essay in Cosmology*. Corrected edition edited by David Ray Griffin and Donald W. Sherburne. New York: The Free Press, 1978; original edition, New York: Macmillan, 1929.Wieman, Henry Nelson. *The Source of Human Good*. Carbondale, IL: Southern Illinois University Press, 1946.

———. *Man's Ultimate Commitment*. Carbondale, IL: Southern Illinois University Press, 1958.

Wildman, Wesley J. "Theological Literacy: Problem and Promise." In Rodney L. Petersen and Nancy M. Rourke, editors, *Theological Literacy for the Twenty-First Century*, 335–351. Grand Rapids, MI: Eerdmans, 2002.

———. "Neville's Systematic Theology of Symbolic Engagement." In Amos Yong and Peter G. Heltzel, editors, *Theology in Global Context*, 3–27.

———. "Global Spiritual Confusion and the Neglected Problem of Excess Spiritual Information." In Charles L. Harper Jr., *Spiritual Information*, Chapter 6.

———. "The Significance of the Evolution of Religious Belief and Behavior for Religious Studies and Theology." In Patrick McNamara, editor, *Where God and Science Meet*, Volume 1, Chapter 11, 227–272.

———. *Religious Philosophy as Multidisciplinary Comparative Inquiry: Envisioning a Future for the Philosophy of Religion*. Albany, NY: State University of New York Press, 2009.

———. *Science and Religious Anthropology: A Spiritually Evocative Naturalist Interpretation of Human Life*. Farnham, Surrey, UK: Ashgate, 2009.

———. *Science and Ultimate Reality: A Multidisciplinary Inquiry*. Farnham, Surrey, UK: Ashgate, 2010.

———. *Religious and Spiritual Experiences: A Multidisciplinary Inquiry into Their Nature, Functions, and Value*. Cambridge, UK: Cambridge University Press, 2010.

———. "The Ambiguous Heritage and Perpetual Promise of Liberal Theology." *American Journal of Theology and Philosophy* 32/1 (January 2011), 43–61.

Wilken, Robert L. *The Land Called Holy: Palestine in Christian History and Thought.* New Haven, CT: Yale University Press, 1992.

Williams, Rowan. *On Christian Theology*. Oxford, UK: Blackwell, 2000.

Williams, William Carlos. *Spring and All*. Paris, FR: Contact, 1923.

Wilson, David Sloan. *Darwin's Cathedral: Evolution, Religion, and the Nature of Society*. Chicago, IL: University of Chicago Press, 2002.

———. *Evolution for Everyone: How Darwin's Theory Can Change the Way We Think about Our Lives*. New York, NY: Bantam Dell, 2007.

———, and Elliott Sober. *Unto Others: The Evolution of Psychology of Unselfish Behavior.* Cambridge, MA: Harvard University Press, 1998.

———, and Jonathan Gottschall, editors. *The Literary Animal: Evolution and the Nature of Narrative*. Evanston, IL: Northwestern University Press, 2005.

Wilson, Edward O. *Human Nature*. With a new preface. Cambridge, MA: Harvard University Press, 2004; originally published 1978.

———. *Consilience: The Unity of Knowledge*. New York, NY: Random House, 1998; Vintage Books, 1999.

Winter, Tim, editor. *The Cambridge Companion to Classical Islamic Theology*. Cambridge, UK: Cambridge University Press, 2008.

Wippel, John F. *The Ultimate Why Question: Why Is There Anything at All Rather than Nothing Whatsoever?* Washington, DC: Catholic University of America Press, 2011.

Wittgenstein, Ludwig. *Tractatus Logico-Philosophicus*. London, UK: Routledge and Kegan Paul, 1922.

Wolter, Allan, O.F.M., translator and editor. *Duns Scotus: Philosophical Writings.* New York, NY: Thomas Nelson & Sons, 1962.

Xunzi. *Xunzi: A Translation and Study of the Complete Works*. Three volumes. Translated and edited by John Knoblock. Stanford, CA: Stanford University Press. Volume 1, Books 1–6 (1988). Volume 2, Books 7–16 (1990). Volume 3, Books 17–32 (1994).

Yong, Amos, and Peter G. Heltzel, editors. *Theology in Global Context: Essays in Honor of Robert Cummings Neville*. New York, NY, and London, UK: T&T Clark, 2004.

Zank, Michael. "Jewish Ethics in a Modern World." In Nicholas de Lange and Miri Freud-Kandel, editors, *Modern Judaism: An Oxford Guide*, Chapter 26. Oxford, UK: Oxford University Press, 2005.

Zizioulis, John D. *Being as Communion: Studies in Personhood and the Church.* Foreword by John Meyendorff. Crestwood, NY: St. Vladimir's Seminary Press, 1993.

Index

[Citations after **"I"** are to *Ultimates: Philosophical Theology Volume One*, those after "**II**" are to *Existence: Philosophical Theology Volume Two*, and those after "**III"** are to *Religion: Philosophical Theology Volume Three*. The Index published in the first volume is somewhat reorganized in this combined Index.]